Education law and

John Ford is a solicitor who has worked in private practice for more than 25 years. He is recognised as a specialist education solicitor in *Chambers' Directory* and *The Legal 500* and was formerly the convenor of the Children Act special interest group of the Education Law Association. He has been a primary school governor for several years.

Dr Mary Hughes is a barrister at 10–11 Gray's Inn Square practising in education, child care and family law. She worked in local authority education before training for the bar and previously taught part-time at the Inns of Court School of Law.

David Ruebain is a solicitor at David Levene & Co where he specialises in education and community care law. He is a council member of the Alliance for Inclusive Education, vice-chair of Disability Equality in Education and honorary legal adviser to the Independent Panel for Special Educational Advice.

The Legal Action Group is a national, independent charity which campaigns for equal access to justice for all members of society. Legal Action Group:
- provides support to the practice of lawyers and advisers
- inspires developments in that practice
- campaigns for improvements in the law and the administration of justice
- stimulates debate on how services should be delivered.

Education law and practice

John Ford, Mary Hughes and
David Ruebain

Legal Action Group
1999

This edition published in Great Britain 1999
by LAG Education and Service Trust Ltd
242 Pentonville Road
London
N1 9UN

© John Ford, Mary Hughes and David Ruebain 1999

British Library Cataloguing in Publication Data
A CIP catalogue record for this book is available from the British Library

ISBN 0 905099 81 8

Typeset by Legal Action Group
Printed in Great Britain by Alden Press, Oxford

Foreword

by Lord Justice Otton

This work is an invaluable addition to the already meritorious Legal Action Group publications. Education law is perhaps the most important cornerstone of our society. It deals with the most valuable national asset – our children and our future. Following the Education Act of 1944, aspirations were high. A depressing and deplorable lack of foresight, energy, resources and interest has meant that we have done less than justice to the young. We are now reaping the whirlwind. There is reason to believe that in the last decade reality has obliged our legislators, local education authorities, educationalists, teachers and perhaps even judges to look more closely at the law of education and its practice.

Parents and pupils need assistance to recognise and to claim their right to education. They are encouraged to do so by the incorporation of the European Convention on Human Rights into our domestic legislation by the Human Rights Act, which will come into force in October 2000. Article 2 of the First Protocol provides: 'No person shall be denied the right to education. In the exercise of any functions which it assumes in relation to education and teaching, the state shall respect the right of parents to ensure such education and teaching in conformity with their own religious and philosophical convictions.'

The authors have wisely divined that parents, pupils and lawyers acting for them need guidance and assistance through this complex body of law. Education law is not a self-contained area of the law. It reaches over into family, housing, community care and also criminal law. The authors are uniquely qualified to take our hands. John Ford is a solicitor specialising in education law, Mary Hughes is a practising barrister who previously worked in local authority education for many years, David Ruebain is a solicitor specialising in education and community care law. Like children, we (local education authorities, teachers, parents, pupils, lawyers and, not least, judges) can reach out with confidence and place our trust in v their joint experience and expertise.

I was particularly gratified that they devote two chapters (9 and 10) to special educational needs and social welfare law, both matters to which I have had occasion, professionally and personally, to address. Others will find them of great assistance. Chapter 14 explains the limitations of judicial review and the scope of statutory appeals. Chapter 15, 'Failure to provide appropriate education' is of topical interest as we await the outcome of *Phelps v Hillingdon LBC* in the House of Lords concerning dyslexic children (in which I was part of the constitution in the Court of Appeal).

Finally, the authors are to be congratulated on their exemplary use of plain and comprehensible English. Perhaps even a lesson for some teachers!

I commend this book without a single reservation.

Acknowledgements

We are grateful to Mary Alexandrou, who overcame John Ford's limited facility with the word processor and kept track of all the drafts and redrafts of the text.

David Ruebain expresses thanks to his secretary, Michelle Campbell, and to his colleagues in David Levene & Co for their advice and support.

This book is dedicated to Edmund and Theodore, Jassy and Anthony.

Contents

Table of cases

Table of statutes

Table of statutory instruments

Table of circulars, guidance etc

Codes of Practice

Code of Practice on LEA-School Relations, DfEE, 1998	8.7
Code of Practice on School Admissions, DfEE, 1999	5.7, 5.10, 5.19, 5.28, 5.31
Code of Practice on School Admission Appeals, DfEE, 1999	5.7
Code of Practice on the Identification and Assessment of Special Educational Needs, DFE, 1994	7.36, 9.8, 9.16, 9.30, 9.49, 9.72, 11.26, 11.73, 16.4, 16.36
EPA 1990: Code of Practice on Litter and Refuse, DOE, 1991	6.10
Revised Code of Practice for Appeals, Association of County Councils, Association of Metropolitan Authorities and Council on Tribunals, 1994	5.7, 5.42
Revised Code of Practice on Procedure, Association of Metropolitan Authorities, the Association of County Councils and the Council on Tribunals, 1994	5.70, 5.71, 5.79, 5.80, 8.61, 8.65

DES Circulars

10/65	The Organisation of Secondary Schools	1.13
11/88	Admission of pupils to county and voluntary schools	5.7, 5.31
1/89	Education Reform Act 1988: Local Arrangements for the Consideration of Complaints	4.65, 4.67, 13.12
2/89	Education Reform Act 1988: Charges for School Activities	4.36, 4.40
15/89	ERA 1988: Temporary Exceptions from the National Curriculum	4.15
17/89	The Education (School Records) Regulations 1989	4.47
10/90	The Education Reform Act 1988: Specific Grant for the Education of Travellers and of Displaced Persons	11.57
6/91	Implementation of more open enrolment in primary schools	5.7, 5.31

DFE Circulars

DfEE Circulars

FEFC Circulars

DES Administrative Memoranda

Guidance

Local ombudsman investigations

Reports etc

xlvi   *Education law and practice / Table of circulars, guidance etc*

List of books, journals and pamphlets

List of abbreviations

ACE	Advisory Centre for Education
CA	Children Act
CCT	City Technology College
CCTA	City College for the Technology of the Arts
CDA	Crime and Disorder Act
CTC	Central Training Council
DCP	Disabled Child's Premium
DDA	Disability Discrimination Act
DES	Department of Education and Science
DFE	Department for Education
DfEE	Department for Education and Employment
DLA	Disability Living Allowance
DPTC	Disabled Persons Tax Credit
DVLC	Driver and Vehicle Licensing Centre
DWA	Disability Working Allowance
EA	Education Act
EAZ	Education Action Zone
EDP	Education Development Plans
EEA	Elementary Education Act
E(No2)A	Education (No 2) Act
EBD	Emotional and behavioural difficulties
EP	Educational psychologist
EPA	Environmental Protection Act
ERA	Education Reform Act
ETA	Employment and Training Act
FE	Further Education
FEFC	Further Education Funding Council for England
FEFCW	Further Education Funding Council for Wales
FHEA	Further and Higher Education Act
GAL	Guardian ad litem
GCSE	General Certificate in Secondary Education
HE	Higher Education
HEFC	Higher Education Funding Council
HEFCW	Higher Education Funding Council for Wales
HMIs	Her Majesty's Inspectors
HND	Higher National Diploma
HNC	Higher National Certificate

HSWA	Health and Safety at Work Act
ICA	Invalid Care Allowance
IT	Information Technology
LAB	Legal Aid Board
LEA	Local Education Authority
LGO	Local Government Ombudsman
LMS	Local Management of Schools
Ofsted	Office for Standards in Education
OLA	Occupiers' Liability Act
PACE	Police and Criminal Evidence Act
PGCE	Postgraduate Certificate in Education
PRU	Pupils Referral Unit
QCA	Qualifications and Curriculum Authority (England)
QCAAW	Qualifications and Curriculum Assessment Authority for Wales
RSC	Rules of the Supreme Court
SACRE	Standing Advisory Council on Religious Education
SATs	Standard Assessment Tasks
SDA	Severe Disablement Allowance
SDP	Severe Disability Premium
SEN	Special Educational Needs
SENCO	School's Special Educational Needs Coordinator
SENT	Special Educational Needs Tribunal
SIA	School Inspections Act
SSFA	School Standards and Framework Act
TEC	Training Enterprise Councils
THEA	Teaching and Higher Education Act
UCAS	Universities and Colleges Admission Service
WEA	Workers' Educational Association

Introduction

This book covers the law of education in England and Wales. Since 1979 more legislation has been passed in this area than in any other field. Education is a major political issue of all political parties and is seen as the key to the future of the nation. Education law has undergone constant change and these changes have made increasing demands on people working in education. There have been increased, and increasingly frustrated, expectations on the part of parents and students and uncertainty about how the law in this area will develop. These make potentially great demands on anyone seeking to advise on an education problem.

We have attempted to state the statute law as at 1 September 1999. We do not attempt to produce a comprehensive source book of education law. An excellent one is already available – the four-volume loose-leaf *Law of Education* (Butterworth). Our aim has been to produce a single volume which will be readily accessible to the high street practitioner who is asked by parents, pupils or students to advise them. We have attempted to deal with the most common problems affecting pupils, their parents and their families where the involvement of a lawyer might be beneficial. In many cases there are practical solutions which can be achieved without recourse to lawyers. Excellent advice is available from the Advisory Centre for Education (ACE) and its publications. We commend them to any user for their clarity and practicality. There are also many useful publications available free from the DfEE. We have suggested practical steps which can be taken by a general solicitor-practitioner, using as a guide the pro forma documentation which we have provided in the appendices.

In a publication of this size we have not attempted to deal with all aspects of education law. For instance, some of the detailed provisions regarding the powers, duties and proceedings of governors have been left out where they are not essential for this book or are readily available elsewhere. The DfEE publishes free guides to the law for use by school governors of all types of schools. We have not attempted to deal extensively with higher education or further education.

The book, although aimed at lawyers and advisers, looks at the law and practice from the point of view of the consumers of educational services rather than the providers. We have tried to arrange the book in the same order as a parent may encounter a problem where a legal point could arise. Most parents and many lawyers would not recognise immediately the precise legal issue in this complex field. We look at what to do when things go wrong and consider the available remedies. It is essential to consider carefully the practical effect of any intended course of action where the welfare and development of a child or young person is involved. It can take years to make good the damage done by a traumatic educational experience or a failure to meet SEN.

Sadly, the most deserving cases are not even in the educational system. A significant proportion of young offenders are people with learning difficulties and/or those whom the education system has failed or excluded. Unfortunately, they and their parents and families are the least likely to recognise and exploit the remaining educational opportunities.

It is hoped that this book will provide a guide particularly for the high street, criminal, family, housing or personal injury practitioner, who can then offer some practical advice and guidance on obtaining specialist evidence and making representations. Social workers providing support to children and families and divorce court welfare officers could find it useful in encouraging pupils and their parents not to give up hope. We believe that this book will have served its purpose if it assists in the recognition of education law problems. This is, however, a highly technical field and specialist advice and assistance will often be required.

We hope that the book will achieve its aim of becoming a practical guide which makes education law accessible to the committed (legal aid) practitioner and his/her client in a way which benefits those whom the education system in England and Wales is supposed to serve.

John Ford, Mary Hughes and David Ruebain
September 1999

CHAPTER 1

A brief history of education in England and Wales

This chapter gives a brief outline of the growth of the education system in England and Wales in order to set the context for the details of the current system described in the rest of the book.

The growth of schools

1.1   Until the latter part of the 19th century, schools were not very common. The churches, both established and nonconformist, were the major providers of various types of schooling. Charitable foundations and endowments were the other chief means of supporting schools, both day and boarding. In addition, there were the 'dame' schools run by local, often old uneducated women, which provided more in the way of childcare than education. The foundations and endowments were often originally targeted at the poor but became subverted to the provision of education for the middle classes, usually boys, in grammar schools. Such education as was provided for disabled children was in predominantly boarding institutions run by different philanthropic foundations. The aristocracy, of course, tended to educate their sons, and sometimes their daughters, at home with private tutors or governesses.

1.2   Central government involvement in the provision of education began in 1833, when the first grants were given to the British and Foreign School Society, connected with nonconformists, and to the National Society, associated with the established church to supplement the educational work of the established and non-conformist churches and for the building of what we now know in various forms as voluntary schools. These soon developed into annual grants. Until 1856 their distribution was administered by the Committee for Education of the Privy Council but, after the Elementary Education Act (EEA) 1870, elected school boards were set up, with the power to raise finance by means of rates where the provision made by the voluntary societies was deemed to be insufficient. It was usual for small fees to be charged in both voluntary and board schools, although it was possible for these to be remitted.

1.3   The EEA 1870 did not make education free or compulsory. It was available for children between the ages of five and ten years, with the possibility of extension to 13. The cost was 9d per child per week. Shortly after this Act, the minimum age laid down for employment was set at ten years. In 1880, elementary education up to the age of ten became compulsory but this was always difficult to enforce while fees remained payable. Fees were not finally abolished for elementary education until the Fisher Act of 1918.

1.4   A central Education Department dating from 1856 gave way to the Board of Education (with a president) in 1899. The Education Act

(EA) 1902 established county boroughs and counties as education authorities, and council schools in place of board schools. From 1890 it was also possible to raise local taxes to provide separate technical instruction. It was recognised that Great Britain was lagging behind some other European nations, notably Germany, in its technical and industrial progress.

1.5   At the end of the 19th century, there was concern at the poor physical health of the nation, which became startlingly apparent at the time of conscription for the Boer War. A range of non-compulsory health and welfare provisions began to be implemented, including school doctors, school meals and milk.

Free state schooling

1.6   From the early 1900s, a diversity of types of school began to develop – elementary, higher elementary, junior technical and senior – which began to compete with the endowed grammar schools, as well as the private and proprietary schools. The partnership between the state and the voluntary sector continued. There was no universal state secondary education. Some children continued their education in the elementary school until they were 14. In most towns, secondary schools, including some new grammar schools, supplemented the endowed grammar schools. In the inter-war years of economic depression, the main way to obtain a free secondary education was by winning a scholarship at 11 to a grammar school. Fees were not abolished entirely until 1944, although the school leaving age was raised to 14 in 1918 and education was made compulsory to this age. In addition, local authorities were empowered to provide nursery education.

1.7   In 1926 there were revised regulations on grants and free places. Independent schools were compelled to choose between having a direct grant from central government, in exchange for providing a percentage of free places to local authority children, or remaining independent. Two hundred and thirty-five schools opted for direct grant status – the beginning of the assisted places scheme. This scheme was abolished for future pupils by the Education (Schools) Act 1997 from 1 September 1997 (see para 6.47).

The 1944 Act

1.8   The Education Act 1944 ('the Butler Act') was the landmark piece of legislation, which still forms the backdrop of much of the current legislative framework. A Minister of Education replaced the President of the Board of Education.[1] It was intended to establish a system of education that would compensate for the rigours of a long period of war. Furthermore, the voluntary and religious authorities were slowly becoming poorer and needed the financial support of the local education authorities (LEAs) in exchange for some loss of control of governors to the local authority. There were now four different types of LEA school, which reflected the varying degrees of local authority financing. These were the county or maintained schools, funded entirely by central and local government, and the voluntary aided, voluntary controlled and special agreement schools, which received funding from the state and some support from, for example, religious bodies or charitable foundations. In addition, there remained the direct grant schools referred to in para 1.7, the 'great' public schools and other private schools. By far the majority of school age children were now educated in the state system.

1.9   EA 1944 provided free schooling for all children from five to 14. In 1947 the leaving age was raised to 15[2] and in 1972 to 16.[3] Provision for milk, meals, clothing and transport was also extended, although this was not free, but means-tested. The primary, secondary and further education (FE) stages were defined, with transfers from primary to secondary taking place between the ages of 10 years 6 months and 12 years. A tripartite system of state school education was established – primary, grammar and secondary modern, with selection at age 11.

1.10   LEAs had a duty to provide both full-time and part-time further education for those over compulsory school age. This was often of a vocational/technical nature, as well a basic skills and social, physical and recreational training (for definition, see EA 1996 s2(3)). There was also the power to provide adult education, including recreational and leisure time activities as well as more erudite subjects.

1.11   Alongside this was an expanding system of higher education. Traditionally there had been the long-established elitist Oxford and Cambridge universities and some university colleges. The 'red brick'

---

1   Superseded by a Secretary of State for Education in 1964.
2   Education Act 1944 s35.
3   Ibid and Raising of the School Leaving Date Order 1972 SI No 444.

universities were established after the second world war, followed from the 1960s by the 'new' universities. Polytechnics were created in the 1960s and 1970s, initially concentrating on subjects with a vocational bias. Higher education has continued to expand, with a range of new institutions and courses. The old polytechnics and colleges of higher education have now all been granted university status by the Further and Higher Education Act 1992.[4]

1.12   There have been about 30 amending Acts in the past 50 years.

Comprehensive secondary schools

1.13   The Labour government of 1964–70 was committed to developing comprehensive non-selective secondary education and engaged in what became known as 'the Great Debate'. In June 1965 it issued a circular[5] which laid the foundation for the reconstruction of secondary education by replacing the tripartite system of separate grammar, technical and modern secondary schools and the abolition of selection at 11-plus. The Conservatives were returned to office in 1970 and they attempted to reverse the process. However, when the Labour party was re-elected in 1974, it continued with its plans for comprehensivisation and by EA 1976 comprehensive education became compulsory. There was considerable parental opposition and litigation, notably the *Tameside* case,[6] where a newly elected council decided not to continue its predecessor's proposals for making all secondary school entry non-selective and the court held that the Secretary of State for Education's view of education policy did not entitle him to make the council obey his direction. Twenty years on, it is interesting to read the judgment of Lord Diplock and speculate whether the secretary of state today would be seen by the courts as having such a limited direct role in providing services and decision-making. The School Standards and Framework Act (SSFA)

4   Courses of higher education include: (a) further training of teachers, youth workers and community workers; (b) post-graduate course, including higher degrees; (c) first degree course; (d) courses for the Diploma of Higher Education; (e) courses for the Higher National Diploma (HND) or Higher National Certificate (HNC) of the Business and Technician Education Council (BTEC) or the Diploma in Management Studies; (f) courses for the Certificate of Education; (g) courses for the preparation of a professional exam at a higher level; (h) courses providing education at a higher level, whether or not for an examination (Education Reform Act 1988 Sch 6 para 1; EA 1996 s579(1)).

5   DES Circular 10/65 *The Organisation of Secondary Education.*

6   *Secretary of State for Education and Science v Tameside MBC* [1977] AC 1014.

1998 has given the secretary of state greater powers to intervene in LEAs. In 1979, the newly-elected Conservative government immediately abolished the duty to give effect to the comprehensive principle.[7]

Education under the Conservatives 1979–97

1.14   The philosophy of the policymakers during the tenure of the Conservative governments until 1997 seems broadly to have been an attempt to reverse the developments which had gestated over the previous 100 years and culminated in EA 1944 which, at the time, commanded universal support from all parties. See, for example, the suggestion made in December 1995, and subsequently dropped, that all denominational schools should opt out of local authority control and become grant-maintained. Another example was the increasing move towards reintroducing more selectivity and streaming, as well as the operation of market forces and competition between schools and the consequences for admissions procedures. Most noticeable, however, has been the progressive removal of power from the LEAs, leaving them with duties which they scarcely have the resources to carry out, effectively becoming victims of political decisions about grants and budgets even where the funding or other power has been transferred from the LEAs to central government or a quango.

1.15   In 1992, what was previously the Department of Education and Science (DES) became the Department for Education (DFE). Since 5 July 1995, the minister responsible for education has borne the title Secretary of State for Education and Employment, when the Department of Employment was disbanded and training came under the newly titled Department for Education and Employment (DfEE).

1.16   Two major Acts came into force in 1996, largely consolidating much previous legislation: the Schools Inspections Act 1996 and the Education Act 1996. In addition, the Education Act 1997, which came into force in March 1997, amended EA 1996 in relation to school discipline. Provision was also made for baseline assessments and targets for pupils' performance, inspection of LEAs and schools, careers guidance and education and the extension of assisted places to primary schools. The Act was passed on 21 March 1997.

---

7   Education Act 1979, which received royal assent on 26 July 1979, only ten weeks after the general election.

Education under a Labour government

1.17   Education has often been, but never more so than today, a major political football and election issue. The Labour government stated on election in May 1997 that its new priorities would be 'education, education, education'. It has already (June 1999) introduced four new Acts and numerous regulations and circulars since it came to power. Its first act was to abolish the assisted places scheme so recently extended by the previous government.[8]

1.18   The Education (Student Loans) Act 1998 allowed the government to sell off a portfolio of student loans to financial institutions. The Teaching and Higher Education Act 1998 established the General Teaching Councils for England and Wales, dealing with such matters as the registration, qualifications and training of teachers and the inspection of such training. It also covered the provision of grants, loans and fees for students in further and higher education.

1.19   The most significant piece of legislation has been the SSFA 1998 and its attendant regulations. This limits the size of infant school classes, sets up education action zones, gives powers to both LEAs and the secretary of state to intervene in schools causing concern, sets up new categories of schools and new arrangements for governing bodies, and makes provision for home-school agreements. The emphasis, as the title of the Act implies, is on improving educational standards and discipline in schools.

1.20   The Human Rights Act 1998 will incorporate the European Convention on Human Rights into UK law during 2000, but the effect of article 2 on education law is likely to be limited as regards parental rights.

8   Education (Schools) Act 1997.

CHAPTER 2

The key players

This chapter looks at the powers and duties of the key players responsible for running the education system in England and Wales and the rights and duties of parents and children within the system.

The current position

2.1   In recent years there has been a distinct shift away from a partnership between central and local government to an increased centralisation of power. This is particularly apparent in relation to the concentration of resources into the hands of the Secretary of State for Education. It is said that the secretary of state acquired over 200 separate powers under the Education Reform Act (ERA) 1988 and several dozen more under EA 1993.[1] At the same time, power has been devolved downwards out of the hands of the LEAs to the governors of individual schools.   This has been largely through financial delegation under local management of schools (LMS). This has increased both the autonomy and the power of school governing bodies.

2.2   Major new agencies have been established which allocate resources to the higher education (HE) and the further education (FE) sector. These are the Further Education Funding Councils for England and Wales (FEFC and FEFCW) and the Higher Education Funding Council (HEFC) established by the Further and Higher Education Act (FHEA) 1992.

2.3   The National Curriculum, which was introduced by ERA 1988, is overseen by the Qualifications and Curriculum Authority, created by EA 1997 ss21 and 33. This has a wider remit in the advancement of education and training than the School Curriculum and Assessment Council, which it replaced. It also reviews external qualifications (EA 1997 s24). There is a separate authority for Wales, the Qualifications, Curriculum and Assessment Authority for Wales (EA 1997 s27).

2.4   The state education system has been subject to privatisation and competitive tendering in certain key areas, not only in relation to inspections but also in the provision of support services such as school meals, cleaning, maintenance and transport.

2.5   Furthermore, although the reality is somewhat hollow, through its Parents Charter,[2] the government has attempted to develop the concepts of partnership with parents and parental choice. Unlike other areas of child law, this has detracted from the independent rights of children themselves.

2.6   A summary of the roles and powers of the key players follows.

---

1   Neville Harris *The Law Relating to Schools*, 2nd edn, Tolley, 1995, p4.
2   *Our Children's Education: the Updated Parents' Charter*, DFE, 1994.

Secretary of State for Education and Employment

2.7 The secretary of state has the following duties:

1) to promote education, generally (EA 1996 s10);
2) to provide public funds to all bodies responsible for securing educational provision (EA 1996 s11);
3) to issue a code of practice on special educational needs (SEN) (EA 1996 s313);
4) to make arrangements for securing that sufficient facilities are available for training teachers for schools, FE and HE (EA 1994 s11A);
5) to pay grants to persons other than LEAs for educational services or research (EA 1996 s485);
6) to pay LEAs and others grants for the teaching of Welsh or the teaching of other subjects in Welsh (EA 1996 s487);
7) to pay each LEA a grant equal to the amount given in mandatory grants by the LEA (ERA 1988 s209);
8) to revise the National Curriculum when s/he considers it necessary or expedient (EA 1996 s356);
9) (as well as LEAs, governing bodies and headteachers) to ensure that the curriculum for maintained schools is balanced and broadly based (EA 1996 s351);
10) to issue a code of practice in relation to special educational needs (EA 1996 s313);
11) to issue a code of practice in relation to admission arrangements and consult on this (SSFA 1998 ss84 and 85);
12) to issue a code of practice in order to ensure effective relationships between LEAs and maintained schools (SSFA 1998 s127); and
13) to make regulations imposing limits on infant class sizes (initially 30) (SSFA 1998 s1) and to reimburse LEAs for any expenditure in this regard (SSFA 1998 s3).

2.8 The secretary of state has the following powers:

1) to make grants to the FEFC and the HEFC (FHEA 1992 s7; see also Teaching and Higher Education Act 1998 s26);
2) to give education standards grants to LEAs (EA 1996 s484);
3) to give grants to bodies whose objects are the promotion of learning or research (EA 1996 s486);
4) to give grants for the education of travellers and displaced people (EA 1996 s488; ERA 1988 s210);

5) to give grants to LEAs, CTCs and CCTAs to provide for ethnic minorities (Local Government Act 1966 s11; EA 1996 s490); and to give grants to governing bodies of further education institutions for the same (ERA 1988 s211);

6) to give grants for teacher training (E(No2)A 1986 s50);

7) to prescribe the staffing of schools and the qualifications required for teachers (ERA 1988 s218) (NB it is the prime minister and not the secretary of state who establishes a review body to consider teachers' pay and conditions of service (School Teachers' Pay and Conditions Act 1991);

8) to require LEAs, or other persons, to appraise the performance of teachers (E(No2)A 1986 s49);

9) to establish education action zones (EAZs) to improve standards in particular schools (SSFA 1998 s10);

10) to appoint additional governors to a school requiring special measures (SSFA 1998 s18) (for special measures, see SSFA 1998 s15);

11) to direct closure of a school requiring special measures (SSFA 1998 s19);

12) to require closure of a community or foundation special school in the interests of health, safety or welfare of pupils (SSFA 1998 s32);

13) to direct the rationalisation of school places (SSFA 1998 s34 and Sch 7);

14) to approve any significant change in the character or the closure of a school (SSFA 1998 ss28-31);

15) to cause a local enquiry to be held in connection with any of his/her powers or duties under EA 1996 (EA 1996 s507);

16) to determine disputes between LEAs and governing bodies (EA 1996 s495);

17) to prevent the unreasonable exercise of functions where s/he believes that an LEA or governing body has acted or is proposing to act 'unreasonably' (EA 1996 s496);

18) where satisfied that an LEA or governing body has failed to discharge its duty, to give directions to enforce the performance of that duty; such directions are enforceable by mandamus (EA 1996 s497); to use the same power in relation to funding authorities (EA 1996 s24(4)); to direct an officer of an LEA to discharge the function (EA 1996 s497A; the powers of this person are set out in s497B);

19) to require LEAs, governing bodies and headteachers to provide

such information as is required by regulations (EA 1996 s408);

20) to set attainment targets, programmes of study and assessment arrangements in relation to the National Curriculum (EA 1996 s356);

21) to transfer functions of LEAs re provision of lunches to governing bodies (EA 1996 s512A, inserted by SSFA 1998 s116);

22) to require governing bodies to set annual targets for the performance of pupils (EA 1997 s19); and

23) to require governing bodies and headteachers to perform certain functions in relation to baseline assessments (EA 1997 s18).

Chief Inspector of Schools and Ofsted

2.9 The position of Chief Inspector of Schools in England was established under SIA 1996 s1. The chief inspector is also head of the Office for Standards in Education (Ofsted), which was set up by the government under the Education (Schools) Act 1992 (since repealed) to administer school inspections. There is a similar system of inspections of schools in Wales under the Chief Inspector of Schools in Wales (SIA 1996 s4). For more details of the inspection system, see chapter 4, paras 4.51–4.60.

2.10 The Chief Inspector of Schools has the following duties:

 – to keep the secretary of state informed on quality, standards, efficient use of resources and the spiritual, moral, mental, physical and cultural development of pupils (SIA 1996 s2);

 – to administer school inspections at prescribed intervals by registered inspectors (SIA 1996 s10).

2.11 The Chief Inspector of Schools has the following power:

 – under EA 1997 s38, on direction of the secretary of state, to make arrangements to inspect an LEA.

Local education authorities

2.12 Local education authorities have the following duties:

1) to ensure the provision of 'sufficient schools' for the provision of primary and secondary education in their area (EA 1996 s14, previously EA 1944 s8);

2) to ensure, along with secretary of state, that education is

organised in three stages: primary, secondary and FE (EA 1996 s1);

3) as far as powers permit, to 'contribute towards the spiritual, moral, mental and physical development of the community by securing that efficient primary education, secondary education and further education are available to meet the needs of the population of their area' (EA 1944 s7, now EA 1996 s13(1));

4) to secure adequate facilities for FE (EA 1996 ss15 and 15A);

5) to make arrangements for the education of children who may not receive this at school for whatever reason (EA 1996 s19);

6) to promote high standards in primary and secondary education (EA 1996 s13A, inserted by SSFA 1998 s5);

7) to secure that facilities for primary, secondary and further education include adequate facilities for recreation, social and physical training (EA 1996 s508);

8) to be responsible for maintenance of schools (SSFA 1998 s22) – but see governors' responsibilities;[3]

9) to delegate functions to committees and subcommittees under their general powers under Local Government Act 1972 ss101–102, as amended;[4]

10) to appoint a chief education officer (EA 1996 s532) to whom functions can be delegated by the LEA, its committees and subcommittees;

11) to produce plans showing arrangements to be made to reduce class sizes (SSFA 1998 s2);

12) to provide such information as is required by regulations (EA 1996 s408);

13) to produce education development plans (EDPs) detailing proposals for education in their area by raising standards or improving the performance of schools; to consult with headteachers and governing bodies of maintained schools and, if appropriate, the diocesan authority and any other person thought appropriate (SSFA 1998 s6);

14) to establish a school organisation committee including at least one member from the LEA, one from the Diocesan Board of Education and a person nominated by the bishop of any Roman

---

3   See *Local Management of Schools* DFE Circular 2/94, Annex G, which suggests a division of responsibility between LEA and governors; it is essential that these divisions are incorporated in LMS schemes.

4   There is no longer a need to have an education committee (EA 1993 s296, not reproduced in EA 1996).

Catholic Church (SSFA 1998 s24);

15) to prepare a school organisation plan (SSFA 1998 s26);

16) to publish proposals if it intends to establish, alter or close a community, foundation, voluntary or special school (SSFA 1998 ss28, 29 and 31);

17) to determine the dates of school terms and holidays for community, voluntary controlled or community special schools (SSFA 1998 s41);

18) to give a financial budget to all maintained schools (SSFA 1998 s45);

19) to employ all staff in community, voluntary controlled or community special schools (SSFA 1998 s54), or foundation, voluntary aided and foundation special schools (SSFA 1998 s55);

20) to exercise its functions to ensure a broad and balanced curriculum (EA 1996 s351);

21) (along with governing bodies and headteachers) to prohibit: political indoctrination in maintained schools and ensure the balanced treatment of opposing political views (EA 1996 ss406 and 407);

22) to be responsible with the governing bodies of maintained schools for approving the instruments of government (SSFA 1998 Sch 12 para 3);

23) to provide training and support for governors (SSFA 1998 Sch 11 para 7);

24) to be the admissions authority for community and voluntary controlled schools, except where this is delegated to the governing body (SSFA 1998 s88);

25) to publish information each school year about admissions (SSFA 1998 s92);

26) to establish a complaints procedure approved by the secretary of state to deal with complaints of unreasonableness by an LEA or governing body in relation to such matters as the curriculum, the provision of information, collective worship or religious education (EA 1996 s409);

27) to make arrangements for admissions appeals (SSFA 1998 s94);

28) to make arrangements for appeals against exclusions (SSFA 1998 s67) and to make arrangements for governing bodies to appeal against an LEA decision to place a pupil who has been permanently excluded from two schools in two years (SSFA 1998 s95);

29) to identify and be responsible for children with special

educational needs in their area (EA 1996 s321) (see associated duties in chapter 9);

30) to have regard to the code of practice on SEN (EA 1996 s313);

31) to make the arrangements for the educational provision in statements of special educational needs (EA 1996 s324);

32) to establish a standing advisory council on religious education (SACRE) (EA 1996 s390);

33) to enforce school attendance (EA 1996 s437);

34) to prepare and maintain a statement with arrangements or proposals to be made for the education of children with behavioural difficulties (EA 1996 s527A, inserted by EA 1997 s9);

35) to make mandatory awards for higher education (EA 1962 s1);

36) to prepare plans for the reduction of infant class sizes (SSFA 1998 s2); and

37) to select an accredited baseline scheme (EA 1997 s16).

2.13   Local education authorities have the following powers:

1) to arrange nursery education (EA 1996 s170);

2) to appoint some governors to maintained schools (SSFA 1998 Sch 9);

3) to enter and inspect maintained schools 'for the purpose of enabling them to exercise any function of theirs' (SIA 1996 s25(1)(a)) – this is only allowed if 'it is not reasonably practicable to obtain information in any other manner' (SIA 1996 s25(1)(b));

4) to establish a school inspection service to tender for school inspections (SIA 1996 s24);

5) to provide boarding or the cost of this (EA 1996 s14(6)(c) and s514);

6) to provide transport (EA 1996 ss509 and 509A), clothing (s510), milk and meals (EA 1996 s512, as amended by SSFA 1998 s115, also SSFA 1998 s114);

7) to pay the cost of children taking part in school activities, to pay all or part of the fees at fee paying schools and to grant scholarships etc to people over compulsory school age (EA 1996 s518);

8) to give discretionary awards for attendance at courses not covered by EA 1962 s1 for people over compulsory school age (including teacher training) (EA 1962 s2);

9) to direct that a child be admitted to a particular school (SSFA 1998 s96);

10) to take such steps as are required to prevent breakdown or continuing breakdown of discipline in a maintained school

(SSFA 1998 s62);

11) to intervene in maintained schools if a school has been subjected to a formal warning (SSFA 1998 s15(1), has serious weaknesses identified in an inspection under SIA 1996 (SSFA 1998 s15(4)), or requires special measures identified in an inspection under SIA 1996 (SSFA 1998 s15(6)) (see SSFA 1998 s15); to appoint additional governors (SSFA 1998 s16) (not applicable if secretary of state has appointed additional governors under SSFA 1998 s18 or directed closure of a school under SSFA 1998 s19); and to suspend the right to a delegated budget (SSFA 1998 s17);

12) to give directions about occupation and use of community and community special schools (SFA 1998 Sch 13); and

13) to make allowances for governors' travelling and subsistence where the governing body does not have a delegated budget (EA 1996 s513).

Further Education Funding Councils

2.14   The FEFC and the FEFCW have the following duties under the Further and Higher Education Act (FHEA) 1992:

1) to secure sufficient provision for full-time education for people over compulsory school age up to their 19th birthday (s2);

2) to ensure the provision of part-time education for people over compulsory school leaving age (s3);

3) to ensure the provision of full-time education falling within the categories identified in FHEA 1992 Sch 2 for those over 19 (s3);

4) to have regard to the needs of people with learning difficulties (s4);

5) to provide information to the secretary of state as required (s8);

6) to be responsible for assessing quality control (s9).

2.15   The FEFC has the following power:

– to give financial support to governing bodies of either FE or HE institutions for the provision of facilities for either FE or HE (FHEA 1992 s5).

Higher Education Funding Council

2.16   The HEFC has the following duties under FHEA 1992:

- to administer funds to HE institutions for education and research (s65);
- to provide information to the secretary of state as required (s69);
- to ensure the assessment of quality control in HE institutions (s70).

School governing bodies

2.17   All maintained schools (see SSFA 1998 s20) must have an incorporated governing body (SSFA 1998 s36 Sch 9). No governor may be under 18 (EA 1996 Sch 8 para 8). School governing bodies have the following duties:

1) to operate under instruments of government (SSFA 1998 s37);

2) to be responsible for the conduct of a maintained school and to conduct the school in a manner which ensures high standards of educational achievement; regulations may set out terms of reference for governing bodies, confer functions on them and define the respective roles and responsibilities of governing bodies and headteachers (SSFA 1998 s38);

3) (in community and community special schools) to control the occupation and use of school premises during and outside school hours subject to any direction given by the LEA (SSFA 1998 Sch 13 para 1) (cf foundation and foundation special schools where governing bodies do not have to have regard to directions from the LEA (SSFA 1998 Sch 13 para 3));

4) to set up a procedure for dealing with complaints not dealt with by any other statutory mechanism, ie, exclusions (SSFA 1998 s39);

5) to comply (along with the headteacher) with directions given by an LEA in relation to health and safety of persons on school premises or taking part in school activities elsewhere (SSFA 1998 s39);

6) (in community, voluntary controlled or community special schools) to determine the times of school sessions; (in foundation, voluntary aided or foundation special schools) to determine the days and times of school terms and holidays and the times of school sessions (SSFA 1998 s41);

7) to prepare and make available a governors' report annually; and to provide reports for the LEA as required (SSFA 1998 s42);

8) to hold an annual parents' meeting (SSFA 1998 s43)

9) to enter pupils for public exams (EA 1996 s402);

10) to maintain a written policy on sex education (EA 1996 s404) and ensure (along with the LEA and headteacher) that sex education includes the teaching of moral principles and the value of family life (EA 1996 s403);

11) to forbid (along with the LEA and headteacher) political indoctrination (EA 1996 s 407) and to secure (along with the LEA and headteacher) the balanced treatment of political issues (EA 1996 s407);

12) to manage a delegated budget (SSFA 1998 s49) (governors will not incur personal liability if they act in good faith (SSFA 1998 s50);

13) to make and review a written statement on good behaviour and discipline (SSFA 1998 s61);

14) to perform various duties in relation to excluded pupils (SSFA 1998 s66);

15) to secure (with the LEA and headteacher) religious education (SSFA 1998 s69) and collective worship (SSFA 1998 s70);

16) to act as the admissions authority for foundation and voluntary aided schools (this function may be delegated to the governing body by the LEA in relation to community, or voluntary controlled schools: SSFA 1998 s88); to publish yearly information about admissions (SSFA 1998 s92); and (in foundation or voluntary aided schools) to make arrangements for admissions appeals (SSFA 1998 s94);

17) to adopt a home-school agreement with a parental declaration (SSFA 1998 ss110–111);

18) to ensure (with the LEA and headteacher) a balanced and broadly based curriculum (EA 1996 s351);

19) (in foundation or voluntary schools) to publish proposals for any prescribed alterations (SSFA 1998 s28) or proposed discontinuance and to consult (SSFA 1998 s29); at least two years' notice of discontinuance must be given (SSFA 1998 s30) (for foundation special schools, see SSFA 1998 s31);

20) to observe duties in relation to pupils with special educational needs (SEN) (EA 1996 s317);

21) to admit a child whose SEN statement names their school (EA 1996 s324(5));

22) to have regard to the code of practice on SEN (EA 1996 s313);

23) to be responsible for health and safety (Health and Safety at Work Act 1974 s4(2));

24) to set school attendance targets if directed by regulations (SSFA 1998 s63);

25) to pay to governors allowances determined in accordance with regulations (SSFA 1998 Sch 11 para 6); and

26) to chose a baseline assessment scheme if this is not chosen within a reasonable time by the headteacher (EA 1997 s16(5));

2.18   Governing bodies have the following powers:

1) to delegate any powers with respect to the budget to the headteacher (SSFA 1998 s50(3));

2) to appoint staff to community, voluntary controlled and community special schools where they have a delegated budget, although the LEA remains the employer (SSFA 1998 s54) (cf foundation, voluntary aided and foundation special schools, where the governing body is the employer: SSFA 1998 s55);

3) to appeal against the admission of a child who has been excluded twice (SSFA 1998 s95)

4) to require pupils to attend any place outside the school to receive instruction or training as part of the secular curriculum (SSFA 1998 s39); and

5) to do anything necessary or expedient relating to the conduct of the school (SSFA 1998 Sch 11 para 3).

2.19   The DfEE provides a series of free publications on the functions of governing bodies (telephone 0845 6022260).

Headteachers

2.20   All maintained schools must have a headteacher.[5] The headteacher is generally a member of the governing body although this is not obligatory. S/he is an ex officio member (EA 1996 s225; SSFA 1998 Sch 9).

2.21   Headteachers have the following duties:

1) to determine measures to promote self discipline and good behaviour by pupils; to prevent bullying having regard to the statement of the governing body in respect of this; these

---

5   Education (Teachers) Regulations 1993 SI No 543 reg 6(2)(a).

measures must be written and published (SSFA 1998 s61);

2) to decide on exclusions, either fixed term or permanent (SSFA 1998 s64);

3) to comply with any directions of the LEA (along with the governing body) regarding the health and safety of people on school premises or taking part in school activities (SSFA 1998 s39);

4) to secure the implementation of the National Curriculum (EA 1996 s357);

5) to make arrangements for children to be assessed at key stages 1, 2 and 3;[6]

6) to secure the provision of religious education (SSFA 1998 s69 and Sch 19; EA 1996 s352(1)(a))

7) to ensure that all pupils take part in a daily act of collective worship (SSFA 1998 s70), unless excused by SSFA 1998 s71;

8) to take such steps (with the LEA and the governing body) as are reasonably practicable to ensure that any sex education given is given in such a manner as to encourage pupils to have due regard to moral considerations and the value of family life (EA 1996 s403);

9) to comply with any regulations which set out the respective roles and responsibilities of governing bodies and headteachers, including regulations in relation to the curriculum and any regulations which confer functions on headteachers (SSFA 1998 s38);

10) to provide such information as may be required by regulations to parents and others about the education provided and about the results of assessments (EA 1996 s 408);

11) to provide the governing body or the LEA with any reports relating to the discharge of his/her functions as they may require; the LEA must inform the governing body if it requires such a report and the headteacher must give the governing body a copy of any report (SSFA 1998 s42(4))

12) to forbid (with the LEA and the governing body) political indoctrination and ensure the balanced treatment of political issues (EA 1996 ss406 and 407); and

13) to chose a baseline assessment scheme for his/her school (EA 1997 s16(5)).

6   Education (National Curriculum) (Key Stage 1 Assessment Arrangements) Order 1996 SI No 2114; Education (National Curriculum) (Key Stage 2 Assessment Arrangements) Order 1996 SI No 2115; Education (National Curriculum) (Key Stage 3 Assessment Arrangements) Order 1996 SI No 2116.

2.22 Headteachers have the following power:

– to exempt pupils from all or part of the national curriculum on a temporary basis (EA 1996 s365).

Teachers

2.23 Teachers have the following powers:

1) to use reasonable force (along with other school staff) to restrain pupils under certain circumstances (EA 1996 s550A, inserted by EA 1997 s4);
2) to be elected to the governing body as a representative of the teaching body, as may non-teaching staff (SSFA 1998 Sch 9);
3) to sit on certain exclusion panels (SSFA 1998 Sch 18); and
4) to sit on admission appeals panels, but not those relating to the school in which they teach (SSFA 1998 Sch 24).

Parents

2.24 The term parent is defined as a natural parent, someone with parental responsibility or someone who cares for the child (EA 1996 s576).

2.25 Parents have the following duties:

1) to ensure that a child of compulsory school age receives efficient full-time education suitable to his/her age, ability and aptitude and any special needs s/he may have, either at school or otherwise (EA 1996 s7); this can be enforced by a school attendance order (EA 1996 s437), an education supervision order (Children Act (CA) 1989 s36), criminal sanctions (EA 1996 s444) or the enforcement of a parenting order (presently being piloted in certain areas: Crime and Disorder Act 1998 ss7 and 8); and
2) if required, to sign a home-school agreement in relation to a registered pupil (SSFA 1998 s110).

2.26 Parents have the following rights:

1) to be a school governor (SSFA 1998 Sch 9);
2) to be a parent governor on education committees (EA 1996 s499 as amended by SSFA 1998 s9);
3) to request an assessment of their child in relation to SEN (EA 1996 s329);

4) to appeal to the Special Educational Needs Tribunal (EA 1996 s336);
5) to express parental preference about to the school they wish their child to attend (EA 1996 s9); this does not apply where a child has been excluded from two or more schools in last two years (SSFA 1998 s87) or where an education supervision order is in place (CA 1989 Sch 3 para 13 (2)(b));
6) to appeal in relation to admissions (SSFA 1998 s94) but not where a child has been excluded from two or more schools in the last two years (SSFA 1998 s95);
7) to appeal in relation to exclusions (SSFA 1998 s67);
8) to withdraw their child from religious education and worship (SSFA 1998 s71);
9) to see a governing body's statement on sex education (EA 1996 s404) and to remove their child from sex education (EA 1996 s405);
10) to one parents' meeting a year (SSFA 1998 s43);
11) to have access to information (EA 1996 s408);
12) to complain to the governing body (SSFA 1998 s39);
13) to complain to the LEA about curriculum questions (EA 1996 s409); and
14) to complain to the secretary of state (EA 1996 ss496 and 497).

Children

2.27   Children are defined as people not over compulsory school age (EA 1996 s579(1). But for children with special educational needs the definition is those under 19 who are registered school pupils (EA 1996 s312(5)). These definitions should be compared with CA 1989 in which, for most purposes, children are defined as people under 18. Education law fails to recognise the independent rights of children, at variance with the philosophy of the Children Act.

2.28   A child has no independent appeal right separate from her/his parents; though in relation to exclusion appeals s/he will be a relevant person if over 18 and hence able to appeal (SSFA 1998 s65(5)).

2.29   A child cannot withdraw him/herself from sex or religious education – see chapter 4 paras 4.22–4.31.

2.30   A student of an FE institution may become a governor before reaching the age of 18 (E(No2)A 1986 s61).

CHAPTER 3

Structure of the school system

This chapter looks at the framework for the provision of education in schools in England and Wales. It maps out the provisions which govern the different types of school available, the structure and roles of governing bodies, the staffing and funding of schools, the ways in which schools are opened, closed and changed, the requirements of school premises and which LEAs are responsible for which pupils and students.

Types of school

3.1   'School' is defined in EA 1996 s4(1) as an educational institution which is:

- outside the further and higher education sectors, and which
- provides primary education and/or secondary education and/or full-time education for those over 16 and under 19.

Accordingly, it covers institutions both within and outside the state sector.

3.2   The School Standards and Framework Act (SSFA) 1998 s20 introduced new categories of LEA-maintained schools from September 1999. The new categories are (s20(1)):

- community schools
- foundation schools
- voluntary schools
- community special schools
- foundation special schools.

These are described in more detail below. SSFA 1998 Sch 2 makes provision for the allocation of the previous classification of schools – county, voluntary controlled, voluntary aided, special agreement, special and grant maintained schools – to the new classifications and makes provision for balloting in certain circumstances, where an allocation to a new category is disputed by the governing body of the school. In addition, SSFA 1998 Sch 8 makes provision for a school to change its category by way of a procedure requiring the publication of statutory proposals (see para 3.48).

Community schools

3.3   SSFA 1998 Sch 2 allocates schools which were known as county schools to be community schools. In general, community schools are wholly maintained by their LEA. LEAs are also the employers of community school staff (SSFA 1998 s54 and Sch 16).

Foundation schools

3.4   Foundation schools are those which had, before the establishment of the new types of school, been designated as grant maintained or grant maintained special schools, providing that before those schools were established as such, they were previously either county or voluntary controlled schools or special schools. Foundation schools will have a body of persons other than an LEA, whether incorporated or not but excluding the governing body itself, which holds land on trust for the purposes of the school. LEAs will be wholly responsible for maintaining foundation schools but foundation school staff are employed by their school governing body (SSFA 1996 s55 and Sch 17).

Voluntary schools

3.5   There are two kinds of voluntary school: controlled and aided schools. SSFA 1998 Sch 2 allocates controlled schools to voluntary controlled schools; aided and special agreement schools to voluntary aided schools; and grant maintained schools which had hitherto been either aided or special agreement schools or had been established by promoters within the meaning of EA 1996 Part III, to voluntary aided schools. Voluntary controlled schools will be wholly maintained by their LEAs, who are also voluntary controlled school staff employers. On the other hand, voluntary aided schools are mainly, but not wholly, maintained by their LEAs and the voluntary aided governing bodies are the employers of voluntary aided school staff (SSFA 1998 s55 and Sch 17).

Special schools

3.6   Special schools are those schools which either were previously maintained special schools or are not maintained but are approved by the secretary of state. They are, of course, schools specially organised for children with special educational needs (see chapter 9 and paras 11.20–11.24).

Change to the new system

3.7   In many respects, the previous designations are similar to the new designations. The principal change arising from the new designations is that grant maintained schools, which were hitherto outside of the local education authority sector, are now brought within its purview. Grant maintained schools accordingly cease to exist. However, the few City Technology Colleges and City Colleges for the Technology of the Arts will remain as independent schools, albeit ones funded by central government (see para 13.58).

Nursery schools

3.8   Nursery schools are schools which, in accordance with EA 1996 s6(1) are primary schools used mainly for the purpose of providing education for children between the ages of two and five. Nursery schools may be classified in accordance with any of the above stated provisions, or, indeed, be independent.

Pupil referral units

3.9   These are, technically, schools, established by EA 1996 s19(2) and Sch 1 to make provision for children of compulsory school age who, by reason of illness, exclusion from school or otherwise, may not for any period receive suitable education at another school. They are maintained by LEAs see paras 8.74 and 11.28–11.31).

Independent schools

3.10   These are wholly outside the state sector and may be run for charitable purposes or for profit. They may receive public funds through the old assisted places scheme (now abolished and being phased out, see para 6.47) and arising from agreements to provide for children with special educational needs, but remain responsible for their own conduct and governance (EA 1996 s463).

Further education colleges

3.11   These are defined by the FHEA 1992 and provide post-16 education. For more details about further education (and higher education), see chapter 12.

Governing bodies

3.12   SSFA 1998 Part II chapter III provides for the government of maintained schools. Broadly, responsibility for the provision of education in schools rests with head teachers and governing bodies, subject to detailed provision dividing responsibility. SSFA 1998 Sch 9 determines the constitution of governing bodies, Sch 10 details their incorporation and powers, Sch 11 establishes their membership and proceedings and Sch 12 establishes instruments of government (note that, unlike the framework preceding that introduced by the SSFA 1998, there are no formal articles of government for each school). In addition, the Education (School Government) (Transition to New Framework) Regulations 1998[1] deal with the transition of instruments and articles of government for schools before reclassification under the SSFA, to the new framework, described above. The Education (Government of New Schools on Transition to New Framework) Regulations 1998[2] determine provision for instruments for new schools.

3.13 Schedule 9 determines categories and numbers of governor, for each type of school. Depending on the classification, governors may be co-opted, foundation, LEA, parent, partnership, staff and teacher. In addition, the headteacher is appointed to every governing body, ex officio (EA 1996 s225 and SSFA 1998 Sch 9).

3.14 Schedule 10 incorporates governing bodies and gives them powers to borrow, acquire and dispose of land and other property, contract, invest, accept gifts and do anything incidental to the conduct of the school.

3.15 Schedule 11 determines the membership and proceedings of governing bodies; including the procedure for election or appointment of governors, their qualifications and tenure of office, meetings and proceedings, information as to meetings and proceedings, expenses and training and support of governors. By and large, the detail is dealt with by subsequent regulations.

3.16 Schedule 12 establishes instruments of government, each of which must set out:

- the name of the school;
- the category of the school;
- the name of the governing body of the school;
- the manner in which a governing body is constituted (specifying categories of governor and the number of governors in each category, the categories of persons from whom or from amongst whose members nominations for the appointment of any additional governors are to be sought, the number of such governors for whose appointment, nominations are to be sought in the case of each such category of person, any representative, governor and the total number of governors);
- the name and details of any foundation governors;
- the name of any body or bodies by whom any representative

---

1   1998 SI No 2763.
2   1998 SI No 3097. See also Education (Transition to New Framework) (New Schools, Groups and Miscellaneous) Regulations 1999 SI No 362.

governor is appointed in the case of a community school;
- (where the school is a foundation or voluntary school which has a religious character) a description of the ethos of the school; and
- the date when the instrument takes effect.

3.17   The schedule also establishes the procedure for making an instrument: broadly, the governing body must prepare a draft and submit it to the LEA for approval. Foundation schools must first seek the consent of the draft from the foundation governors, any trustees under a trust deed and, in the case of a church school, the appropriate diocesan authority. Upon receiving a draft, the LEA must consider whether it complies with the relevant statutory provisions and, with agreement, revise the draft and then make the instrument accordingly. If there is no agreement, except in the case of foundation schools, the LEA must consult further and, notwithstanding any lack of agreement, may then finalise the draft. In the case of a foundation school, however, if agreement is not reached, the matter is referred to the secretary of state. Instruments of government may be reviewed and must be reviewed on such occasions as may be prescribed. Similar procedures arise in respect of amending instruments, following a review.

3.18   The Education (School Government) (Transition to New Framework) Regulations 1998 establish time limits which require that new instruments of government be established by 1st June 1999. The regulations also make transitional arrangements for governors holding office under the pre-existing arrangements.

3.19   DfEE Circular 15/98: *New Framework Governing Bodies* provides guidance. In addition, the DfEE *Code of Practice on LEA-School Relations*, made under the provisions of SSFA 1998 s127, provides useful information on the overlap of responsibilities between schools and LEAs. The DfEE publishes a range of other, free, publications for governors (telephone 0845 6022260).

Staffing

3.20   SSFA 1998 Part II chapter V deals with staffing and conduct of schools. In the case of community, voluntary controlled and community special schools, the number of teachers and non-teaching staff is determined by the LEA, which is also the staff employer. The LEA may also appoint, suspend and dismiss teachers and other staff as it thinks fit, subject to the general duty to consult with the governing body. Schedule 16 establishes the detail for appointment of headteachers, deputy headteachers, teachers and non-teaching staff, and for discipline, suspension and dismissal of staff in community, voluntary controlled and community special schools. Broadly, the governing body will take responsibility for recruitment and selection, subject to the oversight of the LEA.

3.21　In the case of voluntary aided, foundation and foundation special schools, again, the number of teachers and non-teaching staff is determined by the LEA, whose consent is required for the appointment or dismissal of a teacher. However, the governing body of the school employs the staff and SSFA 1998 Sch 17 makes detailed provisions with respect to the appointment and dismissal of such staff.

3.22　The provisions of the School Teachers' Pay and Conditions Act 1991 and the relevant Teachers Pay and Conditions Order currently in force determine duties, grading and rates of pay of teaching staff.

Finance of schools

Local management of schools

3.23　Since the implementation of local management of schools (LMS) (originally introduced by the ERA 1988, re-enacted in EA 1996 Part II chapter V and now contained within the SSFA 1998) most schools maintained by LEAs have had responsibility for the great majority of their expenditure, through the LMS scheme. In effect, this provides for the funding of most schools maintained by LEAs to be managed by governing bodies. SSFA 1998 Part II chapter IV and the Financing of Maintained Schools Regulations 1999,[3] set out the revised funding arrangements for the new categories of school.

3.24　Each LEA is required to establish a scheme which provides for the allocation of resources to and between schools and which also defines the respective roles and responsibilities of LEAs and governing bodies of those schools.

3.25　Most schools maintained by LEAs (that is, community schools, foundation schools, voluntary schools and special schools) are covered by the LMS scheme (save in exceptional circumstances) but nursery schools and pupil referral units are not. LEAs are required

3　1999 SI No 101. See also Education (Budget Statements) (Wales) Regulations 1999 SI No 440 and Education (Budget Statements and Supplementary Provisions) Regulations 1999 SI No 486.

to allocate to those schools a budget share determined in accordance with a scheme. To determine a school's budget share, the LEA must ascertain its local schools budget for each financial year; in effect, this is the amount appropriated for meeting all expenditure by the LEA in that year for prescribed purposes. From the local schools budget, the LEA must identify the individual schools budget; in effect, this is the local schools budget minus certain planned expenditure determined in accordance with the 1999 regulations (see para 3.23). From this individual schools budget, each maintained school's budget share is determined, again, in accordance with the regulations.

3.26   Every school covered by a scheme must have a delegated budget. The budget remains the property of the LEA until spent by the governing body or headteacher but the governing body may spend that amount as it thinks fit, providing that it is for a purpose connected with the school or for such other purpose as may be prescribed. ('Purposes of the school' does not include those relating to part-time education for people over compulsory school age or full-time education for those over the age of 19.) Meanwhile, the governing body of a school may delegate to the headteacher its powers to spend delegated budgets, to the extent that it considers appropriate, providing that it is permitted by the LEA's scheme (SSFA 1998 s50(3)).

3.27   Governors will not incur any personal liability in respect of anything done in good faith in the exercise or purported exercise of their powers under this framework (SSFA 1998 s50(7)).

3.28   The regulations define the local schools budget as including expenditure:

1) incurred in connection with the LEA's functions in relation to the provision of primary and secondary education;
2) in relation to the LEA's chief education officer and personnel staff;
3) in relation to planning for the education service as a whole;
4) in connection with the administration of committees of the LEA dealing with education;
5) in connection with revenue budget preparation, the production and publication of accounts and external audit;
6) in connection with legal services relating to the statutory functions of the LEA;
7) in connection with the preparation and review of plans involving

collaboration with other local authority services or with public or voluntary bodies; and

8) in connection with the preparation, modification and revision of an early years development plan for the area of the LEA in accordance with SSFA 1998 ss120 and 121.

3.29 Expenditure is specifically excluded from the local schools budget if it is:

1) defrayed by fees and charges and collected by the governing body of a maintained school specifically required or permitted to be collected by any provision of the Education Acts;

2) defrayed by fees and charges collected by the governing body of a maintained school in respect of the use of school premises or equipment;

3) in connection with nursery schools;

4) in connection with any provision for children under the age of five, except where this is made at a maintained school or the expenditure is by way of fees paid for provision for children with special educational needs;

5) in making payments to another LEA concerning recoupment between LEAs;

6) capitalised by the LEA in its accounts in accordance with proper practices pursuant to any enactment or recognised code or otherwise (for example under Local Government and Housing Act 1989 s66(4));

7) offset by income received from HM Chief Inspector of Schools in England or HM Chief Inspector of Schools in Wales; and

8) for the purposes of Road Traffic Regulations Act 1984 s26 (arrangements for patrolling school crossings).

3.30 From this local schools budget, an LEA is permitted to deduct any or all of the following, in order to determine the individual schools budget, expenditure:

1) supported by specific grants;

2) related to special educational provision (or, in Wales, specialised provision);

3) relating to access to education; and

4) relating to strategic management.

(Note that this is particularised in further detail in the 1999 regulations[4] Schs 1 and 2.)

4   1999 SI No 101.

3.31   The regulations also determine each individual school's budget share and its allocation.

3.32   Schedule 14 of the SSFA 1998 establishes procedures for approval, imposition and revision of LEA schemes and schedule 15 deals with suspension of financial delegation to schools in certain circumstances. Those broadly relate to instances of mismanagement, defined as:

– substantial or persistent failure to comply with any delegation requirement or restriction, or

– where money is not managed in a satisfactory manner.

3.33   The provisions allow for review and appeal. In addition, SSFA 1998 s17 gives a separate power to LEAs to suspend a school's right to a delegated budget where the school:

– is subject to a formal warning,

– has serious weaknesses, or

– requires special measures

in accordance with SSFA 1998 s14.

Best value

3.34   Compulsory competitive tendering (CCT) (whereby certain designated activities carried out by local authorities must be subjected to competitive tendering) has now been replaced in schools by much looser arrangements known as 'best value'.

Education action zones

3.35   Under SSFA 1998 Part I Chapter III, funds may be directed at education action zones. The secretary of state may make an order establishing an education action zone with a view to improving standards in the provision of education at particular maintained schools. An order establishing an education action zone must provide for the establishment of an education action forum: a body corporate including one person appointed by the governing body of each of the participating schools (unless the governing body of any such school chooses not to so appoint) and either one or two persons appointed by the secretary of state. Regulations may allow for any statutory provisions relating to governing bodies to apply, with any prescribed modifications, to an education action forum, including that relating to financing of schools.

Opening, closing and changing schools

3.36 There are complex provisions relating to any opening, closure or change of school and this section will seek to guide the reader through key issues. The provisions of SSFA 1998 Part II chapter II and Schs 6–8 re-enact, in a simplified form, the provisions hitherto contained in EA 1996. Guidance is provided in DfEE Circular 9/99 *Organisation of School Places.*

3.37 The general duty to provide schools rests with LEAs in accordance with EA 1996 ss14 and 16, which require them to secure sufficient schools for primary and secondary education and also permits them to establish and maintain such schools and to maintain or assist schools not otherwise established by them. In addition, SSFA 1998 s26 requires the publication by every LEA of school organisation plans, setting out how these duties will be discharged.[5]

3.38 Statutory proposals under the SSFA 1998 are required in the following circumstances:

1) where an LEA proposes to establish a new community school (SSFA 1998 s28(1)(a));

2) where an LEA proposes to establish a new foundation school (SSFA 1998 s28(1)(a));

3) where an LEA proposes to make any prescribed alteration to a community school (SSFA 1998 s(28(1)(b));

4) where an LEA proposes to make any prescribed alteration to a foundation school consisting of an enlargement of the premises of the school (SSFA 1998 s28(1)(c));

5) where any promoters propose to establish a new foundation school (SSFA 1998 s28(2)(a));

6) where any promoters propose to establish a new voluntary school (SSFA 1998 s28(2)(a));

7) where the governing body of a foundation school proposes to make any prescribed alteration to the school (SSFA 1998 s28(2)(b));

8) where the governing body of a voluntary school proposes to make any prescribed alteration to the school (SSFA 1998 s28(2)(b));

9) where an LEA proposes to discontinue a community school

---

5 See also Education (School Organisation Plans) (Wales) Regulations 1999 SI No 499 and Education (School Organisation Plans) (England) Regulations 1999 SI No 701.

(SSFA 1998 s29(1)(a));

10) where an LEA proposes to discontinue a foundation school (SSFA 1998 s29(1)(a));

11) where an LEA proposes to discontinue a voluntary school (SSFA 1998 s29(1)(a));

12) where an LEA proposes to discontinue a maintained nursery school (SSFA 1998 s29(1)(b));

13) where the governing body of a foundation school proposes to discontinue the school (SSFA 1998 ss29(2) and 30(1));

14) where the governing body of a voluntary school proposes to discontinue the school (SSFA 1998 s29(2) and 30(1));

15) where an LEA intends to establish a new community special school (SSFA 1998 s31(1)(a));

16) where an LEA intends to establish a new foundation special school (SSFA 1998 s31(1)(a));

17) where an LEA intends to make any prescribed alteration to a community special school (SSFA 1998 s31(1)(b));

18) where an LEA intends to make any prescribed alteration to a foundation special school (SSFA 1998 s31(1)(b));

19) where an LEA intends to discontinue a community special school (SSFA 1998 s31(1)(c));

20) where an LEA intends to discontinue a foundation special school (SSFA 1998 s31(1)(c));

21) where the governing body of a foundation special school proposes to make any prescribed alteration to the school (SSFA 1998 s31(2)(a)); and

22) where the governing body of a foundation special school proposes to discontinue the school (SSFA 1998 s31(2)(b)).

Promoters include LEAs, governing bodies and others.[6]

3.39   Before publishing proposals, relevant bodies must consult those persons that appear to them to be appropriate, having regard to any guidance given by the secretary of state.

3.40   Once proposals have been published, they must be sent, together with prescribed information, to the school organisation committee for the area of the LEA concerned in England, or to the Secretary of State for Wales for any school in Wales.

3.41   Where a governing body is proposing to discontinue a foundation or voluntary school, it must give the secretary of state and the LEA at

6   For special schools, see also Education (Maintained Special Schools) (England) Regulations 1999 SI No 2212.

least two years' notice of its intention to do so and, if expenditure has
been incurred on the school premises (otherwise than in connection
with repairs) by the secretary of state, the Funding Agency for
Schools or any LEA, no such notice may be served without the
consent of the secretary of state. In addition, in certain
circumstances, before serving a notice, the governing body must
consult the appropriate FEFC.

3.42 There are separate provisions, contained within SSFA 1998 s32,
enabling the secretary of state, if s/he considers it expedient to do so
in the interests of the health, safety or welfare of pupils at a
community or foundation special school, to give a direction to the
LEA by which the school is maintained requiring the school to be
discontinued on a date specified in the direction. Before giving any
such direction, the secretary of state must consult the LEA, any other
LEA affected by the discontinuance of the school, in the case of a
foundation special school which has a foundation – the person who
appoints the foundation governors, and anyone else that the
secretary of state considers appropriate. In addition, SSFA 1998 s34
gives the secretary of state powers to give directions to LEAs and
governing bodies to bring forward proposals for the rationalisation
of school places.

3.43 Once proposals have been published, objections to the proposals
may be lodged by any person. Where the proposals were published
by an LEA, the objections must be sent to that LEA within a
prescribed period and that LEA must send to the relevant school
organisation committee, copies of all objections made and not
withdrawn in writing, within the objection period, together with the
LEA's observations on them. Where the proposals were published by
a governing body or other promoter any objections must be sent
direct to the relevant school organisation committee within the
prescribed period.

3.44 Proposals require approval if:

– they were published by an LEA and either objections have been
made and not withdrawn, or
– they were published by an LEA and, while no objections were
lodged, the LEA failed to make a determination whether the
proposals should be implemented, or approval is required for
other miscellaneous circumstances (as set out in SSFA 1998 Sch
6 para 4(5)(b)).

3.45 Proposals requiring approval must be considered by the relevant
school organisation committee, which may reject, approve or

approve with modifications. If the school organisation committee fails to vote on the question of whether to give any approval or does so but, in certain circumstances, is not unanimous, it must refer the proposals to the relevant adjudicator, who will then decide on the proposals.[7] Detailed provisions requiring LEAs to determine whether or not to implement proposals and when they must do so are set out in SSFA 1998 Sch 6. In Wales, the arrangements are amended to require proposals to be sent to the Secretary of State for Wales instead of a school organisation committee or adjudicator.

3.46   Where the secretary of state brings forward proposals to rationalise school places, there are arrangements for involving the school organisation committee and adjudicator, who may hold a local inquiry. However, in Wales, it is the secretary of state him/herself who will consider the matters, rather than any school organisation committee or adjudicator (SSFA 1998 Sch 7).

3.47   SSFA 1998 Sch 8 deals with changes of category of school, as follows:

1) A community school may become a foundation school in pursuance of proposals published by the LEA.
2) A community school may become a foundation, voluntary aided or voluntary controlled school in pursuance of proposals published by the governing body.
3) A foundation school may become a community, voluntary aided or voluntary controlled school in pursuance of proposals published by the governing body.
4) A voluntary aided school may become a community, foundation or voluntary controlled school pursuant to proposals published by the governing body.
5) A voluntary controlled school may become a community, foundation or voluntary aided school pursuant to proposals published by the governing body.
6) A community special school may become a foundation special school in pursuance of proposals published by the LEA.
7) A community special school may become a foundation special school in pursuance of proposals published by the governing body.
8) A foundation special school may become a community special school in pursuance of proposals published by the governing body.

7   See also Education (Adjudicators Inquiry Procedures, etc) Regulations 1999 SI No 1286.

9) If the governing body of a voluntary aided school is unable or unwilling to carry out its duties under SSFA 1998 Sch 3, it must publish proposals for the school to become either voluntary controlled or a foundation school (depending on prescribed circumstances).

The schedule requires that proposals are published and implemented subject to regulations.

3.48   Finally, SSFA 1998 Sch 22 makes arrangements for disposals of land and disposals on discontinuance. The schedule restricts the powers to dispose of land by requiring the written consent of the secretary of state in certain circumstances.

3.49   Which bodies or people are entitled to be consulted depends on the step proposed and the interrelation between common law and statutory requirement, but may include: LEAs, governing bodies, parents, FEFCs and others. In *R v Brent LBC ex p Gunning*,[8] the court determined that all those affected by a decision to close a school, particularly parents of children at the school, have a legitimate expectation to be consulted before the decision is made. In *R v Sutton LBC ex p Hamlet*,[9] Webster J concurred with the view of Hodgson J in *Gunning*, that the basic requirements of consultation are:

> First, that consultation must be at a time when proposals are still at a formative stage. Second, that the proposer must give sufficient reasons for any proposal to permit of intelligent consideration and response. Third, ... that adequate time must be given for consideration and response and, finally, fourth, that the product of consultation must be conscientiously taken into account in finalising any statutory proposals.

3.50   However, in *R v Secretary of State for Education and Employment and North East London Education Association ex p M and Others*,[10] the court constrained the doctrine of legitimate expectation so as to remove any public law duty to consult subsequently in those circumstances where consultation had arisen previously, prior to proposals being firmed up.[11]

---

8   (1985) 84 LGR 168, QBD.
9   (1986) 26 March (unreported).
10 [1996] ELR162, QBD and CA.
11 See also *R v Leeds City Council ex p N and Others* [1999] ELR 324, an unsuccessful judicial review over the obligations to consult over school closure.

School premises

3.51   School premises are not clearly defined in legislation. However, EA 1996 s579(1) provides that premises include playing fields but not accommodation for teachers.

General requirements

3.52   Requirements for educational premises are set out in EA 1996 ss542–543 and the consequent Education (School Premises) Regulations 1999.[12] These regulations state:

1) There are minimum requirements for washrooms for pupils, which must contain sanitary fittings and washbasins. Where schools have pupils over the age of 11 who undertake physical education, there must be changing accommodation with showers. For staff, there must be an adequate number of washrooms, separate from those for pupils (although washrooms that are accessible for disabled people may be provided for the use of pupils, staff and visitors).

2) Medical accommodation must be provided in each school, including a washbasin and a lavatory reasonably close.

3) Every nursery school, special school and every other school with more than 120 pupils (other than a pupil referral unit) must have a headteacher's room and every school (other than a pupil referral unit) must have a staff room.

4) Generally, school buildings must be sufficient for safe and convenient passage, for storing and drying pupils' outdoor clothing, for preparing food and drink, and for washing crockery and utensils.

5) In the case of boarding schools, each school must have adequate sleeping accommodation such that boys and girls over the age of eight do not share rooms with those of the opposite sex. There must also be sufficient bathroom accommodation accessible to the sleeping accommodation, having regard to the ages, sex and numbers of pupils and to any special requirements that they may have. There are minimum standards of accommodation for private study and social purposes and accommodation for the preparation of meals. Each boarding school must have at least one sick room and, if the school has more than 40 boarding

---

12   1999 SI No 2.

pupils, one isolation room together with ancillary facilities. There must be sufficient separate accommodation for staff in order that they may take meals, be able to sleep and have associated facilities. Finally, every boarding school must have adequate storage facilities.

6) There are general requirements for schools relating to the load-bearing structure of school buildings, weather protection, health and safety and welfare – especially in respect of fire and safe escape, acoustics, lighting, heating, ventilation, water supplies and drainage. In addition, Education (Schools and Further and Higher Education) Regulations 1989[13] reg 7 makes provision for the restriction of use in schools of radioactive substances and certain apparatus in which electrons are accelerated.

7) With respect to playing fields, there are detailed minimum requirements depending on the age and type of school.

3.53   In *Reffell v Surrey CC*,[14] it was held that there might be a private law action for damages for personal injury arising from a breach of statutory duty under EA 1944 s10 (EA 1996 ss542–543) (see the discussion on negligence actions in chapter 15). However, it may well also be the case that failure to comply with the minimum requirements may lead to an action in judicial review (see chapter 14).

Disabled people

3.54   Chronically Sick and Disabled Persons Act 1970 s8 requires providers of school buildings to ensure that appropriate provision is made to meet the needs of disabled people in terms of access to the building, parking facilities and sanitary conveniences. In addition, Town and Country Planning Act 1990 s76 requires planning authorities to draw the attention of developers to the provisions of both the 1970 Act and Design Note 18.[15] EA 1996 s317 (which incorporates the provisions of Disability Discrimination Act 1995 s29) requires that the annual report of a school includes information about, among other things, 'the facilities provided to assist access to the school by disabled people'. Note that, otherwise, the Disability Discrimination Act 1995 does not apply to the provision of education

13 1989 SI No 351.
14 [1964] 1 All ER 743, QBD.
15 *Access for the Physically Disabled to Educational Buildings* (1984, published by Secretary of State for Education).

to disabled children in schools. Finally, Administrative Memoranda 2/85[16] and 1/86[17] and DfEE Circular 3/97[18] all provide guidance.

Areas to which pupils and students belong

3.55   LEAs have a variety of powers and duties towards pupils and students; including those concerning special educational provision, admissions and exclusions arrangements and appeals, provision of support services including transport, grant giving, etc. However, it is not always entirely clear which LEA is responsible for which pupil or student. Accordingly, the Education (Areas to Which Pupils and Students Belong) Regulations 1996, as amended,[19] made in accordance with the provisions of EA 1996 ss414(3)(d), 492 and 495(3), establish a general rule and a series of exceptions to that rule.

3.56   The general principle is that:

1) A school pupil or FE student 'belongs' to the LEA in whose area s/he is ordinarily resident.

2) 'Ordinarily resident' refers to the address at which that person is habitually and usually resident, apart from temporary or occasional absences. However, a school pupil is not to be regarded as ordinarily resident in the area of an LEA by reason only of his/her residing as a boarder at a school in that LEA's area.

3) Where a school pupil or FE student has no ordinary residence (for whatever reason) then s/he belongs to the LEA in whose area s/he is for the time being resident.

3.57   Exceptions to the rule are as follows:

1) **School pupils with statements of SEN living in boarding accommodation (reg 4)** Except where a child is looked after by a local authority (in which case, see below (4)), where s/he has a statement of special educational needs (SEN), attends a boarding school or is provided with boarding accommodation, and does

---

16   *Constructional Standards for Maintained Educational Buildings in England* DES Administrative Memorandum 2/85.

17   *Modification of Approval Procedures for LEA Schools and FE Building Projects* DES Administrative Memorandum 1/86.

18   *What the Disability Discrimination Act (DDA) 1995 means for schools and LEAs* DfEE Circular 3/97.

19   1996 SI No 615, amended by Education (Areas to Which Pupils and Students Belong) (Amendment) Regulations 1997 SI No 597.

not spend holidays with the person responsible for him/her, then the LEA responsible is that in whose area the person responsible ordinarily resides. Where no such person has such ordinary residence, then the LEA responsible is that which maintains the pupil's statement of SEN.

2) **School pupils with statements of SEN and pupils at special schools (reg 5)** Except where a pupil with a statement of SEN lives in boarding accommodation (in which case, see above (1)) or where a pupil is in hospital or is looked after by a local authority (in which case, see below (3) and (4)) then where a pupil has a statement of SEN or is otherwise registered as a pupil at a special school, the LEA responsible is that in whose area the person responsible is ordinarily resident. Where such a person does not have such ordinary residence but is otherwise resident in England and Wales, then the LEA responsible is that in whose area the person responsible is for the time being resident. If the person is not resident in England or Wales, then the LEA responsible is that in whose area the person who has care for the pupil is ordinarily resident. Where none of the above applies, the LEA responsible for the pupil is that which is responsible for making provision for the pupil's education.

3) **School pupils resident in hospital (reg 6)** Except where a pupil is looked after by a local authority (in which case, see below (4)), where a pupil receives education while a patient in a hospital, the LEA responsible is that in whose area the person responsible for the pupil is ordinarily resident. Where such a person has no such residency, then the LEA responsible is that in whose area the person responsible for the pupil is for the time being resident. Otherwise, the LEA responsible is that in whose area the hospital is situated.

4) **Children looked after by a local authority (reg 7)** Where a child is looked after by a local authority in accordance with the provisions of Children Act 1989 s22(1) and either has a statement of SEN or is otherwise registered as a pupil at a special school or is a patient in a hospital and receives education there, or is a FE student, the LEA responsible is that whose area coincides with or includes the area of the local authority which looks after the child or student.

5) **Further education students becoming ordinarily resident for educational purposes (reg 8)** Where a student attends a FE course and has moved to become ordinarily resident in the area

of a LEA for the purpose of attending that course or a previous FE or HE course (which immediately precedes the current course, disregarding any intervening vacation) then the LEA responsible for the student is the LEA in whose area the student lived immediately before moving to attend the course. Where the student had no such residence, s/he belongs to the LEA in whose area s/he attends his/her current course.

6) **Further education students who change ordinary residence while attending courses (reg 9)** Where a student changes his/her ordinary residence while attending a course of FE (or a previous FE or HE course – as in (5) above), then where the student was treated as belonging to the area of an education authority immediately before his/her change of ordinary residence, s/he continues to be treated as belonging to that area for so long as s/he attends his/her current course.

7) **Further education students in receipt of awards (reg 10)** Where a FE student is in receipt of an award otherwise than under EA 1962 s1 (awards by LEAs for designated courses such as those at universities, degree courses, diplomas of higher education, initial training of teachers, higher national diplomas etc), the LEA responsible for the student is that from whom the award was made, so long as the student attends the course in question.

CHAPTER 4

School curriculum, standards and inspections

This chapter considers the curriculum in all maintained schools, explaining the National Curriculum and discussing particular aspects, including political issues, sex education, religious education and careers advice. Charges which can be applied in relation to the curriculum, provision of information and the system of school inspections are discussed. Finally the chapter deals with complaints about the curriculum and the appeal process.

The curriculum in general

4.1   Unlike in other parts of Europe (apart from France), the British government did not prescribe what was taught in schools and the methods of teaching until relatively recently. Although EA 1944 laid down a legal framework for religious education and collective worship, the rest of the curriculum was left in the hands of individual LEAs and the teaching profession. Under the Thatcher government in the 1980s concern was expressed about so-called political bias and purported promotion of homosexuality by LEAs and teachers, and about falling standards. The response came in a number of Education Acts.

4.2   The Education (No 2) Act 1986 removed much power from the LEAs and placed it in the hands of governing bodies. LEAs were still expected to develop and publish curriculum policies. However, the most dramatic change came with the Education Reform Act (ERA) 1988. This introduced the National Curriculum as well as changes in the law governing religious education and collective worship. Also, parents were given the means to complain about curricular issues and rights of access to information.

4.3   Under EA 1996 s351(1), the secretary of state, LEAs, governing bodies and headteachers must exercise their functions so that the curriculum is 'balanced and broadly based' and:

(a) promotes the spiritual, moral, cultural, mental and physical development of pupils at the school and of society, and
(b) prepares pupils at the school for the opportunities, responsibilities and experiences of adult life.

This is called the 'whole curriculum'. There is an emphasis on a thematic approach and the learning of specific skills.

4.4   Since 1986 LEAs have not had formal control of the secular curriculum but, in practice, they still have considerable influence. Although they are no longer required to make statements of curricular policy, they now have the duty of promoting high standards in primary and secondary education.[1] Governing bodies are responsible for the conduct of maintained schools and they must conduct schools in a manner which ensures high standards of educational achievement (SSFA 1998 s38(2)). SSFA 1998 s38(3) provides for regulations to define the roles and responsibilities of governors and headteachers in relation to the curriculum.

---

1   SSFA 1998 s5 creates a new s13A to EA 1996.

Clarification of the governors' role is needed following the repeal of EA 1996 ss370–374. The headteacher is responsible for the implementation of the curriculum and must ensure the implementation of the National Curriculum (EA 1996 s357). Each school must provide a prospectus which contains, among other things, a statement on the curriculum and the organisation of education and teaching methods in the school including its special educational needs policy.[2] This also has to include details of attainment targets at each key stage and results of examinations taken.

The National Curriculum

4.5 Under EA 1996 s352(1), every maintained school must have a basic curriculum which conforms with EA 1996 s351 (see para 4.3). The provisions do not apply to independent schools where there is, therefore, no government control over the curriculum. The National Curriculum is published and revised by the Qualifications and Curriculum Authority (QCA) (in England) and the Qualifications, Curriculum and Assessment Authority for Wales (QCAAW). See further para 4.62.

4.6 The National Curriculum is divided into core subjects and foundation subjects for each of the four 'key stages' of pupils' school careers, defined by EA 1996 s355. These are:

Key stage 1 (5–7 years) from compulsory school age to the school year in which the majority of children in a class reach age seven (infants).

Key stage 2 (8–11 years) from the school year in which the majority of children in a class reach age eight until the end of the year in which the majority reach age 11 (juniors).

Key stage 3 (12–14 years) from the school year when the majority in the class reach age 12 until the end of the year when the majority

---

2   Education (School Information) (England) Regulations 1998 SI No 2526, as amended by 1999 SI No 251; Education (School Information) (Wales) Regulations 1999 SI No 1812; and Education (Special Educational Needs) (Information) Regulations 1994 SI No 1048. See also DfEE Circulars 11/96 *School Prospectuses and Governors' Annual Reports in Primary Schools* and 12/96 *School Prospectuses and Governors' Annual Reports in Secondary Schools* and DfEE Circulars 7/98 *School Prospectuses in Primary Schools* and 8/98 *School Prospectuses in Secondary Schools.*

reach age 14 (secondary).

Key stage 4 (15–16 years) from the school year when the majority in the class reach age 15 until the year when the majority reach the compulsory school leaving age (secondary).

4.7   The core subjects are (EA 1996 s354(1)):

- mathematics
- English
- science
- Welsh (in Welsh-speaking schools).

4.8   The other foundation subjects are (EA 1996 s354(2)):

- technology
- physical education
- history, geography, art and music at key stages 1, 2 and 3
- modern foreign language at key stages 3 and 4
- Welsh in non-Welsh-speaking schools in Wales.

4.9   Each subject has specified attainment targets, programmes of study and assessment arrangements for each key stage. These are set by the QCA and QCAAW and are contained in numerous orders and statutory instruments. Since its introduction, it has become apparent that the original demands of the National Curriculum were too ambitious and left little in the way of flexibility. There has been considerable paring down, mostly outside the core subjects. 20 per cent of curriculum time at key stages 1 to 3 is to be used at the school's discretion, and 40 per cent at key stage 4.

4.10   The following table[3] shows which subjects pupils have to study at each key stage. Pupils who entered key stage 4 before September 1996 do not have to study design and technology, information technology or a modern foreign language. The government intends to issue regulations making it compulsory for pupils over the age of 11 to spend 5 per cent of their school time learning citizenship from 2002.

---

3   Taken from leaflet *The School Curriculum: a brief guide* (DfEE, 1995). Many related publications are available from the DfEE Publications Department, telephone 0845 6022260.

	Key stage 1	Key stage 2	Key stage 3	Key stage 4
English	✓	✓	✓	✓
mathematics	✓	✓	✓	✓
science	✓	✓	✓	✓
physical education	✓	✓	✓	✓
design and technology	✓	✓	✓	✓
information technology	✓	✓	✓	✓
modern foreign language			✓	✓
history		✓	✓	✓
geography		✓	✓	✓
music		✓	✓	✓
art		✓	✓	✓

Assessment

4.11   Assessment of pupils is a vital part of the National Curriculum. At the end of key stages 1, 2 and 3, standard assessment tasks (SATs) are required in the core subjects only. English and mathematics are tested at the end of key stages 1 and 2 and science is added at key stage 3. The headteacher must make arrangements for children to be assessed at key stages 1, 2 and 3.[4] Furthermore, headteachers in primary schools are now required to undertake baseline assessments of children when they start school.[5] This is intended to aid educational planning for particular children and to measure their future educational achievements. Most 16-year-olds will take GCSEs or similar qualifications. Teachers' own assessments continue to play an important role, particularly in the foundation subjects. The government has confirmed that teacher assessment and national test results will be given equal weight in the publication of results.

4.12   Governing bodies of maintained schools are now required to set and publish annually targets for the performance of pupils in public examinations and in assessments related to the National Curriculum.[6]

---

4   EA 1997 s17.

5   EA 1997 s17 and Education (Baseline Assessment) (England) Regulations 1998 SI No 1551; Education (Baseline Assessment) (Wales) Regulations 1999 SI No 1188.

6   EA 1997 s19, Education (School Performance Targets) (England) Regulations 1998 SI No 1532 and Education (School Performance Targets) (Wales) Regulations 1998 SI No 2196.

4.13   Following *Wandsworth LBC v NAS/UWT*,[7] where 88 per cent of teachers who belonged to the National Association of School-masters/Union of Women Teachers in Wandsworth balloted to boycott testing and assessment procedures, the government has taken more powers to audit and verify standards of assessment and gain access to school documents and records.[8]

Exemption from the National Curriculum

4.14   Where an LEA or governing body wants to carry out curriculum development work or experiments at a particular maintained school the secretary of state may direct, under EA 1996 s362, that the National Curriculum shall not apply or shall be modified for a specified period. The Qualifications and Curriculum Authority (see paras 4.9) can also apply for this, if the LEA and the governing body of a community, voluntary controlled or community special school both agree. The agreement of the LEA is not a prerequisite to an application by a foundation, voluntary aided or foundation special school.

4.15   In the case of an individual pupil, regulations[9] made under EA 1996 s365 empower the headteacher of a maintained school to disapply or modify the National Curriculum for up to six months at a time if s/he thinks that it is inappropriate to offer it for the time being and either:

- it is likely to be temporary,[10] or
- there needs to be an assessment with a view to making or amending a statement of special educational needs.

The disapplication or modification is done by means of a written direction and parents, the LEA and the governors must be given information, including reasons. Parents can appeal to governors (EA

---

7   [1994] ELR 170, CA.
8   EA 1996 s356(5)–(8), Education (School Performance Information) (England) Regulations 1999 SI No 1178, and Education (School Performance Information) (Wales) Regulations 1998 SI No 1867 as amended by 1999 SI No 1470.
9   Education (National Curriculum) (Temporary Exceptions for Individual Pupils) Regulations 1989 SI No 1181; Education (National Curriculum) (Temporary Exceptions for Individual Pupils) (Wales) Regulations 1999 SI No 1815.
10 DES Circular 15/89 *ERA 1988: Temporary exceptions from the National Curriculum* states that these cases, for example where the pupil has come from a different educational system, or has been out of school or in hospital, will be rare.

1996 s367(1)–(4)). The headteacher must concur with any ruling of the governors.

4.16   In the longer term a statement of special educational needs may disapply or modify the National Curriculum for an individual pupil.

4.17   EA 1996 s363 also gives the secretary of state power to make regulations providing for all or part of the National Curriculum not to apply to certain groups. For example, the requirements concerning English are disapplied for pupils in Wales who receive more than half their teaching in Welsh.

4.18   It is clear that, when children are receiving home tuition because, for example, they have been excluded from school, they are unlikely to be receiving the full National Curriculum. There will have been no disapplication and so an LEA would appear to be in breach of its statutory duty to provide the national curriculum.

4.19   Where a pupil is unable to access particular lessons, for example because of physical disability or discipline problems, the issue of unauthorised disapplication of the National Curriculum may arise.

4.20   The National Curriculum is disapplied in pupil referral units (EA 1996 Sch 1 para 6), which are required to provide a broad and balanced curriculum. (see chapter 11).

Particular aspects of the curriculum

Political issues

4.21   Political bias in the curriculum is prohibited by EA 1996 s406. It may be difficult to decide how political an issue is, eg, environmental awareness. However, s406 prohibits the 'pursuit of partisan political activities' to pupils under 12 and the promotion of overtly partisan political views in any subjects taught, whether on or off site. EA 1996 s407 requires LEAs, governing bodies and headteachers to take reasonable, practical steps to ensure that pupils are offered a balanced presentation of opposing views.

Sex education

4.22   DFE Circular 5/94[11] provides guidance on this area. In primary

---

11 DFE Circular 5/94 *Education Act 1993: Sex Education in Schools*. A draft circular will be issued at the end of 1999 for consultation to replace Circular 5/94. In autumn 2000, Ofsted inspections will cover sex relationship education and a good practice guide will be issued to all schools by summer 2001.

schools, sex education is not compulsory, though governing bodies have to consider the question and have a written policy on sex education and its provision (EA 1996 s404). Likewise, governing bodies of all maintained schools must have policies for providing sex education. The LEA, governing bodies and the headteacher of maintained schools which provide sex education must ensure that this has due regard to moral considerations and the value of family life (EA 1996 s403). All pupils receiving secondary education must receive it as part of the basic curriculum (EA 1996 s352(1)). Sex education includes education about AIDS, HIV and any other sexually transmitted disease (EA 1996 s352(3)). This may well be part of a human and social awareness course.

4.23   EA 1996 s405 empowers parents to withdraw their child unconditionally from sex education lessons but a pupil cannot remove him/herself. Consequently sex education is not a part of the science curriculum: all pupils continue to learn the biological facts of life in science but no other aspects of human sexual behaviour.[12]

Contraception

4.24   Circular 5/94 paras 38 to 41 attempt to deal with the conflicts highlighted by the *Gillick* case,[13] that is, the difficulty facing an independent professional in advising a child about sexual behaviour

---

12 EA 1996 s356(9) and Education (National Curriculum) (Attainment Targets and Programmes of Study in Science) Order 1995 SI No 53 reg 3.

13 *Gillick v West Norfolk and Wisbech AHA* [1985] 3 All ER 402, HL. In this case the Department of Health and Social Security issued a circular to area health authorities containing advice to the effect that a doctor consulted at a family planning clinic by a girl under 16 would not be acting unlawfully if s/he prescribed contraceptives for the girl, so long as in doing so s/he was acting in good faith to protect her against the harmful effects of sexual intercourse. In exceptional cases the girl's parents did not need to be consulted if in the doctor's clinical judgment it was desirable to prescribe contraceptives. The plaintiff, who had five daughters under 16, sought assurance from her health authority that it would not give such advice or treatment to her daughters. The authority refused to give her such assurances and she took the matter to court. The House of Lords held that a child became increasingly independent as it grew older and parental authority dwindled. Accordingly, the law did not recognise any rule of absolute parental authority until a fixed age. Parental rights were recognised by the law only as long as they were needed for the protection of the child. These rights gave way to the child's right to make decisions when s/he reached sufficient understanding and intelligence to be capable of making up his/her own mind. A girl under 16 did not lack the legal capacity to consent to contraceptive advice and treatment merely because of her age.

which would not meet with the parents' approval. The implication in the circular is that teachers (of pupils under 16 at least) must not usurp 'the proper exercise of parental rights and responsibilities'. Paragraph 40 of the circular advises that where a teacher is approached by an individual pupil for specific advice on contraception or other aspects of sexual behaviour the pupil should be encouraged to seek advice from his/her parents and if appropriate from health professionals. If it is apparent that the child has embarked on or is contemplating a course of conduct that is in breach of the law or would put the child at moral or physical risk then the headteacher should be informed. S/he should arrange counselling, if appropriate, and for the parents to be informed, preferably by the pupil if the pupil is under age.

4.25   Teachers are not health professionals, and the legal position of a teacher giving contraceptive advice has never been tested in the courts (para 39). Paragraph 40 of the circular advises that where the pupil is 'under age' the parents should be made aware and suggests a limitation of the kind of advice which teachers can give, particularly to pupils under 16. Perhaps this would vary depending on whether the advice was given to an individual pupil or to a group. It could be easier to ascertain whether an individual child were '*Gillick* competent' rather than a whole group. Even so, the overall tone of the circular guidance seems to indicate a retreat from *Gillick* principles in the field of education.

Homosexuality

4.26   Local Government Act 1988 s28 introduced a new s2A into Local Government Act 1986, which prevents LEAs from intentionally promoting homosexuality or publishing materials which promote homosexuality or promoting the teaching in any maintained school of homosexuality as a pretended family relationship. This section does not apply directly to schools or to education to prevent the spread of disease, for example, AIDS. Circular 5/94 makes no reference to homosexuality although the law on buggery is summarised in appendix B. With the prospect of the age of consent for homosexual acts being reduced to 16 in the near future, it seems likely that this subject will need to be addressed more positively in the sex education curriculum. There is nothing to prevent homosexuality being raised in schools, for example, through literature.

Worship and religious education

4.27   LEAs, governing bodies and headteachers have a duty under SSFA 1998 s70 to ensure that all pupils attending community, foundation or voluntary schools take part in an act of collective worship each school day. This may be a single act of worship for all pupils or separate acts for different groups (SSFA 1998 Sch 20 para 2(2)). In community and foundation schools without a religious character, this must be of a broadly Christian character without being distinctive of any particular denomination (SSFA 1998 Sch 20 para 3(3)). It does not matter that non-Christian children would be participating.[14] In a foundation or voluntary school with a religious character the collective worship will be in accordance with any trust deed or in accordance with a specific religious denomination (SSFA s69(4) and Sch 20 para 5). Parents have the unqualified right to withdraw children from such worship and from religious education (SSFA 1998 s71(1)). Where the parents cannot agree between themselves whether the child should be withdrawn, the court will follow the checklist in Children Act 1989 s1(3).[15]

4.28   A headteacher of a maintained school may, after consultation with the governing body, which may consult parents, apply to the local standing advisory council on religious education (SACRE)[16] to lift or modify the Christian requirement of collective worship for any class or description of pupil (EA 1996 s394; SSFA 1998 Sch 20 para 4). This happens in schools where there are children of different and often non-Christian faiths. The decision must be reviewed on any application of the headteacher and in any event every five years (EA 1996 s395). The secretary of state can intervene if s/he considers that a SACRE is acting unreasonably in this regard (EA 1996 s396).

4.29   LEAs, governing bodies and headteachers must ensure that religious education is provided as part of the basic curriculum (SSFA 1998 s69). There must be an agreed syllabus for an LEA approved by the SACRE (EA 1996 s375 and Sch 31). This must reflect England's mainly Christian background but must consider the other main religions. In community, foundation and voluntary schools without

---

14   *R v Secretary of State for Education ex p R and D* [1994] ELR 495, QBD.

15   *Re T and M (minors)* [1995] ELR 1.

16   Every LEA must constitute a SACRE to advise on religious worship and education including an agreed syllabus. The membership consists of representatives of Christian denominations including the Church of England (but not in Wales), and other religions representative of religions in an area. There are also representatives of teachers and the LEA (EA 1996 ss390–94).

a religious character, no religious catechism or formulary distinctive of any particular denomination may be used in the religious education syllabus.[17] Facilities should be provided for children to withdraw from lessons to receive education of a particular religion, unless it would be unreasonable to do so (SSFA 1998 Sch 19 para 2).

4.30   In foundation and voluntary controlled schools with a religious character, if parents request religious education of this denomination, the governors must ensure that this is provided during not more than two periods a week (SFA 1998 Sch 19 para 3). In voluntary aided schools of a religious character, religious education will reflect the specific religious denomination. Education in accordance with an LEA's agreed policy can be provided where this is requested by parents and the children cannot with reasonable convenience attend a school where the LEA syllabus is in use (SSFA 1998 Sch 19 para 4). See generally, Circular 1/94 *RE and Collective Worship*.

4.31   Religious education is not part of the National Curriculum, so attainment targets cannot be set by the secretary of state. Nevertheless, model syllabuses containing attainment targets exist. Again, parents can withdraw their children.

Careers education

4.32   Careers education is defined as education designed to prepare people for taking decisions about their careers and to help them implement such decisions (EA 1997 s43(6)). All maintained schools, including special schools (other than those in hospitals), city technology colleges and city colleges for the technology of the arts and pupil referral units, must provide a programme of careers education for children in the last three years of compulsory schooling (EA 1997 s43(5)).

4.33   EA 1997 s44 gives careers advisers rights to information. They must be provided with names and addresses of relevant pupils, the parent's address if different from the pupil's, and information held by the school which is needed to provide the pupil with advice and guidance about his/her career. A parent or pupil over 18 can prevent such information being released. Advisers have access to pupils and students, both individually and in groups, in order to provide careers advice.

17 This appears to be the earliest specific provision in our education legislation (Elementary Education Act 1870) which survives intact.

4.34   By EA 1997 s45 students must have access to guidance material and a wide range of up-to-date reference material. There is guidance to schools on making these arrangements available on the premises.[18] For example, there must be a dedicated careers library which must be open at all reasonable times.

4.35   EA 1997 s44(11) defines a careers adviser as a person employed by a body providing services in pursuance of arrangements made or directions given under the Employment and Training Act 1973 s10. They are often employed by a company contracted to the LEA, rather than by the school or college.

Charges for education

4.36   Since the early 1900s it has not been permitted to charge for education in maintained schools. The blanket prohibition in EA 1944 s6 was watered down in Education Reform Act 1988.[19] With certain exceptions it is not possible to charge for education provided for registered pupils during normal school hours.

4.37   Education outside school hours cannot be charged for if it is a necessary part of a syllabus, an examination, part of the National Curriculum or religious education which complies with the basic curriculum (see EA 1996 s384) (EA 1996 s351(4)).

4.38   Charges can be made for the following:

– individual and small group (up to four) music tuition in school hours (EA 1996 s451(3)–(5)), unless it is part of preparation for an examination, part of the National Curriculum or religious education within the basic curriculum;

– board and lodging on residential trips (EA 1996 ss452(6) and s455(1)(d)).

4.39   Conversely, no charge may be made for:

1) the National Curriculum or religious education (EA 1996 ss357 and 451; SSFA 1998 s69);

2) any part of a syllabus for a public examination for which the school is preparing the pupil (EA 1996 s453(1));[20]

18 DfEE Circulars 5/97 *Careers Education and Guidance in Schools: Effective Partnerships with Careers Services* and 5/98 *Careers Education in Schools: Provision for Years 9–11.*

19 See now EA 1996 s450–456, DES Circular 2/89 *Education Reform Act 1988: Charges for School Activities* and DFE Circular 2/94 *Local Management of Schools,* paras 147–155.

3) entry to a public examination (EA 1996 s453(1));
4) materials (unless parents have said in advance that they wish to keep any end product), books, instruments or other equipment, which is defined in EA 1996 s462 as not including clothing (EA 1996 s454(1) and (2));
5) transport which is incidental to education for which no charge can be made or in relation to preparation for public examinations (EA 1996 s454(3) and (4)).

4.40   Charging in kind is also prohibited (EA 1996 s454). The governing bodies of maintained schools may request or invite voluntary contributions. Any such request must explain that this is not obligatory and that pupils will not be treated differently according to whether parents contributed or not.[21]

4.41   Governors may charge for 'optional extras' under EA 1996 s455 if parents agree and they do not come under s451 (see above). These include education not included by EA 1996 s451, ie, outside the National Curriculum or basic curriculum, transport, examination fees, and the cost price of board on residential trips. Only the actual cost may be charged. The cost is determined by governors (if they have control of funds) or the LEA. Both must have a charging and remissions policy. Without a policy they are unable to charge. There must be complete remission for board and lodging on residential trips if the parents are on benefit and the education comes under s451.

4.42   Where educational activities take place partly in and partly outside school hours, different arrangements apply, see EA 1996 s452. If 50 per cent or more of the period of the activity, including travelling time, falls during school hours then any education provided outside school hours will be treated as coming under EA 1996 s451 and will not be chargeable. If less than 50 per cent of the education and related travelling time takes place inside school hours it shall be treated as taking place outside school hours. If the number of school sessions taken up by a residential trip equals or exceeds the number of half days (ie, 12 hours) spent on the trip then the education will be deemed to come under EA 1996 s451 and not be chargeable. If the opposite applies then the education will be deemed to take place outside school hours.

---

20   Education (Prescribed Public Examination) Regulations 1989 SI No 377.
21   EA 1996 s460(1)–(2); DES Circular 2/89 *Education Reform Act 1988: Charges for School Activities* para 15.

Information

Pupils' achievements

4.43   In the Parents' Charter (see para 2.5) the government promised parents written information on their child's progress at least once a year. This is now covered by regulations.[22] The information must take into account matters in the specific regulations relating to each key stage including, where appropriate, the success rate for other pupils in the school.

4.44   A headteacher must prepare a report on a child's academic achievement for the head of a new school when a child transfers. This must be received within 15 days of departure from the school.[23]

4.45   All school leavers also have to have a report set out in a prescribed way. The governors' annual report must contain the details of public examinations and assessments, the continuing education of pupils leaving school and employment details.[24]

4.46   Under EA 1997 s19 governing bodies are required to set annual targets from the 1998/9 school year.[25] Regulations under EA 1996 s537A require governing bodies of every school, including independent schools, to provide information on individual pupils or former pupils.[26]

Education records

4.47   All maintained (including special) schools have to keep a curricular record which transfers with the individual pupil throughout his/her

22   Education (Individual Pupils' Achievements) (Information) Regulations 1997 SI No 1368; Education (Individual Pupils' Achievements) (Information) (Wales) Regulations 1997 SI No 573, as amended by 1999 SI No 1497.
23   1997 SI No 1368 (n22) reg 7.
24   SSFA 1998 s42; Education (School Performance Targets) (England) Regulations 1998 SI No 1532; Education (School Performance Targets) (Wales) Regulations 1998 SI No 2196.
25   Education (School Performance Targets) Regulations (for England and Wales), see n24.
26   Education (Information About Individual Pupils) (England) Regulations 1999 SI No 989; Education (Individual Pupil Information) (Prescribed Persons) Regulations 1999 SI No 903; Education (School Performance Information) (England) Regulations 1998 SI No 1929; Education (School Performance Information) (Wales) Regulations 1998 SI No 1867; Education (Individual Performance Information) (Prescribed Bodies and Persons) Regulations 1997 SI No 2440; Education (Individual Performance Information) (Prescribed Bodies and Persons) (Wales) Regulations 1998 SI No 1120.

school career.[27] It should be noted that records dating from before 1 September 1989 are likely to be hard to find, because reg 6 gives governing bodies a discretion to decide what is appropriate to transfer and the new school or college must make a written request. Governors have to ensure that this record is updated each year.

4.48 Parents of pupils under 16, the parents or pupils themselves if 16 or 17, and the pupil if over 18 can receive copies of the curricular records. A request must be made in writing and any fee not exceeding the cost of supply of the copies must be paid for (EA 1996 s563). A request must be complied with within 15 'school' days, ie, days when the school meets. Schools may not disclose statements of SEN, reports to magistrates' courts or racial details (reg 12). These regulations only apply to information compiled after 1 September 1989 (reg 13).

4.49 If any inaccuracies (other than assessment of achievement) are pointed out, the governors must either correct the record or attach the parents'/pupil's letter to the record. No change can be made to an assessment of special educational needs. Disclosure does not have to be made where it might be detrimental to the child (regs 9–13). Where the decision not to disclose is taken by a teacher, the governing body must make arrangements to hear appeals relating to disclosure. It is probably not appropriate for the headteacher or teacher governors to hear such appeals.

4.50 There is some confusion about precisely what information is accessible to parents and pupils. It can include 'other educational records ... kept at the school' (reg 7(1)(a)). This includes the teacher's record, defined as 'any record kept at the school by a teacher other than a record kept and intended to be kept solely for that teacher's own use' (reg 7(2)). This seems to limit the amount of information potentially accessible to parents. The regulations cannot be used to obtain access to files and documents held centrally by the LEA.

Inspection and review

Inspection of schools

4.51 Previously, school inspections, which included curricular issues, were the province of Her Majesty's Inspectors (HMIs) and, to some

27 Education (School Records) Regulations 1989 SI No 1261 as subsequently amended and Circular 17/89 *The Education (School Records) Regulations* 1989.

extent, the LEAs. This was changed by the Education (Schools) Act 1992, which set up the Office for Standards in Education (Ofsted). HMIs now work for Ofsted, the head of which is the Chief Inspector for Schools.

4.52   The role of HMIs includes:

1) monitoring inspection teams and registered inspectors (see para 4.54);
2) training inspectors;
3) inspecting some schools (including independent schools);
4) monitoring schools which are failing to carry out their statutory duties (see para 4.59);
5) inspecting LEAs (see para 4.61).

4.53   The chief inspector has to ensure that schools are inspected every five years in England[28] and every six years in Wales.[29] Teams of inspectors contract with Ofsted to carry out inspections of individual schools. Contracts are awarded following submission of tenders, on the basis of 'value for money'. The contractors are private companies, which usually select from a pool of qualified inspectors for each particular inspection.

4.54   Inspectors gain qualification by attending a course and passing tests. Each inspection must be led by a 'registered inspector', who has passed further tests, worked on a number of previous inspections, been inspected by HMIs and paid a registration fee. At least one member of an inspection team ('the lay member') must have no personal experience of the management or provision of education in a school, other than as a governor or in a voluntary capacity. Neither may this person be employed primarily to provide financial or business expertise (SIA 1996 Sch 3 para 3).

4.55   Under SIA 1996 s24, LEAs may maintain a school inspection service to inspect their own or other schools on a full cost basis and subject to the tendering arrangements (see para 4.53). They also have a duty and a power to inspect the arrangements made for pupils who are being educated at home (see paras 7.15–7.17). They retain a restricted power under SIA 1996 s25 to inspect in order to obtain information about any matter in connection with any school maintained by them. This power should only be used where it is not

---

28 Education (School Inspection) Regulations 1997 SI No 1966.
29 Education (School Inspection) (Wales) Regulations 1998 SI No 1866, as amended by 1999 SI No 1440.

reasonably practicable to obtain the information in any other manner.

4.56   In carrying out an Ofsted inspection, a team considers:

1) whether the school is fulfilling its statutory duty to deliver the National Curriculum;
2) the breadth and range of the whole curriculum;
3) the management and leadership of the school, and
4) whether the school is providing 'value for money'.

4.57   There is a separate system of inspection of denominational education and collective worship in denominational schools (SIA 1996 s23). In practice, in Roman Catholic and Church of England schools, this is carried out at the same time as an Ofsted inspection, by an inspector nominated by the diocese. The SACRE has no direct role in inspections. When inspecting both denominational and non-denominational schools, Ofsted teams will look at the school assembly to see if the school is fulfilling its statutory duty (see paras 4.27–4.28).

4.58   After an Ofsted inspection, which lasts about one week, depending on the size of the school, the team's report is published. The team may consider that the school has 'serious weaknesses' or 'requires special measures', the latter meaning that it is failing in its statutory duties.

4.59   In either case, the team's judgment must be confirmed by HMIs. If they agree, HMIs will monitor the school regularly until they judge that the comment no longer applies. The governing body will be required to draw up action plans (SIA 1996 s17) as will the LEA (SIA 1996 s18).

4.60   Various measures will be taken if a school requiring special measures fails to improve (SSFA 1998 s15). The secretary of state may appoint additional governors (SSFA 1998 s18) or direct that the school be closed (SSFA 1998 s19). The LEA may also intervene (SSFA 1998 s15); it may appoint additional governors (SSFA 1998 s16) or suspend a school's delegated budget (SSFA 1998 s17).

Inspection of LEAs

4.61   EA 1997 ss38–39 empowers the Chief Inspector of Schools to review the way in which LEAs are performing any of their functions relating to pupils of compulsory school age and registered pupils. Ofsted has a rolling programme to inspect every LEA by 2001. This involves both investigating the LEA officers and interviewing the schools. If the resulting report identifies problems, the LEA must draw up an action plan for improvement. In a similar operation to that for a failing school (see paras 4.59–4.60), HMIs may take 'special measures' to improve an LEA.

Monitoring the curriculum

4.62   EA 1997 ss21 and 27 set up the Qualifications and Curriculum Authority and the Qualifications Curricular and Assessment Authority for Wales. These have the job of promoting quality and coherence in relation to education and training. Their functions are spelt out in detail in ss23(2) and 29(2) but essentially they are charged with keeping all aspects of the school curriculum, examinations and assessments under review.

Complaints about the curriculum etc

4.63   EA 1996 s409 establishes a local machinery for dealing with complaints about the performance of the LEA or governors over such matters as the curriculum or the provision of information. This has to have the approval of the secretary of state, who will not consider complaints under EA 1996 s496 or s497 (see paras 13.34–13.45) until this local mechanism has been exhausted.

4.64   Informal resolution must be attempted first. It is apparent that many complaints need never arise as such if there were better liaison between the school and the parent in the first place. Many LEAs incorporate this informal resolution into their education complaints procedure.

4.65   Guidance says that LEAs have to show that they have plans for general publicity of their complaints procedure.[30] In addition, EA 1996 s408 requires information on the complaints procedure to be included in school prospectuses and for copies of the arrangements to be available in schools. Unfortunately, this does not always happen[31] and most parents, and perhaps too many governing bodies, are ignorant of the procedure. Consequently there have been very

---

30 Circular 1/89 *Education Reform Act 1988: Local Arrangements for the Consideration of Complaints* Appendix A para 6.

31 Harris *Complaints About Schooling* (National Consumer Council, 1992, at p121) found that only 18% of primary schools and 28% of secondary schools had this information in their prospectus.

few formal complaints and the overwhelming majority of these were unsuccessful.

4.66   Apparently LEAs and governors are still largely unclear about what types of problem are covered by this machinery. EA 1996 s409 deals with unreasonably exercising any power or performing any duty concerning religious worship, religious education, the National Curriculum or the provision of information, or failing to discharge any such duty in maintained schools. Schools will soon have to have procedures in place for dealing with all other types of complaint in any event.[32]

Procedure for complaints

4.67   Circular 1/89 required LEAs to consult governing bodies and gave guidance on the drafting of complaints procedures, and was followed up by a model prepared by the Association of Metropolitan Authorities and the Association of County Councils. These have been closely followed by all LEAs.

4.68   Usually it is the parents who complain about an issue that affects their child's education. However, there is no legal reason why a child under 16 should not be entitled to make a complaint.

4.69   The LEA has to administer the procedure. There is supposed to be a designated officer (or the clerk to the governing body), who is the first point of contact and who has to decide whether the complaint comes within EA 1996 s409.

4.70   There are various stages:

1) **Informal resolution** This will be through discussion between the parent and teacher or headteacher.

2) **Discussion with those with direct responsibility for the matters involved** However, there is unlikely to be any purpose in discussing with the headteacher a complaint about the governing body, as s/he is likely to be a member of it.

3) **Formal complaint to the governing body (where appropriate)** This will have been referred by the designated officer to a meeting of the governing body.

4) **Formal complaint to the LEA** However, the LEA has no jurisdiction over religious education or collective worship in denominational schools.

32 See para 13.6.

4.71   At stage 3, the parent may speak at the meeting and present a written statement. Provided matters of English or Welsh law are at issue, the advice and assistance scheme may be used for a practitioner not only to advise and prepare the written submissions but, if appropriate, to attend the meeting and address the governors (since these are not 'proceedings'[33]). If the question is important, serious consideration needs to be given to representation. The other side will be represented in all such meetings, if not by a lawyer by a person with great knowledge of educational administration and experience of advocacy. It is not surprising that complaints have historically met with little success. No time limits are set and it is unlikely that the procedure can cope with an urgent complaint.

4.72   At stage 4, the designated officer will become involved in investigating the complaint. The results of the investigation are then considered by a panel of three members of the LEA. Presumably the results must be disclosed to the complainant, who, again, is entitled to make an oral presentation and be represented.

4.73   A successful complainant is entitled to be told of recommended corrective action.

4.74   Only after this local machinery has been exhausted may an unsuccessful complainant pursue a further complaint to the secretary of state (EA 1996 s496–497), see chapter 13.

33 See chapter 16 paras 16.54–16.55.

CHAPTER 5

School admissions

This chapter looks at school admissions policies and arrangements. It considers parental preference, choosing a school and the duties of admission authorities. Finally, it deals with admission appeals by parents, explaining the procedure and advising on preparation.

For complete chapter contents, see overleaf

Government policy

5.1   Government policy on greater parental choice has fostered the misconception that parents are free to choose their children's school. The reality has not borne this out. A report by the Audit Commission (December 1996)[1] stated that one in five parents failed to obtain their first choice of school, while up to £100 million was being wasted on spare capacity in other schools. This policy has led to larger class numbers in popular schools as they are forced to take pupils to a notional capacity. The report indicated that, in a survey of ten LEAs, the number of admission appeals had risen by 44 per cent in the previous three years.

5.2   Popular schools will always be oversubscribed. This problem may well be exacerbated by the reduction in class sizes in infant schools (SSFA 1998 s1). The vast majority of children in England and Wales will continue to be educated in the nearly 24,000 maintained schools – comprising community, foundation, voluntary controlled and voluntary aided schools as well as community and foundation special schools – not counting private schools and public schools.

5.3   The Conservative government (see EA 1997 s10) allowed schools to give selection on aptitude a higher priority in their admission procedures. The School Standards and Framework Act (SSFA) 1998 has not altered this approach markedly and grammar schools have been retained (ss99–109). Legislation, however, allows for ballots of parents to decide whether grammar schools should remain. The effect of this will probably make it more difficult for parents to obtain their first choice place for their children.

Admission authorities

5.4   For community or voluntary controlled schools, the admission authority is the LEA, unless the LEA has delegated this responsibility to the governing body.[2]

5.5   For foundation or voluntary aided schools, the admission authority is the governing body.[3]

5.6   The admission authority for a school has responsibility for

---

1   *Trading Places: the supply and allocation of school places* Audit Commission, 1996.
2   SSFA 1998 s88(1)(a)(ii).
3   SSFA 1998 s88(1)(b).

determining the arrangements for admission of pupils to the school, including the school's admission policy.[4]

Admission policy

Guidance

5.7   SSFA 1998 s84 requires the Secretary of State for Education to issue a code of practice on school admissions, to give guidance to LEAs, governing bodies, appeal panels and adjudicators.[5] Guidance on formulation and application of policy (where not otherwise covered by a code of practice) is contained in statutory instruments and circulars.[6]

5.8   Policy must, in theory, be reasonable and non-discriminatory. Also, it must not be too rigid.[7] Cases show that any reasonable criteria may be used to meet local circumstances, as long as they have a practical or educational justification.[8] The kinds of criteria used are siblings, distance, religion (see para 5.17), health concerns, special educational needs, aptitude and ability.

---

4   SSFA 1998 s88(2).

5   *Code of Practice on School Admissions*, DfEE, 1999. This came into force on 1 April 1999 and applies to arrangements for primary and secondary school intakes from September 2000. It supersedes Circular 12/98 *Admissions: Interim Guidance*. It is intended that there will be a *School Admission Appeals Code of Practice* in force by 1 September 1999. This will supersede the *Revised Code of Practice for Appeals*, Association of County Councils, Association of Metropolitan Authorities and Council on Tribunals, 1994.

6   Two statutory instruments deal with interim arrangements until the new framework for schools is fully operational: SSFA 1998 (Admissions) (Modifications No 2) Regulations 1998 SI No 3130 and Education (Determining School Admission Arrangements for the Initial Year) Regulations 1998 SI No 3165. Other regulations came into effect on 1 April 1999 alongside the Code of Practice, which determine future policy: Education (Relevant Areas for Consultation on Admission Arrangements) Regulations 1999 SI No 124, Education (Objections to Admission Arrangements) Regulations 1999 SI No 125, Education (Determination of Admission Arrangements) Regulations 1999 SI No 126, Education (School Information) (England) (Amendment) Regulations 1999 SI No 251 and Education (Aptitude for Particular Subjects) Regulations 1999 SI No 258. See also, DES Circular 11/88 *Admissions of pupils to county and voluntary schools* and DES Circular 6/91 *Implementation of more open enrolment in primary schools*.

7   *R v Greenwich LBC ex p Governors of John Ball Primary School* [1990] 88 LGR 589, CA.

8   *R v Lancashire CC ex p F* [1995] ELR 33, QBD; *R v Lancashire CC ex p M* [1994] ELR 478, QBD.

5.9   SSFA 1998 s99 prohibits the selection of pupils for admission to a maintained school on the basis of ability unless the school is a grammar school under s104, or the selection by ability is in a 'permitted form'. This means one or more of the following:

1) there are pre-existing selection procedures in operation (s100);
2) under s101 banding is used to secure that the pupils admitted are representative of all levels of ability and no level is substantially over or under represented;
3) selection relates to pupils over compulsory school age (s99(1)(c));
4) selection of up to 10 per cent of pupils is by reference to aptitude in a subject in which the school specialises (s102).[9]

5.10   Academic selection should not be used for primary school admissions.[10] Schools or admissions authorities should not interview parents as any part of the application or admission procedure.[11]

Admission numbers

5.11   The admission number for any year group in a school is the number of pupils in that age group which it is intended to admit to the school in a particular year.[12] It is fixed by the admission authority for the school (ie, the LEA or the governing body). The admission number cannot be less than the relevant 'standard number'. The standard number is calculated from historical data about the school by a complicated formula.[13] It can be increased or decreased on application by various bodies or by order of the secretary of state.

5.12   The admission number can be greater than the standard number. A proposal to increase the admission number can be made to the admission authority by the LEA (if the governing body is the admission authority) or the governing body (if the LEA is the admission authority).

---

9   Permitted subjects are modern foreign languages, performing arts, visual arts, physical education or sport, design and technology and information technology (Education (Aptitude for Particular Subjects) Regulations 1999 SI No 258).
10 *Code of Practice on School Admissions* para 5.9.
11 Ibid para 5.25.
12 SSFA 1998 s93(10).
13 EA 1996 ss417–420.

5.13   SSFA 1998 s1 and the Education (Infant Class Sizes) (England) Regulations 1998[14] limit infant class[15] sizes in England to a maximum of 30, commencing in the school year 2001/2. In Wales the situation is slightly different. The Education (Infant Class Sizes) (Wales) Regulations 1998[16] require there to be classes of 30 in the school year 1999/2000 in classes where the majority of children will be five during the year; in the year 2000/1 this will be extended to classes of six-year-olds and in the following year to seven-year-olds. There are certain exceptions, such as children with a school named in a statement of special educational needs or children allowed in on appeal, both of these for their admission year only.

Catchment areas

5.14   One commonly used criterion for admissions is for the admission authority to define a catchment area for a school. This is probably drawn up in conjunction with the school. However, it may be expressed by reference to neighbourhoods or population centres or boundaries, and any home-school distance criterion may not be stated clearly, even though this is the most easily understood factor. Some children may not be in any school's catchment area.[17]

5.15   It has been held that it was not unlawful to deny a place to a child living outside an oversubscribed school's catchment area and outside the LEA boundary who had been offered a place in his own area.[18] Even where a child from outside the catchment area is included in the admission process, it is very difficult to counter the effect of a proper consideration of the distance of his/her home from school and this is likely to produce the same negative result for the applicant in the absence of other factors.

5.16   But parents of children (whether inside or outside the catchment area) must be permitted to express a preference and give reasons.[19] Parents who express a preference must be given priority over those who express no preference.

---

14   1998 SI No 1973.

15   This means a class containing pupils the majority of whom will attain the age of five, six or seven during the course of the school year (SSFA 1998 s4).

16   1998 SI No 1943.

17   *R v City of Bradford MBC ex p Sikander Ali* [1994] 2 ELR 299 QBD.

18   *R v Wiltshire CC ex p Razazan* [1997] ELR 370, CA.

19   *R v Rotherham MBC ex p Clark and Others* [1998] ELR 152, QBD.

Religion

5.17 A foundation or voluntary aided school which has a religious character can make admission arrangements to preserve that religious character (SSFA 1998 s91). These are known as 'special arrangements'. In theory, there is no discrimination against any religion but, in practice, foundation or voluntary aided schools will be largely Roman Catholic, Church of England or nonconformist. There are a number of Jewish schools and a few Islamic schools.

5.18 In *R v Lancashire CC ex p F*,[20] a policy which excluded Roman Catholic children from a non-denominational school because a Roman Catholic school was available to them was upheld in the High Court. In *R v Lancashire CC ex p M*,[21] Popplewell J held that the LEA was entitled to maintain a policy under which Roman Catholic children who had attended Roman Catholic primary schools were not considered for non-Roman Catholic secondary schools until non-Roman Catholic children had been offered places. This was despite the fact that the DFE had expressed its disapproval of the evident discrimination against Catholic children. The LEA was entitled to maintain its policy because it was being fully reviewed by an appropriate body, probably a working party.

Consultation and challenges

5.19 The admission authority must engage in consultation before drawing up its admission arrangements. Consultation has to be completed before 1 March for admissions in the September 18 months after that.[22] LEAs with other admissions authorities should set up local admissions forums for consultation and discussion of issues around admissions.[23] The following must be consulted:

1) the LEA (if the admission authority is the governing body) – it must consult with any LEA within a five-mile radius of the main entrance to the school if it is a secondary school and two miles if a primary school;

2) the admission authorities for all other maintained schools in the relevant area (usually the LEA area) or prescribed classes of them;

20 [1995] ELR 33, QBD.
21 [1994] ELR 478, QBD.
22 Education (Determination of Admission Arrangements) Regulations 1999 SI No 126.
23 *Code of Practice on Admissions* para 4.4.

primary schools need only consult with primary schools;

3) the admission authorities for maintained schools of any prescribed description.[24]

Where the LEA is the admission authority it must consult with all neighbouring LEAs.[25]

5.20 SSFA s105 permits parental ballots to determine admission arrangements for the 163 remaining grammar schools in England and Wales.

5.21 A challenge to policy will be to the secretary of state or adjudicator. SSFA 1998 s90 permits certain bodies and parents to object to changes to policy. If parents of children of compulsory school age or others consulted about admission arrangements object to any admission arrangements made by an admission authority they may refer the matter to the adjudicator (a creation of SSFA 1998 s90(1)–(2)). This machinery does not apply to nursery or special schools, children under compulsory school age or children with statements of special educational needs. The adjudicator can also determine disputes between local admission authorities over individual criteria or arrangements. Regulations make provision for determining the allocation to particular adjudicators of matters referred to the adjudicator. A person who has worked in any authority in the previous ten years is ineligible to adjudicate in any dispute involving that authority.[26] The procedure followed by the adjudicator is also determined by regulations.[27]

Admission arrangements

Publication

5.22 Under SSFA 1998 s92(1), each LEA must publish annually information about arrangements for admission to the maintained schools in its area and, in some cases, schools outside its area or private schools. Objections must be made within six weeks of the publication of the arrangements.[28] These regulations allow the

---

24 SSFA 1998 s89(2).

25 Education (Determination of Admission Arrangements) Regulations 1999 SI No 126.

26 Education (References to Adjudicator) Regulations 1999 SI No 702.

27 Education (Adjudicators Inquiry Procedure etc) Regulations 1999 SI No 1286.

28 Education (Objections to Admission Arrangements) Regulations 1999 SI No 125.

adjudicator to decide objections from parents or admission authorities over partially selective admission criteria and potentially to abolish these. Ten parents must register substantially the same objection before an adjudicator has to make a determination. In certain prescribed cases, eg, where admissions criteria relate to a person's religion (SSFA 1998 s90(10)), the objection is referred direct to the Secretary of State. The adjudicator and the secretary of state must publish their findings, which are binding on all parties.

5.23   The information published by LEAs must include:

1) the admission number for the age group in each school (see para 5.11);
2) the admission functions of the LEA and the governing body;
3) the admissions policy (see paras 5.7–5.9);
4) arrangements for pupils from outside the LEA area;
5) arrangements for appeals (see paras 5.42–5.87).

Regulations determine the procedure to be followed by LEAs before publishing such information and also the timing and manner of such publication (SSFA 1998 s92(5)). A composite prospectus covering admission arrangements in its area should be published before 1 October and no later than six weeks before the date when parents can express a preference for any school in the prospectus.[29]

5.24   Under SSFA s92(2), governing bodies of foundation and voluntary aided schools must publish information about their school in addition to that published by the LEA. This may be published on their behalf by the LEA with their agreement (SSFA 1998 s92(5)).

5.25   Regulations under EA 1996 s408 deal with the content of documents explaining policy and provision at the school. Governors have to provide additional information on special needs provision on request.[30]

5.26   The admissions authority does not have to publish every nut and bolt of the policy, as long as the information can be elicited by questions.[31]

29 Education (School Information) Regulations 1998 SI No 2526, as amended by Education (School Information) (England) (Amendment) Regulations 1999 SI No 251, and Education (School Information) (Wales) Regulations 1999 SI No 1812.

30 Education (Special Education Needs) (Information) Regulations 1994 SI No 1048.

31 *R v Bradford MBC ex p Sikander Ali* [1994] ELR 299 QBD.

Procedure

Primary schools at age 5

5.27   Usually a parent will visit the nearest primary school and put his/her child's name on the waiting list some considerable time before s/he is due to start school. In some areas there may be only one school in close proximity to a child's home. In others there may be several and it would be wise to put a child's name down on more than one, particularly if a school is popular. Being on the waiting list is no guarantee of a place because the admissions criteria will still be applied. There is a deadline for putting a child's name down.

Secondary school transfer at age 11

5.28   Most secondary schools arrange a series of open days or evenings when prospective parents may find out more about a school. In addition, LEAs usually put on events publicising provision in their area. Parents usually indicate their choice on a form, available from the admission authority, though often distributed via primary schools. They are usually given three choices but tactically they need to consider if it is a good idea to name three schools or concentrate on only one. Where LEAs ask parents to express more than one preference and to rank these the LEA must consider each a valid preference but there is no requirement that parental ranking must take priority over other means of allocating places.[32] The admission authority for most maintained schools will be the LEA; although foundation and voluntary aided schools may have their own forms, being admission authorities. This means that parents may have more than three choices and, since they can apply to more than one LEA, more than one selection procedure. The government requires admission authorities in an area to have common timetables, forms and arrangements in relation to the September 2000 intake.[33] The amount of information required from the parents is minimal and, although there is the expression of parental preference, it seems that the allocation of secondary school places is largely an administrative exercise based on limited formalised criteria falling short of full consideration of the complete admissions criteria. In practice, this is only challenged during admission appeals in relation to individual children.

32   Code of Practice para 3.14.
33   Ibid paras 3.9–3.12.

Admission at other times

5.29 When a family moves into an area and requires a school place it is usual for them to approach the LEA, which is able to tell them of any vacancies and pass their details on to appropriate schools. If, however, parents want to transfer a child from one school in an LEA to another they must usually approach the prospective school direct in order to establish whether there are vacancies.

Parental preference

5.30 By SSFA 1998 s86 the admissions authority must have arrangements enabling parents (including those living outside its area – s86(8)) to express a preference for their child's school, at any stage of the education cycle, and to give reasons for this.

Obtaining information

5.31 Information about schools and their admission policies can be obtained from the following sources:

1) visiting the school;
   - There is no substitute for visiting all the schools being considered, during the school day, to obtain the feel of the school and see the pupils and staff at work. Observe the general behaviour of the children coming out of school at the end of a day, talk to other parents, and interview the headteacher.

2) school prospectuses;
   - It is essential to obtain a copy of the school prospectus, which should contain a comprehensive range of information, such as arrangements for prospective parents' visits, a statement on the curriculum, organisation of the education and teaching methods used, the content and organisation of sex education, special educational needs, the ethos and values of the school, unauthorised absences, attainments achieved and, in secondary schools, examination results.[34]

---

34 Education (School Information) Regulations 1998 SI No 2526, as amended by Education (School Information) (England) (Amendment) Regulations 1999 SI No 251, and Education (School Information) (Wales) Regulations 1999 SI No 1812.

3) annual reports of governing bodies;
   - These must contain various prescribed matters,[35] including details of the arrangements for disabled pupils, the steps taken to ensure that they are not treated less favourably than other pupils and the facilities provided to assist access.[36]

4) school inspection reports[37] (see paras 4.51–4.58);
   - These are available from the appropriate authority, which is the governing body or the LEA for a school without delegated budget. They can now also be obtained on the Internet.

5) LEAs (not necessarily only the one in which the child lives) (see paras 5.12–5.16);
   - In relation to performance information about primary schools, see Education (School Performance Information) (England) Regulations 1999[38] para 14.[39]

6) other parents;

7) teachers at the child's existing school;

8) the local press;

9) league tables;[40]
   - These are published annually in the national press; and are found in the LEA-published information relating to secondary transfer and in the prospectus of individual schools.

---

35 Determined by regulations made under SSFA 1998 s42. See Education (Governors' Annual Reports) (Wales) Regulations 1999 SI No 1406. See also DfEE Circulars 11/96 (Primary Schools) and 12/96 (Secondary Schools).

36 EA 1996 s317(6).

37 Reports of any school inspections and action plans must be made available for inspection by members of the public at such times and places as may be reasonable (SIA 1996 s16(4)(a)); a copy of a report and summary must be given to any person who asks free of charge or in prescribed cases on payment of a fee no higher than the cost of supply (SIA 1996 s16(4)(b)). In addition, every parent of a pupil must receive a copy within 10 working days of receipt of the report: SIA 1996 s16(4)(c) and Education (School Inspection) Regulations 1997 SI No 1966 reg 7(3) and Education (School Inspections) (Wales) Regulations 1998 SI No 1866 reg 7(3).

38 1999 SI No 1178 and Education (School Performance Information) (Wales) Regulations 1998 SI No 1867.

39 Under Education (School Information) (England) Amendment Regulations 1999 SI No 251 all LEAs must publish in each school year a prospectus of admissions information for all the schools in its area.

40 EA 1996 s408; Education (School Performance Information) (England) Regulations 1999 SI No 1178 and Education (School Performance Information) (Wales) Regulations 1998 SI No 1867, as amended by 1999 SI No 1470.

10) DES Circular 11/88 *Admission of pupils to county and voluntary schools* and DES Circular 6/91 *Implementation of more open enrolment in primary schools*;
11) *The Code of Practice on School Admissions*, DfEE, 1999;
12) *Our Children's Education*;[41]
13) *School choice and appeals*.[42]

Parent or 'person responsible' for pupil

5.32   Under EA 1996 s576 'parent' includes anyone who has parental responsibility or care of the child. The area where a child belongs is determined by s579(4) and Education (Areas to which Pupils and Students Belong) Regulations 1996.[43] Regulation 2(3) introduced a new term – 'person responsible' for a school pupil – to deal with the situation where the parents are abroad or in different areas. The regulations do not affect the rights of parents as regards admissions. The test is the child's habitual and normal residence. If this is shared equally between parents with parental responsibility, the responsible person under this regulation is the one nearest the child's current school. This could be relevant to the effect of the admissions policy.

Tactics on expressing preference

5.33   Careful thought should be given to how preference for schools is stated. If a school is very popular and over-subscribed, parents should consider whether it is worth choosing it at all. If a popular school is put as first choice, the net result might be to lose a place at a second preference school to those who nominated it first.

Exceptions

5.34   The parental preference rule does not apply to:
1) nursery education for under-fives (unless they are seeking a reception class place at four-and-a-half plus), see chapter 12, 'Children under school age';

2) special schools;
   – Regulations may make admission arrangements for community or foundation special schools and the allocation of

41   Publicity leaflet, DFE, 1994.
42   Advisory Centre for Education (ACE), 1991.
43   1996 SI No 615. See also paras 3.56–3.58.

functions between the LEA and the governing body (SSFA 1998 s98(5)).[44]

3) pupils with statements of special educational needs (see chapter 9);
   - The LEA must still take account of the wishes of the parents (EA 1996 s9) when deciding which school to name in a statement.[45]

4) Where an education supervision order is in force with respect to the child, by virtue of Children Act (CA) 1989 Sch 3 Part III para 13(2)(b).

Authorities' duty to comply

General duty

5.35   By SSFA 1998 s86(2), admission authorities (LEAs or governors) must comply with parental preferences unless to do so would:

1) prejudice efficient education or the efficient use of resources;
2) be incompatible with admission arrangements designed to preserve the character of a foundation or voluntary aided school; or
3) be incompatible with arrangements for selection by ability and aptitude where arrangements are based on admitting only pupils with high ability or with aptitude (s86(3)).

Prejudice to efficient education cannot be claimed unless the standard or admission number is exceeded.

5.36   An admissions authority may not refuse to accede to parental preference which is based on grounds which are arguably racist. It can only rely on the grounds contained in s86(2). In *R v Cleveland CC and Others ex p Commission for Racial Equality*,[46] the parent of an English-speaking child asked to move her daughter from a predominantly Asian school to one where most of the children had English as their first language and the LEA, after taking legal advice, complied with her request. It was held that the mandatory duty to comply with parental preference overrides any duties under Race Relations Act 1976.

---

44 Education (Maintained Special Schools) (Wales) Regulations 1999 SI No 1780.
45 See *C v Buckinghamshire County Council and Special Educational Needs Tribunal* [1999] ELR 179, CA.
46 [1994] ELR 44, CA.

5.37   Children living outside the LEA's area should not be treated less favourably than those within it.[47] This seems to outweigh the LEA's general statutory obligation, under EA 1996 ss14–17, to provide sufficient schools to meet the needs of the residents of its area.

Excluded children

5.38   SSFA 1998 s96 gives power to the LEA to direct a school to admit a child if s/he has been permanently excluded from or refused admission to any school providing suitable education within a reasonable distance from home (see chapter 6). A particular school cannot be specified if the provision of efficient education or use of resources would be prejudiced (s96(4)). This is particularly appropriate when a child has been permanently excluded from a school and there are difficulties finding another place. The parent, the school governing body and any other authority maintaining the school must be consulted. Governors can refer the matter to the secretary of state within 15 days of notification and the secretary of state may give a direction. This is only a discretionary power and its practical value is doubtful. It may well be of little use to the parents of a child whose educational problems and needs are the subject of disagreement with the LEA and there may be delay while the secretary of state considers representations by the governing body.

5.39   Admission authorities' duty under SSFA 1998 s86(2) to comply with parental preference does not apply where a child has been permanently excluded from two or more schools, for two years from the date on which the latest exclusion took place. The date runs from the school day on which a headteacher decided that the child should be permanently excluded. The parent is unable to appeal against a refusal to admit in a decision when s86(2) applies. Furthermore, under SSFA 1998 s95 and Sch 25, an LEA acting as admission authority must make arrangements for the governing body of a community or voluntary controlled school to appeal against a decision of the LEA to admit a child who has been excluded twice. The decision of the appeal committee is binding.

Special educational needs

5.40   Parents of children with statements of special educational needs

---

47 *R v Greenwich LBC ex p Governors of John Ball Primary School* (1990) 88 LGR 589, CA; confirmed in *R v Wiltshire CC ex p Razazan* [1997] ELR 370, CA.

(SEN) have a quite separate machinery regarding choice of school (see chapter 9). SSFA 1998 s98 states that a child with SEN must be admitted to any school named in his/her statement. The governing body has a duty to admit the child.

School attendance orders

5.41   If a school attendance order is made with respect to a child (see chapter 6), a school will be named in the order. An LEA should not name a school in an order if it would cause the number of pupils to exceed the fixed number or if the child had been permanently excluded from the school, unless the LEA is the admission authority. The governing body, and, if appropriate, another LEA must be consulted. Either can apply to the secretary of state for a direction, which is final (EA 1996 s439).

Admission appeals

Right to appeal

5.42   In the case of a community or voluntary controlled school the LEA arranges the appeal. The governing body arranges the appeal for foundation and voluntary aided schools. Joint arrangements can be made by two or more foundation or voluntary aided schools. An LEA and the governing bodies of foundation or voluntary aided schools can also make joint arrangements (SSFA 1998 s94). The procedure is the same for all schools.[48] The exact procedure may be determined by the body which arranges the appeal. The procedure outlined by the *Revised Code of Practice for Appeals*[49] will continue to be a guide until the secretary of state issues a new code under SSFA 1998 ss84 and 85. The parents will be informed of their right of appeal when they are informed in writing that they have not obtained a place for their child.

5.43   The right of appeal belongs to the parent as defined in EA 1996 s576 (see para 5.32). If the parents are unmarried or living apart, this does not mean that only the residential parent has the right of appeal. Anyone with parental responsibility under CA 1989 s2 has

48   SSFA 1998 Sch 24 Part II paras 8–16. Note that the secretary of state has power to amend this schedule.
49   Association of County Councils, Association of Metropolitan Authorities and Council on Tribunals, 1994.

the right of appeal. This cannot be surrendered but it can be delegated to, for example, the other parent (s2(9)). The question of parental rights has been inconsistently treated in the legislation and, in the absence of a ruling by a court, schools and admission authorities may adopt working arrangements in the interests of practicality. It is submitted that a carer could present an admission appeal.

Making an appeal

5.44   An appeal must be made in writing setting out the grounds of appeal. This must be submitted within the timescale laid down by the LEA or governing body. It should not be less than 14 days from notification of the decision. This can be extended in exceptional circumstances.

5.45   A late appeal, if accepted, should be heard at the same time as, or as soon as possible after, any other appeals in relation to the same school, preferably by the same panel.

Appeal panels

5.46   Until 1 April 1999, appeals were heard by appeal committees, whose constitution was dealt with under EA 1996 Sch 33. There are now panels constituted under SSFA 1998 Sch 24. Their conduct is subject to the guidance (see para 5.42).

5.47   Under Sch 24 Part I, there may be three or five members on an LEA or governing body panel hearing an appeal, including:

1) at least one lay member with no experience of management or providing education in a school other than in a voluntary capacity (which includes experience as a governor); this person cannot:
    –   be a member of the LEA or governing body;
    –   be a non-teacher LEA employee; or
    –   have past or present connections with the LEA or any member or employee of it which might raise doubts about impartiality.
2) other members who are:
    –   people with experience of education;
    –   people with knowledge of local education conditions; or
    –   parents of children attending any school.

5.48   LEA employees are allowed to sit if they are teachers from a different school. There is nothing in Sch 24 which prevents parents with children registered at a school sitting on an appeal at the school at which their child attends, but this would be contrary to natural justice and should not be permitted. Paragraph 1(8) prevents a person sitting on an LEA appeal panel if s/he was involved in any aspect of the decision under appeal. On the other hand, primary school governors can hear appeals concerning a particular secondary school for which their school is a feeder, in the absence of overt evidence of bias.

5.49   LEAs and governing bodies are required to advertise for appeal panel lay members (Sch 24 para 6).[50] Members of appeal panels are paid allowances (para 5) and must be legally indemnified by the admissions authority (para 7).

5.50   Appeals tend to be heard during the summer months and it is quite common for more than one panel to sit at the same time.

Procedure before a hearing

5.51   At least 14 days' notice of a hearing should be given. This should be in writing and sent by first class post. Parents can agree to a shorter date.

5.52   At least seven days before the hearing, the chief education officer or the governors should send the following documents to the clerk and the parents by first class post:

1) a written statement summarising how the admissions policy has been applied to the particular case – this should include relevant background information and, in the case of a foundation or voluntary aided school, any arrangements pertinent to SSFA 1998 s91 re religious character;
2) a summary of the reasons for the decision explaining why a factor in SSFA 1998 s89(3) applies; and
3) copies of any information or documents to be put to the hearing.

Preparing for the hearing

5.53   The parent may be eligible for advice and assistance (see chapter 16). Much of the information required at this stage can be collected by the parent. It may even be possible to brief the parent on finding out informally from the education officers concerned the way in which they have apparently applied the admissions criteria and assessed the capacity of the school in declining to offer a place; this could be

50 Education (Lay Members of Appeal Committees) Regulations 1994 SI No 1303.

of value in questioning the witness for the admissions authority at the appeal hearing. On balance, the value of getting the information at the pre-hearing stage outweighs the element of surprise gained by raising these questions for the first time at the hearing – and there is a danger that the information will not be available to the appeal panel otherwise. Usually it will not be possible to find evidence to challenge the policy or its application. A decision must then be taken about whether there is any merit in pursuing an appeal and, if so, whether the parent should be represented.

Representation

5.54   LEAs tend to discourage parents from being represented, apparently because it is felt that this could make the hearing too formal or even counterproductive. Certainly due deference needs to be paid to the needs of a largely lay tribunal, but the importance of the process and the increasing competition for school places would seem to indicate that an increase in representation is inevitable. Some parents are capable of presenting their own appeal but better results are likely to be achieved using an advocate or lawyer, at least as a McKenzie friend.[51] Many parents are just too emotionally involved to present their case effectively. This does not mean making the proceedings excessively daunting or formal. But the examination of the LEA's case is likely to be much more effective if done by a third party.

Evidence

5.55   Parents can decide how to present their appeal. Unfortunately, despite the guidance which has been issued by the secretary of state and the High Court, appeal panels still seem to want to focus on why the the particular child in question should be admitted in preference to others who are appealing. One could take along school reports, examples of work and details of extra-curricular activities to stress why the admission of this child would be an advantage. If the school one is appealing for is some distance away from the child's home it would be necessary to emphasise the ease and duration of the journey. If appropriate, refer to other children who are already at the school and known to the child. Hearsay evidence is acceptable. It is not usually expected that the child or other witnesses will attend. However, witnesses may be allowed to speak if they do attend.

---

51 There is no longer an unqualified right to a McKenzie friend in private hearings: see *R v Bow County Court ex p Pelling* (1999) *Times* 18 August, CA.

5.56   The following matters should be considered (paras 5.57–5.70).

Reasonableness of admissions policy

5.57   Study the admissions policy of the admission authority. This can be obtained from the LEA or the governing body. Examine the criteria for reasonableness and to see how closely a particular child fulfils them.

Proper application of the admissions policy

5.58   Check that the policy has been properly applied. For example, in *R v Dame Alice Owen's School ex p S*,[52] the policy defined three groups of applicants for entry and allocated different percentages to these. The admission authority decided to take more pupils under band B, which reduced the numbers able to be accepted under under band C. This was held to be unfair.

5.59   In practice, problems are possible when a child has a disciplinary history or has suffered exclusion from a school. It appears to be lawful for a headteacher or admissions authority to take such factors into account in deciding whether a place at a new school is available, quite apart from the provisions of EA 1996 s95. The headteacher can obtain the child's curricular records (excluding assessment of achievement) when an application is under consideration and there is nothing to stop this information being shared with the LEA.[53] It would be fanciful to imagine that such information is not available for exchange, although most schools do protect the confidentiality of information relating to individual pupils before their education records are formally passed on. It is most unlikely that a pupil's disciplinary record would be raised explicitly in opposition to a parental appeal.

5.60   In *Investigation No 98/C/2730* (Cumbria County Council) the local government ombudsman decided that the school's representations about previous difficulties with the parents were not relevant to the consideration of whether their third child should be admitted and should not have been taken into account. However, in *R v Secretary of State for Education and Employment and the Governors of Southlands Community Comprehensive School ex p W*,[54] it was held lawful to consider the behaviour of a parent in deciding on

---

52 [1998] COD 108; [1998] 1 Ed CR 101, QBD.
53 Education (School Records) Regulations 1989 SI No 1261 reg 6(3).
54 [1998] ELR 413, QBD.

admission. There were undoubtedly other factors which influenced this decision. The parents had complained about an appeal committee upholding a decision not to offer a place to a 12-year-old girl and the secretary of state issued a direction to the governing body to admit the child. The governing body refused to comply. Relief was refused in all the circumstances – which included threats of industrial action by teachers as a result of the father's conduct.[55]

Admissions criteria

5.61   Consider the admissions criteria applied in the decision refusing admission. The most common one is that the school is oversubscribed and admission would prejudice efficient education. Consider arguments to show how these may be overcome. First, check whether the absolute statutory limit on class sizes (see para 5.13) is yet effective.

Roll numbers

5.62   Obtain from the LEA details of:

- current and previous year roll numbers for the age group in question and compare these with the standard number to see if they have exceeded the standard number at any time;
- the number of successful appeals in relation to each year group so that it can be argued that the standard number has been exceeded before without any evident detriment.

If time permits a standard letter can be written (see appendix L) but the LEA staff will usually be prepared to give the information over the telephone. Information about other identifiable pupils can never be obtained.

Other facts about the school and their relevance

5.63   By approaching the clerk to the appeal panel, whose details should be included with information about the appeal arrangements, it should be possible to obtain details of the following:

1) the attendance record/absenteeism of the school;
    - There will always be some children away and this is a useful point to make. It is unlikely that there will be full attendance at any one time and this relieves the pressure on desks,

---

55   It seems that these could be relevant factors in exclusion decisions, although there is no specific case-law on the subject: see chapter 8.

equipment and subsidiary facilities. On the other hand if discipline and attendance is good it can be argued that this means that the teachers are not having to cope with unruly pupils or having to recap for pupils who are often absent.

2) the number of exclusions and the discipline record of the school;
   - It may be possible to argue that a school with a good behaviour record should be able to accommodate more pupils. Better discipline and an older age range means that less teacher time is being spent on discipline. If the child who is appealing has a good attendance/work pattern it can be argued that s/he would have a positive effect on other pupils.

3) the number of children with special educational needs;
   - This often attracts additional funding. It is also apparent (though not openly acknowledged) that schools with statemented pupils benefit generally from the funds that often follow them. Apart from easing the pressure on delegated budgets, the existence of support staff (although aimed at specific pupils) is also another resource to help within the class/school.
   - Stress that, if it is a secondary school, the pupils are often taught in sets and there is less need for the direct attention of the teacher. The children should by this stage have learnt how to study. They also tend not to need a desk of their own, usually carrying their belongings around with them.

4) the number of children for whom English is not their first language;
   - Again, this attracts additional funding.
   - If most of the children have English as a first language they may need less teacher attention.

Physical characteristics of the school

5.64   From a visit to the school (which may be by the parent or possibly the adviser using a Claim 10 extension) prepare information about the physical characteristics of the relevant classrooms, space, facilities etc, in order to show the effect of adding a desk, for example. If there is a reluctance to give access, it should be sufficient to remind the school and the LEA of the need to obtain evidence for the hearing and the importance of apparent fairness.

Catchment area

5.65   Whether or not the catchment area has been used in the decision, it is usually worth trying to find out how many other pupils have already been admitted from outside the catchment area specified in the admissions criteria. This is best done by letter in advance to the LEA as the information will not be readily available at the hearing.

5.66   It is possible that the parent will have heard of other pupils who have been admitted from further afield than their child and the appeal panel may be confronted with the details of such children. It is sometimes possible to have the distances measured precisely if this may show that a child's home address is in fact on or just within the boundary.

5.67   It is important to make sure that there were no other reasons for admission of the other children, such as priority for siblings or statements of special educational needs. There is a developing tendency for parents to arrange for children to live with a relative who is closer to the desired school, or even to obtain a second home in the area. It would seem that these meet a residence criterion, but ultimately it depends on the wording.

Reasons for admission

5.68   Make a list of all the personal reasons why the school should admit this child. These may include siblings on the roll, friends, travel and collection arrangements, medical reasons, any particular vulnerability which this school could appropriately handle and other family circumstances, eg, working lone parent.

The panel

5.69   Find out in advance from the LEA the names of the panel members who are to sit, their interest and their capacity. This provides a check on compliance with the code of practice and also an indication of how the appeal might be targeted.

Procedure at the hearing

5.70   The procedure is governed by the *Revised Code of Practice on Procedure* (1994) (see para 5.42).

5.71   The conduct is largely at the discretion of the appeal panel and should be based on fairness coupled with informality. It is a good idea to have someone other than the parent/advocate making notes of what is said, in case there is a dispute about the evidence or a complaint about the procedure. The Code of Practice suggests that tape recording is unlikely to assist this process but, unless someone can be present to take full notes, it might be worth asking for permission.

5.72 Sufficient time should be allowed for the appeal but, in reality, usually only a short time is allowed so the parent or representative may need to be politely forcible to get all the necessary points across.

5.73 The order of hearing is likely to be:

1) the case for the LEA or governing body;
2) questioning by the parents;
3) the case for the parents;
4) questioning by the LEA or governing body;
5) summing up by the LEA or governing body;
6) summing up by the parents.

5.74 The panel may ask questions at any time if it requires clarification or more information in order to reach its decision. At no stage should one party be present alone with the appeal panel.

Points of law

5.75 Generally the issue will come down to the 'provision of efficient education or the efficient use of resources' (SSFA 1998 s86(3)(a) and Sch 25 para 11). The key to a successful appeal is often to show that there is no evidence that exceeding the standard number will prejudice efficient education, etc.

5.76 The committee has to apply the well-established two-stage test propounded by Forbes J in *R v South Glamorgan Appeals Committee ex p Evans*.[56] The LEA must first show that the admission of one more child would prejudice efficient education or the efficient use of resources. If it does not discharge this burden of proof, the appeal should succeed. Given the existing class sizes and other factors over the past few years which have taxed the resourcefulness of schools and LEAs in coping with changes to budgets, it may prove quite difficult for the LEA to demonstrate that an additional pupil would be detrimental. In reality it seems that appeal committees accept as a fact the LEA's argument in relation to stage one even though this is usually extremely thin and unsupported by evidence. For example, the chair of the committee said during one appeal, without consulting her colleagues, that she found that the LEA had made a

56 (1984)10 May Lexis CO/197/84.

case. This prompted the wingers to agree with her without any consultation or discussion.

5.77   If the committee thinks there would be prejudice, it is still required to conduct a balancing exercise to see if the arguments of the parents or other known circumstances outweigh this.[57] The selection provisions of what is now SSFA 1998 s86(3)(c) were interpreted in 1993 by Glidewell LJ in the Court of Appeal as distinguishing between 'genuine academic selection – the grammar school type of selection' and a decision that admitting a pupil (with special educational needs) might prejudice the welfare and educational needs of other children in the school.[58] Nowadays, parents of pupils with statements of special needs, who cannot use this appeal process, may feel more fortunate in that they can take their disputes about choice of school to the Special Educational Needs Tribunal (see chapter 9). More recently, the appeal committee applied the test correctly in *R v Education Appeal Committee of Leicestershire CC ex p Tarmohamed.*[59]

5.78   Paragraph 12 of SSFA 1998 Sch 24 allows an appeal panel to offer a place to a child refused entry on class size 'prejudice' grounds only where it is satisfied that the decision to refuse admission was not one which a reasonable admission authority would have made in the circumstances of the case or that the child would have been offered a place if the school's admission arrangements had been implemented properly. In *R v Sheffield City Council ex p Hague and Another,*[60] the majority of the Court of Appeal considered that the appeal panel does have jurisdiction to consider the legality of the admissions arrangements (see paras 14.28–14.29) as well as the matters dealt with in SSFA 1998 Sch 24 para 11.

Multiple appeals

5.79   The procedure in para 5.70 may have to be adapted for multiple appeals relating to the same school, which ought to be heard by the same panel.[61]

57   *R v Local Commissioner for Administration ex p Croydon LBC* [1989] 1 All ER 1033, QBD, affirming Forbes J's test. See also *W (a minor) v Education Appeal Committee of Lancashire CC* [1994] ELR 530, CA, and *R v Appeal Committee of Brighouse School ex p G and B* [1997] ELR 280, CA.

58   *R v Governors of Hasmonean High School ex p N and E* [1994] ELR 343, CA.

59   [1997] ELR 48.

60   (1999) *Times* 20 August, CA.

61   *R v Camden LBC ex p X* [1991] COD 195. See Revised Code of Practice 1994 para 23.

5.80   The revised Code of Practice (see para 5.42) suggests that the stage one approach can be used where the panel hears all the appeals relating to a particular school and then decides how many children can be admitted without causing prejudice etc. The panel must make its own findings under the stage one test. It may decide that a number of additional pupils could be admitted.

5.81   It must then decide which of the appellant children are to be admitted, using the objective admissions criteria of the admissions authority. It must hear or consider all the parents' arguments in relation to individual prejudice. The panel should note the main features of individual cases. The chair should sum up the salient features after the appeal and, after the parties have withdrawn, the panel should discuss briefly the personal circumstances, perhaps reaching a provisional list of priorities as the appeal proceeds.

Decision of the appeal panel

The decision letter

5.82   The decision may be made at the hearing but it must be sent in writing. If appropriate, the chair has a casting vote.

5.83   The decision letter must set out the grounds for the decision, but there need not be a detailed statement of reasons.[62] It is enough for the parties to know why they have won or lost.[63] Thus, evidence that an appeal panel may have misdirected itself may initially have to be gleaned from sources other than the decision letter.

5.84   In multiple appeal cases, however, the decision letter must make reference to the two-stage process, indicating the position regarding the establishment of prejudice, and stating, with an adequate explanation, why the parents' case did or did not outweigh the prejudice arguments of the LEA/governing body. In *R v Birmingham City Council ex p M*,[64] Scott Baker J quashed the decision of the independent appeal committee because the decision letter was in a standard form which did not give the basis for the decision beyond a ritual incantation of the two-stage test.

5.85   Decisions are binding on governors or LEAs (EA 1996 s423(5)).

---

62 *R v Lancashire CC ex p M* [1995] ELR 136, QBD.
63 Popplewell J at first instance in *R v Lancashire CC ex p M* [1994] ELR 478, QBD, and Court of Appeal in *W (a minor) v Education Appeal Committee of Lancashire CC* [1994] ELR 530.
64 [1999] ELR 305, QBD.

Challenging decisions

5.86   Appeal panels are amenable to both judicial review and complaint to the local government ombudsman.[65] Time is of the essence in seeking to challenge an appeal panel's decision by way of judicial review, all the more so when there was a group of appeals.[66] The interests of good administration and consistent application of admissions arrangements are likely to tell against an individual who may have been prejudiced by an act of unfairness leading to the withdrawal of a school place. This was emphasised in *R v Beatrix Potter School ex p K*.[67] The parent's appeal had been dismissed by the committee on the ground of prejudice to efficient education. Subsequently two pupils left the school and the head teacher offered a place to the applicant whose other child was already a pupil at the school. The LEA realised that this was a breach of the admissions policy (because of failure to consider the merits of other unsuccessful appellants, the LEA being anxious to avoid parents perceiving the application of the admissions policy as unjust and arbitrary following correct admission appeal procedures). The offer was promptly withdrawn, but not before the parent had bought a school uniform. Popplewell J found that there had been a legitimate expectation, but that it had not been Wednesbury unreasonable of the LEA to withdraw the offer after such a short time. In a case such as this a sensible course might have been for the appeal committee to have listed the relative merits of all the unsuccessful appellants in case further places became available for some reason.

Further appeals

5.87   Unless there are significant and material changes, parents may not appeal again in the same academic year for a place in the school. If the LEA or governing body has a policy not to consider repeat applications without a change in circumstances, this must be published in the admission arrangements. If there have been material or significant changes in circumstances the full appeal procedure has to be adhered to. The LEA or governing body can decide if this should be to the same or a different committee.

65   *R v Commissioner for Local Administration ex p Croydon LBC* [1989] 1 All ER 1033, QBD.
66   *R v Leicestershire CC Education Appeals Committee ex p Tarmohamed* [1997] ELR 48, QBD, per Sedley J at 61.
67   [1997] ELR 468, QBD.

CHAPTER 6

Health and safety, pastoral care and welfare

This chapter looks at the general provisions for health and safety issues affecting LEAs and governing bodies. It then considers the often vexed question of bullying in the context of pastoral care. There is a review of provision for the welfare of individual pupils, including clothing grants and other financial provision, school medicals, meals and milk, and travel arrangements.

For full list of contents, see overleaf

Health and safety

Occupiers' Liability Acts 1957 and 1984

6.1   The Occupiers' Liability Acts (OLA) 1957 and 1984 put a duty on an occupier to take reasonable care to ensure that visitors will be safe while on its premises. 'Occupier' has not been specifically defined in relation to schools but it is likely to be the governing body and/or the LEA, depending on the nature of the defects. DFE Circular 2/94,[1] Annex G describes the division of responsibility for building and ground maintenance between LEAs and schools since local management of schools (LMS) has been introduced.

6.2   Visitors to schools would include pupils,[2] parents[3] and teachers. Visitors can also include trespassers. Under the Occupiers Liability Act (OLA) 1984, if an occupier has reasonable grounds to believe that a danger exists on his/her premises and the risk is one that in all the circumstances s/he may be reasonably expected to offer some protection against, then s/he owes a duty to trespassers whom s/he has reasonable grounds for supposing may be in the area (s1(3)). The duty is to take such precautions as are reasonable in all the circumstances to see that they are not injured (s1(4)). It is clear, however, that the extent of the duty would differ in the case of a child, a burglar or an adult. In *Ratcliff v McConnell*,[4] the Court of Appeal overturned a High Court judgment finding Harper Adams Agricultural College 60 per cent liable for injuries sustained by a student at the college. The swimming pool had been closed for the winter. It was walled and locked and there were notices prohibiting its use at night. The student entered the pool with two friends at 2.30 am. He had been drinking but was not drunk. He took a running dive into the pool and suffered tetraplegic injuries. It was held that no duty was owed to the trespassers under OLA 1984 s1 because he had knowingly and willingly accepted the risk.

6.3   OLA 1957 specifically states that 'an occupier must be prepared for children to be less careful than adults' (s2(3)(a)). A risk willingly accepted means that the occupier will not be liable (s2(5)). It is unlikely that pupils, because of their age, will have the capacity to accept risks. This may, of course, be arguable for older children.

1   DFE Circular 2/94 *Local Management of Schools*.
2   *Woodward v Mayor of Hastings* [1944] 2 All ER 565, CA; *Ward v Hertfordshire CC* [1969] 114 Sol J 87, CA.
3   *Griffiths v Smith* [1941] AC 170, HL.
4   (1998) *Times* 3 December; (1999) 4 Ed CR 523, CA.

Education Act 1996

6.4   Schools may be under a duty to take reasonable precautions to protect teachers and pupils from the unlawful intentions of unwelcome visitors. This area may well be tested in the courts more frequently in future. A person who causes or permits a nuisance or disturbance on school premises (including outdoor spaces), to the annoyance of those who lawfully use the premises, whether they are there or not, commits a summary offence under EA 1996 s547. This is punishable by a fine up to level 2. The offender need not be a trespasser ab initio before the offence arises. If a police officer or a person authorised by the LEA has reasonable cause to suspect that an offence is being or has been committed, the suspect may be removed from the premises. The governing body of a foundation, voluntary aided or foundation special school may also authorise someone to remove an offender. The LEA can also authorise removal, but only with the agreement of the governing body. Prosecutions may be brought by someone authorised by the governing body; this may apply to the police. The LEA, in order to prosecute, requires consent of the governing body of a foundation or voluntary aided school (s547(8)). There are analogous provisions applicable to other education institutions such as colleges and universities, under the Local Government (Miscellaneous Provisions) Act 1992.

Common law

6.5   The common law jurisdiction to obtain an injunction to restrain a criminal act has been used on occasions to prevent undesirable persons entering school and LEA premises. School premises are under the control of the governing body, although in practice the LEA and the governing body will have authorised the headteacher to determine access questions. It seems that a local authority has an unfettered right to give or withhold permission to visitors to enter any of its property which members of the public have no right to visit without invitation.[5] The LMS scheme would have to be studied to determine the rights of the governing body as occupier of school premises in a particular case.

---

5   *R v Brent LBC ex p Assegai* (1987) *Independent* 12 June, QBD.

Health and Safety at Work Act 1974

6.6 The Health and Safety at Work Act (HSWA) 1974 and numerous regulations made thereunder also place certain duties on those responsible for schools. LEAs and governing bodies as employers must take reasonable steps to ensure that employees and others on the premises are not exposed to risks to their health and safety. The Health and Safety Executive inspectors enforce this Act in schools. Under the Management of Health and Safety at Work Regulations 1992,[6] the LEA as employer must make a written assessment of the risk of its activities. The governing body and headteacher of a community or voluntary controlled school must comply with any directions given to them by the LEA concerning the health and safety of people on school premises or taking part in school activities anywhere (SSFA 1998 s39(3)).

6.7 DfEE Circular 14/96[7] (para 8) points out that, where pupils have medical needs, the school may need to take additional steps to safeguard their health and safety; the relevant staff have to be aware and, if necessary, trained to provide any additional support they need. A privately-owned children's play centre was held to come within the provisions of HSWA 1974 s4(1) in *Moualem v City of Carlisle Council*.[8]

6.8 It is possible that LEAs or governors could be criminally liable under HSWA 1974 s37, although this section does not appear to have been used in relation to schools.

Environmental Protection Act 1990

6.9 The Environmental Protection Act (EPA) 1990 s89(1)) imposes a duty on the governing body of a school in respect of land under its control, and on the 'principal litter authority' (generally the LEA) in respect of land under its direct control and to which the public have access, 'to ensure that the land is, so far as is reasonable practicable, kept clean of litter and refuse'. This includes dog excrement. The section does not cover heath and woodland not usually open to the public.

6.10 *EPA 1990: Code of Practice on Litter and Refuse*[9] sets out the

6   1992 SI No 2051.
7   DfEE Circular 14/96 *Supporting pupils with medical needs in school.*
8   [1995] ELR 22, QBD.
9   Department of the Environment, January 1991.

expected standards of cleanliness. On receiving a complaint from any person, a magistrates' court can impose a litter abatement order requiring the litter or refuse to be removed within a specified time (EPA 1990 s91(6)). If this is not complied with, 'without reasonable excuse', a maximum fine of £2,500 can be imposed on the relevant authority, plus a further £125 for each day the offence continues after conviction (s91(9)). Section 91(12) also allows magistrates to order costs against the defendant. Alternatively, it is possible for the principal litter authority to issue a litter abatement notice.

6.11   Section 87 makes it an offence punishable by a maximum fine of £2,500 for a person to throw down, drop or otherwise deposit litter on relevant land of a designated education institution, excluding an independent or nursery school.

Other health and safety issues

6.12   See para 3.53 for a discussion of the statutory requirements of the safety of school premises. If an accident happens because of a breach of the Education (School Premises) Regulations 1999,[10] parents and teachers may have a claim for breach of statutory duty.[11]

6.13   See para 8.29 for police powers under the Offensive Weapons Act 1996 in relation to offensive weapons and bladed or pointed instruments.

Pastoral care and negligence

6.14   Apart from the obvious need to take care of its pupils and ensure that they are not placed in danger or at risk, there are few enforceable legal obligations governing the content and application of pastoral care arrangements in schools. They are likely to be more developed in special schools, particularly those which are residential or cater for pupils with emotional or behavioural disturbance.

Supervision

6.15   The courts have held that a teacher is 'in loco parentis', meaning that s/he acts in the place of the parent. Under Children Act (CA) 1989 s3(5), s/he would be a person without parental responsibility but

10   1999 SI No 2.
11   *Reffell v Surrey CC* [1964] 1 All ER 743, QBD.

who has care of the child and may do what is reasonable in the all the circumstances to safeguard or promote the child's welfare.However, it has been held necessary to apply the careful, prudent parent test in the context of a school, where a teacher has far more children to care for than a parent will have in the home.[12] On the other hand, where the pupil was disabled and mentally handicapped, it was held at trial that a deputy headteacher owed a higher duty – that of a responsible parent – and not solely that of a teacher.[13]

6.16   It is important to assess the degree of risk involved in the conduct which has caused the damage. This probably hinges on the degree of supervision given at any one time to a particular activity. As Neville Harris suggests:

> There is clearly a trade-off between inhibiting activities which are
> known to carry some risk of injury, and permitting children to
> benefit from the lesson of experience in the course of growing up
> and from the enjoyment of childhood.[14]

6.17   Another factor that determines the standard of care expected from teachers is the social utility of the act engaged in. In *Jeffrey v London CC*[15] McNair J said that a balance had to be struck 'between the meticulous supervision of children ... and the very desirable object of encouraging their sturdy independence'. This approach has been followed in other cases.

6.18   The question of social utility is particularly relevant to sporting activities which carry intrinsically higher risks than other activities. In *Van Oppen v Clerk to the Bedford Charity Trustees*,[16] a case concerning a serious injury sustained while playing rugby, Balcombe LJ approved the remarks of Boreham J at first instance:

> There are risks of injury inherent in many human activities, even of
> serious injury in some. Because of this, the school, having the
> pupils in its care, is under a duty to exercise reasonable care for
> their health and safety. Provided due care is exercised in this
> sphere, it seems to me that the school's duty is fulfilled.[17]

6.19   In this case the Court of Appeal found that there was no duty on the school to insure against personal injury of its pupils, or against

12   *Lys v Middlesex CC* (1962) 61 LGR 443, QBD.
13   *T v North Yorkshire County Council* [1998] ELR 625, CA.
14   Harris *The Law Relating to Schools* Tolley, 1995, p332.
15   (1954) 52 LGR 521, QBD, at 523.
16   [1989] 3 All ER 389, CA.
17   Ibid at 410–412.

negligence. At first instance, the judge considered that in certain situations the duty owed by a school may be higher than a parental duty, because a school might have knowledge which the parent does not have.

6.20   A more recent case, *Smolden v Whitworth*,[18] decided on its own particular facts, may still change the balance of duties. Here, a rugby player aged 17 and a half successfully brought an action against the referee in a local game for the multiple injuries he received during a scrum. This succeeded because it was a game for under 19s and the rules had been modified for such games. The referee had presided over an unacceptably high level of collapsed scrums. Nevertheless, Bingham LCJ said that the threshold of liability was a high one and would not easily be crossed. A referee could not properly be held liable for errors of judgment, oversight or lapses which might happen in a fast-moving game.

6.21   Even if an activity carries risks, teachers must ensure that it is carried out in a safe manner which has regard to any reasonably foreseeable risk. It is clear that, if a pupil is told or encouraged to take part in an activity which the teacher should reasonably have known was beyond his/her capabilities, negligence may be established. In *Moore v Hampshire CC*[19] a 12-year-old girl broke her ankle while attempting a handstand during a PE lesson. She suffered from congenital dislocation of the hips and the teacher knew that she was not to do PE. Negligence was proved.

School trips

6.22   When children are on educational visits or school trips, teachers have to be exceedingly vigilant about supervision. They also need to check bookings, accommodation and equipment beforehand with care. Professional associations have issued various guidance on this. Following the tragic accident a few years ago where several pupils were killed while visiting an activity centre, the government has issued guidance on these in DFE Circular 22/94.[20] Centres must now be licensed under the Adventure Activities Licensing Regulations 1996.[21]

---

18   [1997] ELR 249, CA.
19   (1981) 80 LGR 481, CA.
20   DFE Circular 22/94 *Safety in Outdoor Activity Centres: Guidance.*
21   1996 SI No 772.

Outside school hours

6.23 Teachers do not have to supervise children during the lunch break as part of their contract of employment but the LEA or the school must provide adequate supervisory staff for this purpose.

6.24 Generally, schools have no responsibility for children arriving at school before the usual time for the beginning of the school day. Where pupils are allowed into the grounds from a certain time there may be responsibility and liability. Prudent headteachers should ensure that school gates are not opened unless or until a member of staff is present in the playground to supervise activities.

6.25 Schools have to ensure that they have an adequate system for handing children over to their parents or carers at the end of a school day. This is, of course, more important with younger children. If a parent fails to collect a child, the school is not liable but should make sure that the child is handed to a responsible adult known to the child. Failing this, the child should be handed to the social services or the police to avoid the situation of allowing a young child to wander off. Teachers or other members of a school's staff should do what is reasonable to safeguard or promote the child's welfare (see para 6.15).

6.26 Children should never be let out of school early unless parents are informed well in advance. In *Barnes (infant) v Hampshire CC*,[22] the children were let out early. One five-year-old girl wandered into the street before her mother arrived and was injured on the road at 3.29 pm, leaving time being 3.30 pm. The LEA was held liable.

6.27 *Nwabudike v Southwark LBC*[23] established that the threshold for a breach of the duty of care for the safety of pupils is high. There is no breach if the school has taken all reasonable steps to ensure safety. The claim of a child who ran out of the school gates and was run down by a car was dismissed.

6.28 In *Wilson v Governors of Sacred Heart Roman Catholic Primary School, Charlton*,[24] the court held that a school was not in breach of its duty of care when a child was injured by another child on school premises while leaving at the end of a school day. Schools do not need to provide adult supervision at this time. The lunch break is different.

---

22 [1969] 1 WLR 1563, HL.
23 [1997] ELR 35, QBD.
24 [1998] ELR 637, CA.

Child abuse by staff

6.29   Where abuse of boys in an approved independent school by the headmaster was not foreseeable in the absence of knowledge about his proclivities, the LEA was held to owe no duty of care to them.[25]

Negligence by pupils

6.30   An LEA may be liable for the negligent action of pupils to themselves or to others. This will largely depend on the age and understanding of the child involved. There may well be cases where the child in question could be held contributorily negligent and any damages against the LEA or governors would consequently be reduced. In *Butt v Cambridgeshire and Ely CC*[26] a large class of nine- and ten-year-olds were using scissors and one child accidentally poked another in the eye with scissors. The Court of Appeal decided that the LEA was not liable, on the ground that there was no fault in the system of supervision. But in *Black v Kent CC*,[27] £13,000 damages was awarded against the LEA to a seven-year-old who jabbed a pair of sharp scissors in his own eye. The injury would not have happened if blunt scissors had been used. If clear warnings are given about unavoidable risks and safety precautions are taken – again, depending on the age of the children – liability may be avoided.

Bullying

6.31   Bullying is potentially a form of negligence. It involves a pattern of dominance over one pupil by another, or a group of others. The victim's life is made miserable and, in extreme cases, can be threatened by suicide.

6.32   DfEE Circular 10/99[28] says that schools need to be clear in their policies about strategies to deal with the prevention of and sanctions for bullying behaviour, which often takes place at break times. The governing body must review the school policy on bullying regularly and school prospectuses should explain the arrangements whereby pupils can report instances of bullying in confidence.[29] Since 1 April

25   *P v Harrow LBC* [1993] 2 FCR 341; [1993] 1 FLR 723; [1993] Fam Law 21, QBD, Potter J. A similar ruling was made by the Court of Appeal in *T v North Yorkshire CC* [1998] ELR 625, CA.

26   [1970] 68 LGR 81, CA.

27   [1983] 82 LGR 39.

28   DfEE Circular 10/99 *Social Inclusion: Pupil Support*.

1998, under EA 1996 s154 (now SSFA 1998 s61), the governing body and headteacher have had new statutory duties concerning discipline (see chapter 8).

6.33   It is not sufficient that a school only provides disciplinary measures against the perpetrators – there needs to be an ethos of care not only for the individual child victim, but also concerning the reasons why a pupil should adopt anti-social behaviour.[30] Sometimes the bully or aggressor may be suffering some form of physical or emotional deprivation or even abuse, which makes it necessary for the school to carry out a very difficult and delicate balancing act. The disciplinary code is to be applied in the interests of good order, discipline and morale throughout the school. In particular, the school has duties to all pupils with special educational needs, including any who are bullying.

6.34   The headteacher and the governing body have a heavy responsibility for being alert to bullying and its consequences, and risk a judicial review if they are not seen to be prepared to investigate and take action[31] (see chapter 14). Note that, where the child will no longer be attending the school, the court is likely to refuse relief.

6.35   According to the principles of negligence, an LEA (as vicariously liable for the negligence of teachers) or the governing body could be liable for the consequences of bullying amounting to assault. However, it is unlikely that a school or LEA would easily be found by a court to be liable for damages if a victim of bullying cannot demonstrate physical injury or psychological harm. This is mainly because of the problem of causation.[32] However, parents of a boy who suffered persistent bullying at a school in Richmond received £30,000 from the LEA in an out of court settlement despite the fact that liability was not admitted.[33]

6.36   Schools have jurisdiction over behaviour outside school hours and off the school premises. This extends to behaviour of pupils towards other pupils of the school, at least where there is an element of bullying or assault.[34]

6.37   A criminal assault on a pupil by another pupil or a teacher, even if not prosecuted, would entitle the pupil to an award from the Criminal Injuries Compensation Authority.

29 Ibid para 56.
30 Ibid paras 44–52.
31 *R v Solihull BC ex p W* [1997] ELR 489, QBD.
32 *Walker v Derbyshire CC* (1994) *Times* 7 June, QBD.
33 News report, *Times* 18 November 1996.
34 *R v Newham LBC and Another ex p X* [1995] ELR 303, QBD.

6.38   Circular 8/94 (see paragraph 6.31) encourages the development of whole-school behaviour policies and approaches. The policy is to be worked out in a spirit of co-operation with the headteacher and the whole of the teaching and non-teaching staff. Pupils are found to play a positive role, for example, in exposing bullying and establishing schools' councils. Guidance on features of appropriate pastoral care can be found in the ACE information sheet *Pastoral Care Guide*.[35] See also the pamphlet *Bullying, A Guide to the Law* by the Children's Legal Centre.[36]

Welfare of pupils

Grants and awards

6.39   It is possible for LEAs to make various sorts of grants or allowances available to pupils in connection with their education.

Minor awards

6.40   EA 1996 s518 (as substituted by SSFA 1998 s129) and the Local Education Authority (Payment of School Expenses) Regulations 1999[37] allow for 'minor awards' to be made to children with parents on low incomes so that they can participate in educational activities, both during and outside school hours.

6.41   Minor awards made under EA 1996 s518(6) may be available to people over compulsory school leaving age attending either full-time or part-time courses other than full-time secondary schooling or a course for which a mandatory grant is available. These are in the form of scholarships, exhibitions, bursaries and other allowances.[38]

Educational maintenance awards

6.42   Under the Scholarships and Other Benefits Regulations 1977,[39] all tuition fees or part of board and lodging fees at direct grant and fee paying schools are to be paid on a means-tested basis. The

35 *Pastoral Care Guide* by Chris Watkins, ACE, undated.
36 Children's Legal Centre, October 1996.
37 1999 SI No 1727.
38 See Local Education Authority (Post Compulsory Education Awards) Regulations 1999 SI No 229. See also paras 12.58–12.73.
39 1977 SI No 1443 (as amended by 1979 SI Nos 269 and 542, 1989 SI No 1278 and 1999 SI No 86) reg 4(b)–(d).

Chancellor of the Exchequer has put forward proposals to be piloted in 12 areas where the school leaving rate is well above the norm. This would provide up to £40 per week, payable directly to a child between the ages of 16 and 18, in households where the family income is less than £13,000 pa, to stay on at school or college.

6.43   Regulation 6 states that no payment shall be made unless:

– it prevents or relieves financial hardship, and
– the authority is satisfied that the course to which it relates is suitable for the pupil.

Fees at independent schools

6.44   Arrangements can also be made for children to attend independent schools. EA 1996 s517(1)–(5) lays down conditions which require the LEA to pay the whole of the fees (including board and lodging) at such schools. Fees can be paid if the school is one supported by a grant from the secretary of state under EA 1996 s485 and there is no maintained school reasonably convenient which is suitable to a pupil's age, ability and aptitude and any special needs s/he might have. Board and lodging will be paid for if the LEA is satisfied that suitable education would not be available unless this were provided. An LEA will have acted illegally and fettered its discretion if it refuses to consider exceptional circumstances in relation to paying fees under this discretionary provision.[40]

6.45   These duties are distinct from any duty which the LEA may have to pay for independent educational provision under the special educational needs legislation (see chapter 9). They are also distinct from the payments made by central government under the assisted places scheme (see para 6.47).

LEA policies

6.46   LEAs can be quite subjective in the formulation of their policies regarding these discretionary awards. However, in *R v Lambeth LBC ex p G*,[41] Potts J held that a policy of making awards to persons attending out-of-district schools only where there was no suitable course in the LEA's own area was unlawful. The policy also failed to have regard to the principle of parental preference in EA 1996 s411. This violated the provisions of EA 1944 ss76 and 81 (now EA 1996 ss9 and 518) and was accordingly ultra vires.

40   *R v Hampshire Education Authority ex p J* (1985) 84 LGR 547, QBD.
41   [1994] ELR 207, QBD.

Assisted places

6.47   This scheme, under which central government paid fees for children at independent schools, was abolished from the end of the school year 1997/98 by Education (Schools) Act 1997 s1. Transitional arrangements are in place for existing pupils (s2). If a child had an assisted place for primary education this will cease when s/he completes that stage of education unless the secretary of state is satisfied in relation to that particular pupil that s/he should continue to be assisted until the end of the secondary stage (s2(2)). Below an annual income of £10,670, no fees are payable.[42] The similar scheme for providing places at music, ballet and choir schools under EA 1996 s485 will not be affected.[43] It should be noted that, as a result of *R v Cobham Hall School ex p S*,[44] judicial review may be available in respect of any dispute between an independent school and an assisted pupil (see chapter 11).

Clothing

6.48   LEAs can provide clothing and footwear to pupils in certain situations (EA 1996 s510 and 579(1)). These are for boarders at maintained schools and for pupils for whom an LEA provides board and lodging, pupils in nursery schools or classes and pupils for whom special educational provision is made. In addition, an LEA may provide clothing if it appears that a pupil cannot take full advantage of educational opportunities because of the inadequacy of his/her clothing.

6.49   LEAs also have the power to provide clothing for physical training, including activities specified in EA 1996 s508 such as holiday camps and play centres. EA 1996 s511 allows LEAs to provide clothes as a gift or a loan. They can also charge parents some or all of the cost.

Milk and meals

6.50   EA 1996 s512 has been amended by SSFA 1998 s114 so that LEAs shall not be required to provide meals if it would be unreasonable for

---

42 Education (Assisted Places) Regulations 1997 SI No 1968 as amended by Education (Assisted Places)(Amendment) Regulations 1998 SI No 1726.

43 Education (Grants) (Music, Ballet and Choir Schools) (Amendment) Regulations 1999 SI No 1503.

44 [1998] ELR 389, QBD.

them to do so. Furthermore, they do not need to provide them to children under school age who are only attending school part time. SSFA 1998 s114 allows for regulations to be made setting nutritional standards for meals. LEAs have a duty to provide meals at no charge to pupils whose parents are on income support or income-based jobseeker's allowance (EA 1996 s512(3)). In other cases, LEAs can charge whatever they deem fit but every pupil must be charged the same amount. There appears to be no power to remit charges in individual cases.

6.51   Section 512(4) requires LEAs to provide facilities for pupils to eat their own food at the school. SSFA 1998 s116 inserted a new s512A to EA 1996, empowering the secretary of state to order the responsibility for meals etc to be transferred to governing bodies of schools with delegated budgets. The provision of school meals in specified LEAs in England has been transferred to governing bodies.[45] The LEAs are named in three schedules according to whether the order is to apply to secondary, primary and secondary, or primary, secondary and special schools in an area. In Wales, from 1 September 1999, lunches in all former grant maintained schools with delegated budgets will be the responsibility of governing bodies, and by 1 April 2000, this will extend to all secondary schools.[46]

Medical and dental inspection and treatment

6.52   Under EA 1996 s520 it is the duty of the LEA:

> to make arrangements for encouraging and assisting pupils to take advantage of the provision for medical and dental inspection and treatment made for them in pursuance of s5(1) or (1A) of the National Health Service Act 1977 or paragraph 1(a)(i) of Schedule 1 to the Act.

Usually medicals are provided at a school but dental inspection and treatment would more usually be held in a school's dental centre. Section 5(1A) also includes education in dental health. Accommodation for medical or dental examination or treatment, for the care of pupils, must be made available under Education (School

---

45   Education (Transfer of Functions Concerning School Lunches) (England) Order 1999 SI No 604.

46   Education (Transfer of Functions Concerning School Lunches) (Wales) Order 1999 SI No 610 and Education (Transfer of Functions Concerning School Lunches) (Wales) (No 2) Order 1999 SI No 1779.

Premises) Regulations 1999[47] reg 5.

6.53   Unless a child's parent notifies that s/he objects to this encouragement the LEA must make arrangements for encouraging and assisting the child to avail her/himself of this provision.

6.54   National Health Service Act 1977 Sch 1 also allows this provision to be made available to senior pupils attending an establishment other than a school, including a further education college, and for any child who by EA 1996 s19 is receiving education otherwise than at a school. The LEA can also make this provision available to junior and senior pupils educated at a school not maintained by the LEA.

6.55   Circular guidance on administering medicines at school is somewhat equivocal.[48] While the in loco parentis principle is acknowledged, especially in an emergency, it is pointed out that 'there is no legal or contractual duty on school staff to administer medicine or supervise a pupil taking it' (para 13). There should be insurance cover for 'staff willing to support pupils with medical needs' (para 13) and 'staff should not, as a general rule, administer medication without first receiving appropriate information and/or training' (para 21). Reliance is placed on the school nurse provided by the local NHS Trust, for advice.

6.56   Schools are to make known their policies and procedures, which will usually involve the headteacher deciding what to do. The circular is clear on the need to keep some medication readily available in an emergency and not locked away. Relevant school staff and the pupil concerned should know where this is kept (paras 27–28) By Children Act 1989 s3(5), teachers are able to take action in an emergency (para 14). Parents remain responsible for their child's medication (para 18) but the headteacher usually decides if the school can assist in administering this, having regard to the encouragement of regular attendance and participation. Arrangements for the administration of medication can be a source of difficulty between parents and schools, particularly in mainstream schools.

47   1999 SI No 2.
48   See DfEE Circular 14/96 *Supporting Pupils with Medical Needs in School.*

Provision of transport

To and from school

6.57 In line with his/her duty to ensure a child's attendance at school (see chapter 7), a parent should, where reasonably practicable and prudent, accompany a child to school where it would not be safe for the child to go alone.[49]

6.58 Under EA 1996 s509(1)–(2) LEAs have to make appropriate arrangements to provide free transport for children to attend school, including boarding schools. Parents have a defence to failing to send their child to school under EA 1996 s444 if the school at which the child is registered is not within walking distance and no suitable arrangements have been made by the LEA for the child's transport (but see para 6.66). Section 509A, inserted by SSFA 1998, extends this provision to nursery education not provided at a school.

6.59 Walking distance is defined as two miles, or three miles where the child is aged eight or over. This is measured by the 'nearest available route'. In *Rogers v Essex CC*,[50] the House of Lords held that, where a child could not walk on her own without risk of danger, the route was still 'available'.

6.60 In *Re S (minors)*,[51] the children attended a school in Wales, some distance away from their home, where predominantly English was spoken. They received free transport to the school. The LEA withdrew this transport, which meant that the children were unable to remain at the school. They were forced to move to a school nearer their home where more Welsh was spoken. It was held that it was not appropriate for the court to decide whether the new school was suitable and it was not perverse for the LEA to refuse to continue providing free transport. The Court of Appeal said that the objective suitability of the proposed local school could not possibly assist a defence under EA 1996 s444(4), which deals with lack of suitable arrangements for ensuring attendance. Therefore, the court had no obligation to consider the suitability of the local school.

6.61 Following *Rogers*, EA 1996 s509(4)(a) provides that:

> In considering whether or not they are required by subsection (1) to make arrangements in relation to a particular person, the local education authority shall have regard (amongst other things) to the

---

49 *George v Devon CC* [1988] 3 All ER 1002.
50 [1986] 3 All ER 321, HL.
51 [1995] ELR 98, CA.

age of the person and the nature of the route, or alternative routes, which he could reasonably be expected to take ...

6.62   EA 1996 s509(4)(b) requires the LEA also to take into account any religious preferences of the parents in considering whether it should make transport arrangements under s509(1). This followed *R v Rochdale MBC ex p Schemet.*[52]

6.63   *Ex p Schemet* also emphasised that, if an LEA wants to provide education at a school nearer than the one proposed by the parent, it has to show not that the transport facilities are suitable but that the school is suitable for the particular pupil. While an LEA must take into account the parental preference in reaching a decision, the parents did not in effect have a right of veto over a suitable school. This was confirmed by the Court of Appeal in *R v Essex CC ex p C.*[53] Russell LJ said that parental choice was subject, inter alia, to 'the avoidance of unreasonable public expenditure' under EA 1944 s76 (now EA 1996 s9). The LEA can look at the reasons underlying the parental preference and must consider the inherent suitability of the respective schools.[54] Where the school is named in a statement of special educational needs, the LEA must help with transport if requested and cannot refuse this on the ground that there may be other nearer schools which could accommodate the child.[55]

6.64   By EA 1996 s509(3), LEAs may, 'as they think fit' provide funding for 'reasonable travelling expenses' in whole or in part for people for whom transport arrangements are not made under s509(1) (see para 6.61).

6.65   If LEAs provide transport under EA 1996 s509 (1)–(2) it must be 'non-stressful'.[56] There is no prescribed maximum limit to journey times and each case will turn on its own facts and expert opinion, if appropriate. Some LEAs still follow the guidance given in the *Manual of Guidance (School No 1)* which was issued 1950, but withdrawn in 1981.[57] This stated that the journey time in normal conditions for primary pupils should not exceed three-quarters of an hour, and for secondary children one and a half hours (para 24). The

---

52   [1994] ELR 89, QBD.

53   [1994] ELR 54, QBD, and [1994] ELR 273, CA.

54   DFE Circular 1/94 *Religious Education and Collective Worship* gave guidance which is consistent with this decision. See also *R v Kent County Council ex p C* [1998] ELR 108, QBD.

55   *R v Havering LBC ex p K* [1998] ELR 402, QBD.

56   *R v Hereford and Worcester CC ex p P* [1992] 2 FLR 207, QBD.

57   DES, 1950.

guidance did not deal with children attending special schools or boarding schools (para 2).

6.66   *Ex p Schemet* (see paras 6.62–6.63) made it clear that, if LEAs changed their policies on transport, this could have a significant impact on parents with children already attending a particular school, and might in some circumstances mean that parents had to move their children. Roch J said that parents whose children were already getting free transport to a school in another district had a legitimate expectation to be consulted over proposed changes. They had a legitimate expectation that the situation would remain the same unless and until they had been informed of, and given the opportunity to comment on rational arguments for a change of policy.

Road safety

6.67   In *R v Gwent CC*,[58] Macpherson J held that the LEA in 1993 was not obliged to install seatbelts in order to ensure that the children would be reasonably safe. However, from February 1997 it has been compulsory for mini-buses (9–16 seats) and coaches (more than 16 seats, over 7.5 tonnes and with a maximum speed in excess of 60 mph) to have seat belts.[59] No vehicle without seat belts can be used to transport children up to the age of 16 without a lap belt, child restraint or a disabled person's harness, with support for the provision of a lap and diagonal seat belt where practicable. Children must be on an organised school trip, which means being carried to or from school or from one part of their school premises to another.

6.68   Consequently most single and double decker buses typically used in local scheduled bus services will be excluded.

6.69   Difficulties may arise in the enforcement of the wearing of seat belts, the safety aspect of lap belts as distinct from over the shoulder types and the lack of regulation of the quality of fixings for the seats.

Drivers

6.70   If LEAs hire buses to drive large numbers of children, no checks will be made on drivers because they will not be employed by the LEA. Where children are transported by LEA drivers in LEA transport

---

58 [1995] ELR 27, QBD.
59 Road Vehicles (Construction and Use) Regulations 1986 SI No 1078 as amended by 1996 SI No 163.

then criminal records are checked. Unfortunately, driving records are not part of a routine police check. A check can be made via DVLC Swansea, but it can take several weeks and a fee is payable. Parents may well feel that someone's driving record is just as important as any criminal convictions.

6.71   Generally, where cars pick up children they are either taxis or mini-cabs. The former are licensed with local authorities and checks are carried out on drivers and vehicles. The latter are licensed outside London. If LEAs employ temporary drivers they may not carry out checks. It is necessary to look at an LEA's transport policy.

6.72   The standard of care to be adopted is that of the reasonable, prudent parent. This is illustrated in *Myton v Woods*.[60] Here, the LEA paid a taxi firm to take the child to and from school. Contrary to instructions given by the authority, the driver set the child down in a busy main road and he was hit. The local authority was held not liable. The Court of Appeal found that it had acted in accordance with its duty under EA 1944 (now EA 1996) and at common law to provide suitable arrangements for transport and was not liable for the negligence of the driver.

Escorts

6.73   By EA 1996 s509 (1)–(2) LEAs make arrangements for transport 'and otherwise'. This appears to require LEAs to employ escorts where necessary. In addition, it seems from *Shrimpton v Hertfordshire CC*[61] that, where an LEA provides transport, there is a requirement that a second person be provided to assist the driver to get the children in and out as necessary. The age, needs and temperament of the child are significant factors in determining whether an escort is required. In *Jacques v Oxfordshire CC*[62] no adult supervisors were provided. It was held that, in all the circumstances, despite a boy being injured by a pellet, there had been adequate supervision by prefects.

6.74   Some LEAs are better than others in checking and training escorts. In a case involving an escort, or lack of one, it is essential again to look at the LEA's transport policy.

---

60 (1980) 79 LGR 28, CA.
61 (1911) 104 LT 145, HL.
62 (1967) 66 LGR 440 (Oxfordshire Assizes).

CHAPTER 7

Attendance

This chapter looks at the law relating to attendance, including the duties of schools to register school pupils, the duties of parents and the powers of local education authorities to ensure pupils' attendance at school.

Introduction

7.1   It should not be surprising to those involved in the legal system that a recent Home Office publication[1] directly links non-attendance at school through truancy and/or exclusion to the incidence of crime amongst young offenders. It makes depressing yet predictable reading. It is not uncommon for those who represent young offenders to find that they also have an education law case on their hands. At the very least, an LEA may be in breach of its statutory duty under EA 1996 s19 in not providing any or an adequate education. Unfortunately, the young people themselves are often so alienated and distanced from the schooling system that they are not interested in seeking any remedy, and neither are their parents.

7.2   No one knows precisely how many children are out of school at any one time because of truancy or exclusion, but each year at least one million children truant, and over 100,000 children are excluded. Some 13,000 are excluded permanently.[2] The government has recently initiated a series of measures to combat truancy and improve attendance. The secretary of state is empowered to require governing bodies of maintained schools with a truancy rate of three per cent or more above the national average for that type of school for two years to set targets for the reduction of unauthorised absences for the following three years.[3]

7.3   The other main types of case in which attendance is an issue are those where parents deliberately keep their children out of school because they have not been offered a place at the school of their choice (see paras 5.30–5.41). These parents may be in the process of making an admissions appeal (see paras 5.42–5.87) or an appeal to the Special Educational Needs Tribunal (see paras 9.69–9.94) or their appeal may have been refused. Parents may also decide to educate their children at home or outside the formal school system (see paras 7.13, 7.16 and 7.17).

---

1   *Young People and Crime*, Home Office Research Study 145, 1995.

2   Graham and Bowling *Truancy and School Exclusion* Cm 3957, Social Exclusion Unit, May 1998.

3   SSFA 1998 s63; Education (School Attendance Targets) (England) Regulations 1999 SI No 397; Education (School Performance and Unauthorised Absence Targets) (Wales) Regulations 1999 SI No 1811.

Duty to register pupils

7.4   LEAs have various powers designed to ensure that children of school age are registered on the roll of a school and that they attend school (see paras 7.18 onwards). Unfortunately, for a variety of reasons, in which lack of resources plays a significant part, LEAs substantially fail to exercise their statutory powers to these ends. Many of the parents and pupils affected by this are unlikely to complain, since they are either indifferent or opposed to the pupil's attendance at the school offered by the LEA. Therefore, the issue of registration may only rarely be raised by a parent, for example in judicial review or (possibly) negligence proceedings or by making a complaint to the secretary of state or the local ombudsman (see chapter 13). It may arise in defending criminal proceedings but is rarely pursued by the parent.

7.5   Rights to education depend to some extent on registration of the pupil and it is, therefore, important to understand the strict rules which apply, particularly to young people under 16. Schools and LEAs have been known to neglect the formalities, with the result that vulnerable young people sometimes disappear from the educational system, and new guidance[4] goes into detail as regards recording absence.

7.6   Under EA 1996 s434(1) the proprietor of every school, both state and independent, must keep the particulars which are prescribed by the Education (Pupil Registration) Regulations 1995.[5] A proprietor is usually the governing body. The LEA is the proprietor of a pupil referral unit (PRU) and in some independent schools the proprietor would be the owner or the trustees. All schools must keep an admission register and an attendance register except schools where all the pupils are boarders and they are excused an attendance register (reg 5). Names may only be deleted from the register on prescribed grounds. Breach of the regulations is a criminal offence, attracting a Level 1 fine on summary conviction (EA 1996 s434(6)). There is DFE guidance[6] regarding the attendance register (reg 7) and dealing with absence (reg 8).

7.7   The names and addresses of every parent known to the school

---

4   DfEE Circular 10/99 *Social Inclusion: Pupil Support.*

5   1995 SI No 2089.

6   DFE Guidance *School Attendance: Policy and Practice on Categorisation of Absence,* May 1994, has been superseded by DfEE Circular 10/99 *Social Inclusion: Pupil Support* Annex A.

must be included in the admission register, with emergency contact telephone numbers for the pupil's home (reg 6). Under reg 9, the permitted grounds for deletion of the name of a compulsory school-age pupil from the admissions register are:

1) revocation of school attendance order or change of school in an order (see paras 7.18–7.23);
2) registration at another school;
3) notification from parent to governing body that pupil is receiving education otherwise than at school (written notice of withdrawal of the pupil from the school is not sufficient) – the school has a statutory obligation to notify the name and address of the pupil to the LEA within ten school days (reg 13(3));
4) day pupil has ceased to attend and no longer lives within a reasonable distance of the school;
5) unexplained failure of pupil to return for more than ten school days following holiday with leave of absence;
6) certified unlikely to be fit to attend whilst of compulsory school age;
7) pupil absent for more than four weeks and cannot be found, despite reasonable enquiry by both school and LEA;
8) pupil absent for more than four weeks and detained under a court order;
9) death of pupil;
10) pupil will be over compulsory school age next term and does not want to return;
11) pupil at non-maintained school has ceased to be a pupil;
12) pupil has been permanently excluded from maintained school (Circular 10/99[7] page 43 requires any appeal procedure to be completed first);
13) nursery pupil fails to transfer to a reception class (see SSFA 1998 s98).

7.8   Generally, names may not be removed from special school registers without the consent of the LEA which arranged the placement (reg 9(2)). Where the pupil has dual registration (eg, PRU and school, special and mainstream schools) proprietors of both schools must agree (reg 10).

7.9   In the case of a pupil not of compulsory school age the grounds for deletion from the admissions register are modified (reg 9(3)):

1) pupil has ceased to attend or board at the school;

7   DfEE Circular 10/99 *Social Inclusion: Pupil Support.*

2) pupil absent for more than four weeks and cannot be found, despite reasonable enquiry by the school;
3) death of pupil;
4) pupil has been permanently excluded from maintained school;
5) nursery pupil fails to transfer to a reception class.

7.10   If a child who is over compulsory school age ceases to be registered at a school s/he will not be entitled to special educational provision under EA 1996 Part IV unless s/he already has a statement of special educational needs (see EA 1996 s321(3)).

7.11   LEAs and schools are required to keep records of pupils who fail to attend regularly or are continuously absent without sickness, leave of absence etc, for more than ten school days (reg 13).

Duties of parents

7.12   EA 1996 s7 provides that:

> It shall be the duty of the parent of every child of compulsory school age to cause him to receive efficient full-time education suitable to his age, ability, and aptitude, and to any special educational needs he may have either by regular attendance at school or otherwise.

'Parent' means anyone who has parental responsibility for or care of the child (EA 1996 s576(1) – the same definition as in Children Act (CA) 1989).

7.13   A child begins to be of compulsory school age on the 'prescribed day' on or after which s/he reaches the age of five (EA 1996 s8(2)). The prescribed days are 31 March, 31 August and 31 December.[8] There is no obligation on parents to send their child to school until this date if it is not practicable to register the child at a school.

7.14   A person remains of compulsory school age until the school leaving date (the last Friday in June[9]) in the school year in which s/he becomes 16 (EA 1996 s8(3)).

Suitable education

7.15   'Suitable education', in relation to a child, means efficient full-time education suitable to his/her age, ability and aptitude and to any special educational needs s/he may have (EA 1996 ss19 and 437(8)).

8   Education (Start of Compulsory School Age) Order 1998 SI No 1607.
9   Education (School Leaving Date) Order 1997 SI No 1970.

In *Harrison v Stevenson*,[10] the Crown Court heard an appeal against convictions under EA 1944 s40 for failure to comply with school attendance orders (see para 7.22). Education was held to be suitable to a child's age, ability and aptitude only if the education prepared a child for life in modern civilised society and enabled a child to achieve his/her full potential. In *R v Secretary of State for Education and Science ex p Talmud Torah Madizikei Hedass School Trust*,[11] Woolf J held that education is suitable if it primarily equips a child for life in a community of which s/he is a member as long as it does not foreclose the child's option later to adopt some other form of life if s/he wishes to do so.

7.16   The phrase 'or otherwise' allows the possibility of parents educating their children at home permanently (see paras 11.40–11.50) or providing tuition for children who do not attend school for a reason such as illness, exclusion, or travelling. If it appears to an LEA that a child of compulsory school age is not receiving suitable education, it may issue a notice requiring a parent to satisfy it that the child is receiving satisfactory education (EA 1996 s437(1). The words 'if it appears' were considered in *Phillips v Brown*.[12] Donaldson LJ considered what an LEA could do in this situation and suggested that it could ask the parents for information although there was no compulsion on them to provide the information. If no information was given, Donaldson LJ said the LEA would then have to consider again whether it felt that the child was receiving suitable education. The LEA does not have the right to go into a home to check on educational provision. If a parent refuses a request for a visit or information, then the LEA has the power to serve a school attendance order (see paras 7.18–7.23). There is no statutory guidance on the extent to which matters such as the National Curriculum must be covered at home.

7.17   The phrase was considered in *R v Gwent CC ex p Perry*.[13] The Court of Appeal looked at the procedures followed by the LEA to satisfy itself about whether a child educated at home was receiving suitable education. Once the LEA had allowed the parent sufficient time to set in motion his arrangements for home education, it was sufficient for two education advisory officers to visit an eight-year-old boy at home to inspect the syllabus and facilities for teaching,

10   (1981) Worcester Crown Court (unreported).
11   (1985) *Times* 12 April, DC.
12   (1980) 20 June, DC (unreported).
13   (1985) 129 Sol Jo 737, CA.

interview him and test his mathematics and reading, in order to see the end product as reflected in the child's intellectual and other development. There was no general obligation to bring to the parent's attention all the adverse impressions gained by the LEA. The parent failed in a challenge to the LEA's decision to prosecute him despite two reports he had submitted to them about the boy's response to home education. The European Court of Human Rights in *H v UK*[14] held that a state was entitled to make education compulsory and to require parents who educated their children at home to co-operate in the assessment of standards reached.

Powers of LEAs to enforce attendance

School attendance orders

7.18 A school attendance order requiring the parent to register a child at a named school must be served on the parent if the parent fails on not less than 15 days' notice to satisfy the LEA that the child is receiving suitable education (EA 1996 s437(1)).

7.19 The LEA must inform the governors and the head of the proposed school that it has made a school attendance order. The school must admit the child but its exclusion powers (see paras 8.35–8.53) are unaffected. The parent has the right under EA 1996 s438 to be offered alternative schools unless the child has a statement of special educational needs, but the LEA need not offer a school that is full (EA 1996 s439).

7.20 The order continues in force while the child remains of compulsory school age unless it is revoked by the LEA or a magistrates' court directs that it shall cease to apply. The parent can have the named school changed by agreement with the LEA. The secretary of state will not intervene if there is in reality a dispute about choice of school (in a statement of special educational needs).[15] A school attendance order cannot apply when an education supervision order is in force or a care order is made (CA 1989 s91(5)).

7.21 In the case of a child with a special educational needs statement, if the statement specifies a school, this must be named in the school attendance order. If no school is named, the statement must be amended to name the school in the school attendance order.

14 (1984) 38 DR 105.
15 *R v Secretary of State for Education ex p G* [1995] ELR 58, QBD.

Criminal liability

Failure to comply with school attendance order

7.22   It is a criminal offence for a parent to fail to comply with a school attendance order (EA 1996 s443). Prosecutions are brought by the LEA. On conviction the penalty is a fine on level 3 (£3,000) in the magistrates' court. The power to impose a prison sentence was abolished by Children Act 1989 Sch 15. A parent can only be prosecuted once in relation to any one school attendance order.

7.23   Under EA 1996 s443(1) there is a defence to the failure to comply with a school attendance order if the parent proves that the child is receiving suitable education out of school.

Failure to secure regular attendance of a registered pupil

7.24   For the majority of children, who are not subject to school attendance orders, the parent is guilty of an offence under EA 1996 s444 if a registered pupil 'fails to attend regularly at school'. This means attendance at the times prescribed by the LEA. Pupils arriving after the register has closed are treated as absent.[16] Prosecution is a comparatively straightforward remedy for the LEA, and the initiation of criminal proceedings may in itself act as a sufficient incentive for school attendance to be resumed in time for a decision to be taken to offer no evidence at the substantive hearing.

7.25   There are a number of statutory excuses:

1)   leave of absence, given by an authorised person;
2)   sickness of the child (not the parent);
3)   unavoidable cause affecting the child,[17] usually an emergency;
4)   day of religious observance;
5)   no suitable transport arrangements made by the LEA, when the school is not within walking distance (paras 6.57–6.66);

16   *Hinchley v Rankin* [1961] 1 All ER 692.
17   In *Bath and North East Somerset District Council v Warman (Jennifer)* (1999) ELR 81, QBD the child was nearly 16 when the prosecution started. She had left home to live with her boyfriend some distance away. Her mother did not approve of this but did not know where she was living until after her 16th birthday. She had contacted the police but they would do nothing because they did not think the child was at risk. The magistrates found the mother not guilty. The prosecution appealed and Rose LJ remitted the case back to them with a direction to convict. He said that the unavoidable cause related to the daughter and not the mother and there was nothing stopping the daughter attending school. He did, however, suggest that an absolute discharge would be appropriate.

6) child is of no fixed abode, and:
   - parent has itinerant trade etc;
   - child has attended as regularly as trade permitted; and
   - child is over six years of age and has over 200 attendances in the 12 months before the summons.

This is an absolute offence and parents will be found guilty even if they have taken all reasonable steps to ensure attendance and they were unaware that their child was not attending school.[18]

Education supervision orders

7.26 An LEA may not prosecute under EA 1996 ss443 and 444 unless it has first considered whether to apply to a family proceedings court for an education supervision order with respect to the child (EA 1996 s447). A magistrates' court which is dealing with a young person in criminal proceedings has the power to direct the LEA to apply for an education supervision order before conviction under s444 or after conviction under s443, unless the LEA has decided after consultation with the social services department that the child's welfare will be safeguarded without an order.

7.27 This provision may mean that judicial review could be available against an LEA which was determined to prosecute without showing that it had first ruled out the option of an education supervision order. In such a case, however, an alternative remedy may lie in the powers of the magistrates court and this would make it difficult to obtain civil legal aid for judicial review

Obtaining an order

7.28 Under CA 1989 s36 a magistrates' (family proceedings) court may make an education supervision order where the child 'is of compulsory school age and is not being properly educated'. This is the same test as 'suitable' in EA 1996 s7 (see para 7.15). A child is only being properly educated 'if he is receiving efficient full-time education' suitable to his age, ability and aptitude and to any special educational needs he may have' (s36(4)).

7.29 The order lasts one year and enables a supervisor (usually an education welfare officer) or education social worker 'to advise, assist and befriend, and give directions to' the supervised child and the person with parental responsibility. The order can be extended once

18 *Crump v Gilmore* (1968) LGR 56, QBD, a prosecution under EA 1944 s36.

only by up to three years on application when there is less than three months to run (CA 1989 Sch 3 para 15). There is no limit to the number of orders that can be made but if after an order has been made a child is still not being educated properly this may suggest that alternative methods should be tried.

7.30   An education supervision order may not be made if a child is already in the care of an LEA (CA 1989 s36(6)). An order ceases to have effect if the child goes into care (Sch 3 para 15(6)) or is no longer of compulsory school age.

7.31   The child's parent may appeal to the High Court against an education supervision order (CA 1989 s94).

7.32   The LEA is obliged to show that it has consulted the appropriate local authority before it applies for an education supervision order (CA 1989 s36(8) and (9)). In practice, this means the social services department. However, it does not require the consent of the local authority before applying for an order. Not infrequently this consultation is cursory or non-existent. The appropriate local authority is the local authority where the child lives, or will live. If accommodation is being provided by or on behalf of a local authority, it is that authority. This is because the local authority is supposed to consider whether support should be given to the child and the family under CA 1989 Part III (Local authority support for children and families). This deals with children in need. The local authority does not have a part in an investigative process.

Help from the local authority or health authority

7.33   The intention of the Children Act 1989 is clearly that appropriate support should be available where there is a child 'in need' under s17. A child is held to be 'in need' if s/he is unlikely to achieve or maintain, or to have the opportunity of achieving or maintaining, a reasonable standard of health and development without services provided by a local authority under CA 1989 Part III, or is disabled (s17(10)). See paras 11.15–11.19.

7.34   Any child who is not being educated is by definition in need. The social services department has a statutory duty to carry out an assessment of such a child's needs. In theory, this may be carried out at the same time and using some of the same resources as an educational assessment under EA 1996 s323 (see CA 1989 Sch 2 para 3). But, in practice, this seems to be a rare occurrence. If education problems are evident when a local authority investigates a case, it must consult the LEA (CA 1989 s47(5)).

7.35 An LEA has limited powers to insist on help[19] from the local authority or district health authority. It has a discretion to make a request (EA 1996 s322(1)). But there are generous exemptions from compliance on the part of the authority:

1) where is considers that help is 'not necessary' under CA 1989 Part III;
2) where the district health authority, in the light of its own resources for use in exercising its functions under the National Health Services Act 1977, decides that it is not reasonable to comply;
3) where a local authority considers that the request is not compatible with its own statutory or other duties and obligations or unduly prejudices the discharge of its functions.

7.36 Even if the LEA has decided to assess for special educational needs (see chapter 9) it may only ask the social services department of the (usually same) authority to provide advice in the statutory form.[20] But, if the child is not already known to the department, there will be no substantive advice.

Assessment of special needs following an order

7.37 The result is that in many cases an LEA can obtain an education supervision order without there having been an exhaustive investigation of the reasons for the child's non-attendance at school. Inevitably, lack of parental commitment or interest is a factor in many cases, but the role of learning difficulties is perhaps underestimated. This is not relevant to the court's decision to make an order, but there is an expectation that the order will facilitate a proper assessment of special needs. This is much more meaningful if carried out while the child is attending school.

7.38 A conflict can arise if an assessment is considered desirable but the parent does not want it.

7.39 When a parent feels that there should be further investigation of special educational needs, it may be worth considering whether an independent report from a child psychiatrist or psychologist or educational psychologist would assist in disposal of family proceedings. It might be useful as an independent guide for the LEA in its future assessment of the child. However, legal aid must not be

19 See CA 1989 Sch 2 Part 1 for the range of services potentially available.
20 *Code of Practice on the Identification and Assessment of Special Educational Needs* DFE, 1994, para 3.116–119.

abused. Leave of the court must be obtained before papers can be shown to an outside expert[21] or to have the child seen by another expert.[22]

7.40   The court may well regard the LEA's educational psychologist as a sufficiently detached independent expert and refuse to give leave. Such a decision could, in principle, be challenged in the High Court. Care should be taken at an early stage to consider the various matters set out in *Re G (minors) (expert witnesses)*.[23]

Operation of an education supervision order

7.41   The court appoints a supervisor, probably an education welfare officer or a social worker, who issues directions to ensure that the child is properly educated. These may apply to the child as well as the parent. Criminal sanctions (fine on Level 3) apply where a parent persistently fails to comply with a direction (CA 1989 Sch 3 para 18).

7.42   There is a defence under CA 1989 Sch 3 para 18 if the parent can prove that:

1) s/he took all reasonable steps to ensure the direction was complied with;
2) the direction was unreasonable; or
3) s/he had complied with a requirement in a supervision order (imposed by a criminal court), or directions given under such a requirement and it was not reasonably practicable to comply with the supervision order and an education supervision order.

7.43   In one case,[24] a mother was prosecuted in 1993 because of truancy by two of her sons. She was fined £90 and an education supervision order was imposed. This was not renewed after a year. The school attendance of the boys rapidly declined, as did that of their sister. The mother was again prosecuted in 1996 and was placed on probation for three years by Solihull magistrates. This is believed to be the first order of its kind in these circumstances. There have also been instances where magistrates have deferred sentencing, presumably to see if attendance improved.[25]

7.44   The LEA must notify the local social services department if the child persistently fails to comply with an education supervision

21 Family Proceedings Courts (Children Act 1989) Rules 1991 SI No 1395 r23.
22 Ibid r18.
23 [1994] 2 FLR 291, FD.
24 *Guardian* news report, 17 April 1996.
25 *Guardian* news report 24 April 1996.

order. The department must investigate the circumstances and decide whether intervention under CA 1989 Parts III or IV is required.

7.45   At this point the social services department might consider applying for a care order on the ground that the child is suffering or is likely to suffer significant harm (CA 1989 s31(9)). In fact, in appropriate cases, the local authority may be able to apply directly for a care order without first trying an education supervision order.[26]

7.46   While an education supervision order is in force, a parent loses the right under EA 1996 s9 to have his/her child educated in accordance with parental wishes. (CA 1989 Sch 3 para 13(2)(b)). Furthermore, SSFA 1998 ss86 and 94, which relate to parental preference and appeals against admission decisions, are disapplied (see para 5.34).

Parenting orders

7.47   The government is currently (summer 1999) piloting parenting orders under the Crime and Disorder Act (CDA) 1998 s8 in certain parts of the country for a period of 18 months.[27] These can be used when a parent is found guilty of failure to comply with a school attendance order or has failed to secure the regular attendance of a registered pupil at school (CDA 1998 s8)

7.48   A parent has to comply with any requirements in a parenting order for a period not exceeding 12 months. Furthermore, where an order is made for a second or subsequent time, parents may be required to attend weekly counselling and guidance sessions for a maximum of three months.

7.49   If a parent fails without reasonable excuse to comply with the requirements of a parenting order s/he is liable on conviction to a fine up to level 3 (CDA 1998 s9). There is a right of appeal to the Crown Court or the Divisional Court (CDA 1998 s10).

7.50   It remains to be seen how this order will dovetail with the education supervision order. While the requirements attached to it may be similar in relation to the parent, unlike the education supervision order there will be no requirement to consider the welfare checklist in relation to the child.

26 See *Re O (a minor) (care proceedings: education)* [1992] 2 FLR 7, FD, where the High Court had no doubt that truancy would result in significant harm.

27 These are Hammersmith and Fulham, Kensington and Chelsea, Westminster, Hampshire including Portsmouth, Southampton and the Isle of Wight, Wolverhampton and Sheffield, Lewisham, Bedfordshire including Luton, Devon, St Helens and Sunderland.

Home-school agreements

7.51   SSFA 1998 ss110–111 make provision for home-school agreements. These came into force on 1 September 1999[28] and will apply only to parents of children registered in a school. It is the responsibility of the governing body to prepare these agreements. There is no guidance in the regulations about what these should cover.

Truancy centres

7.52   Police have new powers under CDA 1998 s16 to deal with truants. Local authorities can designate premises where children can be taken by the police if they suspect that someone of compulsory school age is in a public place and is absent from school without lawful authority. An LEA must notify the chief of police for an area of these premises (which cannot be police stations). An officer above the rank of superintendent can authorise the use of these powers for a specified period.

7.53   The child can be taken to these designated premises or to a school from which s/he is absent. These powers apply only to pupils registered at a school. Therefore, children educated at home or permanently excluded from school are not covered. Pupils on fixed-term exclusions are not covered either, because they are lawfully absent.

7.54   It is intended that there be a joint local approach to tackling truancy. The Home Office and the DfEE have issued guidance on these powers.[29] This guidance suggests that police officers should be aware of the categories of children who may have a justifiable reason for not being at school (see EA 1996 s444). There are a range of legitimate reasons why children are off school premises: for example, on the way to or from a medical or dental appointment, en route to off-site sporting facilities, moving between split sites, on work experience.

7.55   The police will need to be informed of school holidays, training days and the like. Thought will need to be given to children truanting across LEA boundaries. Many truants are out in the company of adults and it will be interesting to see how the police deal with this. It is not a crime for a child to truant but it is an offence for a parent

---

28 School Standards and Framework Act 1998 (Home-School Agreements) (Appointed Day) Order 1998 SI No 2877.

29 *Crime and Disorder Act 1998: Police Power to Remove Truants Guidance* Home Office/DfEE, 1998.

not to secure his/her regular attendance (see paras 7.24–7.25).

7.56   It is the LEA and not the police who bring the prosecution. LEAs have the power to disclose to police the names of persistent truants (CDA 1998 s115).

7.57   It is unclear how thorough police enquiries have to be before an officer has reasonable cause to exercise this power lawfully. The guidance recommends that police officers be in uniform and, where practicable, accompanied by a representative of the LEA. It will be possible for an officer to use such force as is necessary to remove a child to a designated centre. If a child resists with violence this could be an offence and other powers would come into play. There could be claims for wrongful arrest and false imprisonment if a child with a justifiable reason for being out of school is taken to designated premises.

CHAPTER 8

Discipline and exclusion from school

This chapter deals with questions of discipline in schools, including school and LEA policies on discipline, the powers of teachers and other staff and types of punishment. Finally, it covers exclusion from school, both fixed-term and permanent, and the exclusion appeal procedure.

For full list of contents, see overleaf

Advising in discipline cases

8.1   Parents sometimes seek advice about rules of the school or treatment of their children which they consider unacceptable or even unlawful. Sometimes this is occasioned by the institution of some disciplinary process towards their child and for this reason the situation must be examined particularly critically. Complaint may be made about a particular member of staff or his/her methods. It is important that such matters are investigated and pursued in a way which allows all parties to feel able to make concessions without feeling a loss of face.

8.2   A second cardinal principle is that nothing is ever as simple as it is presented. Caution should, therefore, be exercised in accepting a client's account of an incident (especially when it is essentially a hearsay rendition of the child's account) until there has been an opportunity to test it against external factual material.

8.3   Third, where the child is of 'sufficient age and understanding', it is best to avoid having to take instructions from or in the presence of the parent. Some parents are all too quick to condemn their own children for not following some rule, without enquiring as to why this might be. Others seem pathologically unable to accept that their child might be capable of errant, foolish or downright criminal behaviour. Either way there is great pressure on the child not to disappoint the parent's expectations.

8.4   For these reasons, even in an emergency, it is wise to try to obtain from the other party as full an account of the problem as possible before committing instructions to the record in correspondence. Most parents cannot be expected to have retained correspondence or reports from the school. This may contain important material relevant to disciplinary measures and it may be that the school's reliance on the child to deliver such material would not be adequate for the purposes of statutory publication. The extent to which parents have been informed of disciplinary measures is rarely clear, nor indeed how much consultation was appropriate.

8.5   Parents sometimes demand that a teacher be disciplined or cease to have contact with their child or even be dismissed, or that their child be moved to a different school. Sometimes such an outcome is sadly inevitable, but often the understandable sense of outrage on behalf of the child makes it very difficult for the parent to appreciate and weigh up the possible disadvantages for the child held by one of the more drastic options. S/he may be generally happy in the school and a complaint of some nature could prejudice his/her relationship with staff or other pupils. S/he might suffer considerably by being removed from her/his peer group. These dilemmas are not easy to resolve. As time passes the parent is usually able to discuss the approach which is likely to be in the child's best interests. It may be sufficient merely to discuss the legal merits of the parent's position so that the parent can deal with an informal meeting with the headteacher or another teacher with a feeling of strength, having an understanding of the procedures and realistic options. See also chapter 16, 'Practical considerations in running an education case'.

Statements of policy on discipline and exclusions

Schools

8.6   The governors of maintained schools are legally responsible for the conduct of the school (SSFA 1998 s38). This includes not only its government, but also its management and day-to-day running.

8.7   Until recently the constitution of schools was contained in their articles of government which were determined by the LEA. Now legislation is going to govern the powers and duties of governing bodies. Under SSFA 1998 s37 there are new instruments of government for all maintained schools, whose content is determined by Schedule 12.[1] Under SSFA 1998 s38(3) regulations may set out the terms of reference for governing bodies including the respective roles and responsibilities of governing bodies and headteachers and confer functions on these.[2]

8.8   Under SSFA 1998 s61(2)(a) governing bodies are required to make and review periodically a written statement of general principles to which the headteacher must have regard when deciding measures for promoting good behaviour and discipline. A DFE Circular[3] gives guidance on what should be included in a written whole-school behaviour policy. If a governing body considers that the headteacher should determine particular measures or have

---

1   See Education (School Government) Transition to New Framework Regulations 1998 SI No 2763. See para 3.12.

2   See also DfEE *Code of Practice on LEA-School Relations* 1998 and Annex B of DfEE Circular 10/99.

3   DFE Circular 9/94 *The Education of Children with Emotional and Behavioural Difficulties*.

regard to particular matters s/he could be given guidance on this (SSFA 1998 s61(2)(b)). Governing bodies must have regard to any guidance from the secretary of state (SSFA 1998 s61(2)(b)). Any revision of the written statement of the governing body can only take place after the headteacher and parents have been consulted (SSFA 1998 s61(3)).

8.9　　The secretary of state can require governing bodies to set attendance targets in order to reduce unauthorised absences.[4]

8.10　　The headteacher has to decide on standards and rules of behaviour and their enforcement (SSFA 1998 s61(4)). S/he must act in accordance with the written statement of the governing body and any guidance from it (SSFA 1998 s61(5)). The rules and disciplinary measures must be publicised by the headteacher within the school and to parents of pupils. This must be done at least once a year (SSFA 1998 s61(7). It is no longer necessary for the LEA to be consulted about any proposed measures which might increase LEA expenditure or affect its employment responsibilities.[5]

Local education authorities

8.11　　Under EA 1996 s527A, LEAs must issue a statement setting out arrangements for children with behavioural difficulties, including the support available to schools and for children not in school and, by EA 1996 s527A(2)(c), any other arrangements made or to be made by them for assisting children with behavioural difficulties to find places at suitable schools. This covers all phases of education from the pre-school provision included in an LEA's early years development plan to preparation for transfer to post-16 provision.

8.12　　The Local Education Authority (Behaviour Support Plans) Regulations 1998[6] came into force on 1 April 1998 and DfEE Circular 1/98[7] gives guidance on their operation. The regulations require LEAs to formulate behaviour support plans for the following types of pupil, who have already demonstrated behavioural difficulties:

1)　excluded pupils (both permanent and fixed-term);
2)　pupils at risk of permanent exclusion;
3)　persistently disruptive pupils;
4)　pupils involved with bullying others;

4　See para 7.2.
5　Previously in EA 1996 s154(8).
6　1998 SI No 644.
7　DfEE Circular 1/98 *LEA Behaviour Support Plans*, March 1998.

5) violent or abusive pupils;
6) pupils repeatedly absent without permission;
7) school refusers and school phobics;
8) pupils with challenging behaviour (including that associated with learning difficulties);
9) pupils on schools' special educational needs (SEN) registers for behavioural difficulties;
10) pupils with statements of SEN for behavioural difficulties;
11) pupils who have committed criminal offences.[8]

8.13   It must be emphasised that LEAs' policies are not of direct application to an individual pupil, but they give an indication of how the system should work. Paragraph 10 of the circular points out that pupils with emotional difficulties are a vulnerable group who ought to be able to benefit from these policies. They might include the following:

1) pupils with emotional difficulties;
2) looked after children;
3) children on the child protection register;
4) pupils with family difficulties;
5) pupils who feature disproportionately in exclusions figures, such as African-Caribbean boys or travellers' children;
6) pupils with significant trauma histories, such as refugees;
7) pupils with drug problems or those from drug using families;
8) pupils with mental health problems;
9) pupils who are or have been bullied.[9]

8.14   LEAs are required to consult widely in preparing their plans. In their implementation there is intended to be close co-ordination between schools and the LEA.

8.15   An LEA can intervene in a school to prevent the breakdown or continuing breakdown of discipline. This may occur when the behaviour of pupils or any action by pupils or their parents would prejudice the education of other pupils and the governing body have been informed in writing of this by the LEA (SSFA 1998 ss15 and 62).

8   Ibid para 12.
9   Ibid para 13.

Powers of teachers to discipline

8.16 In recent years, particularly since the advent of the Children Act (CA) 1989, it has been increasingly appropriate to treat teachers as acting in loco parentis (see paras 6.15–6.21). A prudent headteacher will make specific reference to this in the published measures. It can be argued that the teacher is a person caring for the child and as such may do what is reasonable in safeguarding the child's welfare. This could include disciplining other pupils.

8.17 Under EA 1996 s9, children are to be educated in accordance with the wishes of their parents, so far as that is compatible with the provision of efficient instruction and training and the avoidance of unreasonable public expenditure. However, there has never been any suggestion that parents can influence individual disciplinary matters since by definition discipline is required so that a school can run smoothly. The European Court has recently held that some form of punishment, with no adverse effects on the child's physical or moral integrity, is not unlawful.[10]

School uniform and clothing

8.18 A school is entitled to have rules in relation to uniform which are notified to parents on admission. Parents who genuinely cannot afford uniforms are entitled to be treated sensitively and the school should have policies to cover this. Financial assistance may be available from charitable funds or the LEA.[11] Problems may occur where the uniform rules appear to conflict with anti-discrimination legislation. The leading case on this point is *Mandla v Dowell Lee*,[12] where Sikhs were defined as an ethnic group and the headmaster of an independent school could not justify the imposition of a 'no turban' rule. A rule requiring girls to wear skirts may offend against the sex discrimination and race relations legislation. The position will be markedly different where there are health and safety considerations and rules are made which can be justified as reasonable in the light of the school's duties of care (see chapter 6). Examples would be certain jewellery and bracelets, footwear, toys,

---

10 *Costello-Roberts v UK* [1994] ELR 1, ECHR.
11 See paras 6.48 and 6.49. Some schools keep stocks of secondhand garments.
12 [1983] 1 All ER 1062, HL.

food and sweets and certain hair fashions. Home-school agreements[13] will no doubt help to prevent conflict over these rules.

Corporal punishment

8.19   Corporal punishment was abolished in maintained schools and for pupils supported from public funds by the Education (No 2) Act 1986. It is now illegal in all schools, including the private sector (EA 1996 s548, as substituted by SSFA 1998 s131). This applies to all members of staff, not just teachers.

Restraint

8.20   A new s550A was added to EA 1996 by EA 1997 s4, dealing with the restraint of pupils. School staff may use such force as is reasonable in the circumstances to prevent a pupil doing or continuing to commit an offence, causing personal injury or damage to property (including their own) or by s550A(1)(c):

> engaging in any behaviour prejudicial to the maintenance of good order and discipline at the school or among any of its pupils, whether that behaviour occurs during a teaching session or otherwise.

This section applies to off-site and on-site activities but nothing must be done which contravenes EA 1996 s548 regarding corporal punishment. 'Staff' here means teachers at the school and any other person whom the headteacher authorised to be in charge of the pupils.

8.21   This widening of staff powers to use force in less extreme situations is likely to cause problems and has been criticised.[14] Furthermore, the Guidance issued by the DfEE[15] misses the opportunity to involve pupils in consultation about disciplinary procedures which apply to them. Circular 10/98 states that it is important that all schools have a policy on the use of force. This is the responsibility of the headteacher, who must refer to any guidance from the DfEE and the LEA. All staff, governors, pupils and parents must be familiar with the policy. If a school is aware of

---

13   See para 7.51.
14   'DfEE: Draft Guidance on Section 550A of the 1996 Education Act: The use of reasonable force to control or restrain pupils' in *Childright*, March 1998, Children's Legal Centre.
15   DfEE Circular 10/98 *Section 550A of the Education Act 1996: The use of force to control or restrain pupils.*

the potential need to control or restrain a pupil, there should be advance planning in consultation with his/ her parents. This circular looks at the application of force and what would be considered acceptable and unacceptable (paras 21–27). It is accepted that a complaint about the use of force could lead to the investigation of a member of staff under disciplinary procedures, by the police or the social services under child protection procedures (para 31).[16]

8.22   The question of restraint was considered in Circular 9/94[17] para 115, which states:

> On rare occasions there is no alternative to restraining pupils physically, in their and others' interests and safety. In such instances no more than the minimum necessary force should be used, taking into account all of the circumstances. Such interventions should be made only when they are likely to succeed. Desirably more than one adult should be present (although this is not always possible). Physical restraint is normally necessary only to prevent a pupil causing harm to him or herself or to others, seriously damaging property, or committing some criminal act which risks harm to people or property, where verbal commands will not control the behaviour. The purpose of intervention is to restore safety, and restraint should not continue for longer than is necessary. Physical contact and restraint should never be used in anger, and teachers should seek to avoid any injury to the child.

8.23   This circular is specifically directed at children with emotional and behavioural difficulties but has universal application. It does state, however, that:

> Parents with children in special schools should be told how restraint is being exercised. Children who require complex or repeated physical management should have a prescribed, written handling policy. Staff dealing with them should be trained in proper and safe methods of restraint.

The DfEE intends to issue guidance in the near future to help staff choose strategies to restrain pupils with challenging behaviour within the special educational needs setting.

8.24   Anything that is done must be 'reasonable'. In practice, acts amounting to a battery are unlikely to result in any criminal, civil or disciplinary proceedings against the teacher, but see para 8.21.

16 See DfEE Circular 10/95 *Protecting Children From Abuse*, which gives guidance and procedures for dealing with allegations against teachers.
17 DFE Circular 9/94 *The Education of Children with Emotional and Behavioural Difficulties*.

Detention

8.25   On the parental principle, detention is not unlawful if it is not 'for such a period or in such circumstances as to take it out of the realm of reasonable parental discipline'.[18] It had hitherto been thought prudent to obtain the parent's implied consent to individual or group detention, eg, by notifying the proposal and inviting dissent within a time limit. However, a new EA 1996 s550B (inserted by EA 1997 s5) states that a period of detention will not be unlawful without parental consent if the following conditions are adhered to (s550B(3)):

1) The headteacher must have previously determined and made known within the school and to parents the fact that detention after the end of a school session is a disciplinary option.
2) The detention must be reasonable.
3) Parents must have been given at least 24 hours' written notice that the detention was due to take place.

8.26   Section 550B(4) states that the following matters must be taken into account in determining if a detention is reasonable:

(a) whether the detention constitutes a proportionate punishment in the circumstances of the case; and
(b) any special circumstances relevant to its imposition on the pupil which are known to the person imposing it (or of which he ought reasonably to be aware) including in particular
   (i) the pupil's age,
   (ii) any special educational needs he may have,
   (iii) any religious requirement affecting him, and
   (iv) where arrangements have to be made for him to travel from the school to his home, whether suitable alternative arrangements can reasonably be made by his parent.

8.27   Guidance has been given to supplement these new statutory powers.[19] It emphasises the need for schools to take care to avoid legal action, for example over the supervision and travel arrangements for detained children. A parent who is dissatisfied with a detention decision can use the school's complaints procedure – see para 13.6.

18   *R v Rahman* (1983) 81 Cr App R 349, CA.
19   DfEE Circular 10/99 *Social Inclusion: Pupil Support* Annex C.

Investigating and preventing crimes

8.28   The headteacher has the task of investigating breaches of discipline. There is no requirement to caution a pupil before questioning him/her.[20] The investigation need not involve carrying out searching enquiries and calling bodies of oral evidence. Technical rules of criminal court evidence and procedure were not to be imported into inquiries of this nature and there is no objection in principle to the acceptance of hearsay even if that is the only evidence of the pupil's misbehaviour.[21] Headteachers can invite the police in to investigate suspected criminal activities but good practice, not always followed, suggests that children should not be interviewed about specific events without the presence of a parent or someone with parental responsibility.

8.29   In the wake of the stabbing of the London headteacher Philip Lawrence and the Dunblane massacre, the police have been given new powers to enter schools without invitation to search pupils for knives and other weapons. The Offensive Weapons Act 1996 s1 makes it an offence to be in possession of a bladed instrument on school premises without reasonable excuse. There is a power to arrest without a warrant for having a blade or point or other offensive weapon on school premises.

8.30   The following sections of the EA 1996 have been repealed by the SSFA 1998 but it is anticipated that they will be largely replicated by regulations under SSFA 1998 s38. The governing body of a school was required to foster good relations with its local police and to consider how the ethos and standards promoted by a school can affect the incidence of juvenile crime in an area. It also had to take note of any representations from the chief officer of police in relation to the exercise of its responsibility in relation to the curriculum (EA 1996 s371(4), s372(3) and s373(2)). Reference had to be made in the annual report to the steps taken to foster links with the police (EA 1996 Sch 17 para 8).

20 Because a headteacher is not a person 'charged with the duty of investigating offences or charging offenders' under PACE s67(9): *DPP v G* (1997) *Times* 24 November, QBD.

21 *R v Roman Catholic Schools ex p S* [1998] ELR 304, QBD. This will create a tension with article 6 of the European Court of Human Rights when the Human Rights Act 1998 comes into force.

Confiscation of property

8.31   Confiscation by a teacher or other member of staff is not unlawful and may be necessary if the property concerned is dangerous or obscene or if it is drugs. It may well be that the property should be handed over to the police. Destruction of property could, however, be unlawful unless it is necessary in the interests of safety. Confiscation could also amount to a theft if goods are retained for the confiscator's personal use. Any confiscated property that is not dangerous etc should be returned to the child or a parent at the earliest opportunity, ie, at the end of a school day, unless there is an agreement or policy permitting continued retention.

Exclusion from school

8.32   Exclusion should be regarded as a draconian remedy of last resort. Yet the number of exclusions has risen over the years, which must be a sign of failure.[22] Precisely what has failed or, more significantly, the reasons for it, may be difficult to determine. A recent report by the Commission for Racial Equality[23] found that it is twice as expensive to educate excluded pupils and they are likely to get less than a tenth of full-time education in the year they are excluded. The report also found that between three and six times more Afro-Caribbean boys are excluded than their white peers. An article in the *Times Educational Supplement* stated that children in care are ten times more likely to be excluded from school than other pupils.[24] It is also recognised that children excluded are in grave danger of getting involved in anti-social and criminal activities.

8.33   In March 1996 the government indicated its intention to run pilot projects in 43 local authorities. 'Flying squads' of educational psychologists, social workers and local authority advisers were to go into schools to try to tackle the problem of disruptive pupils. Units

---

22   See Graham and Bowling *Truancy and school exclusion* Cm 3957, Social Exclusion Unit, May 1998, and *Banished to the Exclusion Zone* Children's Legal Centre, 1996. The first statistical release prepared by the DfEE indicated that in 1997/98 the number of permanent exclusions dropped by 3 per cent to 12,300. See SFR 11/1999, 16 June 1999. The rate for pupils with statements of special educational needs was seven times as high as for other pupils. Interim annual reviews should be considered in these cases – see DfEE Circular 10/99 para 6.10.

23   *Exclusion from School and Racial Equality: A Good Practice Guide* CRE, 1996.

24   TES 5 March 1999, page 22.

were to be established in schools for those in danger of being excluded. It remains to be seen how these initiatives will work in practice and what effect they will have on the exclusion level. Some results of these pilots have been incorporated in the guidance in Circular 1/98 (see para 8.10).

8.34   Unfortunately, children who place undue demands on teachers' time, whether because of emotional or behavioural disturbance or other special needs, may all be treated in the same way. For some children, exclusion can be a blessed release, providing an incentive to all concerned to find a more appropriate school, but there is a danger that the process will lead to antagonism of the parents, alienation, apathy and a feeling of failure on the part of the child. This is highly relevant to the difficult decisions which have to be taken after exclusion, about whether to appeal and seek reinstatement or whether simply to look for another school. With the increased pressure on school places, the second option may not be realistic if an early return to school is wanted. Parents may be tempted to give up the present school so as to avoid being seen as trying to ingratiate themselves again. On the other hand, there is often a desire to put the record straight, even if it has been decided not to take up the chance of reinstatement following a successful appeal.

The decision to exclude

8.35   The power to exclude rests with the headteacher alone (SSFA 1998 s64). This includes a duly appointed acting headteacher (EA 1996 s579(1)). It is not possible to set out hard and fast rules about when a headteacher is justified in using his/her discretion in favour of exclusion. Any school punishment must be moderate and reasonable in relation to the behaviour complained of.[25] As part of its drive to reduce the number of exclusions by one-third by 2001, the latest guidance by the DfEE, issued in July 1999, raises the threshold for exclusion decisions.[26]

8.36   An exclusion must be either permanent (SSFA 1998 s64(1)) or, under SSFA 1998 s64(2), for a fixed period. A pupil can be excluded on one or more occasions in any school year up to a maximum of 45 school days. Long fixed-term exclusions should only be used where a period of more than 15 days is needed for the pupil's reintegration

25 *R v Hopley* (1860) 2 F & F 202.
26 DfEE Circular 10/99, in particular paras 6.2–6.4.

into school.[27] It is usual for pupils to be excluded for only a few days. There can be no indefinite exclusion as was the case previously. It is sometimes the case that a pupil is excluded initially for a fixed period and this is changed to a permanent exclusion after a headteacher has had time fully to investigate the circumstances leading to the exclusion.

8.37   In addition, it seems that some schools are developing ways of effectively excluding children from lessons without actually excluding them, eg, confining them to the library or canteen.

8.38   Another ploy is to ask parents to remove children voluntarily. Although this excludes the parent from any right to appeal or to make formal representations, parents could consider this option where a satisfactory alternative school place is being offered. Otherwise, there is too great a danger of less than full-time education being available for an unspecified period following withdrawal.

8.39   The following are examples of behaviour which has led or could lead to exclusion.

Off school premises:
−   removing another boy's trousers, underpants and socks;[28]
−   shooting pupil with airgun;
−   brandishing an open penknife at a bus stop;
−   shoplifting;
−   spitting on bus passengers.

At school:
−   possession of air weapon, knife (even a penknife), controlled drug, matches, bicycle chain;
−   fighting;
−   assault on staff or pupil;
−   indecent assault.

8.40   SSFA 1998 s65 states that, after excluding a pupil, a headteacher must (without delay) take reasonable steps to inform the relevant person (ie, the parent, or the pupil if over 18) about

1)   the period of the exclusion;
2)   the reasons for the exclusion;
3)   the reasons for converting a fixed term into a permanent exclusion;
4)   the right and means by which representations may be made to the governing body.

27   Circular 1/98 para 68.
28   *R v Newham LBC and Another ex p X* [1995] ELR 303, QBD.

This may initially be orally but should be followed up in writing.[29]

8.41 Where the headteacher excludes a pupil for more than five school days in any one term, a pupil loses the opportunity to take a public examination, is excluded permanently or a fixed term exclusion is made permanent, s/he must inform the governing body and the LEA without delay (SSFA 1998 s65(4)).

Representation to governing body in first instance against either fixed-term or permanent exclusion

8.42 In maintained schools the relevant person, ie, parent or pupil over 18, must make representations in the first instance to the governing body against any exclusion, be it fixed-term (even when for five days or fewer), or permanent (SSFA 1998 s65(1)(c)(d)). There does not have to be a meeting with oral representation when the exclusion is for fewer than five days.

8.43 Where a pupil has been excluded

1) for more than five days in any one term
2) and loses an opportunity to take a public exam
3) permanently
4) and a fixed-term exclusion is made permanent,

the governing body or its discipline committee (SSFA 1998 Sch 11 para 4) must consider the circumstances surrounding the exclusion. It must also consider both written and oral representation from the relevant person and the LEA (SSFA 1998 s66). The Education (Exclusions from School) (Prescribed Periods) Regulations 1999[30] may provide time scales in relation to these representations and procedures (SSFA 1998 s66(8)).

8.44 If a parent wishes to make representations, a meeting should be convened by the governing body as soon as practicable. The pupil will often be back in school before the meeting is held but parents have the chance in some circumstances to have their voice heard and perhaps set the record straight. The meeting should be of at least three members of the governing body (or discipline committee), excluding the headteacher. The headteacher must not take part in the decision-making but a teacher governor who was not involved

---

29 *R v Governing Body of Rectory School and Richmond LBC ex p WK (a minor)* [1997] ELR 484, QBD.
30 1999 SI No 1868.

with the pupil may do so.[31] The rules of natural justice apply and so a parent should not be denied an opportunity to make representations.[32] The meeting should be clerked by the governors' clerks department of the LEA.

8.45   The governing body can order reinstatement either immediately or at a future date. It can also decide not to reinstate (SSFA 1998 s66(3)). It has the power to allow a pupil back into school during a period of exclusion to take a public examination.

8.46   The headteacher must comply with any direction of the governing body. The relevant person and the LEA must be informed of any decision. Under the previous legislation (EA 1996 ss158–159 and Schs 15 and 16), in county, controlled or maintained special schools, the LEA had a right to order reinstatement and the governors had a right to appeal against this decision to an independent appeal committee. This did not apply to grant maintained, voluntary aided or special agreement schools.

8.47   The headteacher is entitled to take account of the parent's attitude to the headteacher and/or the governors in deciding whether to make an exclusion permanent.[33] If the headteacher decides to extend a fixed-term exclusion for more than five days or to make a fixed-term exclusion permanent, the relevant person should be informed of his/her right to make further (ie, oral) representations.

8.48   There is no further right of appeal against a fixed-term exclusion See para 8.56 in relation to further appeals against permanent exclusions.

8.49   The headteacher must arrange for the excluded pupil to receive work to do at home and to arrange for it to be marked (see para 11.50). The governing body should keep this under review. If a child is permanently excluded and has unsuccessfully appealed against this, or the time laid down for appeals has gone, then s/he is taken off the school roll. It then becomes the responsibility of the LEA under EA 1996 s19 to provide education.

---

31   *R v Board of Governors of Stoke Newington School ex p M* [1994] ELR 131, QBD.

32   *R v Newham LBC and Another ex p X* [1995] ELR 303, QBD.

33   *R v Neale and Another ex p S* [1995] ELR 198, QBD. There appear to be no reported cases giving guidance on the extent to which parental behaviour may be taken into account. It is certainly a factor relevant to the background.

Permanent exclusions

8.50   A child may be permanently excluded by the headteacher for a serious breach of discipline such as an assault or bringing drugs or a weapon into school. It may result from a course of bad behaviour which merited various fixed-term exclusions and finally culminated in a permanent exclusion.

8.51   The headteacher must inform the relevant person of the reason for the exclusion and the right to appeal initially to the governing body. This is the same procedure as for a fixed-term exclusion (SSFA 1998 s65).

Advising parents about exclusions

8.52   If consulted by parents about an exclusion, whether as soon as it has happened, before a governors' meeting or before an appeal (see paras 8.54–8.68), advisers should consider the following factors when taking instructions:[34]

1) whether it was reasonable for the headteacher to have concluded that the pupil is guilty of the conduct complained of;
2) the pupil's age;
3) the pupil's intellectual ability and curricular achievement;
4) the pupil's state of health – physical and psychological;
5) the pupil's previous behaviour record;
6) the pupil's domestic situation and family changes;
7) parental pressure;
8) peer group pressure leading to misbehaviour;
9) degree and severity of the offence;
10) the likelihood of recurrence;
11) whether the pupil acted alone or as part of a group;
12) scapegoating;
13) whether there are symptoms of emotional or behavioural difficulties necessitating assessment for SEN;
14) cultural factors, including indirect racial discrimination;
15) provocation;
16) treatment given to other offenders on this or earlier occasions;
17) whether behaviour of any staff involved was acceptable;
18) special needs provision in the school affecting other offenders with statements of SEN;

---

34 See ACE information sheet, *Exclusion from School, Parents' Information Checklist.*

19) the pastoral care system in the school and the personal tutor arrangements;

20) whether there is an effective system for pupils to air grievances.

8.53   In addition, it is necessary to establish whether the school's documented behaviour and discipline policy has indeed been adequately publicised by the headteacher (see para 8.10). It is not unknown for some sanctions for misbehaviour to be omitted. There should be an immediate request for access to the pupil's curricular record. This right exists for all pupils (see paras 4.47– 4.50) but will be of little use with short fixed-term exclusions because 15 school days' notice must be given to obtain a record.[35] Parents will, therefore, not be able to have this information in time to make representations to the governors – see below, paras 8.54–8.55.

Exclusion appeal procedure

Governors' meeting

8.54   There is a right to make oral representations at a meeting of the governing body, which can order reinstatement, order a fixed-term exclusion, uphold a permanent exclusion or decide on a permanent instead of a fixed-term exclusion (SSFA 1998 s66). Decisions may sometimes be based on evidence (eg, statements from other pupils) which is produced after the date of the original exclusion decision. This may be relevant to the reasonableness of the headteacher's decision and the grounds on which it was based. The chronology of events may need to be examined.

8.55   If the governing body decides that a pupil should not be reinstated, it must inform the relevant person, the headteacher and the LEA. It must give the relevant person notice in writing stating the following (SSFA 1998 s66(6)):

1) the reasons for its decision;

2) the right to appeal to an independent appeal panel;

3) the person who should be notified of an appeal;

4) the necessity of putting grounds of appeal in a notice of appeal;

5) the last date for an appeal (15 days after notification in writing of the unsuccessful appeal to the governors (SSFA 1998 Sch 18 para 1(1)).

---

35   Education (School Records) Regulations 1989 SI No 1261 reg 6(2).

A notice in writing from a relevant person saying s/he does not wish to appeal is final (SSFA 1998 Sch 18 para 1(2)).

8.56 An LEA has the responsibility of arranging an independent appeal panel in relation to permanent exclusions from all maintained schools (SSFA 1998 s67 and Sch 18). This has simplified the procedure with effect from 1 September 1999. Previously the governors of grant-maintained, voluntary aided and special agreement schools were responsible for arranging an appeal committee for their schools and the LEA for arranging the appeal committees against decisions of non-grant maintained schools. The panel may order reinstatement immediately, reinstatement at a specified date or uphold the permanent exclusion. Its decision is binding on a governing body, the headteacher and the LEA (SSFA 1998 s67(3)).

8.57 The parent or pupil, if over 18, may appeal to an independent appeal committee established by the LEA (SSFA 1998 s67). Notice of appeal must be given within 15 days of receipt of written notification of the governing body's decision (SSFA 1998 Sch 18 para 1(1)).[36]

Composition of independent appeal panel

8.58 The appeal is heard by an appeal panel constituted under SSFA 1998 Sch 18. It shall consist of three or five members appointed by the LEA from:

1) people eligible to be lay members, defined as someone without personal experience in the management of any school or the provision of education in any school except as a governor or in a voluntary capacity;
2) people with experience in education, people with knowledge of educational conditions in an LEA area or parents of registered pupils at a school.

There must be at least one each from these two categories (SSFA 1998 Sch 18 paras 2–4).

8.59 The following are disqualified from membership:

1) any member of the LEA or governing body of the school in question;
2) an employee of the authority, except a teacher;
3) anyone with any connection with the LEA, the school or any teacher on the panel or the pupil if this might raise doubts about his/her impartiality (SSFA 1998 Sch 18 paras 6–7).

36 These sections came into force on 1 September 1999.

It is essential to check the membership and background of the panel thoroughly before the hearing. Details can be obtained from the LEA panel clerk. Challenges have arisen in the past because of an undeclared interest on the part of a member.

8.60   Written grounds of appeal must be submitted by the parents (SSFA 1998 Sch 18 para 7).

8.61   The panel is supposed to meet within 15 school days of the appeal being lodged (SSFA 1998 Sch 18 para 8(2)). The LEA must take reasonable steps to ensure that the relevant person and anyone else entitled to give oral evidence is able to attend (SSFA 1998 Sch 18 para 9). There can sometimes be difficulty obtaining the full details of the case to be met, particularly if it depends on evidence of other pupils whom the school does not wish to identify, but in the interests of the excluded pupil it may be undesirable to seek anything more than a short adjournment in order to prepare the case adequately. Usually the parent will be unwilling to take up an offer of a place at another school while an appeal is pending, and the LEA is also unlikely to offer much, if any, alternative tuition at this stage. The rules of natural justice apply, as does the *Revised Code of Practice on Procedure.*[37]

8.62   Appeals are usually in private. The relevant person is able to make oral representations, take a friend or be represented. The headteacher, the LEA and the governing body are able to make written and oral representations (SSFA 1998 Sch 18 para 10).

8.63   Legal representation at the hearing is clearly appropriate in view of the importance to the pupil and his/her family and the complexity of the legal and factual issues which usually arise. In practice, even with the best will in the world, the lay persons involved in the exclusion procedure are likely to have fallen foul of some rule of procedure or fairness. For example, in one case there was no advance notice of witness statements and the chair also failed to control the parents' own advocate.[38]

8.64   Written submissions may be given at the hearing. Some of the material may be better understood if delivered in written form beforehand. There is no control on when this is actually delivered to the members of the panel, but the panel clerk at the LEA will usually give a deadline for receiving written material and this can be used by

---

37   Issued by the Association of Metropolitan Authorities, the Association of County Councils and the Council on Tribunals (1994). This will be superseded by a new Code of Practice on exclusions due to be issued by the DfEE in September 1999. See also DfEE Circular 10/99 Annex D.

38   *R v Governors of Bacon's City Technology College ex p W* [1998] ELR 488, QBD.

the appellant to get it delivered to the panel in good time. The parent or representative should insist on being provided in advance with copies of all documents to be considered by the panel and of all written representations made by other parties and details of any witnesses who may appear.

8.65 The 1994 Code of Practice (see para 8.61) states that the committee (now panel) should do everything possible to ensure informality so that the parties can put their case simply (para 14). The Code states that it is likely that witnesses will need to be called to describe what happened leading to the exclusion. Where the headteacher has not personally witnessed an incident, and where those who have are reluctant to attend an appeal, the presentation of their evidence by the headteacher may seem unfair and written statements should be sought from witnesses (para 18). The Code warns that the committee (panel) should be mindful that written statements can be challenged but not questioned (para 18(d)).

8.66 Careful thought needs to be given as to whether the pupil attends the hearing. It may be useful in any event to have written representations from him/her. If the child is old enough not to be too stressed by the proceedings it is probably wise for the child to attend.[39] Usually it will be desirable for the committee to hear from the excluded pupil.[40]

8.67 Bearing in mind the need for informality, the order of hearing should be along the lines of:

1) the case for the authority;
2) questioning by the parent or pupil;
3) the case for the parent or pupil;
4) questioning by the authority;
5) representations by the governing body;
6) questioning by the parent or pupil;
7) questioning by the authority (if necessary);
8) summing up by the authority;
9) summing up by the parent or pupil.

8.68 It would appear that a victim of misbehaviour has no right to be heard in proceedings relating to an exclusion decision. In a case relating to Camden LEA, a father initially failed in his application for judicial review of the appeal committee which ordered the

39 *R v Governors of St Gregory's RC School and Appeals Committee ex p M* [1995] ELR 290, QBD.
40 See, for example, *R v Governors of Bacon's City Technology College ex p W* [1998] ELR 488, QBD.

reinstatement of two boys, one of whom who had brought a pellet gun into school and another who had fired it at his son. In dismissing the application, Tucker J said that the governors and the LEA had received letters from the victim's father and had considered very carefully the effect of the incident, and of reinstatement, on his well-being. The father appealed and the Court of Appeal ruled[41] that there had been insufficient enquiry into what had occurred in the incident. Also, the school and LEA should have obtained more information about what would now happen to the victim, and investigated the effect of interfering with the headteacher's decision on the victim and the future of the school.

8.69   In *R v Governors of St Gregory's RC School and Appeals Committee ex p M*,[42] Turner J emphasised that, if the school operates a strict disciplinary regime, the court had to assess whether or not a reasonable headteacher could arrive at the decision reached in the instant case. The appeal committee must enquire about the quality of the evidence relied upon by the headteacher and make its own judgment about the reliability of the evidence.[43]

8.70   In *R v Solihull BC ex p H (a minor)*,[44] Latham J ruled that the permanent exclusion of a 12-year-old child with learning difficulties for brandishing an open penknife at a bus stop at an older pupil, who may have been bullying him, was justified.

8.71   The decision of the appeal panel and the grounds for such a decision must be communicated in writing to the relevant person, the LEA, the governing body and the headteacher by the end of the second school day after the conclusion of the hearing (SSFA 1998 Sch 18 para 14). The appeal panel must explain why the child has been excluded and must not leave it to the parents to assume that its grounds are the same as the headteacher's.[45] In *R v Governors of Bacon's City Technology College ex p W*,[46] Collins J said that this was an area where reasons needed to be given, because it might be necessary to see to what extent the pupil's past record was relied on in deciding whether permanent exclusion was the appropriate sanction.

---

41   *R v Camden LBC ex p H (a minor)* [1996] ELR 360, CA.
42   [1995] ELR 290, QBD.
43   See *R v Roman Catholic Schools ex p S* [1998] ELR 304, QBD.
44   [1997] ELR 489, QBD.
45   *R v Northamptonshire CC ex p W* [1998] ELR 291, QBD.
46   [1998] ELR 488, QBD.

8.72   The decision of the appeal panel is binding and there is no further right of appeal for either side.[47]

8.73   The pupil's name remains on the school roll until it is clear that any appeal procedure has concluded.

Exclusions from PRUs

8.74   This should happen only rarely but EA 1996 Sch 1 para 7 allows for both fixed-term and permanent exclusions on disciplinary grounds.[48] pupil referral units (PRUs) are not maintained schools as defined by SSFA 1998 s20 and, accordingly, the statutory exclusion appeal machinery is absent. Non-attendance is unhappily tolerated by all parties concerned and for practical purposes exclusion rarely becomes an issue. The legal significance of pupil registration should not be overlooked – see chapters 7 and 9.

8.75   It may be that if a child is excluded from a PRU the LEA should consider whether, if there is not already one in place, a statement of special educational needs is appropriate (see para 11.26).

8.76   The guidance in DfEE Circulars 1/98 and 10/99 is thin on detail. Advisers may consider that the best practical solution will be to utilise the duties and powers of the LEA concerning excluded PRU pupils, who have the same rights as other pupils out of school by virtue of EA 1996 s19. See chapter 11 generally.

47 But see *R v South Tyneside Education Department and the Governors of Hebburn Comprehensive School ex p Cram* [1998] ELR 508, QBD, where Ognall J refused to endorse the decision of an appeal committee which had reinstated a boy who had been permanently excluded for hitting a teacher in the light of a ballot of teachers who were refusing to teach him if reinstated. See also *R v Secretary of State for Education and Employment and the Governors of Southlands Community Comprehensive School ex p W* [1998] ELR 413, QBD and para 5.60 (re admission appeals).

48 Circular 11/94 *The Education by LEAs of Children Otherwise Than at School* paras 65–65 provided guidance which has now been superseded and not specifically replaced by DfEE Circular 10/99.

CHAPTER 9

Special educational needs

This chapter looks at the rights of, and duties towards, children who have special educational needs. It covers assessments and statements of special educational needs and describes how to take a case to the Special Educational Needs Tribunal.

For complete chapter contents, see overleaf

Introduction

9.1   Of all the aspects of education law, special educational needs (SEN) is probably the most litigated, not least because the matters concerned raise not only issues of law but also of practice and policy, in respect of which there is a variety of opinion. For example, for those parents who seek support for their children so as to enable them to attend a mainstream school, the law gives what is known as a qualified right for a mainstream place (see para 9.55). Statistically, some LEAs 'mainstream' a greater percentage of children with SEN than others and disputes will, therefore, arise. At the other end of the spectrum, some parents (especially those of children with specific learning difficulties, such as dyslexia, or with autistic spectrum disorder) may seek independent specialist places and LEAs may resist this, ultimately on the ground of cost.

9.2   The provisions currently contained in EA 1996 Part IV were first introduced (in a much simplified form) in EA 1981, which came into force in April 1983. They were expanded and replaced by EA 1993 Part III, which itself was re-enacted in EA 1996 Part IV. The law prescribes, in detail, processes and procedures with regard to the identification of and provision for children with SEN.

Definitions

9.3   Special educational needs are defined in EA 1996 s312 as arising when a child has a learning difficulty which calls for special educational provision to be made. A learning difficulty is subsequently defined in s312(2) as arising if:

- the child has a significantly greater difficulty in learning than the majority of children of the same age;
- the child has a disability which either prevents or hinders him/her from making use of educational facilities of a kind generally provided for children of the same age in schools within the area of the LEA; or
- the child is under the age of five years and is, or would be if special educational need was not made, likely to fall within the above categories when over that age.

9.4   However, a child does not have a learning difficulty merely because his/her home language is different from that which is or will be taught at school, in other words, where the child has English as a second language.

9.5   Special educational provision is defined in s312(4) as follows:

-   for a child aged two years and over, educational provision additional to, or otherwise different from, the educational provision made generally for children of the same age in schools maintained by the LEA (other than special schools) in the area, and
-   for a child aged under two years, educational provision of any kind.

9.6   Accordingly, there are elements of objectivity and subjectivity in the definition.[1] For example, while the fact of a disability may be an objective test, whether or not educational facilities within an area are available to meet the needs of the disabled child is, ultimately, subjective.

9.7   LEAs have duties toward children with SEN if the child is under the age of 19 and registered at a school or under the age of 16 otherwise (EA 1996 s312(5)).

Legislation

9.8   Apart from EA 1996 Part IV, the principal legislation is contained in the Education (Special Educational Needs) Regulations 1994[2] (the 1994 Regulations) and the *Code of Practice on the Identification and Assessment of Special Educational Needs*.[3] The Code of Practice is issued under EA 1996 ss313–314, which require LEAs and others to 'have regard to the provisions of the Code'. At the time of writing, the government has announced that the Code of Practice will be amended early in the year 2000 (see para 9.15.)

9.9   The principles of the Code are that:

-   The needs of all pupils who may have SEN, either throughout or at any time during their school careers, must be addressed. The Code recognises that there is a continuum of needs and a continuum of provision, which may be made in a wide variety of forms.
-   Children with SEN require the greatest possible access to a broad and balanced education, including the national curriculum.
-   The needs of most pupils will be met in the mainstream, and

1   See *Bromley LBC v Special Educational Needs Tribunal* [1999] ELR 260, CA, for a discussion on what constitutes special educational provision.
2   1994 SI No 1047. See appendix E.
3   DFE, 1994.

without a statutory assessment or statement of ?
SEN, including children with statements of SE'
appropriate and taking into account the wishe
educated alongside their peers in mainstrear'
- Even before s/he reaches compulsory schoc'
  SEN requiring the intervention of the LEA as ㆍ.
  and/or social services.
- The knowledge, views and experience of parents are vital. ㄴ
  assessment and provision will be secured where there is the grea.
  possible degree of partnership between parents and their children
  and schools, LEAs and other agencies.

9.10   Accordingly:
- All children with SEN should be identified and assessed as early as
  possible and as quickly as is consistent with thoroughness.
- Provision for all children with SEN should be made by the most
  appropriate agency. In most cases this will be the child's
  mainstream school, working in partnership with the child's parent:
  no statutory assessment will be necessary.
- Where needed, LEAs must make assessments and statements in
  accordance with the prescribed time limits; must write clear and
  thorough statements, setting out the child's educational and non-
  educational needs, the objectives to be secured, the provision to be
  made and the arrangements for monitoring and review; and ensure
  the annual review of the special educational provision arranged for
  the child and the updating and monitoring of special educational
  targets.
- Special educational provision will be most effective when those
  responsible take into account the ascertainable wishes of the child
  concerned, considered in the light of his/her age and
  understanding.
- There must be close co-operation between all of the agencies
  concerned and a multi-disciplinary approach to the resolution of
  issues.

9.11   The code introduces five stages of need as follows:

Stage 1 Class or subject teachers identify or register a child's SEN
and, consulting the school's special educational needs co-ordinator
(SENCO), take initial action.

Stage 2 The school's SENCO takes lead responsibility for gathering
information and for co-ordinating the child's special educational
provision, working with the child's teachers.

It is anticipated that, in the amended Code of Practice (which is
likely to be issued early in the year 2000), stages 1 and 2 will be

– see para 9.15.

e 3 Teachers and the SENCO are supported by specialists from
side the school.

Stage 4 The LEA considers the need for a statutory assessment and,
if appropriate, makes a multi-disciplinary assessment.

Stage 5 The LEA considers the need for a statement of SEN and, if
appropriate, makes a statement and arranges, monitors and reviews
the provision.

9.12 A common misconception is that all children with SEN must have a
statement of SEN. In fact, the five-stage model shows that only those
children at stage 5 require statements. This model flows from the
approach taken by Dame Mary Warnock's Royal Commission[4] which
led to the introduction of the EA 1981. This identified that, in total,
up to 20 per cent of school children will have SEN at some time
during their school career but that only around two per cent of those
children will require statements. In fact, the percentage of children
in receipt of statements in most LEAs is in excess of two per cent but
the broad principles remain true. The approach was affirmed in *R v
Hereford and Worcester CC ex p Lashford*.[5]

9.13 However, in practice, many parents of children with SEN will
seek statements not only to obtain extra help or different schooling,
but also because, by virtue of EA 1996 s324(5)(a)(i), the LEA has an
absolute duty to arrange the provision set out in the statement,
enforceable, if necessary, through the courts.[6] Note, however, that
the duty to 'arrange' does not necessarily mean 'pay for' (although it
may) since, if the LEA can persuade another body (such as the school
concerned or a health authority) to make provision, then the duty is
discharged.

9.14 It should be noted that, before the current legislative framework
came into force in April 1983, the legal and policy framework for
considering disabled children and others with SEN was wholly
different. Then, LEAs tended to maintain schools for different types
of impairment (for children who were blind, deaf, 'backward',
physically handicapped, 'maladjusted', 'delicate', etc) and children
were placed either in one of those schools or in a mainstream school.

---

4   *Report of the Committee of Enquiry into the Education of Handicapped Children
    and Young People*, 1978 (The Warnock Report).
5   [1987] 1 FLR 508, QBD.
6   See *R v Harrow LBC ex p M* [1997] ELR 62, QBD.

The statutory regime which was implemented by the EA 1981 is one which encourages a child-centred approach – to consider the individual needs of the child rather than the 'label' which may be attached to that child.

9.15　　At the time of writing, the government had concluded a consultation paper on SEN.[7] Following the consultation, the government has indicated that a revised Code of Practice will be produced, expanding the guidance on a number of topics and issues. This revised Code is likely to include more guidance on:

1) a more inclusive approach to SEN;
2) better co-operation between education, health and social services;
3) support for looked after children;
4) the role of governing bodies in relation to SEN;
5) support for children aged under 5, and the links with the Early Years and Sure Start Initiatives;
6) exclusion from school, and 'Education Otherwise';
7) the interface between the national curriculum and the literacy hour;
8) the rights of disabled children to personal support;
9) conciliation arrangements;
10) the implications for SEN of the National Child Care Strategy and changes to the NHS and the new school framework.

In addition, the revised Code is likely to include further guidance on

1) secondary schools,
2) special educational needs co-ordinators (SENCOs);
3) individual education plans;
4) the merging of the three pre-assessment stages to two stages: school support and support plus;
5) procedures for statutory assessments and statements and monitoring;
6) children whose first language is not English;
7) the need to have regard to the child's views;
8) parents as partners;
9) transport;
10) speech and language therapy;
11) transitional reviews; and
12) amending statements in good time before transfer from one school to another (in fact, the government has indicated that it is

7　*Excellence for all Children, Meeting Special Educational Needs* DfEE.

likely to amend the Special Educational Needs Regulations to make this a statutory requirement).

General duties of LEAs

9.16 Much of SEN law and practice focuses on assessing and 'statementing' children with SEN (stages 4 and 5 of the Code of Practice). However, a number of other duties arise which directly affect children with SEN as follows (paras 9.17–9.34).

9.17 EA 1996 s9 gives a general obligation on LEAs to have regard to parental wishes in the provision of education. In *Catchpole v Buckinghamshire County Council and the Special Educational Needs Tribunal*,[8] the Court of Appeal considered the extent to which this applies to children with special educational needs. In summary, the requirement does apply but in practice it will be of limited benefit and use, given the detailed provisions relating to arrangements for children with SEN, in EA 1996 Part IV.

9.18 EA 1996 s14(6)(b) requires LEAs to have regard to the need for securing that special educational provision is made for pupils who have SEN, when undertaking their duties to secure provision of sufficient schools.

9.19 EA 1996 s15(5) requires LEAs to have regard to the requirements of persons over compulsory school age who have learning difficulties when carrying out their duties to provide further education (see chapter 12).

9.20 EA 1996 s510 empowers LEAs to provide clothing for pupils with statements of SEN when they are providing board and lodging (see para 6.48).

9.21 EA 1996 ss348 and 517 provide that LEAs must pay the fees for independent boarding provision for pupils who have SEN where it is expedient that the required special educational need should be made at that school. They further require the LEA to pay for the board and lodging as well, where the education cannot be provided unless board and lodging are also provided, having regard, among other things, to the pupil's SEN (see para 6.44). Note also that under EA 1996 s320, LEAs have a power to make arrangements for the education of children with SEN outside England and Wales. Following *R v Cheshire CC ex p C*,[9] unusually, it may be lawful for

8 [1998] ELR 463, CA.
9 [1998] ELR 66, QBD.

part of the costs of such education to be met privately so as to make the cost to the LEA no greater than domestic provision – see paras 9.51–9.57.

9.22 Further and Higher Education Act 1992 s4 requires the Further Education Funding Councils for England and Wales to exercise their functions with regards to the requirements of persons having learning difficulties – see paras 12.30–12.39.[10]

9.23 EA 1996 s317(1)(a) requires that governing bodies of schools must use their best endeavours to make any special educational provision that a pupil requires.

9.24 EA 1996 s317(1)(b) requires that governing bodies of schools must secure that, when a chair or other designated governor (or headteacher in the case of a nursery school) is informed by the LEA that a pupil has SEN, those needs are made known to all who are likely to teach the pupil.

9.25 EA 1996 s317(1)(c) requires that governing bodies of schools are required to secure that teachers are aware of the importance of identifying and providing for pupils with SEN.

9.26 EA 1996 s317(3) provides that governing bodies must consult with each other, the LEA and the funding authority in order to co-ordinate provision for children with SEN.

9.27 EA 1996 s324(5)(b) provides that governing bodies of maintained schools must admit a child whose statement names that school.

9.28 EA 1996 s317(4) provides that generally, those concerned with provision must ensure that a child with SEN engages in the activity of the school together with children who do not have such needs, insofar as it is compatible with that child receiving the special educational provision that s/he requires, the provision of efficient education for the children with whom the child will be educated and the efficient use of resources.

9.29 EA 1996 s316 provides that those concerned with provision must integrate children with SEN in mainstream schools, subject to certain qualifications.

9.30 EA 1996 s313 provides that those concerned with provision must

---

10 For a discussion on the overlapping responsibilities of LEAs and the FEFCs, see *R v Dorset CC and FEFC ex p Goddard* [1995] ELR 109, QBD, and *R v Oxfordshire CC ex p B* [1997] ELR 90, CA. See also *R v FEFC and Bradford MDC ex p Parkinson* [1997] ELR 204, QBD.

have regard to the Code of Practice (see para 9.8).

9.31   EA 1996 s321 provides that LEAs must exercise their powers to ensure that they identify any child in their area whose SEN require the LEA to make special educational provision if the child:

- is a pupil at a maintained special school;
- is educated at an independent school at the expense of the LEA or funding authority;
- is registered at a school and has been brought to the LEA's attention as having (or probably having) SEN; or
- is not under the age of two years or over compulsory school age and has been brought to the LEA's attention as having (or probably having) SEN.

9.32   EA 1996 s315 provides that LEAs must keep under review the arrangements made for special educational needs.

9.33   Generally, EA 1996 Part IV, and Schs 26 and 27, provide that LEAs must assess and make and maintain a statement where appropriate.

9.34   There are a number of important decided cases on these general duties. For example, in *R v Lancashire CC ex p M*,[11] the Court of Appeal determined that speech therapy may be educational provision and therefore the responsibility of the LEA to arrange. See also *Bromley LBC v Special Educational Needs Tribunal*[12] for a discussion on the meaning of special educational provision and a review of the case-law. In *R v Harrow LBC ex p M*,[13] a case in which the Special Educational Needs Tribunal held that occupational therapy, physiotherapy and speech and language therapy were – in that case – special educational needs, subsequently the court held that the therapy required as special educational needs must be arranged by the LEA. A number of cases have examined the effects of an LEA's policy on a child. Most of these determine that, providing an authority does not fetter its discretion, it may develop and establish broad funding and allocation policies.[14]

9.35   EA 1996 s322 requires district health authorities and local authority departments separately to assist and co-operate with LEAs over special educational needs.

---

11 [1989] 2 FLR 279, CA.
12 [1999] ELR 260, CA.
13 (1997) ELR 62, QBD.
14 See *R v Cumbria CC ex p P* [1995] ELR 337, QBD; *R v Newham LBC ex p R* [1995] ELR 156, QBD; and *R v Cumbria CC ex p NB* [1996] ELR 65, QBD.

Statutory assessments of SEN

9.36 It is not a prerequisite that a child progresses from stage 1 through to stage 3 before s/he may have an assessment and attain a statement of SEN (stages 4 and 5). Accordingly, it may be the case that a child may immediately be assessed, as soon as the LEA is made aware of the child's learning difficulty or potential learning difficulty, especially if the impairment is initially considered to be severe. Either way, the procedure for assessing is laid out in detail in EA 1996 s323 and the 1994 Regulations, see paras 9.39–9.43.

9.37 EA 1996 s323(1) requires an LEA to carry out a statutory assessment if it considers that a child has, or probably has, SEN requiring the LEA to make special educational provision which any or all of the child's learning difficulties call for.

9.38 At the same time, EA 1996 s329 provides that a parent can ask for an assessment and, in that event, the LEA must comply with the request unless:

– an assessment has been made within six months ending with the date on which the request is made; or
– it is not necessary for the LEA to make an assessment.

Procedure for assessment

9.39 The LEA must first serve a notice on the child's parent informing him/her:

– that it proposes to make an assessment of the child's SEN;
– of the procedure to be followed in making the assessment;
– of the name of the officer from the LEA from whom further information may be obtained;
– of the parent's right to make representations and to submit written evidence to the LEA within not less than 29 days (or such greater period as is specified in the notice).

9.40 The LEA must send copies of the notice to:

– the social services authority responsible for the child concerned,
– the district health authority responsible for the child concerned, and

– the headteacher of any school at which the child is registered.

9.41   After the expiry of the notification period and consideration of any representations, if the LEA remains of the opinion that the child has or probably has SEN requiring special educational provision to be made, it must then undertake an assessment. The LEA must give notice in writing to the child's parent of its decision and the reasons for it. The LEA must send copies of the notice to those persons identified in paragraph 9.40.

9.42   When making an assessment, the LEA must seek advice from:

– the child's parent (1994 Regulations reg 6(1)(a));
– the child's headteacher, teacher with experience of teaching children with SEN or with knowledge of the differing provision which may be called for in different cases to meet those needs or, where the child is not attending school, other persons responsible for his/her education. (reg 7(1));
– if the child is hearing impaired and/or visually impaired, a person qualified to teach such children (reg 7(5));
– a registered medical practitioner appointed by the district health authority responsible for the child (reg 8);
– an educational psychologist engaged or employed by the LEA (reg 9);
– the social services authority;
– anyone else that the LEA considers appropriate for the purpose of arriving at a satisfactory assessment;
– the child, if possible.

9.43   The LEA must take into account all advice and representations made. However, essentially, it is not obliged to comply with any recommendations offered in all or any of the advices.

Statements of SEN

9.44   Once an assessment is concluded, the LEA must then consider whether, in the light of the evidence obtained, a statement of SEN must be maintained. This decision is of great importance because a statement will be prepared and maintained if the child requires special educational provision (as defined). Unlike children without statements, this gives the child a direct and personal right to receive

15   For an explanation of the phrase 'target duty', see *R v ILEA ex p Ali* [1990] COD 317, DC.

(as opposed to the LEA having a 'target duty' to provide)[15] the provision set out in the statement.

Procedure for 'statementing'

9.45 Once the LEA has determined to prepare a statement following an assessment, it must serve on the parent of the child:

- a copy of the proposed statement;
- a written notice (including a list of schools) explaining how a school will be chosen, what representations can be made and the rights of appeal.[16]

At this stage, no school will be named in the draft statement.

9.46 The parent then has an opportunity to:

1) express a preference as to the school at which s/he wishes his/her child to be educated;
2) make representations or further representations;
3) require the LEA to arrange a meeting and then further meetings.

The parent must make his/her requests within 15 days.

9.47 The LEA must then make the statement of SEN in the prescribed form.[17] The final statement may be in identical terms to the draft statement served on the parent in para 9.45 or with such amendments as the LEA agrees to make.

9.48 The LEA must then serve a copy of the statement on the parent of the child and give notice in writing of the parent's right of appeal and of the name of the person to whom the parent may apply for information and advice about the child's SEN.

9.49 In *R v Secretary of State for Education and Science ex p E*,[18] the Court of Appeal held that, once an LEA has determined that it should maintain a statement, all of the child's needs and the provision to meet those needs must be included in the statement, including those needs for which provision can be made by the school (see also

---

16 The notice is prescribed in Part A of the Schedule to the 1994 Regulations (see appendix E) or, for children in Wales, in the Education (Special Educational Needs) (Prescribed Forms) (Welsh Forms) Regulations 1995 SI No 45.

17 Set out in Part B of the Schedule to the 1994 Regulations (or the Welsh equivalent, see note 12).

18 [1992] 1 FLR 377, CA.

19 [1996] ELR 153, QBD.

para 4.28 of the Code of Practice). Furthermore, in *R v Oxfordshire CC ex p P*,[19] the Divisional Court confirmed that, under EA 1996 s324(5)(a)(i), the LEA retained a duty to make the special educational provision required by a statement regardless of any funding arrangements with the school.[20] In general, special educational provision must be specific and quantified.[21]

Form of the statement

9.50   A statement of SEN is prescribed as follows:

Part 1 Contains basic details of the child including his/her name, address, telephone number, details of the parent and any religious affiliation.

Part 2 Contains details of the child's SEN.

Part 3 Contains details of the special educational provision to meet the SEN, including the objectives of the special educational provision and the monitoring arrangements.[22]

Part 4 Will name the school or type of school or other institution at which the provision will be made.[23]

Part 5 Sets out any non-educational needs that the child may have (these may be medical needs, such as nursing,[24] but note that some ostensible non-educational needs, such as a need for speech and language therapy, may in fact be educational needs and, therefore, properly set out in parts 2 and 3.[25]

Part 6 Sets out any non-educational provision (again, beware of some provision which may in fact be educational provision).

20   See also *R v Hillingdon LBC ex p Governing Body of Queensmead School* [1997] ELR 331, QBD, and *R v Harrow LBC ex p M* [1997] ELR 62, QBD.
21   *L v Clarke and Somerset CC* [1998] ELR 129, QBD, and *Bromley LBC v Special Educational Needs Tribunal* [1999] ELR 260, CA.
22   Note, in particular, *R v Secretary of State for Education and Science ex p E* [1992] 1 FLR 377.
23   *Richardson v Solihull MBC and Another; White and Another v Ealing LBC and Another;* and *Hereford and Worcester CC v Lane* [1998] ELR 319, CA.
24   See *City of Bedford v A* [1997] ELR 417, QBD, which held that nursing was not special educational provision.
25   *R v Lancashire CC ex p M* [1989] 2 FLR 279, CA. For a discussion on what is and what is not special educational provision, see *Bromley LBC v Special Educational Needs Tribunal* [1999] 260, CA, although even that case did not fully clarify the divide.

Appendices These should include all of the reports and information obtained as part of the statutory assessment.

Choice of school

9.51 The procedures for expressing a preference and for obtaining a place at a school, described in chapter 5, do not apply to children with SEN. Instead, EA 1996 Sch 27 sets out the procedure as follows.

9.52 When an LEA serves a draft statement on the parent of a child with SEN, it must also serve a list of schools, together with a request that the parent expresses a preference within 15 days of:

– service of the written notice, or
– any meeting which has been fixed to discuss the matter.

9.53 Once a preference has been expressed, where that preference is for a state school, the LEA is required to name that school in the statement unless:

– it is unsuitable having regard to the child's age, ability, aptitude or SEN, or
– the attendance of the child at the school would be incompatible with the provision of efficient education for the children with whom s/he would be educated or the efficient use of resources.

9.54 In *B v Special Educational Needs Tribunal*,[26] the Court of Appeal determined that the reference to 'resources' was not confined to those of the LEA maintaining the statement but could, as in this case, also include the resources of the different LEA which maintains the school of the parents' choice. This may make a difference when comparing the costs of two schools in different LEAs (EA 1996 Sch 27 paras 3 and 8).

9.55 In addition, EA 1996 s316 gives a qualified duty to all those involved with the provision of education for children with statements of SEN to ensure that they are educated in ordinary or mainstream schools (ie, not special schools). The duty is qualified because it does not arise in the following situations:

1) if this is incompatible with the wishes of the child's parent;
2) if the child will not receive the special educational provision which his/her learning difficulty calls for, at the mainstream school;

26 [1998] ELR 351, CA.

3) if this is incompatible with the provision of efficient education for the children with whom the child will be educated; or

4) if this is incompatible with the efficient use of resources.

9.56   In *C v Lancashire CC*,[27] the court elaborated on the extent of the duty to 'integrate' children with statements of SEN in mainstream schools. It held that the test of what constitutes 'efficient use of resources' is not a strict one, and that that needs to be balanced against the interests of the child. In *Jules v Wandsworth LBC*,[28] the court held that the s316 duty did not require the Special Educational Needs Tribunal, of its own volition, to consider alternative mainstream schools which had not been sought by either party to the appeal.

9.57   Once a maintained school is named, the governing body of the school must admit the child (EA 1996 s324(5)(b)). Where an independent school is requested, a LEA need only name it if, in effect, it is necessary (in practice, where no state school is suitable).[29]

Time limits

9.58   As a result of provisions introduced in the EA 1993 and the 1994 Regulations, there are now time limits within which the assessment and statementing procedure must be concluded. Hitherto, it was not uncommon for LEAs to take years to conclude an assessment and produce a statement. In any event, the time limits are now as follows.

9.59   Where the LEA serves a notice informing the parent that it proposes to make an assessment, or receives a request for an assessment by the parent, the LEA must decide whether or not to make an assessment within six weeks. Within this period, the parent has 29 days in which to make representations.

9.60   Where the LEA has given notice to the parent of its decision to make an assessment, it must complete that assessment within ten weeks. Within this period, a district health authority and a social services authority must provide advice to the LEA within six weeks.

9.61   Once an assessment has been made, the LEA must either serve a copy of a draft statement or give notice of its decision not to make a

27 [1997] ELR 377, QBD.

28 [1998] ELR 243, QBD.

29 See *Catchpole v Buckinghamshire County Council and Special Educational Needs Tribunal* [1998] ELR 463, QBD.

statement within two weeks.

9.62   After service of a copy of the proposed statement, the LEA must serve a copy of the final statement within eight weeks. Within this period, the parent has 15 days to make representations or request a meeting.

9.63   Accordingly, the period between informing a parent of a proposal to carry out an assessment, or receiving a request from a parent to carry out an assessment, and producing a final statement of SEN must be no more than six months in total. Moreover, an LEA may conclude the various stages within shorter periods and there may be good reason to ask them to do so (although they may not be compelled so to do).

9.64   However, there are a number of exceptions which permit the time limits to be exceeded (paras 9.65–9.68).

9.65   Exceptions to the six-week limit for LEAs to tell a parent whether it will or will not make an assessment are:

1) where the LEA has requested advice from the headteacher of a school during a period between one week before the school closes for a continuous period of not less than four weeks (in effect, the summer vacation) and ending one week before it reopens;
2) where there are exceptional personal circumstances affecting the child or his/her parent during the six-week period (for example, family bereavement);
3) where the parent or child are absent from the area of the LEA for a continuous period of not less than four weeks.

9.66   Exceptions to the ten-week limit within which the LEA must make an assessment are:

1) where further advice or reports are exceptionally needed;
2) where the parent wants to provide advice for an assessment more than six weeks after the date on which the LEA's request for advice was received;
3) where the LEA issues a request for educational advice during a period beginning one week before the school closes for a continuous period of not less than four weeks (in effect the summer vacation) and ending one week before it reopens;
4) where the district health authority or social services authority have not replied to a request for advice within six weeks;
5) where the LEA is aware of exceptional personal circumstances affecting the child or his/her parent during the process of assessment (for example, family bereavement);

6) where the parent or the child are absent from the area of the LEA for a continuous period of not less than four weeks; or

7) where the child fails to honour an appointment for an examination or test.

9.67   Exceptions to the six-week limit within which the district health authority and social services authority must provide information are:

1) where there are exceptional personal circumstances affecting the child or his/her parent during the process of assessment (for example, family bereavement);

2) where the parent or the child are absent from the area of the LEA for a continuous period of not less than four weeks;

3) where the child fails to keep an appointment for an examination or test;

4) where the district health authority or social services authority has had no relevant knowledge of the child before receiving the LEA's notice or request.

9.68   Exceptions to the eight-week limit for making the statement are:

1) where there are exceptional personal circumstances affecting the child or his/her parent during the making of a statement (for example, family bereavement);

2) where the parent or the child are absent from the area of the LEA for a continuous period of not less than four weeks;

3) where the parent wants to make representations about the content of the statement after the 15-day period allowed;

4) where the parent seeks more than one meeting;

5) where the LEA has asked the secretary of state for his/her consent to the child being educated at an independent school not approved by him/her and where such consent has not been received within two weeks of the date on which the request was sent.

Appeals to the Special Educational Needs Tribunal

9.69   Before the statutory framework for appeals was expanded in EA 1993 Part III, there was a two-stage process when parents were in dispute with LEAs over the contents of statements or related matters. The first stage was an appeal to a panel appointed by the LEA which had advisory powers and could, therefore, make recommendations. However, the LEA did not have to comply with those recommendations. Subsequently, there was an appeal to the secretary of state, whose decisions were binding on the LEA. However, the whole process often took many months, if not years.

9.70   This procedure was replaced by the introduction in EA 1993 Part III (now EA 1996 Part IV) of the new Special Educational Needs Tribunal (SENT). The tribunal falls within the jurisdiction of the Council on Tribunals in accordance with Tribunals and Inquiries Act 1992 s11. It consists of a president appointed by the Lord Chancellor, legally qualified chairs and lay persons.

9.71   Each sitting of the tribunal has three members: one chair and two lay persons. The tribunal may hear appeals against:

1) a decision of an LEA not to carry out a statutory assessment of a child's SEN;
2) a decision of an LEA not to make a statement of SEN, following a statutory assessment;
3) the description of SEN in part 2 of a statement;
4) the description of special educational provision in part 3 of a statement;
5) the school named or not named in part 4 of a statement;
6) The refusal to change the name of the school to another maintained school;
7) the refusal of an LEA to carry out a reassessment of a child's SEN;
8) the decision of an LEA to cease to maintain a statement; and
9) disputes about the identification and provision for non-educational needs in parts 5 and 6 of a statement.

9.72   However, there are a number of matters which concern children with SEN but which may not be appealed to the tribunal. For example:

1) failure of the LEA to have regard to the Code of Practice;
2) failure of the LEA to comply with the statutory time limits;
3) failure of the LEA to meet other requirements for assessments;
4) failure of the LEA to arrange the special educational provision set out in part 3 of a statement;
5) failure of the LEA to keep under review its special educational provision;
6) adoption by the LEA of an unlawful policy in respect of the assessment and statementing procedure;
7) failure of the LEA to carry out an annual review;
8) failure of a governing body of a maintained school named in a statement to admit the child.

Accordingly, such matters may form the subject of an alternative remedy, such as utilisation of an LEA's complaints procedure, reference to the local government ombudsman, reference to the secretary of state, action in negligence or judicial review (see chapters 13–15).

Procedure for appeals

9.73 The procedure for appealing to the SENT is set out in the Special Educational Needs Tribunal Regulations 1995[30] (the 1995 Regulations), as follows.

9.74 Appeals must be lodged by a parent, not a child, with the SENT at Windsor House, 50 Victoria Street, London, SW1H 0NH within two months of receipt of the decision which is being challenged (this period may be extended, very exceptionally, on application to the president). If the two-month period expires during the month of August, the appeal does not have to be lodged until 1 September.

9.75 A booklet entitled *How to Appeal* is available from the tribunal. It contains a form for appeal, which asks all the questions required for lodging an appeal. In addition to lodging the form, the relevant correspondence and documentation (letter refusing assessment, letter refusing a statement, copy statement in respect of which the contents are being appealed, plus covering letter, etc) must also be enclosed.

9.76 Once an appeal is registered, an acknowledgement is sent to the parent (or his/her representative) and a copy of the appeal is sent to the LEA concerned. The LEA has 20 working days to lodge any reply, which must indicate whether or not it opposes the appeal and give a summary of its reasons.

9.77 Any reply is sent to the parent, who then has 15 working days to lodge any response to the reply.

9.78 These time limits are of great importance. Often, a parent may need to obtain his/her own expert evidence in order to support the appeal, for example, in order to support the need for a specific amount of speech and language therapy to be set out in a statement. Care must, therefore, be taken to ensure that any reports or other documentary evidence can be lodged within these time limits and that any expert is instructed in good time, so as to have the report available to meet these time limits.

9.79 Meanwhile, the tribunal will arrange a time and place for the

30 1995 SI No 3113. See appendix G.

hearing. The parent may be accompanied by a representative and up to two witnesses (exceptionally more, on application to the president) and witness summonses may be obtained from the tribunal where necessary. Hearings are usually listed for half a day and the procedure is designed to be informal so as to ensure that each party is able to put his/her views properly. As well as their representative and witnesses, parents may also bring somebody to be with them, but this person may not take an active part in the proceedings.

9.80   The LEA is likely to bring a similar number of people and there will, of course, also be the three members of the tribunal and the tribunal clerk. The tribunal usually reserves its decision which will be issued approximately two or more weeks after the hearing.

9.81   Decisions of the tribunal are binding on all parties and there is no further right of appeal (except on a point of law – see chapter 14) but any party may ask the president to review the decision within ten working days on the ground that:[31]

1) the decision was wrongly made as a result of an error on the part of the tribunal staff;
2) a party, who was entitled to be heard at a hearing but failed to appear or to be represented, had good and sufficient reasons for failing to appear;
3) there was an obvious error in the decision of the tribunal which decided the case; or
4) the interests of justice require a review.

9.82   Usually, no order for costs is made, although the tribunal has the power to do so in exceptional circumstances.[32] In particular, costs may be awarded:

1) against a party, if the tribunal is of the opinion that that party has acted frivolously or vexatiously or that his/her conduct in making, pursuing or resisting an appeal was wholly unreasonable;
2) against a party who has failed to attend or be represented at a hearing of which s/he has been duly notified;
3) against the LEA where it has not delivered a written reply under reg 12 of the 1995 Regulations; or
4) against the LEA where it considers that the disputed decision was wholly unreasonable.

9.83   If a parent appeals for an independent school and a tribunal accedes

---

31 1995 Regulations reg 32.
32 Ibid reg 33.

to the appeal and orders the LEA to amend the statement in question to name the independent school, responsibility for arranging the provision (ie, paying for the school) runs from the date of the order and not the date when the original statement was made.[33]

9.84   Legal aid is not available for representation at the Special Educational Needs Tribunal, although advice and assistance may be available to advise a parent, obtain an expert's report or provide for a McKenzie friend (see chapter 16).

Running an appeal

9.85   The following points (paras 9.86–9.94) should be noted when running an appeal to the tribunal on behalf of a parent.

9.86   When taking instructions from the client, obtain sufficient information so that all parties are clear about precisely what it is that the parent disagrees with. This may be obvious – the refusal of the LEA to carry out an assessment, for example – but it may be that the parent is not, in fact, dissatisfied with the contents of the statement but, rather, about the failure of the LEA to deliver what is set out in the statement. In that event, an appeal to the tribunal may not be appropriate. If the dispute is with respect to the contents of parts 2, 3 or 4 of a statement, ensure that the parent is clear about precisely what s/he would like instead.

9.87   At the same time as clarifying the subject matter of an appeal, consider the deadline – two months from the date of the decision to be challenged. If there is some time to spare, consider instructing an expert. Often, experts – particularly those used to preparing reports for tribunals – are in demand. In order for a report to be obtained in good time to lodge with the tribunal, having regard to the time limit set out, the expert should be instructed as soon as possible. However, bear in mind that an appropriate expert should be instructed. For example, if the matter in dispute is the amount of speech and language therapy specified in part 3 of the statement (or the fact that it is not specified at all) then, more likely than not, a specialist speech and language therapist should be instructed rather than, for example, an educational psychologist.

9.88   Lodge the appeal with the tribunal in good time to ensure that it is received before the two-month time limit. As well as completing the information required by the form contained in the booklet produced by the tribunal, ensure that the tribunal has copies of all

33 *R v Barnet LBC ex p W* [1998] ELR 291, QBD.

relevant documents, including the decision letter/statement and supporting documentation. Ensure also that the appeal is particularised sufficiently so as to enable both tribunal staff and the LEA to know precisely what is in dispute.

9.89   Consider what witnesses to call. The parent may call up to two witnesses and, exceptionally, more with the permission of the president. The witnesses should be persons who can give evidence in support of the substantial matters in issue. Consider also the fact that a witness may be hostile and, although his/her attendance may be required by way of a summons, such a witness may not assist the parent, ultimately, in the appeal.

9.90   Consider also any requirements for further information from the LEA. In the first instance, ask the LEA direct for that further information – whether it be factual information or documents held by the LEA – but, if this is refused or if the LEA does not reply promptly, consider a request for an order from the president of the tribunal in accordance with reg 21(2) of the 1995 Regulations.

9.91   On receipt of the LEA's reply, consider in detail what the outstanding issues in dispute are. It may be that the LEA accedes to some of the matters which form the subject of the appeal. In that event, the matters in issue may be reviewed so as to obviate the need for a particular witness.

9.92   Before the tribunal hearing, ensure that the parent and the witnesses are clear about what is likely to happen (the booklet – see para 9.75 – will assist) and confirm the outstanding matters in issue.

9.93   At the tribunal hearing, be clear and concise. Tribunals are informal and do not lend themselves well to the minutiae of legal procedure. That said, there is no reason why particular points of law and procedure should not be raised if they are directly material. However, different chairs run tribunals differently.

9.94   On receipt of the tribunal decision, if it does not meet with the parents' approval, consider a request for a review (see para 9.81) and an appeal on a point of law (see chapter 14).

Reassessments

9.95   EA 1996 s328(2) gives parents of children who have statements of SEN the right to ask for a reassessment at any time. An LEA in receipt of such a request must comply with it unless:

– an assessment has been made within the period of six months ending with the date on which the request was made (it is not clear precisely when an assessment can be said to have been made although it is likely to be at least before the issue of the draft statement – often LEAs have panels which consider the advices obtained for the assessment but it is unlikely that this consideration forms part of the assessment itself); or

– it considers it not necessary to make a further assessment, in which case a right of appeal arises.

9.96   Should a reassessment occur, the same procedures as set out in paras 9.39–9.43 arise and the same appeal rights apply.

Review of statements of SEN

9.97   The detail of these provisions is contained in the 1994 Regulations (see appendix E).

Child under 14 and at school (reg 15)

9.98   In this case the LEA must review a statement annually as follows:

1) The LEA requests in writing the head teacher to submit a report within two months and sends a copy of this notice to the child's parent.
2) The head teacher then seeks advice from:
   – the child's parent,
   – anyone else as determined by the LEA, and
   – anyone else as determined by the headteacher,
on the following matters:
   – the child's progress towards meeting his/her objectives and targets,
   – the application of the national curriculum or other substituted provision (except where the school is in a hospital or is independent),
   – any amendments which would be appropriate, and
   – whether the LEA should cease to maintain the statement.
3) The head teacher must then arrange a meeting with:
   – an LEA representative,
   – the child's parent,
   – members of the school staff, and
   – anyone else considered appropriate by the headteacher or LEA.
4) At least two weeks before the meeting, everyone invited must

receive written notice of the meeting together with copies of advices submitted and with a request for further comments and advice as appropriate.

5) After the meeting, the headteacher's report must be submitted to:
   - the LEA,
   - the child's parent,
   - any person from whom the headteacher has sought advice,
   - any persons invited to the meeting, and
   - any other persons, as appropriate.

6) The LEA must then review the statement in the light of the report and information. There is, unfortunately, no time limit prescribed for this review. However, within a week of completing the review, the LEA must send copies of its recommendations to:
   - the child's parent,
   - the headteacher,
   - persons from whom advice has been sought,
   - those invited to attend the meeting, and
   - other appropriate persons.

Child aged 14 and over and at school (reg 16)

9.99   The same procedure as set out in para 9.98 applies but, in addition, a representative of the social services authority and a person providing careers services (in accordance with the Employment and Training Act 1973) must also be invited to the meeting. In addition, a transition plan (defined as a document setting out the arrangements which an LEA considers appropriate for a young person during the period when s/he is aged 14 to 19 years, including arrangements for special educational provision and for any other necessary provision, for suitable employment and accommodation and for leisure activities, and which will facilitate a satisfactory transition from childhood to adulthood) must be prepared.

Child who does not attend school (reg 17)

9.100   Where a child does not attend school, similar provisions as set out in para 9.98 arise, except that there is no express obligation to involve a headteacher or school staff.

Amendments to statements of SEN

9.101   An LEA may determine to amend a statement (perhaps following an annual review) without having conducted a full reassessment. The procedure is generally as follows (EA 1996 Sch 27 paras 9 and 10):

1) The LEA must first notify the parent of its proposal and allow him/her to make representations.
2) The parent then has 15 days to make representations.
3) The LEA must then consider those representations and give notice in writing of its decision, including notice of the right of the parent to appeal.

9.102   Any amendment must be made within eight weeks of service of the notice. Again, a parent may appeal against that decision to the Special Educational Needs Tribunal.

Request for a change of named school by a parent

9.103   EA 1996 Sch 27 para 8 gives a parent the right to ask for the named school to be changed to another maintained school (but not an independent school, which may only be requested following a full assessment or reassessment). The LEA must comply with such a request unless:

1) a similar request has been made within the past 12 months;
2) the statement was served within the past 12 months;
3) the statement was amended within the past 12 months;
4) an appeal to the tribunal was concluded within the past 12 months;
5) the school is unsuitable to the child's age, ability, aptitude or SEN;
6) the attendance of the child at school would be incompatible with the provision of efficient education for the children with whom s/he would be educated; or
7) the attendance of the child at the school would be incompatible with the efficient use of resources.

9.104   The LEA must decide within eight weeks whether or not to comply with the request. It must either do so or notify the parent of its refusal to do so and of the parent's right of appeal.

Cessation of statement of SEN

9.105   An LEA may only determine to cease to maintain a statement where it is no longer necessary to maintain it, except where:

- it is no longer responsible for the child (for example, because the child moves to another area or goes to college), or
- it is ordered to cease to maintain a statement by the tribunal (EA 1996 s326(3)(c)).

9.106 If the LEA so determines, it must serve notice of that fact on the parent, together with a note of the right of appeal to the tribunal. In that event, the LEA may only then cease to maintain the statement within a four-week period beginning two months after service of the notice, otherwise, the process has to be commenced again.[34]

Restriction on disclosure of statements of SEN

9.107 Statements (including evidence, advice and representations contained in the appendices to the statement) can only be disclosed:[35]

- to the parent;
- to persons whom the LEA considers ought to receive a copy, in the interests of the child;
- for the purposes of an appeal to the tribunal;
- for the purposes of research which, in the LEA's opinion, will advance the education of children with SEN, provided the identity of any persons involved, particularly the child or his/her parent, is not disclosed in anything published;
- on the order of a court;
- to the local ombudsman regarding an investigation of alleged maladministration;
- to the secretary of state when considering the exercise of his/her powers under EA 1996 s496–498;
- to social services department officers for assessments under Disabled Persons (Services, Consultation and Representation) Act 1986 s5(5);
- to a social services department for the purposes of its duties under Children Act 1989 ss22(3)(a), 85(4)(a), 86(3)(a) and 87(3); or
- to an inspector in accordance with School Inspections Act 1996 s3(3) or Sch 3 para 7.

---

34 *R v Oxfordshire CC ex p Roast* [1996] ELR 381, QBD.
35 Education (Special Educational Needs) Regulations 1994 SI No 1047 reg 19.

CHAPTER 10

Special educational needs and social welfare law

Solicitors who have clients with children who have SEN may find themselves with requests for advice on related matters. These may include the law relating to community care, benefits, discrimination on grounds of disability and adaptations to housing. This chapter deals with some of the related issues that may arise.

Community care law

10.1   The law relating to services to help disabled, elderly and unwell people and others who may require accommodation and/or services is in disarray. There are at least a dozen Acts of Parliament which, through their inter-relation, establish the powers and duties of social services departments and district health authorities towards people who may require services, ranging from the National Assistance Act 1948 to the Community Care (Direct Payments) Act 1996. In addition, practice varies widely throughout the country, and so provision of services may be available in one area but not in another. There is insufficient space in this book to cover all of the detail and the authors recommend, in particular, Legal Action Group's book *Community Care and the Law by Luke Clements*[1] and also *Community Care Assessments* by Richard Gordon QC and Nicola Mackintosh.[2] In addition, LAG publishes *Community Care Law Reports*. Some issues which may arise in cases involving disabled children or young people are discussed in the following paragraphs.

Chronically Sick and Disabled Persons Act 1970 s2

10.2   Section 2 requires social services departments to make arrangements, where necessary, to ensure that people covered by that section (in practical terms, disabled people) receive such assistance as they require:

1) at home;
2) in obtaining a television or radio;
3) in accessing a library or similar facility;
4) in attending recreational and educational facilities outside the person's home;
5) with travelling;
6) with carrying out works of adaptation at home (see also the section dealing with housing, paras 10.30–10.32);
7) with taking holidays;
8) with the provision of meals; and
9) with the provision of a telephone and any special equipment required to use the telephone.

10.3   By s28A of the Act (inserted by Children Act 1989 s108(5) and Sch

---

1   LAG, 1996.
2   FT Law & Tax (now part of Sweet & Maxwell), 1996.

13 para 27), such services also apply to children. Accordingly, a disabled child who may require any, some or all of the above should be advised, through his/her parent, to ask the social services department for an assessment with a view to provision of such services. An assessment may be formally requested in accordance with the Disabled Persons (Services Consultation and Representation) Act 1986. Broadly, the law requires social services departments to carry out an assessment (the manner of which is not prescribed and certainly not with the detail of statutory assessments of special educational needs) and then to reach a relevant service provision decision. Once such a decision has been reached, the local authority is then under a duty to make the provision determined.

10.4 The House of Lords decision in *R v Gloucestershire CC and Secretary of State for Health ex p Barry*[3] established that, in determining what services are necessary to meet the needs of an individual under s2, the resources available to the social services department may be taken into account. However, it is important to note that this is different from a decision by a social services department that an individual needs a service and then that it cannot afford it, which, in the view of the authors, would be an unlawful decision.

10.5 In addition, some of the services set out in s2 may also be provided in other ways. For example, the Children Act 1989 may also make similar provision (see paras 10.6–10.7) or transport for a child may be available in accordance with the provisions of EA 1996 ss501–501A, especially where it relates to education (see chapter 6 paras 6.57–6.74 and paras 11.20–11.55).

Children Act 1989

10.6 This is a comprehensive and consolidating piece of legislation and is the primary source for provision for children. Section 17 and Schedule 2 provide for services for children who are defined as being 'in need' and this includes disabled children. Section 17 requires social services departments to safeguard and promote the welfare of children in need, so far as is consistent with that duty, by promoting their upbringing by their families. The services set out in Schedule 2, which may be provided, include:

1) information;
2) assessments; and

3   (1997) 1 CCLR 40, HL.

3) services to minimise the effect on disabled children of their disabilities and to give them the opportunity to lead lives that are 'as normal as possible'.

10.7   There is little case-law on the extent of the duties set out in s17 and it is the authors' view that such duties are hard to enforce, because of the general way in which they are set out (see paras 11.15–11.19).

Carers (Recognition and Services) Act 1995

10.8   This Act requires that when assessments are carried out; inter alia, in accordance with Children Act 1989 or the Chronically Sick and Disabled Persons Act 1970, the carer may also request the local authority to assess him/her. In *R v Newham LBC ex p Whittingham*,[4] the court confirmed that a carer may include a child who cares for an adult disabled person.

10.9   Generally, the Local Authority Social Services Act 1970 requires social services departments to act under the guidance of the Secretary of State for Health. Although a mass of guidance has been produced, little appears to have been issued under this Act, but the policy guidance issued by the Department of Health[5] is a notable exception. In *R v Islington LBC ex p Rixon*,[6] Sedley J confirmed that local authorities must comply with statutory guidance, except where there are good reasons not to do so. He also determined that local authorities must have regard to even non-statutory guidance.

Benefits

Disability living allowance

10.10   Disability living allowance (DLA) is a non-means-tested benefit that combines mobility allowance and attendance allowance for disabled people under the age of 65. It is for disabled people who require help with personal care and/or need assistance with mobility and cannot walk without difficulty. It comprises two components, the care component and the mobility component. The mobility component cannot be claimed by anyone who is under five years old or over 65,

---

4   (1997) 29 January, QBD CO/3657/96 (unreported).
5   *Policy Guidance : Caring for People – Community Care in the Next Decade and Beyond* DoH, 1990.
6   [1997] ELR 66; (1998) 1 CCLR 168, QBD.

but if claimed before 65 it can be paid for life. This is the only benefit that is available to a child.

Disability working allowance

10.11 Disability Working Allowance (DWA) is aimed at enabling disabled people to start work or return to work by 'topping up' a low amount of earnings. To qualify, the disabled person must be working 16 or more hours a week and can be employed or self-employed. This is a means-tested benefit and the amount awarded depends on the person's total income, working hours and family situation. From October 1999, Disability Working Allowance will be replaced by the Disabled Persons Tax Credit. Most of the rules about who can claim will be the same.

Industrial injuries benefit

10.12 The industrial injuries scheme covers people who are injured in an accident 'arising out of and in the course of' work. It also covers people who contract an industrial disease whilst working. It does not cover self-employed people. the industrial injuries scheme disablement benefit covers people who have actually become disabled through a 'prescribed' industrial accident or disease. People who have become disabled through work in this way may get the benefit, even if they are still able to work.

Disability premium

10.13 This is one of the premiums payable on top of income support. It is paid to disabled people aged from 16–60. To qualify, the disabled person must meet one or more of the disability conditions set out in the rules.

Severe disability premium

10.14 The severe disability premium (SDP) is another of the premiums payable on top of income support. It can be paid on top of the disability premium. Disabled people cannot claim it if someone looking after them gets invalid care allowance or if there are other people over 18 living with them, ie, non-dependants.

Disabled child's premium

10.15   The disabled child's premium (DCP) is another premium that can be claimed on top of income support. This premium can be paid for disabled children as soon as they are three months or older. If the child is blind, s/he is registrable as being blind from the date of his/her birth and can claim the DCP from the date of registration. If there is more than one disabled child in a family, DCP can be claimed for each.

Carer premium

10.16   This is another premium that can be paid on top of income support. It is paid to people who are in receipt of invalid care allowance or would be entitled to invalid care allowance.

Incapacity benefit

10.17   This benefit can be claimed by people whose illness or disability means that they are not able to work. To qualify, the disabled or ill person must have paid the requisite amount of national insurance contributions and be assessed as being incapable for work. This is a non-means-tested benefit. This benefit can be claimed by people who are 16–65 years old.

Severe disablement allowance

10.18   Severe disablement allowance (SDA) can be claimed by disabled people who have not been able to pay enough national insurance contributions to qualify for incapacity benefit and have been incapable of work for at least 28 weeks. It can be claimed by people aged from 16–65 years.

Invalid care allowance

10.19   Invalid care allowance (ICA) can be claimed by any person under the age of 65 who cares for a disabled person in receipt of the disability living allowance care component at the higher or middle rate. The person claiming ICA must give at least 35 hours a week care to the disabled person. The carer claiming this benefit need not be related to the disabled person and need not live with the disabled person. ICA is not means-tested, but is taxable.

Orange badge scheme

10.20 This scheme is intended to enable disabled people with mobility difficulty, or their drivers, to park in places that would otherwise be restricted. Disabled people should apply to their local authority for an orange badge. Orange badges will be issued to disabled people who cannot walk or who have a great deal of difficulty in walking. Orange badges cannot be obtained for children until they are aged two.

Independent Living Funds

10.21 These funds will make cash payments directly to disabled people who need personal assistance, ie, care, in order to enable them to live independently at home. Since 1993, people seeking to claim Independent Living Fund money need to do so in conjunction with their local authority to set up a joint care package.

Disability Discrimination Act 1995

10.22 The Act, substantive parts of which were brought into force on 1 November 1996, seeks to outlaw discrimination towards disabled people in two key areas: employment and the provision of goods, services and facilities. This requires employers and providers of goods, services and facilities to treat disabled people no less favourably than non-disabled people, without justification, and also to make reasonable adjustments. There is no minimum qualifying age for a disabled person and consequently, a disabled child may have rights not to be discriminated against. However, the following limitations should be noted.

10.23 The definition of disability is different from that contained in other legislation covering disabled people. A person is entitled not to be discriminated against if s/he has 'a physical or mental impairment which has a long-term and adverse effect on their ability to carry out normal day to day activities' (Part I). These words have particular meaning and are defined further in regulations and guidance but, broadly, exclude those with relatively minor impairments. The Act also includes those with a history of an impairment, those with progressive impairments, those with severe disfigurements and those who were registered as disabled prior to the Act (which itself, abolished registration) but excludes those

dependent on nicotine, alcohol, any non-prescribed drug or other
substance, those suffering from hay fever and those with certain
propensities arising from a psychiatric condition (eg, pyromaniacs,
kleptomaniacs, etc).

10.24   Employers who are under a duty not to discriminate are those
that have at least 15 staff. The government has announced that, in
due course, this figure is likely to be reduced, and perhaps
withdrawn, so that increasing numbers of employers are brought
within the provisions of the DDA. However, certain categories of
employment – fire fighters, prison officers, police officers, the
armed forces and others – are excluded.

10.25   With respect to the duties on providers of goods, services and
facilities, at the time of writing, only the duty not to discriminate
against disabled people is currently in force. However, from October
1999, various duties to make adjustments will be brought into force
prospectively.

10.26   Critically, the Act excludes most education from its provisions in
respect of goods and services and, therefore, no disabled child or
(indeed) parent has any new or different rights arising from this Act.
However, disabled teachers and other staff may be covered in the
employment provisions.

10.27   In addition, the Act amends EA 1996 s317(5) so as to require
schools, when they publish annual reports, to include information
on:

1) the arrangements for the admission of disabled pupils;
2) the steps taken to prevent disabled pupils from being treated less
   favourably than other pupils; and
3) the facilities provided to assist access to the school by disabled
   people.

10.28   Should a disabled person consider that s/he has been discriminated
against, enforcement will arise in either an employment tribunal (in
respect of employment) or a county court (in respect of goods,
services and facilities).

10.29   Further guidance on the operation of the Disability
Discrimination Act is given in *Notes on the Disability Discrimination
Act* which is updated periodically.[7]

---

7   Available from David Levene & Co Solicitors, Ashley House, 235–239 High
    Road, Wood Green, London, N22 8HF, telephone 0181 881 7777, minicom
    0181 881 6764, fax 0181 829 9747 e-mail info@davidlevene.co.uk. The
    publication and information about the current edition and price are available
    on request.

Housing

10.30 Disabled people may be entitled to assistance in adapting their homes through either or both of the following routes:
- a disabled facilities grant under Local Government and Housing Act 1989 s114;
- under Chronically Sick and Disabled Persons Act 1970 s2(1) (see para 10.2).

10.31 In addition, local authorities have duties towards disabled people, in respect of the provision of accommodation, in accordance with the National Assistance Act 1948.

10.32 In *R v Tower Hamlets LBC ex p Bradford*,[8] the judge determined that it may be possible to require local authorities to provide housing for disabled children and their families, in accordance with the provisions of the Children Act 1989 s17.

8   (1998) 1 CCLR 294, QBD

CHAPTER 11

Special cases

This chapter deals with the less common educational situations where, for a variety of reasons, children are either not living at home or not attending a mainstream school, or where children have particular needs.

For complete chapter contents, see overleaf

Children being looked after by a local authority

11.1 In July 1998 the House of Commons Select Committee on Health reported that the failure to provide adequate educational support and opportunities for looked after children was scandalous. This committee found that 26 per cent of looked after children were receiving no education and around 75 per cent of 16-year-old care leavers had no qualifications compared with 6 per cent of all 16 year olds. Fewer than 20 per cent of care leavers stay at school post 16, compared with 68 per cent of all 16-year-olds. Children looked after by local authorities are ten times more likely to be excluded from school than other children.

11.2 In September 1998 the government launched its 'Quality Protects' initiative aimed at improving the effectiveness of services for children. All local authorities had to produce action plans for reform by January 1999. July 2001 has been set as a target date for 50 per cent of looked after children to achieve one graded GCSE or its equivalent at age 16. This target is raised to 75 per cent by July 2003.

Local authorities' duties and powers

11.3 A distinction needs to be made between a child who has a care order, and for whom the local authority social services department has parental responsibility under Children Act (CA) 1989 s33(3), and a child who is in voluntary care, when the social services department does not have this responsibility. In the former case, the social services department has the power, within certain parameters, to decide the extent to which a parent or guardian can assume his/her parental responsibility.

11.4 CA 1989 s22(3) provides a general duty on a local authority looking after any child:

> ... to safeguard and promote its welfare and to make such use of services available for children cared for by their own parents as appears to the authority reasonable in his case.

Before making any decision the local authority should, where it is reasonably practicable, ascertain the wishes and feelings of the child, his/her parents, anyone with parental responsibility and any other relevant party.

11.5 A local authority may, if it considers it necessary to protect the public from serious injury, use its powers in a way which is inconsistent with its duties under CA 1989 s22 (s22(6)). Furthermore, the Secretary of State for Social Services can direct a local authority to act in the above way (s22(7)–(8)). This might happen when a child is charged with a serious offence, is out of control or is mentally ill, in which case s/he could be placed in secure accommodation. See para 11.11.

Care plans and education

11.6   In May 1994, the DFE and the Department of Health published a circular entitled *The education of children being looked after by local authorities.*[1] This was intended to give advice to class teachers and social workers on the necessity for partnership in caring for these children. It stressed that educational needs should be identified and that a plan should set realistic challenges and academic targets.

11.7   There is a statutory requirement that care plans, regularly reviewed at least every six months and initially more frequently, should be maintained for children in these circumstances.[2] While a care plan is drawn up by the social services department, teachers, the child and the parents should also be involved. Realistic short-term and long-term educational targets should be set. Where appropriate, these will need to take account of any educational plan drawn up in recognition of special educational needs. CA 1989 s27 allows local authorities to request help from other authorities including LEAs, housing authorities and health authorities.

Children's homes

11.8   There are about 100 children's homes in England and Wales which provide education on site, generally for children in the 14 to 16 age group who, for one reason or another, do not attend mainstream schooling. It is often difficult to deliver a broad and balanced curriculum because of the small size of the home, which limits the numbers of teachers that can be employed. The nature of the accommodation may restrict the range of education offered. The staff are usually, but not exclusively, employed by social services departments and may be isolated from the mainstream of education.

11.9   CA 1989 s28 provides that, so far as it is reasonably practicable, an LEA should be consulted about a situation where a child is to live

---

1   DFE Circular 13/94.
2   Arrangements for Placement of Children (General) Regulations 1991 SI No 890; Review of Children's Cases Regulations 1991 SI No 895.

in accommodation which also provides education. The responsible LEA will be either the authority making the placement or, where a child has a statement of special educational needs, the LEA which maintains the statement.

Secure accommodation

11.10   Some children looked after by a local authority may need to be kept in secure accommodation. This can only be for longer than three days if a court is satisfied that certain criteria are met.[3]

11.11   Education has to be provided in these circumstances. Again, this may be somewhat limited because of the small number of pupils, often with special educational needs and/or behavioural problems, and staff. However, while the local authority must maintain the statement of SEN of a child accommodated in a children's home which provides education (see para 11.8), this does not apply to a child in secure accommodation (EA 1996 s562). In fact, this section converts duties to discretions on the part of the LEA in respect of all educational provision as soon as a child is detained by a court or the Home Secretary. The LEA's qualified statutory duty to react to a social services department's requests for co-operation represents a failure to support those children most in need.[4]

Older children leaving care

11.12   CA 1989 s105(1) defines a child as someone under 18, but by CA 1989 s24 a local authority also has a responsibility to provide advice and assistance to a person under the age of 21 who was at any time between the ages of 16 to 18 looked after by a local authority, accommodated or privately fostered for at least three months, but who is no longer looked after, accommodated or fostered. A beneficiary of this duty is defined by s24(2) as a person who was:

... while still a child –
(a) looked after by a local authority;
(b) accommodated by or on behalf of a voluntary organisation;
(c) someone accommodated in a registered children's home;
(d) accommodated –

3   CA 1989 s25; Children (Secure Accommodation) Regulations 1991 SI No 1505.
4   See critical discussion of this problem by Helen Rimington in *Childright*, March 1998.

(i) by any health authority or local education authority; or

(ii) in any residential care home, nursing home or mental nursing home,

for a consecutive period of at least three months; or

(e) privately fostered,

but who is no longer so looked after, accommodated or fostered.

11.13   In relation to categories (c) to (e), local authorities are only empowered to provide advice and assistance if it seems that the person needs advice and to be befriended and if the person asks for help of the kind which authorities must give to those in categories (a) and (b). Section 24(7)–(8) defines the kind of assistance that may be given including, in certain exceptional circumstances, money. Generally local authorities will provide assistance in the form of contributions towards expenses connected to education, training or living expenses connected to the same. This assistance may continue after the age of 21 if a person has not yet completed a course.

11.14   The government has set an objective in Quality Protects to reverse the trend of discharging people from care at 16 and for increasing the support available to young people leaving care. All children over 16 should have a care and aftercare plan, which includes an analysis of educational opportunities and career options. There are proposals to replace the discretion referred to in para 11.12 by a statutory duty. It is also proposed to require local authorities to provide accommodation in the holidays for young people under 24 who are studying.

Other children in need

Local authorities' duties

11.15   As well as their duties towards children they are looking after, local authorities have additional duties under CA 1989 Part III to all children in need. These duties are specified in CA 1989 Sch 2 Part I and include duties to:

1) take reasonable steps to identify the extent of children in need (para 1(1));

2) publicise information about provision provided by themselves and voluntary organisations which the local authorities have power to provide and to disseminate this information to those who might benefit from it (para 1(2));

3) keep a register of disabled children (para 2).

11.16 CA 1989 s17(10) states that a child is defined as in need if:

(a) he is unlikely to achieve or maintain, or to have the opportunity of achieving or maintaining, a reasonable standard of health or development without the provision for him of services by a local authority under this Part;

(b) his health or development is likely to be significantly impaired, or further impaired, without the provision for him of such services, or

(c) he is disabled.

CA 1989 s17(11) states:

For the purposes of this Part, a child is disabled if he is blind, deaf or dumb or suffers from mental disorder of any kind or is substantially and permanently handicapped by illness, injury or congenital deformity or such other disability as may be prescribed; and in this Part –
'development' means physical, intellectual, emotional, social or behavioural development; and
'health' means physical or mental health.

11.17 If a local authority deems a child to be in need, it may assess his/her needs under CA 1989 and, at the same time, under Chronically Sick and Disabled Persons Act 1970, EA 1996 (in relation to SEN), Disabled Persons (Services, Consultation and Representation) Act 1986 or any other Act, such as the Carers (Recognition and Services) Act 1995 (see para 10.8) (the National Health Service and Community Care Act 1990 only covers services for adults).

11.18 Under CA 1989 s18(1) local authorities must provide day care for children in need who are under five and not yet attending school.

11.19 Under CA 1989 s18(5) local authorities must provide care or appropriate supervised activities for children in need who attend school outside school hours and in school holidays. There is also a power to provide such activities for children not deemed to be in need.

Special schools

11.20 A special school is defined by EA 1996 s337 as a school specially organised to make educational provision for pupils with special educational needs and is approved by the secretary of state under EA 1996 s342 (see para 3.6).

11.21 SSFA 1998 Sch 30 para 80 amends EA 1996 s337 to provide for community and foundation special schools from 1 September 1999 and others that do not fall into this category. Any of these latter schools which provide full-time education for five or more pupils of compulsory school age are independent schools, by virtue of the definition in EA 1996 s463. Requirements set out in the regulations[5] must be complied with to ensure approval of those schools that are neither community nor foundation special schools. These schools must not be run for profit. Community and foundation special schools are deemed to be approved by EA 1996 s342(3). Maintained schools under EA 1996 s337 can take children with special educational needs without them necessarily having a statement.

11.22   By EA 1996 s347 the secretary of state may approve independent schools as suitable for the admission of children with statements of SEN under EA 1996 s324. These are governed by the Education (Special Educational Needs) (Approval of Independent Schools) Regulations 1994.[6] No person may make arrangements under EA 1996 Part IV for a child with special educational needs to be educated in such a school unless it is approved or the secretary of state consents to the child being educated there (EA 1996 s347(5)). This would not rule out a private arrangement.

11.23   Special schools cover a range of different difficulties including physical disability, eg, blindness, deafness, mental disability including dyslexia, autism, attention deficit disorder, emotional and behavioural difficulties. Given the development of policy on special needs, schools may not necessarily be established to meet only one particular type of impairment (see para 9.14).

11.24   Some LEAs may not have provision for all the different categories of disability in their area. They may make arrangements for children to be educated in a nearby area or at a boarding school. The latter may be maintained by themselves, another authority, a charitable organisation or be independent. If an LEA places a child outside its own area it is responsible for the cost of this provision. See chapter 9.

---

5   Education (Maintained Special Schools) (England) Regulations 1999 SI No 2212; Education (Non-maintained Special Schools) (England) Regulations 1999 SI No 2257.
6   1994 SI No 651 as amended by 1998 SI No 417.

Children with behavioural difficulties

Behaviour support plans

11.25 Many of the children identified by local authorities as being in need will have behaviour problems. By EA 1996 s27A (inserted by EA 1997 s9) LEAs are required to prepare and review, statements of their arrangements for these children – known as behaviour support plans. A plan must set out the LEA's arrangements for helping schools with pupils with behavioural difficulties and their discipline, and for finding suitable school places for them.[7] These plans will interact with other LEA plans, eg, children's services plan, early years development plan, education development plan and youth justice plan.

11.26 Circular 1/98 gives examples of ways schools may help pupils with behavioural difficulties. These include following the requirements of the Code of Practice on SEN, liaison with health services, parents and carers, providing work when their pupils are on fixed-term exclusion, staff training, following locally agreed procedures in handling absence and exclusions (para 52). Para 58 states that these pupils should have access to a broad and balanced curriculum but that consideration may need to be given to temporarily disapplying the National Curriculum. Careful thought will need to be given to how the curriculum is taught, including a combination of work experience and college courses for pupils at key stage 4.

Education outside mainstream schools

11.27 LEAs are at liberty to provide education for children with behavioural difficulties outside mainstream schools in a variety of ways. Many have pupil referral units (PRUs) – see paras 11.28–11.39. Other LEAs contract with non-LEA providers or with voluntary organisations to provide education for disaffected young people. In these cases, the LEA remains responsible for monitoring the provision. The ultimate aim must be to return children to mainstream schooling as quickly as is appropriate and possible. Education provided in this context does not come out of the General Schools Budget.

7 See Local Education Authority (Behaviour Support Plans) Regulations 1998 SI No 644 and DfEE Circulars 1/98 *LEA Behaviour Support Plans* and 10/99 *Social Inclusion: Pupil Support.*

Children in pupil referral units

Local authorities' duties

11.28   Under EA 1996 s19(1), LEAs must make arrangements for the provision of 'suitable education' for children who:

> ... by reason of illness, exclusion from school or otherwise, may not for any period receive suitable education unless such arrangements are made for them.

11.29   Any school which is specially organised to provide education for such children, which is not a community or special school, is a pupil referral unit (PRU) (EA 1996 s19(2)). See also para 3.9. A PRU is not included under categories of maintained schools under SSFA 1998 s20. LEAs may provide boarding accommodation at a PRU (EA 1996 s19(3)). The Education (Pupil Referral Units) (Application of Enactments) Regulations 1994[8] require LEAs to publish details of their policies to provide education under EA 1996 s19.

11.30   PRUs are not seen as a long-term alternative to other schooling. Therefore, parents are unable to express a preference for a PRU in place of a mainstream school and EA 1996 Sch 1 para 4 allows for dual registration at a PRU and at a mainstream school. Some children may spend part of their time in a mainstream school and part in a PRU. Equally, attendance at a PRU may be suitable for a child who is not on the register of any school and hence, under Sch 1 para 14, it may be named in a school attendance order (see paras 7.18–7.21). Placement in a PRU should never be used instead of making an assessment of a child's SEN under EA 1996 s323. Neither is it appropriate to name a PRU in a child's statement of SEN.[9]

11.31   Now that more credibility and status has supposedly been given to PRUs, curriculum modification and part-time tuition are likely to increase because formerly excluded pupils had either no tuition or 'home tuition' at home or in individual tuition centres. It may well be that a headteacher resorts to excluding a 'difficult' pupil knowing that provision is available in a PRU. This trend has probably also been affected by the current emphasis on school performances and league tables.

8   1994 SI No 2103.
9   *C v Special Educational Needs Tribunal and Greenwich LBC* [1999] ELR 5, QBD.

Status and governance of PRUs

11.32 Surprisingly, given the likelihood that a significant number of PRU referees are children with special educational needs, the statutory obligations to acknowledge and support these have now been watered down by the SSFA 1998.[10] The LEA acts as the governing body of a PRU. But it no longer has any of the obligations under EA 1996 s317(1)–(4)(endeavouring to secure SEN provision and co-ordinating it amongst teachers); nor the s318 power to provide goods or services to PRUs in making SEN provision. This might include educational psychology and specialist teaching and IT services. The SSFA appears to contain no compensating powers to improve the SEN support for PRU pupils and it is difficult to understand the logic of this. As a matter of practice, the very pupils who are most in need of assessment, or reassessment, of their SEN, are the most likely to be passing through the PRU, for example, because of manifest emotional or behavioural difficulties.

11.33 The teacher in charge for legal purposes is regarded as the headteacher of the unit. This allows that person to take any necessary action in relation to health and safety, pupil discipline or exclusions. EA 1997 s48 added para 15 to EA 1996 Sch 1, which allows LEAs to establish management committees for PRUs.

11.34 No formal procedures are laid down in relation to the opening or closing of a PRU. On general administrative law principles there would still need to be consultation over the decision.

11.35 Because PRUS are smaller than schools and have reduced facilities they are excluded from some of the requirements in the Education (School Premises) Regulations 1999,[11] specifically Part V and Sch 2 in relation to playing fields.

Curriculum and inspections

11.36 PRUs do not need to provide the full National Curriculum or to conduct any statutory assessments at the end of each key stage. EA 1996 Sch 1 para 6(1) (as amended by SSFA 1998 Sch 30 para 184) states that the curriculum should satisfy EA 1996 s351, ie, the provision of a broad and balanced curriculum which:

> (a) promotes the spiritual, moral, cultural, mental and physical

---

10 Sch 30 paras 57 and 184(b), and Sch 31, repealing EA 1996 Sch 1 paras 12 and 13.

11 1999 SI No 2.

development of pupils at the school and of society; and

(b) prepares such pupils for the opportunities, responsibilities and experiences of adult life.

11.37   Under EA 1996 Sch 1 para 6(2) (as amended) regulations may make provision for the determination and organisation of the curriculum including the making of a written statement on the curriculum. The LEA must make arrangements for the consideration of complaints against itself or the teacher in charge in relation to the curriculum (EA 1996 Sch 1 para 6(3)).

11.38   There is no need for annual reports as in mainstream schools. But PRUs must provide reports when a child transfers to another school or when a child over 16 leaves school.[12]

11.39   PRUs are subject to modified Ofsted inspections.[13] If a PRU is deemed to require special measures, the LEA must provide a written statement of the action it proposes to take in the same way as a mainstream school.

Children educated at home

'Suitable education'

11.40   Children may be educated at home because their parents choose to do this (see para 11.46) and/or because, for some reason, they cannot attend school (see para 11.47). In either situation, the education they receive must be 'suitable education', defined by EA 1996 s19 as 'efficient education suitable to his age, ability and aptitude and any special educational needs he may have'. See para 7.15 for a fuller description of 'suitable education'.

11.41   In *R v East Sussex CC ex p Tandy* it was held at first instance by Dyson J, by the Court of Appeal[14] and by the House of Lords[15] that the decision about what was suitable education for a particular child was one for the LEA, and not the courts.

---

12   Education (Pupil Referral Units) (Application of Enactments) Regulations 1994 SI No 2103 Sch 1 Part II para 9.

13   Education (School Inspection) Regulations 1997 SI No 1966, as amended by Education (School Inspection) (Amendment) Regulations 1999 SI No 601; also Education (School Inspection) (Wales) Regulations 1998 SI No 1866, as amended by Education (School Inspection) (Wales) (Amendment) Regulations 1999 SI No 1440.

14   [1998] ELR 80, CA.

15   (1998) 1 CCLR 352, HL.

11.42   In this case a 14-year-old girl without a statement of SEN was unable to attend school because she had ME. She sought to challenge the LEA's decision, based on resource grounds, to reduce her home tuition from five hours to three hours a week. The judge said that the LEA's decision must be objective and made a distinction between the House of Lords case *R v Gloucester CC ex p Barry*[16] (relied on by the LEA), which centred on a definition of a person in need under the Chronically Sick and Disabled Persons Act 1970, and the statutory duties imposed by the education legislation.

11.43   The House of Lords also distinguished *ex p Barry*. Lord Browne-Wilkinson said that there was nothing in EA 1993 to suggest that resource considerations were relevant to what was 'suitable education'. That view was much strengthened by the definition of 'suitable education' in EA 1993 s298(7) (now EA 1996 s19) which spelt out expressly the factors relevant to the determination of suitability. All those express factors related to educational considerations and nothing else. There was nothing to indicate that resources available were relevant. Moreover, there were other provisions in the Act which did refer expressly to the efficient use of resources, for example EA 1993 ss160 and 161(4) (now EA 1996 ss316–317). The draftsman had shown that he was alive to the issue of available resources. If he meant such resources to be relevant for the consideration of what constituted suitable education he would surely have said so. Also, the words of EA 1993 s298(7) (now EA 1996 s19) 'efficient ... education suitable to ... age, ability and aptitude and to any special educational needs' echoed the words of EA 1944 s37 (now EA 1996 s7), spelling out a parent's duty to provide education for his/her child. The content of the parental duty to educate could not vary according to the parent's resources.

11.44   The council's statutory duty to make arrangements for what constituted suitable education was owed to each sick child individually and not to sick children as a class. If there was more than one way of providing suitable education, the council would be entitled to have regard to its resources in choosing between different ways of providing suitable education. The council could divert money from other educational or other applications which were merely discretionary so as to apply such diverted money to discharge its statutory duty under EA 1993 s248 (now EA 1996 s19). To permit a local authority to avoid performing a statutory duty on the ground that it preferred to spend the money in other ways was to downgrade

16   (1997) 1 CCLR 40.

a statutory duty to a statutory power. Parliament had chosen to impose a statutory duty, as opposed to a power.

11.45   It is submitted that the position would have been different if the child had had a statement of SEN prescribing a minimum of five hours' tuition, since then there would have been a specific statutory obligation to arrange the provision in the statement under EA 1996 s324(5).

Tuition by parents

11.46   It is estimated that more than 8,000 children in England and Wales are being educated at home by their parents, a figure which has more than doubled between 1988 and 1995.[17] See also paras 7.16 and 7.17.

Home tuition by LEA

11.47   EA 1996 s19(1) placed a duty on LEAs to make arrangements for children of compulsory school age of suitable full-time or part-time education at school or outside school if, '...by reason of illness, exclusion from school or otherwise, they may not for any period receive suitable education unless such arrangements are made for them'. LEAs have a discretion to make such provision for children over school leaving age (EA 1996 s19(4)). EA 1997 s47 deleted the words 'full-time or part-time'. This may be seen as less onerous. But a new subsection (4A) was inserted, with effect from 1 September 1998, requiring the LEA, in determining what arrangements to make under s19(1) or (4), to have regard to any guidance given from time to time by the secretary of state. DFE Circular 11/94 *The Education by LEAs of Children Otherwise than at School* dealt with children in these circumstances but was superseded in July 1999 by DfEE Circular 10/99.[18] This concentrates on exclusion and does not cover other problems (but see para 11.51). It is notable that 're-integration' guidance (chapter 7) occupies only one page and that in the accompanying case study the PRU is co-ordinating the re-integration of excluded pupils. There appears to be no guidance on the nature or quality of education provided in the mean time.

11.48   Where home tuition is provided, there is no minimum amount

---

17 See Amanda J Petrie: 'Home Education and the Law' in *Education and the Law* Vol 10 Nos 2–3:123 for a fuller analysis.

18 DfEE Circular 10/99 *Social Inclusion: Pupil Support.*

which must be provided although ideally this should be daily. Work should also be provided for the child to do on his/her own. Commonly, LEAs provide about five hours per week, and although this might be thought to fall foul of the reduced definition of education in s19, there appear to have been no reported cases on this important question. *Ex p Tandy* made it clear that the courts are not going to enter the arena of indicating the amount of education to which a child out of school is entitled. The reference to 'arrangements' in EA 1996 s19 also suggests that the courts might regard the provision as imposing merely a target duty in considering what is being offered to a particular pupil.[19]

11.49   There is no obligation on LEAs to provide home tuition if a child is out of school for a very short time. In practice, it is unlikely that LEAs will make any arrangements within a matter of days or weeks, and so children subject to short fixed-term exclusions are unlikely to receive formal education.

11.50   In all cases of more than one day's exclusion, the school at which the child is registered must continue to provide and monitor work until the appeal process is finished or any time limit for appeal has passed.[20] See para 8.49.

Sick children

11.51   Under EA 1996 s19, LEAs have a duty to provide education for sick or injured children. The DFE, with the Department of Health and the National Health Service Executive, published a circular on this topic in 1994.[21] No one way is prescribed for LEAs to undertake their duty in this regard. The key element is continuity between the child's school, home and hospital, if appropriate.

Education in hospital

11.52   Hospital schools are defined as special schools. In 1994 there were 40 maintained by 27 LEAs. There are now (1999) only about 20 such schools as LEAs are increasingly providing this through their home tuition service. LEAs may make proposals to establish new hospital

19 Cf the duty on LEAs under EA 1996 s14 to 'secure that sufficient schools...are available for their area', a provision derived from EA 1944 s8.
20 DfEE Circular 10/99 para 6.5.
21 DFE Circular 12/94 *The Education of Sick Children*.

schools under the EA 1996 s339 as well as proposals to alter or discontinue a school. Common law duties to consult may apply. These schools do not have to conform to the Education (School Premises) Regulations 1999.[22]

11.53   Hospital schools must have governing bodies under Education (School Government) Regulations 1989.[23] Because of the transient nature of the patients, EA 1996 s81(2) made special provision for the role of parent governors to be undertaken by appointment by the other members of the governing body rather than by election. This has now been repealed by SSFA 1998 Sch 30 para 69, but is likely to be re-enacted. Likewise, by EA 1996 s350, they did not have to provide the National Curriculum. This has also been repealed but will be re-enacted.

11.54   Education in hospitals may be provided as 'education otherwise' under EA 1996 s19, ie, not in a hospital school. In reality, the provision will probably be very similar, the most significant legal difference being the lack of a governing body. District health authorities have duties to collaborate with LEAs to provide education in hospitals.

Home tuition

11.55   LEAs are able to provide home tuition for sick children (see paras 11.47–11.51). However, it is best practice that their own school should provide work to be done at home if children are absent for periods of up to four weeks. It is desirable for LEAs to have policies on home tuition generally.

Traveller children

11.56   By far the largest group of Travellers are Gypsies, estimated at around 70,000. Other communities include fairground/show people (10,500), circus families (2,000), New Age travellers (6,000), and families living on boats (500). It is estimated that there are about 50,000 travelling children between the ages of 0 and 16.[24] DFE

22   1999 SI No 2.
23   1989 SI No 1503, as amended.
24   *The Education of Travelling Children: a survey of Educational Provision for Travelling Children*, March 1996, HMR 12/96/NS, Ofsted.

Circular 11/92[25] para 11 includes within the definition of Travellers eligible for grant aided facilities under EA 1996 s488 those who have moved into settled housing in the previous two years. Refugees and displaced persons in special camps are included but homeless people in bed and breakfast accommodation are excluded because their accommodation is not specific to displaced persons.[26]

11.57   By EA 1996 s488 and a scheme under the Education (Grants) (Travellers and Displaced Persons) Regulations 1993,[27] the DfEE provides grants to LEAs of 75 per cent of approved expenditure. The schedule to the regulations lists the items eligible for grant aid. These include distance learning, outreach work, transport and uniforms.[28]

11.58   However, these grants, 'must ... be aimed at ensuring unhindered access to, and full integration in mainstream education'.[29] The greater part of this funding is used to employ classroom assistants, peripatetic (but school-based) teachers and specialist education welfare officers.[30] This appears to pay little regard to the lifestyle of Travellers. Furthermore, it fails to address the often entrenched and negative attitudes of the settled population to Travellers, which may result in racism and bullying. School attendance by Traveller children seems to decrease after puberty.[31] The reasons for this are partly the role young people are expected to play within their community, partly the feeling that secondary education is irrelevant to a travelling lifestyle and partly the thought that integration will destroy their ethnic and cultural lifestyle.

Refugees and asylum-seekers

11.59 Further and higher education institutions are not allowed to charge higher fees for refugees or those with exceptional leave to remain.

25 DFE Circular 11/92 *Education Reform Act 1988: Specific Grant for the Education of Travellers and of Displaced Persons.*

26 Education (Grants) (Travellers and Displaced Persons) Regulations 1993 SI No 569 reg 4(c), as amended by 1995 SI No 543.

27 1993 SI No 569.

28 See also DES Circular 10/90 *The Education Reform Act 1988: Specific Grant for the Education of Travellers and of Displaced Persons* para 14.

29 Ibid para 14.

30 'The Ofsted Report on the Education of Travelling Children' *Childright* September 1996 p10.

31 Ofsted report, see note 24.

They are treated as home students.[32] See also para 12.19. Asylum-seekers who are receiving means-tested benefits or receiving support from local authorities through the National Assistance Act 1948 should also be treated as home students.

Prisoners

11.60   Regulation 3(1) of the Young Offenders' Institutions, England and Wales Regulations 1988[33] states that the aim of a young offenders' institution shall be to help offenders to prepare for their return to the outside community. Regulation 3(2) states:

> The aim mentioned in paragraph (1) above shall be achieved, in particular, by –
> (a) providing a programme of activities, including education, training and work designed to assist offenders to acquire or develop personal responsibility, self discipline, physical fitness, interests and skills and to obtain suitable employment after release.

11.61   Regulation 34(1) states that an inmate must be occupied in education, training courses, work and physical education provided in accordance with reg 3. In all such activities, regard shall be paid to individual assessment and personal development (reg 3(2)). An inmate cannot be involved in these activities for more than eight hours a day (reg 3(4)).

11.62   Provision must be made for class teaching or private study within the working week and, as far as is practicable, in the evenings and weekends. Inmates under 17 must participate in education or training for at least 15 hours a week within the normal working week. In the case of those over 17 who are illiterate or backward, appropriate arrangements will be made within the week. Reasonable facilities will be made for women inmates over 21 who are serving a period of imprisonment or who are committed to prison for default (reg 34).

11.63   Training courses will also be provided, in accordance with directions of the secretary of state, which will improve prospects of employment on release (reg 36).

11.64   Arrangements will be made for male inmates to participate in physical education for at least two hours a week on average. For

32   Education (Fees and Awards) Regulations 1997 SI No 1972.
33   1998 SI No 1422.

those under the school leaving age, there will be at least one hour per day of physical education outside the hours allocated to education (reg 38(2)). This does not apply to females over 21. If they are not engaged in outdoor work or detained in an open institution, they will be given the opportunity for exercise in the open air for not less than one hour per day, weather permitting. In special circumstances the secretary of state may reduce this to half an hour. Physical exercise may be indoors instead of outside (reg 38(4))

11.65 Facilities must be provided for inmates in need of remedial physical activity (reg 38(3)).

11.66 The Prison Rules 1999[34] state that, if circumstances reasonably permit, a prisoner over 21 must be given the opportunity to participate in physical education for at least one hour a week (rule 29(1)). Facilities must be provided for prisoners under 21 to partake in physical recreation during the working week as well as in the evenings and at weekends and all convicted prisoners under 21 should have on average two hours per week of such activities (rule 29(2) and (3)). A medical officer must decide on the fitness of each prisoner and the above requirement can be modified (rule 29(4)).

11.67 The Prison Rules 1999 state the following on education and library facilities:

Rule 32
(1) Every prisoner able to profit from the education facilities provided at a prison shall be encouraged to do so
(2) Educational classes shall be arranged at every prison and, subject to any directions of the Secretary of State, reasonable facilities shall be afforded to prisoners who wish to do so to improve their education by training by distance learning, private study and recreational classes in their spare time.
(3) Special attention shall be paid to the education and training of prisoners with special educational needs, and if necessary they shall be taught within the hours normally allocated to work.
(4) In the case of a prisoner of compulsory school age as defined in section 8 of the Education Act 1996, arrangements shall be made for his participation in education or training courses for at least 15 hours a week within the normal working week

Rule 33
A library shall be provided in every prison and, subject to any directions of the Secretary of State, every prisoner shall be allowed to have library books and exchange them.

34 1999 SI No 728.

11.68   The reality is, however, that education in prisons can be disrupted by lack of staff to escort prisoners to classes or security issues which take precedence.

11.69   Education in prisons is the responsibility of the Home Office. Until 1992 LEAs were the providers in individual prisons. Since then it has been put out to tender and is provided by LEAs, FE colleges and private organisations. EA 1996 s562 (which is analogous with FHEA 1992 s60) states that no power or duty imposed under the Act relates to a person detained by the court or on recall but that an LEA, 'may make arrangements for [such] a person ... to receive the benefit of educational facilities provided by the authority'.

Children under school age

11.70   Local authorities must secure that there is sufficient provision in their area for nursery education, whether or not this is provided by themselves. Nursery education is defined by SSFA 1998 s118(1) as education for children under compulsory school age who have attained 'such age as may be prescribed'. This commences at the start of the first term after the child has reached the age of 4. If the child reaches 4 in the period between 1 April and the start of the summer term, between 1 September and the start of the autumn term or between 1 January and the start of the spring term, then the start of the term following is nursery education.[35] This reflects s1 of the Nursery Education and Grant Maintained Schools Act 1996 and Nursery Education (England) Regulations 1998,[36] which provide for the secretary of state to make arrangements for the payment of grants to LEAs and authorities and other persons in respect of nursery education provided by them. The Nursery Education (England) (Amendment) Regulations 1999[37] allow grants to be paid to accredited childminders.

11.71   LEAs are required to establish early years development partnerships for their area (SSFA 1998 s119(1)). They must have regard to any guidance from the secretary of state (s119(2)). These partnerships must work with LEAs to review the sufficiency of

---

35   Education (Nursery Education and Early Years Development) (England) Regulations 1999 SI No 1329 and Education (Nursery Education and Early Years Development) (Wales) Regulations 1999 SI No 1099.

36   1998 SI No 655.

37   1999 SI No 802.

provision in an area and prepare early years development plans under SSFA 1998 s120. These plans must be approved by the secretary of state (s121). It is open to the secretary of state to confer additional functions on the partnerships (s119(6)).

11.72   Under SSFA 1998 s122 and Sch 26, nursery education will be inspected by HM Inspector of Schools and registered nursery education inspectors. Education provided by LEAs, other provision receiving financial assistance from LEAs, education receiving grants under Nursery Education and Grant Maintained Schools Act 1996 s1 and education which LEAs are considering funding are all amenable to inspection. Inspections must take place at four-yearly intervals in England and six-yearly in Wales.[38] Ofsted is to be given new powers to regulate childcare services, which were previously monitored by local authority social services inspectors.

11.73   LEAs, persons providing relevant nursery education and persons employed to provide such assistance must have regard to the *Code of Practice on the Identification and Assessment of Special Educational Needs* (see paras 9.8–9.15) (SSFA 1998 s123). The Code may be expanded to include practical guidance (s123(2). Failing this, the secretary of state must provide such guidance (s123(3)).

11.74   SSFA 1998 s124 added a new s509A to EA 1996, giving LEAs the power to provide assistance with travel arrangements for children receiving nursery education not at a school. This could be by the provision of transport, or assistance with some or all of the travel costs. LEAs are entitled to ask parents for a contribution and to consider whether it is reasonable for other arrangements to be made for a child.

---

38 Nursery Education (England) Regulations 1998 SI No 655 and Education (Inspection of Nursery Education) (Wales) Regulations 1999 SI No 1441.

CHAPTER 12

Further and higher education

This chapter outlines briefly the definitions of further education (FE) and higher education (HE), describing the different institutions in which they are provided. It includes the special responsibilities of LEAs towards students with learning difficulties and the arrangements for funding courses and students. Finally, it discusses the situations when students may have complaints about their treatment by an institution, for instance with respect to admissions, discipline or failure on a course.

For complete chapter contents, see overleaf

Further education

12.1 The Further and Higher Education Act (FHEA) 1992 ss2–3 redefined the FE sector, which is now the responsibility of the Further Education Funding Council for England (FEFC) and the Further Education Funding Council for Wales (FEFCW) (see paras 2.14–2.15). In June 1999 the government issued a white paper, *Learning to Succeed: a new framework for post-16 learning* (Cm 4392), which proposes the abolition of the FEFC and the Training and Enterprise Councils (TECs). These would be replaced by a Learning and Skills Council to cover all post-16 learning except HE.

12.2 Pupils over 16 but under the age of 19 being educated full-time at a school with pupils of compulsory school age are by definition still secondary school pupils (EA 1996 s2(2)). If a pupil begins a course of secondary education before reaching the age of 18 and continues to attend the course, the education remains by definition secondary education even after the pupil attains the age of 19 (EA 1996 s2(5)).

12.3 Further education covers full-time education for those over compulsory school age but who have not reached the age of 19 (EA 1996 s2(4)). It also covers full-time education for those of 19 and over if it is not HE[1] (EA 1996 s2(3)(a)) and part-time education for people over compulsory school age, including vocational, social, physical and recreational training and leisure time activities (EA 1996 s2(3)). This includes what is commonly known as adult education. Those in the FE sector are not pupils because a 'pupil' is defined as a person receiving education at school other than someone of 19 or older receiving further education or part-time education (EA 1996 s3).

12.4 Apart from full-time education for those between the ages of 16 and 18 under FHEA 1992 s2, further education courses are described under s3 and Sch 2 as:

1) courses for vocational qualifications approved by the Secretary of State for Education and Employment;
2) preparation for GCSE, A or AS level examinations;
3) 'access' courses preparing for higher education;
4) 'return to learn' courses;
5) basic literacy in English courses;
6) courses in English for speakers of other languages;
7) basic mathematics courses;
8) courses on literacy in Welsh;
9) courses teaching independent living and communication skills to

1 HE can be provided in the FE sector and vice versa.

people with learning difficulties which prepare them for entry to a course described in (4)–(8) above.

This is known as Sch 2 provision.

FE institutions

12.5   Further education is usually provided not at a school but at a further education institution. These are institutions conducted by further education corporations (FHEA 1992 s91(3)(a)). From 1 April 1993, by FHEA 1992 s15,[2] the following were re-established as independent FE corporations:

– most FE colleges
– LEA maintained sixth form colleges and others which were already grant maintained.

FHEA 1992 s16 allows for the incorporation of other further education corporations under regulations.[3] By FHEA 1992 s47 the secretary of state can transfer a higher education corporation to the further education sector. Much further education provision was consequently taken out of LEA control.

12.6   The secretary of state also has the power under FHEA 1992 s28 to designate certain other educational institutions to receive support from the FEFC. These must cater principally for 16- to 18-year-olds and be one of:

1) a voluntary aided school (eg, sixth form college);
2) a non-school institution assisted by an LEA (eg, agricultural or horticultural college);
3) an institution which is not receiving support from an LEA but is receiving or is eligible for grant aid under EA 1996 s485 (eg art, design or performing arts college or long-term residential college for adults).

Governance and funding

12.7   The status of the institution is relevant to its government, its funding and the involvement of the FEFC.

12.8   All FE corporations have to be governed according to the same constitution which is prescribed by the secretary of state using

---

2   Education (Further Education Corporations) Order 1992 SI No 2097 art 3.

3   Butterworth's *The Law of Education* at B822–3 lists about 30 statutory instruments between 1992 and 1996 incorporating individual institutions.

powers under FHEA 1992 s20.[4] A person under 18 is ineligible for membership of the governing body except as the nominated student member,[5] whose rights to participate and vote are limited in any event.[6] The meetings need not be in public. Minutes and papers are to be open to inspection, though there is a specific provision to exclude any material relating to a named student at, or candidate for admission to, the institution.[7]

12.9   Designated institutions are required by FHEA 1992 s29, as are institutions conducted by a company (FHEA 1992 s30), to have an instrument of government which is effectively approved by the secretary of state. This does not apply to an unincorporated association if the order designating the institution provided for its exemption (FHEA 1992 s29(1)(b)). This covers such cases as the Workers' Educational Association (WEA) which is not a college and does not have an instrument or articles of government. The instruments of government of what was formerly a voluntary aided school must have as the majority of governors those who will preserve the character of the institution at the time of incorporation (FHEA 1992 s30). Broadly the status of the college and the composition of its governing body remain as they were before designation.

12.10   FEFCs have to secure the provision of sufficient full-time education for 16- to 18-year-olds in their area (FHEA 1992 s2). Under FHEA 1992 s2(4), an FEFC has the power to make provision for people not in its area and over 19. It must avoid provision which might give rise to disproportionate expenditure (FHEA 1992 s2(5). It must secure the provision of adequate facilities for Sch 2 work for the population of their area (FHEA 1992 s3(1)). In making provision it must have regard to education of the same kind provided by schools, city technology colleges and city colleges for the technology of the arts (FHEA 1992 s3(6). It can also make provision of Sch 2 work for people not in its area and also non-Sch 2 work, although the duty to secure such provision rests with the LEAs (FHEA 1992 s3(3), as amended by Teaching and Higher Education Act (THEA) 1998

---

4   Education (Government of Further Education Corporations) (Former Sixth Form Colleges) Regulations 1992 SI No 1957 Sch 1 and Education (Government of Further Education Corporations) (Former Further Education Colleges) Regulations 1992 SI No 1963 Sch 1.

5   Education (No 2) Act 1986 s61. A school student under 18 has no such right (see para 2.17).

6   1992 SI No 1957 and 1992 SI No 1963 para 13(6).

7   1992 SI No 1957 and 1992 SI No 1963 para 16(2).

s36). Institutions outside the FE sector can still apply for funding via a sponsoring body within the sector (FHEA 1992 s6(5)). The FEFCs receive grants from the secretary of state on terms and conditions but these must not relate to individual institutions (FHEA 1992 s7).

12.11   By FHEA 1992 s5, financial support is given to governing bodies; it may even be provided for the establishment of an institution (s5(3)). It may also be given to any person other than an LEA, a city technology college or a city college for the technology of the arts for the provision of training or advice or research relevant to the provision of facilities for further education (s5(5)). Only in the case of a person with learning difficulties (see paras 12.30–12.32) may the FEFC pay for individual education and support. The FEFCs must comply with any directions made by the secretary of state (FHEA 1992 s81 and EA 1994 s8).

12.12   Under the Education (Grant) Regulations 1990,[8] the secretary of state may pay grants to the governing body of any FE institution which is non-profit-making and not run by an LEA (regs 7 and 8). S/he may also pay grants to any associations involved in having the promotion of the education of adults, such as the WEA (regs 10 and 11). S/he may also provide grants for informal vocational, social, physical and recreational training not for profit or in an educational institution (reg 12).

12.13   The FEFCs are entitled to whatever information they may require from FE institutions (FHEA 1992 s54). They may make arrangements for persons to carry out studies designed to improve economy, efficiency and effectiveness in any institution (FHEA 1992 s83(1)). Each FEFC must ensure that provision is made for assessing the quality of education in institutions and must set up a 'quality assessment committee' under FHEA 1992 s9(1) to advise on this. Under FHEA 1992 s55, the inspection of local education authority institutions is a matter for HM Chief Inspector of Schools (see paras 12.22–12.25). Under THEA 1998 s34 s/he now has the power to inspect work-based vocational education. Under the white paper *Learning to Succeed* (see para 12.1), Ofsted would be responsible for inspecting FE for 16- to 19-year-olds and there would be a new inspectorate for 19+ provision, work-based training and adult and community education.

8   1990 SI No 1989 as amended by 1997 SI No 678.

Information, admissions and fees

12.14   The governing body of every FE institution is obliged by law to publish annually details of (inter alia) numbers and achievements of GCSE A and AS level entrants and students preparing for vocational qualifications, broken down into the 16–18 and 19 and over age groups.[9] Copies must be provided to anyone who asks in person, as well as to public libraries, training and enterprise councils (TECs) and careers offices. They must also be given to all special schools which provide secondary education and CTCs and CCTAs, for distribution by them. All pupils/students in year 2 of key stage 4 are entitled at least to access to a copy.

12.15   ERA 1988 s159 empowers the secretary of state to make regulations requiring LEAs to publish details of educational provision and achievement in FE institutions maintained by them which offer full-time education. No regulations have yet been issued, which may reflect the fact that, although LEAs have a duty to secure the provision of non-Sch 2 work, there is likely to be a limited amount of full-time provision.

12.16   There is no statutory procedure governing the admission arrangements to FE institutions. Colleges can accept students from any geographical area. Individual colleges may have their own admission criteria, eg, giving priority to students continuing their studies or who had been on a waiting list.

12.17   Paragraph 69 of DFE Circular 1/93[10] emphasises that LEAs must continue to maintain and develop progression routes from courses they provide to those which fall under FHEA 1992 Sch 2.

12.18   The FEFC has power under FHEA 1992 s52 to require an institution in the FE sector which provides full-time education for 16–18 year olds to provide education for a named individual. It is intended that this power is to be used only in exceptional circumstances. See paras 12.32–12.34 for the arrangements established by the FEFC for supporting a place in an institution outside the FE sector.

12.19   Under 1992 SI No 1963 para 16, the further education corporation decides the tuition and other fees paid to itself subject to

9   Education (Further Education Institutions Information) (England) Regulations 1995 SI No 2065; Education (Further Education Institutions Information) (Wales) Regulations 1993 SI No 2169 under FHEA s50. See also DfEE Circular 9/95 *Local publication and distribution of information about the achievements of students in Further Education sector colleges.*

10   DFE Circular 1/93 *Further and Higher Education Act 1992.*

any terms and conditions attached to any grants loans or payments from the FEFCs. Generally, students between the ages of 16 and 18 on a full-time course will not pay tuition fees. Students on benefits will usually get concessionary fees. THEA 1998 s26(1)(2) will allow the secretary of state to impose conditions in relation to grants to the FEFC, which will then put conditions on the payment of grants to governing bodies. The governing body must ensure that, in a particular academic year, a specified class of persons attending courses of specified description shall not pay fees. This does not apply to students not having a specified connection with the UK who, under Education (Fees and Awards) Act 1983 s1, may be required to pay higher fees.[11]

12.20   The Chancellor of the Exchequer is to run pilot schemes in 12 areas where the number of school leavers is above the average. Students aged 16 to 18 at further education institutions (or schools) coming from households with less than £13,000 a year income will receive up to £40 per week.[12]

12.21   By THEA 1998 s32, a new s63A was added to the Employment Rights Act 1996, with effect from 1 September 1999, giving employees aged 16 or 17 reasonable time off work for study or training if they have not attained a sufficient standard of achievement as prescribed in regulations.[13]

Provision of other FE by LEAs

12.22   Under EA 1996 s15, and subject to the above, LEAs still have statutory responsibility for securing adequate facilities in their area for further education. This does not include education to which FHEA 1992 s2(1) applies, that is full-time education for persons over compulsory school age and under the age of 19. Nor does it include education under FHEA 1992 s3(1), that is part-time education for anyone over compulsory school age or full-time education for those over 19 of the type specified in FHEA 1992 Sch 2. However, the LEA may provide this kind of education under EA 1996 s15(3). It may provide for people outside its area (EA 1996 s15(4)). It may, however, take into account educational facilities provided by educational

---

11 Education (Fees and Awards) Regulations 1997 SI No 1972.
12 The areas are Bolton, Nottingham, Cornwall, Doncaster, Gateshead, Leeds, Middlesbrough, Oldham, Southampton, Stoke on Trent, Walsall and the London boroughs of Lambeth, Lewisham, Southwark and Greenwich.
13 See also Right to Time Off for Study or Training Regulations 1999 SI No 986.

institutions and other bodies in their area (EA 1996 s15(5)). By EA 1996 s2, further education is defined as:

(a) full-time and part-time education suitable to the requirements of persons who are over compulsory school age (including vocational, social, physical and recreational training), and

(b) organised leisure-time occupation provided in connection with the provision of such education.

'Organised leisure-time occupation' means cultural training and recreative activities suitable to the requirements of anybody over 16 who is able and willing to profit from the facilities (EA 1996 s2(6)).

12.23   A specific duty is imposed on LEAs by EA 1996 s15(5)(b) to have regard to the requirements of people over 16 with learning difficulties (see para 12.30).

12.24   LEAs' responsibility to provide youth services is described in EA 1996 s508. An LEA shall secure that facilities for further education include adequate facilities for recreation and social and physical training (EA 1996 s508(2)). For that purpose an LEA:

(a) may establish, maintain and manage, or assist the establishment, maintenance and management of –
(i) camps, holiday classes, playing fields, play centres, and
(ii) other places, including playgrounds, gymnasiums and swimming baths not appropriated to any school or other educational institution ...

(b) may organise games, expeditions and other activities ...

(c) may defray, or contribute towards, the expenses of such games, expeditions and other activities.

When making these arrangements, an LEA must co-operate with voluntary organisations who have similar objectives.

12.25   An LEA or the governing body of a school may make arrangements with a further education corporation or designated institution for secondary education to be provided to pupils in key stage 4 (FHEA 1992 s18). By s52A (inserted by SSFA 1998 113(2)), this must be kept separate from the education of those of 19 and over. The Education (Secondary Education in Further Education Institutions) Regulations 1999[14] allow the pupils and students to be taught together as long as there is a teacher in the room. Furthermore, the provision of FE in schools is lawful as long as a school teacher or FE teacher is present.[15]

14 1999 SI No 954.
15 Education (Further Education in Schools) Regulations 1999 SI No 1867.

Careers advice and guidance

12.26   Under EA 1997 ss44 and 45, FE institutions are under the same obligations as schools as regards access by the careers service and availability of materials (see paras 4.32–4.35). Section 46 enables regulations to be issued providing for a programme of careers education. Under the Employment and Training Act (ETA) 1973 s8, the secretary of state now has a duty to secure the provision of services for full-time or part-time FE students to receive free advice and guidance regarding employment, training and education, including further and higher education. People under 21 who have left school or FE up to two years earlier also qualify for free help from the careers service. The Chief Inspector of Schools in Wales now has powers under THEA 1998 s35 to inspect the careers service in Wales.

12.27   These services were provided by LEAs until 1 January 1994 but are now generally contracted out.[16] The secretary of state retains powers to make independent arrangements as well as directing LEAs to contract out this provision.[17]

12.28   One result of this contracting out appears to be a severe decline in the quality and extent of careers advice which is available. It is submitted that the secretary of state and LEAs are now habitually failing in their statutory responsibilities in this area. It is not clear (to the authors) whether such a failure can be judicially reviewed at the instance of an individual student. This is in effect a target duty and there appears to be no direct statutory duty on the secretary of state in the delivery of the service; s/he may give a direction or make arrangements for this with LEAs and others (ETA 1973 s10(8)).

12.29   Circular 1/93[18] seems to envisage that TECs would work closely with LEAs to provide networks of guidance for people at work and the secretary of state may direct LEAs to do so. This development is likely to detract from the ability of the LEA to give guidance about education which is not linked with a job or career plan. The emphasis on work-related training is confirmed by the new power in ETA 1973 s10(10)[19] for LEAs to charge for their services.[20] It is clear,

16 ETA 1973 s10A, inserted by Trade Union Reform and Employment Rights Act 1993 s46.
17 The services and standards applicable to careers services are specified in *The Requirements and Guidance for Careers Services*, DfEE February 1998.
18 DFE Circular 1/93 *Further and Higher Education Act 1992.*
19 Inserted by Trade Union Reform and Employment Rights Act 1993 s45.
20 DFE Circular 1/93 paras 129–131.

however, that the secretary of state and the LEAs must have regard to the requirements of disabled people, including those with learning difficulties, in making arrangements for the provision of services (ETA 1973 s10(1) and (2)).

Students with learning difficulties

General duties

12.30 Under EA 1996 s528, LEAs are required to publish statements about the provision of facilities for FE of disabled persons under Disability Discrimination Act 1995.

12.31 The specific duty imposed by EA 1996 s15(5)(b) to have regard to the requirements of people over 16 with learning difficulties (see para 12.23) was held in *R v Islington LBC ex p Rixon*[21] to be a target duty. However, the court held that the LEA had to take conscientiously into account the guidance issued by the DFE in Circular 1/93 paras 71 and 72:

Students with learning difficulties

71 LEAs' duties and powers in relation to further education ... apply equally to students with learning difficulties. Moreover, in exercising those functions, LEAs continue to be under a specific duty, under s11(8) of FHEA 1992 [now EA 1996 s15(5)(b)], to have regard to the requirements of this group of students. The definition of the term learning difficulty, which is carried over from previous legislation, includes all types of disability. The Government's aim is that, so far as is consistent with LEAs' other obligations, learning difficulties should be no bar to access to further education.

72 It remains a matter for LEAs to determine what facilities they should make available in pursuit of their continuing duty to ensure that adequate provision, of the kind not falling within [FHEA 1992] Schedule 2, is available for those aged 19 and over with learning difficulties. In discharging this duty, LEAs should ensure that adequate arrangements exist for assessing the needs of these students and identifying the provision that will be appropriate, and for the provision of such support services as are necessary. Where students with learning difficulties are moving from LEA provision to the new further education sector, LEAs will need to liaise in appropriate cases with colleges and the Further Education Funding Council to ensure the identification of suitable provision. Information about the individual's needs which has been built up during a period of LEA provision, and possibly incorporated in a

21 [1998] CCLR 119; [1997] ELR 66, QBD.

statement, will be of particular value to the assessment. Account should, however, be taken of the views of the individual concerned about the confidentiality of this information.

Individual students

12.32   Under FHEA 1992 s4, the FEFCs are given a similar duty to that of LEAs to have regard to the requirements of persons with learning difficulties in carrying out their functions in respect of FE. 'Learning difficulties' is defined in s4(6) in the same terms as EA 1996 s312(2).

12.33   If it finds that the facilities available within the FE (or HE) sector are not adequate for an individual under 25 and it is in his/her best interests to do so, the FEFC must secure provision for him/her at an institution outside those sectors (FHEA 1992 s4(3)), including boarding if that is necessary or the only way of obtaining the facilities (s4(4) and (5)). Under FHEA 1992 s5(4) an FEFC may give financial support to an individual (not an LEA, a city technology college or city college for the technology of the arts) for provision under FHEA 1992 s4(3)–(5). Under FHEA 1992 s19(3), a further education corporation may provide facilities of any kind, including boarding accommodation or recreational facilities for students with learning difficulties. An FEFC can require a governing body to provide full-time education for a named individual under the age of 19 as is appropriate to his/her abilities and aptitudes (FHEA 1992 s52). This is intended to secure provision for a young person with special educational needs for whom a place could not otherwise be found.[22]

12.34   For everyone else aged over 16 with learning difficulties, the FEFC is still has a power to secure education outside the FE sector, including boarding provision. Presumably it will have regard to the availability of facilities through the district health authority and social services department. The latter are limited to non-educational facilities.[23]

12.35   The FEFCs issue circular instructions early in each calendar year about the identification of suitable placements and method of application in an individual case. There seems to be no statutory basis for this. An arrangement operates by agreement with the Local Government Association whereby the FEFC appears to be substantially reliant on assessments, information and recommendations provided by the relevant LEA. It is not easy to see whether

---

22   See FEFC Circular 99/02 *Arrangements for Students with Learning Difficulties and/or Disabilities Requiring Provision in 1999–2000.*

23   See FEFC Circular 99/05 *The Council's Aims.*

these arrangements are working satisfactorily. As already mentioned, the careers service of the LEA now has a diminished interest in further education institutions and the available provision. Where the prospective FE student already has the benefit of a statement of special educational needs (SEN) there is still a tendency on the part of the LEA to neglect its ongoing duties under the statement. There will sometimes be scope for court action here.

12.36   The LEA has to carry out the procedures under the current FEFC circular for identifying whether the FEFC or the LEA should fund the education of a 16- to 18-year-old. If the LEA is unable or unwilling to submit a proposal for an individual student, application can be made direct to the FEFC by the student or his/her parents.[24] A statement of SEN refers to the reasonably immediate future and an LEA is obliged to continue the provision in the pupil's statement notwithstanding that s/he is over 16 and no longer on the roll of the school specified in part 4 of the statement. The LEA's duty (under EA 1996 s321) towards a (statemented) child with SEN outweighs that of the FEFC under FHEA 1992 ss2 and 4. An LEA cannot divest itself of this responsibility when the child reaches 16 by failing to include the name of a school in the statement if his/her needs continue to be met most appropriately in a school.[25] The proper procedure would be to amend or cease to maintain the statement.[26]

12.37   However, in *R v Oxfordshire CC ex p B*,[27] where the LEA had an established policy of educating pupils in special schools up to age 16 only and decided to cease the statement of an 18-year-old because it was satisfied that his future special needs would be appropriately met by an FE college under the auspices of the FEFC, the LEA's decision was upheld by the Court of Appeal. That case was decided under EA 1981. The court commented that FHEA ss4(3) and 5(4) had made the system more rigid by withdrawing the option of FEFC funding in a maintained school placement.

12.38   There is a serious practical problem in obtaining useful information for the FEFC from an LEA which no longer maintains a statement of SEN for a person with learning difficulties. The FEFC

---

24 The current circular (FEFC Circular 99/02) contains 26 pages of guidance as well as recommendation forms, which are available on disk. Applications for a particular academic year must reach the FEFC by the preceding May.

25 *R v Dorset CC and FEFC ex p Goddard* [1995] ELR 109, QBD.

26 However, unless the child is a registered pupil, the parent will have no right to pursue an appeal to the Special Educational Needs Tribunal: EA 1996 ss312(5) and 321(a) and (b), and Sch 27 paras 9–11.

27 [1997] ELR 90, CA.

will want to study the defunct statement before deciding whether to undertake its own assessment. There may be serious criticisms of the material in the LEA's assessments. In practice, the FEFC will be slow to agree to make its own assessment in a case where the LEA does not consider that provision outside the FE sector would be appropriate. In such a case, it may be desirable to arrange for an assessment and report from an independent educational psychologist who has had the opportunity to consider what the FE sector offers and can provide a reasoned argument for the chosen provision. This is likely to be a costly exercise because of the amount of work involved.

12.39　　　It should be noted that the secretary of state, in securing careers services for school and college students, is obliged to have regard to the requirements of disabled persons (ETA 1973 s10(1)).

Higher education

12.40　FHEA s62 established a Higher Education Funding Council (HEFC) for England and a separate one for Wales (HEFCW). These replaced the Universities Funding Council and the Polytechnics and Colleges Funding Council established by ERA 1988.

12.41　　　Higher education courses may be distinguished from FE. They are defined in ERA 1988 s120(1) and Sch 6, and reiterated in FHEA 1992 s90(1), as courses for:

1) further training of teachers or youth and community workers;
2) post-graduates (including higher degrees);
3) first degrees;
4) Diploma of Higher Education;
5) HND, HNC (Business and Technician Education Council), Diploma in Management Studies;
6) Certificate in Education;
7) preparation for a professional examination at higher level (ie, a course that is higher than an A level GCE or an HNC or an HND);
8) providing education at a higher level, whether or not in preparation for an examination (ie, the standard is higher than the standard of courses providing education in preparation for any of the examinations in (7)).

This is a only a partial definition and relates to that provision which was provided by LEA institutions prior to the ERA 1988.

HE institutions

12.42 A higher education institution is defined by FHEA 1992 s65(5) for the purposes of funding from an HEFC as a university, an institute conducted by a higher education corporation or a designated institution. A designated institution is defined in ERA 1988 s129 as an institution where the full-time equivalent enrolment number for courses of higher education exceeds 55 per cent of the total.

12.43 Universities are roughly divided into two types. There are those established before 1992 under either a charter or an Act of Parliament and which come under the jurisdiction of the visitor (see paras 12.52 and 12.80). In addition, higher education institutions and designated institutions may now be called universities under FHEA 1992 s77 – but see also THEA 1998 s39–40.

12.44 Before 1988 LEAs were responsible for most higher education which came under the definition of further education (within EA 1944 s41), apart from universities. By that Act, higher education corporations and designated institutions were established outside the control of the LEAs. LEAs still have the power under ERA 1988 s120(3) as amended by FHEA 1992 to secure for their area facilities for higher education as appear appropriate for meeting the needs of their area. They may also provide this for people outside their area. Regard must be had to other provision in their area.

12.45 The government of bodies conducting higher education varies, depending whether it is a higher education corporation established under the ERA 1988, a designated institution or a university founded prior to FHEA 1992.

HE corporations

12.46 These were first established by ERA 1988 s121. New corporations can be established by ERA 1988 s122(1) where, in relation to an institution maintained by an LEA, its full-time equivalent enrolment number on courses of higher education exceeds 55 per cent. Further education corporations may also become higher education corporations if the circumstances referred to above apply (ERA 1988 s122A as inserted by FHEA 1992 s74(1)).

12.47 The constitutions differ depending on when they were established. Those established before 6 May 1992 are subject to provisions specifying the initial constitution of the corporation. Those established after this date have instruments of government prescribed by order of the Privy Council. All corporations must have articles of government as well as an instrument of government (ERA s124A and inserted by FHEA 1992 s71(1)).

12.48   A higher education corporation has the power to provide further and higher education, to conduct research and publish this (ERA 1988 s124).

Designated institutions

12.49   A designated institution is either an institution (see para 12.42 with over 55 per cent of its provision being courses of higher education or an institution conducted by a successor company to a higher education corporation (ERA 1988 s129(5)).

12.50   A designated institution not conducted by a company or established by Royal Charter must have an instrument and articles of government which must be approved by the Privy Council (ERA 1988 s129A, inserted by FHEA 1992 s73).

12.51   An institution conducted by a company must have articles of association which must incorporate instruments and articles of government. The Privy Council, after consulting the persons in control, directs them to amend the memorandum or articles of association (ERA 1988 s129B inserted by FHEA 1992 s73).

Universities established before 1992

12.52   Established by either Royal Charter or Act of Parliament, these all have different constitutions and governing instruments. Many have a 'visitor' who has the power to settle disputes between members, to inspect and regulate their actions and behaviour and generally to correct all abuses and irregularities in the administration of the charity. Where there is a visitor the jurisdiction of the courts is limited.[28]

Funding

12.53   The secretary of state has the power to give grants to the HEFCs on certain conditions (FHEA 1992 s68). These conditions may not apply to individual institutions, courses or research or criteria for the appointment of academic staff or student admissions. THEA 1998 s26(4) allows the secretary of state to impose conditions on the payments of grants, loans or other payments to any specified

28   See *R v Hull University Visitor ex p Page* [1993] AC 682, HL.

institution.[29] These conditions mean that the fees of any prescribed class of person attending courses of a prescribed description[30] must be equal to the prescribed amount (defined in THEA 1998 s22(2)(b) as the maximum amount of grant or loan available to someone in any academic year). This requirement does not apply to 'overseas' students (THEA 1998 s26(7)). The secretary of state is unable to discriminate between different courses of initial teacher training, other courses or research, depending on the subjects studied (THEA 1998 s26(8)).

12.54   The HEFCs provide the above funding for activities carried on by higher education institutions, including pre-1992 universities (FHEA 1992 s65). Grants can also be made for provision in institutions maintained or assisted by an LEA or to institutions in the further education sector for prescribed courses of higher education (FHEA 1992 s65(2)(c). Terms and conditions can be imposed on any payments (FHEA 1992 s65(3)(a)). These may only be imposed after consultation with appropriate bodies (FHEA 1992 s66(1)). It is a requirement of funding that all governing bodies must publish disability statements (FHEA 1992 s65(4A), as inserted by Disability Discrimination Act 1995 s30(6)). In providing funding, the HEFCs must have regard to the desirability of not discouraging institutions from developing funding from other sources (FHEA 1992 s66(3)).

12.55   The HEFCs have a duty to assess the quality of education in the higher education sector (FHEA 1992 s70(1)(a)) and to establish a quality assessment committee (FHEA 1992 s70(1)(b)). The councils have the power to arrange for a person to conduct studies designed to improve economy, efficiency and effectiveness in the management or operations of an institute (FHEA 1992 s83(1)). By FHEA 1992 s69(1), the councils must provide the secretary of state with such information as s/he may require. They are empowered to obtain information from an LEA, the governing body of a higher education institution or of an institution where prescribed courses of higher education are provided (FHEA 1992 s79).

29   Education (Fees at Higher Education Institutions) Regulations 1999 SI No 603, with effect from 31 March 1999.
30   Education (Student Support) Regulations 1999 SI No 496.

Information, admissions and fees

12.56   There is no statutory requirement for the publication of information on the higher education sector. All institutions make their own admissions arrangements and criteria. Most applications for first degree courses and HNDs are made through the Universities and Colleges Admission Service (UCAS), although this is not obligatory. This is essentially a clearing house which is funded by successful applicants and the institutions.

12.57   Institutions are able to make their own fee arrangements. But see para 12.19 in relation to further education and the ability to charge higher fees to certain students.

Grants, loans and maintenance

12.58   Awards for further and higher education were governed by EA 1962 s1 for mandatory grants and s2 for discretionary awards. This Act has been effectively repealed by THEA 1998 Part 2. This proposes a new system of financial support in the form of grants and/or loans to students on courses of further or higher education. Students may now be liable for some of their tuition fees. THEA 1998 s22(2)–(5) include provisions for determining if a student is an 'eligible' student, the maximum grant or loan for any prescribed purpose, how these might vary depending on a student's circumstances, and conditions and terms for making or repayment. The Education (Student Loans) Act 1990 has also been effectively replaced, subject to detailed savings for students already in receipt of loans. Under THEA 1998 s23, the secretary of state can transfer or delegate his/her functions under s22 to another body, ie, an LEA or the governing body of an institution where eligible students are attending courses. See also para 6.41 for the possible availability of grants, bursaries etc under EA 1996 s518.

12.59   The Education (Student Support) Regulations 1999,[31] under THEA 1998 s22, provide for grants for fees, loans for maintenance and supplementary grants for maintenance for eligible students on higher education courses from 1 September 1999. The following courses are designated under reg 5 and Sch 2 of the regulations:

1) first degree course;
2) course for the Diploma of Higher Education;

31 1999 SI No 496.

3) course for an HNC or HND;
4) course for initial training of teachers, including one leading to a first degree;
5) course for the further training of teachers or youth and community workers;
6) course in preparation for a professional exam at standard higher than GCSE 'A' level, or HNC or HND;
7) course providing education of a higher standard than in (6).

12.60 Grants are available for fees up to a maximum amount of £1,025 (para 11); they are also available for living costs (para 12), for disabled students' living costs (para 13), for students who have left care (para 14), for dependants (para 15) and for travel (para 16). These are means-tested. In addition, students are eligible for loans towards their living costs (paras 18 and 19). Eligible students are defined in Schedule 1. The Social Security (Students) (Amendment) Regulations 1999[32] amend regulations on state benefits to take account of the new system of student grants and loans.

12.61 Traditionally the machinery for mandatory awards to be given by LEAs has been set out for each academic year by the Education (Mandatory Awards) Regulations. Under the 1999 regulations,[33] students who began courses before 1 September 1998 and certain other students will be eligible for awards under the old scheme, ie, a full award for tuition fees and a means-tested maintenance allowance to cover approximately half of the overall support for maintenance from public funds. Students who began courses between 1 September 1998 and 31 August 1999 will be eligible for a transitional award of a smaller amount paid first in respect of maintenance and any balance for fees.

12.62 The 1999 regulations also enlarge the category of independent students (reg 3) by including those who are 'irreconcilably estranged' from their parents. Further support is provided to those who have left care or custody.

12.63 Education (Fees and Awards) Act 1983 s2 and Education (Fees and Awards) Regulations 1997[34] reg 5 allow authorities to adopt rules of eligibility for awards. Regulation 13(1) of the Education (Mandatory Awards) Regulations 1999 states that an authority will not be under a duty to give awards if:

32 1999 SI No 1935.
33 1999 SI No 1494 as amended by 1999 SI No 1824.
34 1997 SI No 1972.

1) a person has not been ordinarily resident in Britain for three years before the start of the course (or, in certain circumstances, in the European Economic Area (see reg 13(3));
2) his/her residence has been wholly or mainly to attend full-time education;
3) s/he is not settled in the UK within the meaning of the Immigration Act 1971 (ie, with no restrictions);
4) s/he has, in the opinion of the authority, shown him/herself by his/her conduct to be unfitted to receive an award.

Ordinarily resident is defined in EA 1962 Sch 1 and modified by 1998 SI No 1166 reg 8. This largely adopts (without reference to 'settled purpose') the definition formulated by the House of Lords in *Shah v Barnet LBC*.[35]

12.64   Where the course is not one designated for grant, the LEA must exercise its discretion and allow a proper opportunity for representations for special consideration.[36] A fairly common problem in practice is delay in processing the application. The institution will usually agree not to expel the student if it appears that legal action to obtain the award will be taken if necessary.

12.65   Where the residence test is not satisfied, the LEA for the area where the student is attending the course is required to bestow a 'fees only' award under the Education (Mandatory Awards) Regulations 1998 reg 7(b).

Discretionary grants

12.66   LEAs had a discretionary power under EA 1962 s2 to make awards in respect of attendance at full-time or part-time courses not covered by s1 of that Act for those over compulsory school age, eg, part-time courses at further education institutions but not post-graduate courses except teacher training (PGCE). It is likely that these powers will remain under THEA 1998 ss22 and 23. By EA 1996 s518, as amended by SSFA 1998 s129, and Local Education Authority (Post-Compulsory Education Awards) Regulations 1999,[37] LEAs may grant scholarships, exhibitions, bursaries and other allowances to people over compulsory school age in order that they may take advantage of educational facilities available to them. An LEA may determine not

---

35   [1983] 2 AC 309; [1983] 1 All ER 226, HL.
36   *R v Bexley LBC ex p Jones* [1995] ELR 42, QBD.
37   1999 SI No 229.

to exercise its power in any financial year but must do so in advance of that year. Regulation 5 of the Education (Fees and Awards) Regulations 1997[38] makes it lawful for LEAs to adopt rules confining eligibility in relation to discretionary awards.

12.67   It is important to look at the way in which the LEA has arrived at and formulated its policy on discretionary awards; and how it is applied to a particular application. In *R v Warwickshire CC ex p Collymore*,[39] a policy of making no new discretionary awards prevented consideration of applications. But it is not necessary for the LEA to have a budget for such awards.[40] As with all policy considerations, a challenge by way of judicial review will fail if the LEA can show that it would depart from the policy if there were special circumstances.

12.68   There is some guidance on policy in Circular 1/93[41] paras 101–103. For example, LEAs must not discriminate against institutions on the grounds of their location or source of funding. They are encouraged to support students with learning difficulties who are not on Sch 2 courses, and even to top up the support for those whose Sch 2 educational costs and residential charges are being met by the FEFC. Since there is no statutory provision for a maintenance grant comparable to that in the Education (Mandatory Awards) Regulations 1998, it is arguable that LEAs should have a policy on the maintenance of students, particularly those with learning difficulties.

Other help with maintenance

Minor awards

12.69   Minor awards (see paras 6.40–6.41) are payable by LEAs to enable impecunious students to take advantage of educational facilities without hardship. It is worth noting that, under Scholarships and Other Benefits Regulations 1977[42] reg 4(e)(ii), students pursuing correspondence courses in subjects of FE may be eligible to receive an award.

---

38   1997 SI No 1972.
39   1995] ELR 217, QBD.
40   *R v Warwickshire CC ex p Williams* [1995] ELR 326, QBD.
41   DFE Circular 1/93 *Further and Higher Education Act 1992.*

Benefits

12.70   Under Income Support (General) Regulations 1987 reg 61, a person is a student while s/he is attending a full-time course of study, including periods of vacation within the course. This does not apply to intercalated periods of suspension of studies, so benefit is payable during such periods.[43] In disputes about entitlement to benefit, the description of the course by the education authority (ie, full-time or part-time) is usually conclusive for practical purposes.[44] Where the LEA has demanded repayment of a grant because the student abandoned the course, the amount repayable has ceased to have the character of 'income' and is not to be taken into account by the Benefits Agency as his/her income from the date of the demand.[45] Receipt of a maintenance grant results in limited disregard for travel expenses, the cost of books etc in computing eligibility for income support, even when the whole grant money was spent on travel.[46]

Transport

12.71   FHEA 1992 Sch 8 extended the EA 1996 s509 duty of LEAs (see paras 6.57–6.66) to cover students at any college in the FE sector. They are not permitted to treat FE students less favourably than school students of the same age.

12.72   If the FEFC has placed a student with learning difficulties at an institution outside the FE and HE sectors, the transport duties nonetheless apply to the LEA. Guidance on transport policy is given in Circular 1/93 paras 106–114. It is emphasised that decisions about individuals cannot be taken on policy grounds, without considering the individual circumstances and representations.

12.73   There are also overlapping duties on social services departments to provide transport for disabled students under Chronically Sick and Disabled Persons Act 1970 s2(1).

---

42   1977 SI No 1443.
43   *Chief Adjudication Officer and Secretary of State for Social Security v Clarke* [1995] ELR 259, CA.
44   *Denton v Chief Adjudication Officer* [1999] ELR 86, CA.
45   *Leeves v Chief Adjudication Officer* [1999] ELR 90, CA.
46   Income Support (General) Regulations 1987 SI No 1967 and *Alexander v Chief Adjudication Officer* [1998] ELR 455, CA.

Complaints

12.74   Most complaints concern the assessment of academic performance and rejection of academic or practical coursework. These are sometimes presented as complaints about unfairness in assessment arrangements or denying extensions of time in which to submit written work. They do not usually provide an avenue for legal activity. Others may involve disciplinary decisions, including expulsion, and these are sometimes linked with fees, grants and allowances.[47]

12.75   For FE institutions, the prescribed articles of government (see para 12.8) are the starting point when looking at grievances which students may have. The principal is the chief executive of the institution and is responsible for (inter alia) organisation and management, academic activities, maintenance of student discipline and suspensions. The principal also chairs the academic board, which is responsible for advising him/her on various matters, including the arrangements for admission, assessment and examination of students and procedures for expulsion for academic reasons. Each corporation is required to have a staff grievance procedure, but nothing is stipulated for students. Corporations have the power to make rules and by-laws (which are subject to the articles) regarding the government and conduct of the institution 'as they shall think fit'; and copies must be available for inspection by any student during normal office hours on request. The articles require that any suspension or expulsion of students on disciplinary grounds and expulsion for academic reasons cannot occur unless the rules and procedures provided by the articles have been complied with. This would suggest that no corporation could lawfully decide not to formulate and publish its rules in this area.

12.76   The secretary of state retains jurisdiction to intervene in the event of mismanagement or breach of duty (FHEA 1992 s57). This might be raised initially by way of a complaint to the FEFC, which has a role under the *Charter for Further Education*[48] to consider complaints. The FEFC might then recommend action by the secretary of state (see

---

47   For a useful survey of HE complaints, see article by Parlour and Burwood in *Education and the Law* [1995] (2) 63–78.

48   The charter was first published in 1993. It sets out what can be expected from further education and what to do if it is necessary to complain. Every college should have its own charter.

chapter 13, para 13.31). New procedures for dealing with complaints in the FE sector have recently been issued by the FEFC.[49]

12.77   It is unlikely that a legal challenge by an FE student can be by way of judicial review. Since FE corporations are statutory bodies under FHEA 1992 s15 this, in principle, gives rise to an administrative law route of challenge. But, in practice, the admission arrangements and the conduct of the course are likely to be analogous to a private law contract where there has been consideration. In *Moran v University College Salford (No 2)*[50] (an HE case), it was clear that remedies for breach of contract were available in principle for a failure to confirm a place which a physiotherapy degree student had accepted on a course.

12.78   Furthermore, an institution is likely to have developed a sophisticated and multi-layered appeals and complaints machinery notwithstanding the lack of statutory requirement to do so. This machinery must usually be exhausted before considering taking the matter to court. Where there is a prospect of a student continuing at a particular institution, every effort should obviously be made by all parties to avoid the negative consequences of litigation.

12.79   EA 1996 Sch 37 para 77 applies the power of the secretary of state under EA 1996 s465–468 (in relation to schools) to institutions maintained by LEAs providing FE and HE (ERA 1988 s219).

12.80   A university visitor (see paras 12.43 and 12.52) has exclusive jurisdiction over the application of internal rules and procedures in the university and this ousts that of the courts. This principle applied even where (teacher) training was in partnership with a school and the secretary of state had issued regulations and guidance governing the course.[51] But where an expert academic judgment is involved, eg, the choice of outside examiners, the visitor is entitled to decide not to intrude.[52] However, matters which are subject of a grievance procedure could impact upon a review of a decision made by a board of examiners. For example, an allegation of bias and marking down is not a question of academic judgement.[53] The House of Lords

---

49   *Complaints about Colleges of Further Education and 6th Form Colleges* FEFC, April 1999.
50   [1994] ELR 187, CA.
51   *R v University of Nottingham ex p K* [1998] ELR 184, QBD.
52   *R v HM the Queen in Council ex p Vijayatunga* [1989] 2 All ER 843, CA. See also *R v Liverpool John Moores University ex p Hayes* [1998] ELR 261, QBD, where the court endorsed the university's internal appeal process as academic judgments would be needed to assess the complainant's ability, and *R v Cranfield University Senate ex p Bashir* [1999] ELR 317, CA.
53   *Leeds Metropolitan University ex p Manders* [1998] ELR 502, QBD.

stated in *R v Lord President of the Privy Council ex p Page*[54] that judicial review lies against a visitor who has acted outside his/her jurisdiction, abused his/her power or acted in breach of the rules of natural justice. However, the majority of their Lordships felt that an error of law by a visitor was intra vires and, therefore, not justiciable.

12.81   In the case of the universities established by statute (FHEA 1992), public law remedies are likely to be available in addition to private law ones. *R v Manchester Metropolitan University ex p Nolan*[55] was the first case in which a student succeeded in a judicial review of a statutory university because of an abuse of academic power in its treatment of the allegation that he had cheated in an examination.

12.82   It is notoriously difficult to mount a legal challenge to the exercise of an academic judgment. Even if a breach of natural justice can be found, it must be doubted whether it is worthwhile challenging an academic decision which is simply going to be confirmed by a new board. On the other hand, a failure to observe the principles of natural justice in any disciplinary or expulsion procedure ought to entitle the aggrieved student to bring an action for a declaration in the county court. See *Herring v Templeman*,[56] where it was alleged that the academic board was acting ultra vires.

12.83   This could be coupled with a claim for an injunction, eg, for reinstatement or a favourable reference; and a claim for damages for breach of contract and/or negligence arising from loss of opportunity to complete the course earlier and, possibly, loss of earnings. It may be that such a claim for damages would be ruled out on public policy grounds – see *O'Rourke v Camden LBC*,[57] a homelessness case where damages were sought for breach of a statutory duty to provide accommodation.

12.84   In *R v Board of Governors of Sheffield Hallam University ex p R*[58] the relevant committee of the academic board had no evidence that the requirement of adequate prior warning had been given under the university's own written procedure for the expulsion of students for academic reasons and its decision was, therefore, quashed. In another case, university rules making clear the time limit for submission of a dissertation, which were invoked against a student who was one day too late, were not Wednesbury unreasonable or

54 [1993] AC 682; [1992] 3 WLR 1112.
55 [1994] ELR 380, QBD.
56 [1973] 2 All ER 581, ChD.
57 [1997] 3 All ER 23, HL.
58 [1995] ELR 267, QBD.

irrational as the examination board had a discretion to consider any extenuating circumstances; and awarding no marks for the dissertation was not disproportionate.[59] The Court of Appeal has recently re-emphasised the importance of bringing any judicial review proceedings with the greatest speed, particularly where an academic year was lost to the student, and also that only the clearest and most obvious unfairness or departure from a university's own regulations would justify an attempt by judicial review to impugn an academic decision (confirmed in this case by the academic registrar and an independent member of the academic council who had heard the applicant for over an hour).[60]

12.85   Among the materials which are worth scrutinising in advising the client who has been failed on all or part of a course are:

- prospectus or course handbook;
- establishment and constitution of any assessment board;
- guidance issued to the assessment board by the academic board;
- internal appeal procedure and details of any review panel.

---

59 *R v University of Central England ex p Iqbal Sandhu* [1999] ELR 121, QBD.
60 *R v University of Portsmouth ex p Lakareber* [1999] ELR 135, CA.

Complaints and remedies

This chapter is an overview of the kind of remedies available in education law cases. It concentrates on the non-legal remedies, referring briefly to those which are considered more fully in separate chapters.

Routes for complaints about maintained schools

13.1 Non-legal remedies can sometimes be more effective than the more traditional legal ones or may provide the material for a legal challenge. The following sections (paras 13.2–13.38) describe the possible routes and remedies available to dissatisfied parents and students, apart from going to court.

Local councillors

13.2 In practice, complaint to a local councillor is not likely to be very effective unless the councillor is knowledgeable and persistent; particularly if this involves challenging his/her own party's policies. It may usefully precede a reference to the local government ombudsman (see para 13.22).

Member of parliament

13.3 Complaint to the local MP may be more successful, because someone high up in the education authority is usually called upon to find out what has been going on. Letters written to MPs by LEA officers often contain statements which can be used with advantage at a future date in legal proceedings or in the investigation of complaints against the authority or school.

Parents' association or parent teacher association

13.4 A good practical way of getting information to support objective criticism may be to consult the parents' association. Of course, there may not be one or it may be dominated by the headteacher.

Governing body

13.5 Usually there is a documented complaints procedure, although there has hitherto been no statutory requirement for this. This is not necessarily the case in independent schools.

13.6 Where the complaint concerned some aspect of the curriculum, schools could be involved in the LEA complaints machinery (established under Education Reform Act 1988, now EA 1996 s409). This requires the matter to be raised first with the headteacher, followed by an officer of the LEA deputed to deal with complaints.

The next stage is the complaints unit of the LEA.

13.7   Following the repeal of EA 1996 ss370–374[1] the position will have to be clarified when regulations are made under SSFA 1998 s38. These are likely to deal with curriculum complaints procedure and the role of headteachers, governors and LEAs generally, concerning the conduct of the school. Regulations planned under SSFA 1998 s39[2] were to extend governing bodies' role in the complaints machinery generally, unless there is some alternative statutory machinery. By 28 February 2000, governing bodies were to have procedures for dealing with all other complaints relating to the school and these must be publicised. Usually this will be in the school's prospectus,[3] but reg 29 of the draft s39 regulations also requires the existence of the complaints procedures to be sent with the first publication sent to parents of new pupils. Despite wide consultation, it appears that these regulations are not now to be issued. It may be that they were considered unworkable by schools and LEAs. The detail of the proposed procedure is, however, given below as an indication of what the DfEE considered reasonable in 1998/99.

13.8   The headteacher or his/her designate acts as complaints officer and the governing body must set up a complaints panel who are not governors. Where the complaint is made by a pupil or governor, it is left to individual governing bodies to design the machinery, as long as there is an appeals mechanism. For other complainants (which includes parents) the stages are:

1) Informal mention to staff or governor.
2) Written formal complaint. (Serious or urgent complaints go direct to the headteacher.)
3) Investigation by complaints officer and decision letter within ten school days.
4) Referral to head teacher on notice given within ten further days – headteacher meets complainant.
5) Headteacher sends decision within ten school days.
6) Appeal to governing body on notice to headteacher within ten school days; notice of appeal sent by headteacher within five

---

1   With effect from 1 October 1998, by SSFA 1998 Sch 30 para 91 and 1998 SI No 2212.
2   Education (School Government) (General Complaints Procedures) Regulations 1999 (draft).
3   Education (School Information) (England) Regulations 1998 SI No 2526 regs 8 and 11; Education (School Information) (Wales) Regulations 1997 SI No 1832.

school days to include any statement of complaint.

7) Committee of governing body investigates and holds oral hearing if they think it appropriate. All parties may be represented and written statements submitted at least five school days beforehand. At least one member of the complaints panel sits on the committee (which may not include the headteacher or the complaints officer). The committee sets its own timetable.

13.9 It is not obligatory for the governing body to provide a further right of appeal to the diocese or the LEA. If the complaint is against the headteacher, a governor or the governing body as a whole, the chair acts as complaints officer, and against his/her decision an appeal lies to a committee of the governing body, usually constituted by three members of the complaints panel.

13.10 These procedures certainly would place further burdens on governing bodies' limited time and resources and it is likely that they would have difficulty complying with them. Cynics may rightly say that all these layers of complaints machinery would have the effect of deadening and dissipating the force of the complaint as well as causing extra delay. But where the machinery exists it is essential to utilise it first, or at least consider whether its use is appropriate as a possible resolution to the problem. Failure to do this may make it much more difficult to obtain any relief from a court later on. If the local machinery is absent, the prospect of successful resolution via the secretary of state (see para 13.31) or the courts (para 13.50) is increased.

Local education authority

13.11 Where the complaint concerns the curriculum, religious education or a related matter, it is essential to exhaust the LEA's local complaints machinery (see paras 4.63–4.74). Under EA 1996 s409(2), this must be able to deal with complaints that the LEA or governing body of a maintained school:

(a) have acted or are proposing to act unreasonably in relation to the exercise of a power conferred on them by or under a relevant enactment, or

(b) have acted or are proposing to act unreasonably in relation to the performance of, or have failed to discharge, a duty imposed on them by or under a relevant enactment.

In this context a 'relevant enactment' means a provision in EA 1996

Part V or elsewhere dealing with the curriculum or religious worship in maintained schools.

13.12 The LEA may in fact have developed a complaints procedure which goes far beyond the strict limits of the foregoing and details of this ought to be studied in most cases. It is worth referring to the criteria enacted in annex A to DFE Circular 1/89,[4] because the principles apply to any arrangements which conform with good administration. Thus, all complaints must be investigated speedily, efficiently, fully and fairly, and all aspects of each individual case must be given proper consideration.

13.13 Paragraph 5 of the circular (rephrased) states that there should be:

1) a clear first point of contact in the LEA;
2) a mechanism to identify all relevant complaints and their urgency;
3) arrangements to monitor the stages of all complaints;
4) provision for the complainant (accompanied if desired, and if necessary with the assistance of an interpreter) to make representations in person;
5) definition of the end point of each stage and a mechanism for informing the complainant of progress;
6) notification of the decision taken and the reason for it, the action proposed and any further recourse available.

13.14 SSFA 1996 s14 gives the LEA new powers to intervene where a governing body and the headteacher have been given a warning notice concerning pupil performance, breakdown of management or threats to safety. It would be open to a dissatisfied parent to ask the LEA to invoke this power, which also applies where an inspection has found that the school has 'serious weaknesses' as defined in SSFA 1998 s15(4)–(5) (see para 4.58).

13.15 It is important to watch for occasions where a person may become involved in reviewing in an appellate sense a decision in which s/he may have participated at a lower level. This may provide grounds for a challenge based on a breach of the rules of natural justice. See, for example, *R v Board of Governors of Stoke Newington School ex p M.*[5] The school exclusion panel included a teacher-governor, Mr Davies, who was M's head of year, with some responsi-

---

4   DFE Circular 1/89 *Education Reform Act 1988: The local arrangements for the consideration of complaints.*
5   [1994] ELR 131, QBD (see para 8.44).

bility for her. Potts J accepted that the panel must have had regard to M's conduct over the whole period of her education at the school. Mr Davies was in a position to give direct evidence of this and, on the face of it, he was both judge and witness. The exclusion decision was quashed. In *R v Board of Governors of the London Oratory School ex p Regis,*[6] the headteacher who had excluded the pupil was also the clerk to the governors. However, no request was made for him to withdraw from the meeting of governors considering the exclusion and, in the circumstances, McCullough J refused a judicial review.

13.16   The secretary of state will not entertain a complaint under EA 1996 ss496 and 497 (see paras 13.31–13.33 and appendix B) to which s409(2) applies unless it has been disposed of under the above arrangements.

Special Educational Needs Tribunal

13.17   A separate appeals mechanism exists for children with special educational needs (see paras 9.69–9.94). The tribunal has been dealing with appeals since September 1995 and the subsequent decisions of the High Court suggest that no other forum for determining disputes about assessment, statementing, provision and educational placement will be entertained.[7] There is some dispute about the appropriate machinery where a parent seeks only a change of school placement to a non-maintained school. In the authors' view, this can only be by way of reassessment (see paras 9.95–9.96).

Publicity

13.18   This can be quite effective. The local press will usually be ready and willing to cover a story about a battle with authority by a child or determined parent; and local television news bulletins often feature similar items. But it will tend to alienate LEA professionals and officers for long after the original grievance has been resolved. Parents must be mindful of the need to avoid defaming an individual officer. The effect of publicity on the child pupil must not be underestimated. The long-term position of the parent is likely to be undermined if there is no parallel legal activity or backing from other parents.

6   (1988) *Times* 17 February, QBD.
7   *Re M (a minor)* [1996] ELR 135, CA.

Local authority monitoring officer

13.19 Under Local Government and Housing Act 1989 s5, all local authorities have a duty to appoint an officer whose function is to report to the appropriate committee of the council on the investigation and outcome of a complaint about the failure on the part of the council to discharge its duty or of maladministration. If it appears to this officer that any proposal, decision or omission by the authority or by any committee or subcommittee or officer of the authority has given rise to or is likely to give rise to:

1) a contravention of any enactment or rule of law or of any code of practice, or

2) any maladministration or injustice within the jurisdiction of the local government ombudsman (see paras 13.22–13.25),

the monitoring officer must prepare a report to the authority. In doing this s/he must consult the head of the authority's paid service (ie, the chief executive) and its chief finance officer.

13.20 Copies of the report must be sent to every member of the authority. The authority and any relevant committee must consider the report in a meeting which must be held not more than 21 days after circulation; and it may not implement any step to give effect to the questioned proposal or decision until one day after consideration of the report. The monitoring officer must carry out these duties personally or by a properly nominated deputy.

13.21 The existence of this officer is often not well publicised. It is usually the chief executive or a member of his/ her team, or the head of legal services, who may in effect be wearing two conflicting hats. Complaints addressed to the monitoring officer are usually taken seriously and processed promptly. One reason for this is the threat of subsequent involvement by the local government ombudsman. In any event, it will ensure the involvement of someone at high level and may assist in producing the desired result.

Commissioner for local administration (local ombudsman)

13.22 The powers of the ombudsman (LGO) are derived from the Local Government Act (LGA) 1974 s26 (see appendix A). Where a written complaint is made by or on behalf of a member of the public who claims to have sustained injustice in consequence of maladministration in connection with action taken by or on behalf of an authority in the exercise of administrative functions of that authority, an LGO may investigate that complaint (s26(1)). All local authorities, including LEAs and their appeal committees, are covered by the LGO's jurisdiction. But schools are excluded, as are any secular curriculum policies of the LEA.[8] Many complaints to the LGO are about delay, and the jurisdiction, therefore, applies to inaction as well as action.

13.23   Technically there should first be a complaint to, or referral by, a member of the authority,[9] but in practice the LGO will simply ask that the local authority be given an opportunity to deal with the complaint using any local complaints machinery first.[10]

13.24   There are some important limitations on the LGO's powers. S/he may not investigate:

1) where the complaint was not made within 12 months of the day on which the person aggrieved first had notice of the matters alleged in the complaint – unless s/he considers that there are special circumstances which make it proper to do so (s26(4));

2) where the person aggrieved has a right of appeal to a tribunal or to a minister; or where there is a remedy by way of proceedings – but if the LGO considers that it is not reasonable to expect the person aggrieved to have resort to these rights s/he may still conduct an investigation (s26(6));

3) where in the opinion of the LGO the action complained of affects all or most of the inhabitants of the area of the authority concerned (s26(7)).

13.25   The meaning of 'maladministration' was discussed by Lord Denning MR in *R v Local Commissioner for Administration for the North and East Area of England ex p Bradford MCC*.[11] It covers 'bias, neglect, inattention, delay, incompetence, inaptitude, perversity, turpitude, arbitrariness and so on'. It can deal only with the manner in which a decision is reached or discretion exercised and excludes the merits of the decision or the discretion. The ombudsman will not investigate 'a discretionary decision, properly exercised, which the complainant dislikes but cannot fault the manner in which it was taken'.[12] In the same case, it was held by the Court of Appeal that it

---

8   LGA 1974 Sch 5 para 5. Note that EA 1996 s70 (dealing with LEA curriculum policy) was repealed by SSFA 1998 Sch 30 para 91 and Sch 31 with effect from 1 October 1998.

9   Section 26(2).

10 Section 26(5).

11 [1979] 2 All ER 881, CA, at 898.

12 Ibid.

was unnecessary for the complainant to specify any particular piece of maladministration; merely specifying the action of the local authority was sufficient because the complainant could not know what took place in council offices.

13.26   The investigation by the LGO will usually involve initial correspondence with the complainant and the authority, followed by an examination of the authority's relevant files and interviews with the officers concerned. A draft report is always sent to the authority for comment. The names of the person aggrieved are altered in the report to protect anonymity – even, it seems, when s/he does not desire this. Reports take several months to be prepared.

13.27   If the problem seems likely to lead to legal proceedings, the ombudsman may not be willing to investigate pending those proceedings. It may be necessary to write in some detail to the LGO explaining precisely why it has been decided not to pursue an appeal or court action at that stage. The ombudsman can recommend any particular action and can also recommend the LEA to pay the complainant's costs as well as compensation, but there is no legal obligation on the LEA to do so (LGA 1974 s31(3) – see appendix A). The work of advising a client about these complaints and preparing written representations is covered under the legal advice and assistance scheme.

13.28   For compensation to be awarded the ombudsman must be satisfied that the prejudice suffered by the complainant amounted to an injustice; a finding of maladministration is not enough.[13]

13.29   In many ways the approach of the LGO resembles that of a Crown office judge reviewing an administrative action. Care needs to be exercised in deciding which method of complaint to follow. A recent decision of Turner J shows that where resort was had to judicial review (to obtain a suitable residential school placement for a boy with behavioural difficulties), the LGO no longer has any jurisdiction under LGA 1974 s26, even if an entirely different remedy was sought (compensation for failure to assess SEN). This decision was upheld by Simon Brown LJ in refusing leave in the Court of Appeal in March 1999.[14] The judicial review application and the LGO complaint both related to the same grievance, namely maladministration, and judicial review was necessary to end it. It is not clear whether this would equally affect an application for permission which is withdrawn. A decision must, therefore, be

13   *R v Commissioner for Local Administration ex p S* [1999] ELR 102, QBD.
14   *R v Commissioner for Local Administration ex p H* [1999] ELR 314, CA.

made at an early stage whether to forego a complaint to the LGO. In less clear cases it may be possible to overcome this difficulty by submitting the LGO complaint first and obtaining a result (negative or unsatisfactory) in time for the Order 53 time limit.

13.30   It is worth remembering that the ombudsman is unlikely to be prepared to investigate a complaint about the behaviour of an LEA which unnecessarily opposes a parental appeal or pursues hopeless litigation (for example, by appealing on unsound grounds against an SENT decision in the parents' favour) which has the effect of causing uncertainty, delay or disruption to a child's education. This is because of the element of discretion which is liable to be present in the decision.

Secretary of State for Education

13.31   If there are questions of policy or alleged failure to follow guidance issued by the DfEE, the court is likely to be reluctant to intervene before an approach is made to the secretary of state. Also the courts traditionally regard the secretary of state as the most appropriate person to decide disputes based on a conflict of expert opinion, in the knowledge that in many cases s/he will consult his/her own expert. Usually there is no need for the secretary of state to disclose this advice.

13.32   In *R v Secretary of State for Education ex p S*,[15] an appeal under EA 1981 s8(6) (jurisdiction now superseded by the SENT) against the school named in a statement, the secretary of state did not disclose the specialist advice which he had obtained from an education psychologist and an HMI inspector. The Court of Appeal ruled that the process of government necessarily involves civil servants engaging in a host of consultative exercises involving them applying their individual expertise and experience to a given problem. The ultimate decision of the minister in a case where there had been such consultation was a matter of judgment for the decision-maker. How he reached his decision was essentially a matter for him. It might involve extensive 'in-house' consultation, but, provided the process did not involve a new point with which the interested parties had had no opportunity of dealing, there was no duty to disclose material which was the product of the consultative process. The concept of fairness did not usually require disclosure. If it did, then there should be disclosure. That would only arise in the most

15   [1995] ELR 71, CA.

exceptional circumstances not applicable to the instant case. *Bushell v Secretary of State for the Environment*[16] applied.

13.33   In many cases it is necessary to show that this avenue has been exhausted before the court will entertain a legal challenge.[17]

Unreasonableness

13.34   EA 1996 s496 deals with the unreasonable exercise of powers and duties by LEAs or school governors and funding authorities. If the secretary of state thinks that the body has acted or is proposing to act unreasonably s/he may intervene, even where statute gives the body a discretion in the matter. Thus, it is clear that, in principle, the secretary of state can substitute his/her own opinion. This goes far beyond the role of the court in a judicial review. In *Cumings v Birkenhead Corporation*,[18] the LEA issued a circular stating that pupils in Roman Catholic Primary Schools could not go on to maintained secondary schools, owing to the shortage of secondary school places. The High Court decided that the LEA was entitled in its discretion to adopt a policy which outweighed its parents' wishes (under EA 1944 s76, now EA 1996 s9) and that the proper remedy was to make representations to the minister under what is now EA 1996 s496. There does not actually need to be a complaint under this section before the secretary of state can become involved.

13.35   The question of what is unreasonable on the part of an education body was aired at length in the notorious *Tameside* case.[19] The House of Lords decided that the LEA was entitled to have a policy and the secretary of state was not entitled to make the LEA abandon it merely because he disagreed with it. The secretary of state had decided that he would only give a direction if the LEA were acting unreasonably, apparently without directing his mind properly to the facts disclosed by the LEA's letter stating how it proposed to deal with selection in

---

16 [1980] 2 All ER 608, HL.
17 *R v Northamptonshire CC ex p Gray* [1986] *Times* 13 March, DC (complaint about defective election of parent governors).
18 [1971] 2 All ER 881, QBD.
19 *Secretary of State for Education and Science v Tameside MBC* [1977] AC 1014, HL. The secretary of state approved a scheme by Tameside LEA to make comprehensive schools in its area from September 1976. In May local elections were held and the opposition party took control. It believed that it had a mandate to reconsider the policy on comprehensive schools. It intended to preserve the status quo while considering longer-term proposals. The secretary of state directed the LEA to give effect to the proposals already approved by him.

the time available, or the fact of the considerable local support for the newly-elected authority's proposals. Lord Wilberforce explained how a 'subjective' judgment may be judicially reviewed:[20]

> The section [now EA 1996 s496] is framed in a 'subjective' form – if the Secretary of State 'is satisfied'. This form of section is quite well known, and at first sight might seem to exclude judicial review. Sections in this form may, no doubt, exclude judicial review on what is or has become a matter of pure judgment. But I do not think that they go further than that. If a judgment requires, before it can be made, the existence of some facts, then, although the evaluation of those facts is for the Secretary of State alone, the court must inquire whether those facts exist, and have been taken into account, whether the judgment has been made upon a proper self-direction as to those facts, whether the judgment has not been made upon other facts which ought not to have been taken into account. If these requirements are not met, then the exercise of judgment, however bona fide it may be, becomes capable of challenge: see *Secretary of State for Employment v Associated Society of Locomotive Engineers and Firemen (No 2)* [1972] 2 QB 455 at 493, [1972] 2 All ER 949 at 967, per Lord Denning MR.

13.36 Lord Diplock's judgment in the same case[21] provides a useful analysis of the role of a body which is charged with providing educational services and its relationship to the secretary of state in areas where statutory powers to replace those of the LEA have not yet developed.

Secretary of state or the courts?

13.37 There is often a divergence of views between the interested parties over whether the remedy lies via a complaint to the secretary of state or whether the jurisdiction of the High Court can be invoked instead. In *Watt v Kesteven CC*,[22] the Court of Appeal decided that the duty to provide schools (now EA 1996 s14) is not for the courts to decide on and that the wishes of the parents are only a general principle to be weighed in the balance together with other considerations. See also *R v ILEA ex p Ali*,[23] where the question was whether the LEA had taken the steps necessary to remedy the situation.

---

20 Ibid at 1047.
21 Ibid at 1062–1067.
22 [1955] 1 All ER 473, CA.
23 [1990] COD 317; [1990] 2 Admin LR 822, QBD.

13.38 A very important practical consideration is that complaints to the secretary of state take even longer than going through the courts – two or three years is not unknown. The lack of consultation and feedback is also a disadvantage. An indication of the timescale involved can be seen from *R v Secretary of State for Education ex p Ruscoe:*[24]

16 July 1990: complaint about collective worship dismissed by governing body
17 August 1990: parents' appeals to LEA
13 September 1991: LEA complaints board dismissed appeals
14 October 1991: parents complained to secretary of state
26 February 1993: Divisional Court dismissed challenge to secretary of state's decision.

13.39 It can often be shown that a much more urgent solution to the problem is required if a child's development is not to be prejudiced or efficient education threatened, and this may justify bypassing the secretary of state. But in *R v Mid-Glamorgan CC ex p B,*[25] Harrison J held that, where the EA 1981 appeal committee supported the LEA's decision to change the named school, the LEA did not act unreasonably in refusing to continue to maintain the applicant at the school of the parents' choice pending the determination of the parents' appeal to the secretary of state. The same considerations apply where there is urgency or complex legal issues are involved.[26]

13.40 Where the allegation is that the body has acted ultra vires or contrary to natural justice, it is not appropriate to go to the secretary of state. In *Herring v Templeman,*[27] there was a denial of the right (in the teacher training college's trust deed) to make written or oral representations by a student who wished to challenge a recommendation by the academic board (upheld by the governing body) that he should withdraw from the college forthwith on academic grounds.

Default powers

13.41 If the secretary of state is satisfied that a school or LEA has failed to discharge any duty imposed on it by or for the purposes of this Act, s/he may make an order under EA 1996 s497(1):

24 (1993) 26 February, unreported, QBD.
25 [1995] ELR 168, QBD.
26 *R v North Yorkshire CC ex p Hargreaves* [1997] 1 CCLR 104, QBD.
27 [1973] 2 All ER 581, ChD.

(a) declaring the body to be in default in respect of that duty, and

(b) giving such directions for the purpose of enforcing the performance of the duty as appear to him to be expedient.

Such a direction is enforceable by an order of mandamus (s497(3)).

13.42   Again, there is no need for a person interested to complain, but it seems unrealistic to expect action without such a complaint. Even then, it appears to be unusual for the secretary of state to do more than ask the body complained of to write to him/her explaining what has been going on. The secretary of state may be satisfied with the written answer to this without investigating further and this is unsatisfactory. The section does not oblige the secretary of state to undertake any kind of investigation. S/he may lawfully restrict him/herself to giving only a direction.[28]

13.43   A recent case where the secretary of state used default powers was *R v Secretary of State for Education and Governors of Southlands Community Comprehensive School ex p W*,[29] where the secretary of state in the new government revoked the direction his predecessor had given to the governing body to admit a girl pupil. This may have been because of the threat of industrial action at the school, although another school had been found for the girl by the time the case came on for hearing.

13.44   The SSFA 1998 has added specific new default powers to EA 1996 s497 for the secretary of state to intervene in LEAs' functions regarding the provision of education to registered pupils and those of compulsory school age, and these took effect from 1 October 1998.[30] The failure threshold is lower than under s497. Under s497A(2) it is 'failing (in his opinion) in any respect to perform any function to which this section applies to an adequate standard (or at all)'. Section 497A empowers the secretary of state to direct an LEA officer to secure that that function is performed in such a way as to achieve such objectives as are specified in the direction (s497A(3)). Furthermore, the secretary of state may direct that functions are performed by a particular person at the LEA's expense and under contractual terms specified by the secretary of state (s497A(4)). Additional education functions performed by the same person may be imposed on the LEA by the secretary of state, particularly if

28   *R v Northamptonshire CC ex p Gray* (1986) *Times* 13 March, DC (complaint about defective election of parent governors).

29   [1998] ELR 413, QBD.

30   School Standards and Framework Act 1998 (Commencement No 2 and Supplemental, Savings and Transitional Provisions) Order 1998 SI No 2212.

financial considerations justify it, even where the LEA is not failing under ss2 above (s497A(5)). These directions are thus a severe encroachment on the role of LEAs who do not function effectively and they last indefinitely. It remains to be seen whether the secretary of state will use them extensively to privatise some LEA functions in many areas, but the threat of a complaint to the DfEE may now carry more weight than formerly.

13.45   Associated with this is the power, under s497B, to authorise the specified s497A(4) person to enter LEA premises and inspect and copy any documents and records which the person considers relevant to the performance of the specified function or functions (s497B(2)). LEAs and schools are required to assist the specified person (s497B(4) and (5)).

Questions of policy

13.46   Either the secretary of state or the court will need to address various aspects of the policy which is being challenged.

13.47   Is it unlawful? An LEA is entitled to have policies which in general guide its decisions. This need not be in the form of a policy document. In such a case an applicant for judicial review or a complainant must point to a series of facts from which the court is asked to deduce the existence and terms of the policy.[31] Where the LEA has a wide discretion, the precise level at which the respective cut-off points should be set is a matter for the LEA and not easily subject to challenge in the courts.[32]

13.48   Does it fetter the authority's discretion? An authority must not shut its ears to an application made by someone who does not fulfil the criteria laid down in the policy. It must consider the significance of this failure, bearing in mind all the relevant facts.[33]

13.49   In *R v Hampshire CC ex p W*,[34] a parent's application for a grant for a child to attend a fee-paying school appeared to have been dismissed on the ground that the placement had not been made through the county placement panel (pursuant to a statement).

31   *R v Cumbria CC ex p P* [1995] ELR 337, QBD.
32   *R v Cumbria CC ex p NB* [1996] ELR 65, QBD.
33   See Lord Reid's summary in *British Oxygen Co v Minister of Technology* [1971] AC 610; [1970] 3 All ER 165, HL, at 170.
34   [1994] ELR 460, QBD (see para 14.14).

Legal action

Judicial review

13.50   For consideration of the point at which a judicial review can be justified and more details on judicial review, see chapter 14.

13.51   It must be understood that judicial review is only available where alternative remedies are inappropriate or have been exhausted. In *R v Camden LBC ex p B*,[35] the court was satisfied that a dispute about school placement and the LEA's departure from the appeal committee's findings could be brought to court at least as quickly as the statutory appeal to the secretary of state (six to nine months under the old procedure under EA 1981 s8(6)). On the other hand, *Re M (a minor)*[36] is an example of an unsuccessful application for an injunction restraining implementation of an amended SEN statement pending the parent's appeal to the Special Educational Needs Tribunal under the new procedure.

13.52   It must always be borne in mind that judicial review is a discretionary remedy. In many cases where there has been a serious failure by the LEA, for example, relief will be refused, because the court is satisfied that the LEA is getting its house in order (or is concerned about the expense to the respondent in complying with an order). See para 14.29 for an example where declaratory relief was of little avail in gaining a school place, because of the detriment to good administration. The threat of disruption by teachers breaking their employment contracts was one of the factors which persuaded the court not to grant relief and order reinstatement of an excluded pupil in *R v South Tyneside Education Department and Governors of Hebburn Comprehensive School ex p Cram*.[37] In *R v Gloucester CC ex p P*,[38] Popplewell J declined to grant a declaration that there had been a breach of statutory duty on the ground that it was more of a comment on past events than a relevant factor in future litigation of the dispute. Also the court is not entitled or required by law to decide what was best for the particular child.

13.53   Judicial review is particularly inappropriate where there is a dispute between experts.[39]

---

35   [1994] ELR 490, QBD.
36   [1996] ELR 135, CA.
37   [1998] ELR 508, QBD.
38   [1994] ELR 334, QBD.
39   *R v Newham LBC ex p R* [1995] ELR 156, QBD.

Private law action

13.54 *E v Dorset CC*[40] confirmed that there is no private law action for breach of a statutory duty. There may be a right of action in negligence, see chapter 15.

13.55 Other cases involving torts, eg, personal injuries, assault, nuisance, can be litigated in the usual way.

Complaints about other bodies

Independent schools

13.56 All independent schools must be registered with the Registrar of Independent Schools EA 1996 s466. A school may not remain on the register if its proprietor or premises are disqualified, or if it is employing persons whose employment is restricted on medical grounds or for misconduct, in contravention of the regulations.[41] Rights and remedies are governed by the contractual arrangements between the parents (or those paying for the education of the pupils) and the proprietors of the school. Until recently, it was thought that there can be no public law remedies, even where natural justice is denied.[42] But where the child has obtained a place through the assisted places scheme, public law remedies might apply. In *R v Cobham Hall School ex p S*,[43] Dyson J held that in withdrawing an assisted place on account of the pupil's behaviour the school was exercising a public function. There was no free-standing right to withdraw an assisted place. The application for judicial review was allowed on this ground but it is submitted that a Wednesbury unreasonable decision to exclude an assisted place pupil would be amenable to review. Interestingly, the judge decided that he had the power to order reinstatement on a non-paying basis.

13.57 A dissatisfied parent could make representations to the secretary

---

40 And other appeals in *X v Bedfordshire CC* [1995] 2 AC 633; [1995] 3 All ER 353; [1995] ELR 404, HL.

41 See ERA 1988 s218(6) and Education (teachers) Regulations 1993 SI No 543 reg 10.

42 See *R v Headmaster of Fernhill Manor School ex p Brown* [1994] ELR 67, QBD (an expulsion case). Brooke J suggested that procedural rules should be incorporated to ensure that pupils receive fair treatment in accordance with the rules of natural justice. At the moment this would have to be incorporated in the contract.

43 [1998] ELR 389, QBD.

of state, who has power under EA 1996 s469 to serve notice of complaint on the proprietor of the school on prescribed grounds. The jurisdiction under this machinery concerns:

1) unsuitable school premises;
2) inadequate/unsuitable accommodation in view of number, age and sex of pupils;
3) lack of efficient and suitable instruction;
4) proprietor or teacher not a proper person (this term is not defined);
5) failure to comply with Children Act 1989 s87 (welfare of children accommodated in independent schools).

If it is thought that the fault can be remedied, the notice must specify the remedial measures and impose a time limit of not more than six months for their performance. The person served may then appeal to an independent schools tribunal under EA 1996 s470 with a view to annulling the complaint. The secretary of state is the other party to the appeal and there does not appear to be any machinery for an aggrieved person to appear or make representations, other than as a witness. However, the tribunal may itself call witnesses.[44]

City technology colleges

13.58   CTCs are creatures of statute (ERA 1988 s105, now EA 1996 s482) and so there is no contractual relationship between parent or pupil and school.[45] Judicial review would be the appropriate court proceedings to challenge a decision not to admit a pupil because the state was funding places at that institution.

Further education colleges

13.59   The Further Education Funding Council (FEFC) itself exercises a supervisory jurisdiction over the institutions which it supports, under the Charter for Further Education.[46] Unless the complaint is about a lack of provision in the area, complaints should be made in the first instance to the college concerned. However, the FEFC's role

---

44   Independent Schools Tribunal Rules 1958 SI No 519 r9(2).

45   *R v Haberdashers' Aske's Hatcham College Trust ex p T* [1995] ELR 350, QBD.

46   Published in a leaflet entitled *Complaints about colleges of further education and sixth form colleges* (April 1999), available, free, from the FEFC, Cheylesmore House, Quinton Road, Coventry CV1 2WT. Telephone 01203 863000. Website http://www.fefc.ac.uk.

is somewhat limited. It does not carry out detailed investigations or hold personal discussions with the parties – it can only consider information provided to it in writing. It will not consider personal complaints about members of staff, or where there is a more appropriate form of redress, eg, to an examination body where a qualification is disputed. It should be noted that the complaint must be made within three months of the conclusion of the college's own procedures. The FEFC can only make recommendations to a college and is not empowered to enforce any particular action, though it will monitor the response.

13.60   If an individual can satisfy the secretary of state that the FEFC or an FE institution is not carrying out its duty, the secretary of state may declare it to be in default and give directions to enforce the duty.[47] The secretary of state will usually seek the views of the FEFC before deciding how to respond.

13.61   Most FE colleges are now further education institutions incorporated under FHEA 1992 ss15 and 16 (see para 12.5). These include sixth form colleges. They have instruments and articles of government which are the source of the authority for by-laws containing provisions for disciplining staff and students.[48] There will always be a complaints procedure and a grievance procedure covering disputes about conduct and appealing against academic assessments. Every attempt should be made to follow the internal procedure, to the conclusion of all its appeal stages, before considering a legal remedy, otherwise there will be a claim that all the alternative remedies have not been exhausted.

13.62   It must be stressed that it is always extremely difficult, if not impossible, to challenge the exercise of discretion or judgment concerning academic performance.[49] But, if the procedure adopted by the institution was unfair or the rules of natural justice have been broken, eg, there is the appearance of bias, then in principle judicial review will be available. On the other hand, the issue of a prospectus and course handbook coupled with the student's participation on the course could constitute a contractual arrangement, giving rise to private law procedures and remedies.[50]

---

47 Further and Higher Education Act (FHEA) 1992 s57.
48 FHEA 1992 s20 and Sch 4.
49 See, eg, *R v Universities Funding Council ex p Institute of Dental Surgery* [1994] ELR 506, QBD. See also paras 12.80–12.82.
50 See article in *Education Law* 1994 p72.

13.63   Where the LEA still maintains an institution which provides further education the secretary of state has the corresponding default powers as for schools.[51]

Higher education institutions

13.64   EA 1996 Sch 37 para 77 substitutes the corresponding powers of the secretary of state to deal with unreasonable exercise of function and default powers in the case of schools, as these apply to local authority institutions providing further and or higher education (see ERA 1988 s219 as substituted by EA 1996).

13.65   For a discussion of rights and remedies in HE institutions see paras 12.74–12.85.

---

51 ERA 1988, s 219: i.e. EA 1996 s495(1)(determination of disputes and questions), s496 (preventing unreasonable exercise of functions) and s497 (powers in default of LEAs and governors).

CHAPTER 14

Judicial review and statutory appeals

This chapter deals with High Court challenges against decisions of bodies concerned with the provision of education; principally by way of judicial review under Order 53 and statutory appeals under Order 55 of the Rules of the Supreme Court. Finally, it discusses the possible effect of the Human Rights Act 1998 on education law.

Public law

14.1   The practice of administrative (or public) law is a fast developing specialism; itself spawning particular areas of expertise, not only in education but also in housing, immigration, community care, health, crime, welfare benefits, environmental and commercial areas of judicial review. There is insufficient space in this book to explore in any depth the framework of administrative law and of judicial review but, in essence, judicial review is the remedy available to any legal person (and, possibly, an unincorporated body[1]) against a public body or a body carrying out statutory functions, which has acted unlawfully.

14.2   A number of cases have sought to formulate those circumstances where a public body may have acted unlawfully. Perhaps that which is most commonly used is the classification by Lord Diplock in the House of Lords decision in *R v Minister for the Civil Service ex p Council for Civil Service Unions* (the GCHQ case),[2] which identified three main heads of challenge:

1) illegality, where the public body does something outside its powers;
2) procedural impropriety, which itself can cover a variety of wrongs, including:
   – carrying out the procedure in a way not authorised by the law,
   – breaching natural justice,
   – failing to have regard to legitimate factors, and
   – having regard to illegitimate factors, and
3) perversity, often referred to as Wednesbury[3] unreasonableness.

Alternatives to judicial review

14.3   One principle of judicial review is that it is not available as a remedy where there are alternative effective remedies. Accordingly, many decisions taken in education cases may not be susceptible to judicial review because of the availability of the following potential remedies:

1   *R v London Borough of Tower Hamlets Combined Traders Association* [1994] COD 325, DC; *R v Darlington BC ex p Association of Darlington Taxi Owners and Darlington Owner Drivers Association* [1994] COD 424, DC; *R v Leeds CC ex p Alwoodley Golf Club* (1995) 15 September, DC; and *R v Traffic Commission for the North Western Traffic Area ex p BRAKE* (1995) 3 November, DC.
2   [1984] 3 All ER 935, HL.
3   See *Associated Picture Houses v Wednesbury Corporation* [1941] 2 All ER 680, CA.

1) appeal to an appeal panel against a decision not to admit a child or to permanently exclude a child (see chapters 5 and 8);
2) use of a governing body's complaints procedure (see chapter 13);
3) use of a local authority's complaints procedure (see chapter 13);
4) complaint to the local government ombudsman (see chapter 13);
5) use of the secretary of state's default powers contained in EA 1996 Part IX Chapter 1 (see chapter 13);
6) appeal to the Special Educational Needs Tribunal (see chapter 9);
7) use of the statutory appeals procedure against decisions of the Special Educational Needs Tribunal (see paras 14.90 to 14.94);
8) use of a university visitor (see chapter 12).

14.4   As a result, a practitioner advising a client on an education law matter is likely to consider judicial review proceedings as the exception rather than as the rule. Nevertheless, the following case summaries give examples of circumstances where judicial review may be appropriate.

Judicial review cases

Decisions concerning opening, closing, amalgamating, transferring or changing the character of schools (see chapter 3)

14.5   *R v Secretary of State for Wales and Clwyd CC ex p Russell*
(1983) 28 June, QBD (unreported)

This case concerned the rights of objectors to proposals to reorganise schooling to see answers to those objections from the LEA (in this case, the objectors had no such right).

14.6   *R v Brent LBC ex p Gunning*
[1985] 84 LGR 168

This case concerned the meaning of consultation (see chapter 3, para 3.50).

14.7   *R v Sutton LBC ex p Hamlet*
(1986) 26 March 1986 (unreported)

Again, see para 3.50 because this case dealt with the meaning of consultation.

14.8   **R v Birmingham County Council ex p Kaur**
(1990) *Times* 11 July

This case determined that where consultation was undertaken by an LEA over school reorganisation, the consultation need only be conducted in English and not necessarily in a minority language. (However, further to the introduction of the obligations to make reasonable adjustments contained in Part III of the Disability Discrimination Act 1995, from October 1999, it may well be that consultation arrangements will have to be adapted so as to meet the needs of disabled parents. For example, should deaf parents require it, depending on the circumstances, it may be necessary to provide British Sign Language interpretation for the consultation process, although whether or not this would in fact be required, in any particular case, is a matter of speculation and, in any event, would depend on the particular circumstances.)

14.9   **R v Lambeth LBC ex p N**
[1996] ELR 299, QBD

This concerned, again, the circumstances requiring consultation before the closure of a special school. While the court determined that the precise form of consultation would depend on the proposal in question, here, consultation was inadequate.

14.10   **R v Buckinghamshire CC ex p Milton Keynes BC**
(1996) *Times* 13 November

This case concerned a failed attempt by a new unitary authority to quash a decision by the county council – the previous LEA – to establish a new grammar school.

14.11   **R v Secretary of State for Education and Employment and North East London Education Association ex p M**
[1996] ELR 162, QBD and CA

This was an unsuccessful attempt to prevent the closure of a school, again over the question of consultation (see para 3.51).

14.12   **R v Barnet LBC ex p F**
[1999] ELR 32, QBD

In this case, the court determined that, although there was a breach of statutory duty with regard to the procedure concerning school reorganisation, the court declined to intervene and refused leave (permission) to move for judicial review.

14.13 *R v Leeds City Council ex p N and Others*
[1999] ELR 324

In this case, the applicant sought judicial review over a decision to close a school on the ground that the consultation period was too short. The application failed.

Decisions of admission authorities

14.14 Governing bodies or local education authorities are responsible for determining which children should be admitted to which school (see chapter 5).

14.15 *R v Hampshire Education Authority ex p J*
[1985] 84 LGR 547

This confirmed that, with respect to children with special educational needs, there are, in effect, two classes of children: those who require statements and those who do not. This particular case concerned the refusal of the LEA to pay for an independent school for a child. The LEA's policy was held to be an unlawful fettering of its discretion by refusing to consider independent school provision except for those children with statements. (See also *R v Hampshire CC ex p W* [1994] ELR 460, QBD.)

14.16 *R v ILEA ex p Ali*
[1990] 2 Admin LR 822; [1990] COD 317, DC

This case concerned the extent of a local authority's duties to provide sufficient schools for children within their area (now EA 1996 s14). The court held that such a duty was a 'target duty', rather than one giving a personal right to an individual child.

14.17 *R v Greenwich LBC ex p Governors of John Ball Primary School*
[1990] Fam Law 469; 88 LGR 589, CA

This very important Court of Appeal decision confirmed that, generally, in determining catchment areas for children, admission authorities need not have regard to borough boundaries.

14.18 *R v Hackney LBC ex p T*
[1991] COD 454

This case established that an admissions authority's policy of operating different points of entry for primary age children (depending on their date of birth) was not, of itself, unlawful.

14.19   *R v Head Master of Fernhill Manor School ex p Brown*
(1992) *Times* 5 June

This case confirmed that private schools were not amenable to judicial review. However, it may be the case that some independent schools are subject to judicial review, in so far as they are carrying out functions arising from statutory duties, such as from the (now repealed) assisted places scheme or in respect of children with special educational needs. (See also *R v Governors of Haberdashers' Aske's Hatcham College Trust*, para 14.25.)

14.20   *R v Governors of Bishop Challoner Roman Catholic Comprehensive Girls School ex p Choudhury*
[1992] 3 All ER 277; [1992] 1 FLR 413, HL

This case confirmed that, in circumstances of oversubscription, a denominational school may operate an admissions policy which gives preference to children of that denomination, over others.

14.21   *R v Bradford Metropolitan BC ex p Sikander Ali*
(1993) *Times* 21 October, QBD

The use of the traditional ties between a school and area and the use of catchment areas to allocate places to a school when there is oversubscription was held not to be unlawful (see para 5.26).

14.22   *R v Lancashire CC ex p West*
(1994) 27 July (unreported)

This case confirmed that, in this situation, the use of random selection as part of an allocations procedure for schools was not of itself unlawful.

14.23   *R v Cleveland CC ex p Commission for Racial Equality*
[1994] ELR 44, CA

This case confirmed that where there may be a conflict of requirements between the duties to comply with parental preference and those contained within the Race Relations Act, the former overrides the latter (see para 5.36).

14.24   *R v Governors of the Hasmonean High School ex p N and E*
[1994] ELR 343, CA

This case confirmed that one factor for consideration in allowing a school to refuse admission to a child, on the ground that, otherwise, that would constitute an inefficient use of resources, was the ability of the child, even though the school was not selective.

14.25 *R v Governors of Haberdashers' Aske's Hatcham College Trust ex p T*
[1995] ELR 350, QBD

This confirmed that City Technology Colleges are amenable to judicial review.

14.26 *R v Lancashire CC ex p Foster*
[1995] ELR 33, QBD

This unusual case confirmed that an LEA's preference for non-Roman Catholics over Roman Catholics in circumstances of oversubscription for schools was not, of itself, unlawful, given the preponderance of Roman Catholic Schools available for Roman Catholics in the area (see para 5.18).

14.27 *R v Wiltshire CC ex p Razazan*
[1996] ELR 220, QBD; [1997] ELR 371, CA

This case confirmed that, generally, it was not unlawful for an admissions authority to have catchment areas (but see *R v Greenwich LBC ex p Governors of the John Ball Primary School,* para 14.17).

14.28 *R v Beatrix Potter School ex p K*
[1997] ELR 468, QBD

In this case, an offer of a place was made, in error, and withdrawn very soon after. The court held that, while a legitimate expectation of a place had arisen, this was only one factor to be taken into account in deciding whether there had been Wednesbury unreasonableness. In all the circumstances of the case, the application failed. See para 5.86.

14.29 *R v Rotherham MBC ex p Clark*
[1998] ELR 152, QBD and CA

The LEA adopted a policy providing that, unless parents within a school catchment area notified the LEA otherwise, their children would be allocated to a particular school. Parents of children outside that school's catchment area, whose children had failed to obtain a place, challenged this policy. Both the High Court and the Court of Appeal upheld the challenge on the basis that such a policy did not comply with the duty contained in EA 1996 s411 to enable a parent to express a preference. Doing nothing was held not to constitute such an expression.

14.30   *R v Sheffield County Council ex p H and Others*
[1999] ELR 242, QBD

This case followed the *Rotherham* judgment (see para 14.29 above). Here, the LEA automatically allocated children to their pre-determined schools and in that event, the application forms provided to parents gave no room for parents to give reasons for that choice. The court held that the procedure was unlawful as it was in breach of EA 1996 s411.

14.31   *R v Governing Body of Dame Alice Owens School ex p S*
[1998] COD 108; [1998] 1 Ed CR 101, QBD

This was a successful judicial review over the misapplication of a school's admissions criteria (see para 5.58).

Provision for children with special educational needs (see chapter 9)

14.32   *R v Lancashire CC ex p M*
[1989] 2 FLR 279, CA

This important Court of Appeal decision confirmed that, in most cases, speech and language therapy provision constitutes special educational provision so as to require LEAs to arrange it, in accordance with the provisions of EA 1996 s324(5)(a)(i). See para 9.34.

14.33   *R v Secretary of State for Education and Science ex p Davis*
[1989] 2 FLR 190, QBD

This case (which concerned legislation preceding EA 1996) confirmed that the responsibility for maintaining a statement arose as soon as it was finalised and notwithstanding any outstanding appeal. This principle was affirmed by the Court of Appeal in *R v Barnet LBC ex p G* [1998] ELR 281, QBD and CA.

14.34   *R v Secretary of State for Education and Science ex p E*
[1992] 1 FLR 377, CA

This seminal case confirmed that once it was determined that a child had special educational needs requiring special educational provision, each and every one of those needs should be set out in Part II of the statement, followed by all provision required to meet those needs in Part III, even if some provision could be delivered from resources ordinarily available to the school, without the need for extra support.

14.35 *R v Dorset CC and Further Education Funding Council ex p Goddard*
[1995] ELR 109, QBD

R v Oxfordshire CC ex p B
[1997] ELR 90, CA

These cases considered the overlapping duties of LEAs and the FEFC. Broadly, LEAs maintain responsibility for children and young people with special educational needs while they are at school (see paras 12.36–12.37).

14.36 *R v Hackney LBC ex p GC*
[1996] ELR 142, CA

This case confirmed that a school named in Part III of a statement need not necessarily constitute special educational provision so as to require an LEA to arrange it, in accordance with the provisions of EA 1996 s324(5)(a)(i).

14.37 *R v Newham LBC ex p R*
[1995] ELR 156, QBD

This case concerned the operation of a policy and the way in which it may affect a child. The policy was to educate children with special educational needs in mainstream schools and, broadly, not in independent schools. Here, the policy was held to be lawful, providing it was not applied so as to fetter the LEA's discretion.

14.38 *R v Oxfordshire CC ex p P*
[1996] ELR 153, QBD

The court confirmed that the LEA retained a duty to make the special educational provision required by a statement, regardless of any funding arrangements with the school. (See also *R v Hillingdon LBC ex p Governing Body of Queensmead School* [1997] ELR 331, QBD.)

14.39 *R v Cumbria CC ex p P*
[1995] ELR 337, QBD

This case determined that the fact that an amount of money was stipulated in Part III of a child's statement was not, of itself, unlawful.

14.40   *R v Special Educational Needs Tribunal ex p South Glamorgan CC*

[1996] ELR 326, CA

This case confirmed that appeals from a tribunal to the High Court should be by way of RSC Order 55 (statutory appeals), rather than Order 53 (judicial review). (See also *R v Special Educational Needs Tribunal ex p F* [1996] ELR 213, QBD.)

14.41   *R v Cumbria CC ex p NB*

[1996] ELR 65, QBD

This case also concerned the legality of a policy regarding categories of children for whom LEAs may make and maintain statements. Here, such a policy – which resulted in the applicant not receiving a statement – was held to be lawful.

14.42   *R v Oxfordshire CC ex p Roast*

[1996] ELR 381, QBD

This case considered the construction of the extant Part III of the EA 1993, concerning those circumstances where an LEA may cease to maintain a statement (now contained in EA 1996 Part IV).

14.43   *R v Harrow LBC ex p M*

[1997] ELR 62, QBD

This case confirmed that the duty of LEAs to arrange special educational provision under EA 1996 s324(5)(a)(i) may not be delegated to another body. The issue was the provision of occupational therapy, physiotherapy and speech and language therapy required by Part III of the applicant's statement, but in respect of which the health authority would usually arrange provision. In this case, the health authority did not arrange all of the provision and the LEA was held liable to arrange it.

14.44   *R v East Sussex CC ex p T*

[1998] ELR 251, HL

In this very important case, the House of Lords held that, in determining what home tuition a child unable to attend school is entitled to (under EA 1996 s19), the resources available to the LEA may not be taken into account. In this case, the reduction of home tuition from five hours per week to three hours per week, solely on the ground of a lack of resources available to the LEA, was held to be unlawful (see paras 11.42–11.44).

14.45 *R v Hampshire Education Authority ex p J*
[1985] 84 LGR 547

This confirmed that, with respect to children with special educational needs, there are, in effect, two classes of children: those requiring statements and those not. This particular case concerned the refusal of the LEA to pay for an independent school for a child. The LEA's policy was held to be an unlawful fettering of its discretion by refusing to consider independent school provision except for those children with statements. (See also *R v Hampshire CC ex p W* [1994] ELR 460.)

14.46 *R v Portsmouth City Council ex p F*
[1998] ELR 619, QBD; [1999] ELR 116, CA

This case confirmed, both in the High Court and in the Court of Appeal, that there is no duty on LEAs to fund higher education for students with special educational needs, pursuant to the provisions of Part IV of the EA 1996, because of the provisions of EA 1996 s1(4), which states that apart from s10 (General Duty of the Secretary of State for Education and Employment) nothing in that Act confers any functions with respect to higher education.

The school curriculum (see chapter 4)

14.47 *R v Secretary of State for Education ex p R and D*
[1994] ELR 495, QBD

This case concerned the interpretation of statutory requirements for religious education and worship. The applicants argued, among other things, that the daily act of worship in a particular school was illegal if it was 'multi-faith' and not predominantly Christian. The application failed.

Registration of pupils and maintenance of registers (see chapter 3)

14.48 *R v Gwent CC ex p Perry*
(1985) 129 SJ 737

This case confirmed that, until a child's name is removed from the register on the one of the grounds prescribed by Education (Pupil Registration) Regulations 1995,[4] the parent remains liable for

4   1995 SI No 2089.

prosecution under EA 1996 s444, for failure to ensure the child's attendance.

Exclusion of pupils (see chapter 8)

14.49   *R v Board of Governors of Stoke Newington School and Others ex p M*
[1994] ELR 131, QBD

This case confirmed the importance of complying with natural justice in exclusion procedures. Here, the decision of the exclusion panel was tainted by the presence of a teacher who was in a position to speak as a witness. See para 8.44.

14.50   *R v Newham LBC ex p X*
[1995] ELR 303, QBD

The court held that, in exceptional circumstances, it would be willing to grant interlocutory relief requiring a permanently excluded child to be readmitted prior to, and notwithstanding, the full hearing of an appeal committee.

14.51   *R v Camden LBC and Governors of Hampstead School ex p H*
[1996] ELR 360, QBD and CA

This case confirmed that the legitimate concerns of a victim should also be considered by an appeals panel, in determining whether or not to order reinstatement of a permanently excluded child (see para 8.68).

14.52   *R v Independent Appeal Committee ex p Mayor and Burgesses of the London Borough of Enfield*
(1998) 4 June (unreported)

This case determined that any challenges by the governors to an appeal committee's decision to order a child's reinstatement following a permanent exclusion must be brought very swiftly. Here, the judge set a limit of ten days. (See also *R v Governors of McEntee School ex p Mbandaka* [1999] Ed CR 656, where a judicial review of a decision to uphold a fixed-term exclusion was refused because it was held to have not been brought in time, even though it was brought within three months. However, the situation may be different in the case of permanent exclusions.)

Admission, exclusion and reinstatement appeals (see chapters 5 and 7)

14.53   *R v South Glamorgan Appeal Committee ex p Evans*
(1984) 10 May, QBD (unreported)

R v Commissioner for Local Administration ex p Croydon LBC and Another
[1989] 1 All ER 1033, QBD

Both these cases confirmed the importance of the two-stage process required for admission appeals (see paras 5.76–5.78).

14.54   *R v Camden LBC and Another ex p S*
[1991] COD 195

This case determined that, where an appeal committee member drops out part way through the proceedings, it is not lawful for that person to be replaced by a new member.

14.55   *R v Lancashire CC ex p M*
[1994] ELR 478, QBD

This case concerned the extent to which appeal committees must give detailed reasons for their decisions (see para 5.83). Similar cases include:

- *W (a minor) v Education Appeal Committee of Lancashire CC* [1994] ELR 530, CA;
- *R v Lancashire CC ex p M* [1995] ELR 136, QBD;
- *R v Governors of St Gregory's Roman Catholic Aided High School and Appeals Committee ex p M* [1995] ELR 290, QBD;
- *R v Northamptonshire CC ex p W* [1998] ELR 291, QBD;
- *R v Governors of Bacon City Technology College ex p W* [1998] ELR 488, QBD;
- *McKeown v Appeal Committee and Governors of Cardinal Heenan High School and Leeds City Council* [1998] ELR 578, QBD;
- *R v Birmingham City Council Education Appeal Committee ex p B* [1998] Ed CR 573 (this case expressly distinguished *R v Lancashire CC ex p M* [1994] ELR 478, QBD).

14.56   *R v Appeal Committee of Brighouse School ex p G and B*
[1997] ELR 39, QBD

This case confirmed that the mere fact that a school had reached its admissions number was not, of itself, evidence that the admission of an extra child would automatically constitute an inefficient use of resources.

14.57   *R v Education Appeal Committee of Leicester CC ex p Tarmohamed*
[1997] ELR 48, QBD

This case concerned the way admissions appeals should be conducted in circumstances where there are multiple appeals, ie, where a number of children were appealing for a place at the same school. The court held that it may be necessary to rank children in order of preference rather than treating each appeal individually. In addition, the court held that, while it was not necessary for each parent appellant to know the details of the case of all other parent appellants, if a direct point was made about one parent, then that parent may have a right to know about it and to respond. See para 5.77.

14.58   *R v Roman Catholic Schools ex p S*
[1998] ELR 304, QBD

This case considered the extent to which an appeal committee must examine evidence and call witnesses to establish issues of fault. In this case concerning an appeal against a permanent exclusion, the appeal committee was held to have failed to take such adequate steps and a decision to uphold the exclusion was quashed.

14.59   *R v Wakefield Diocesan Board of Education (Schools Appeal Tribunal) and Holy Trinity School Wakefield ex p J*
[1999] Ed CR 566

In this case, a decision of an exclusion committee to uphold a permanent exclusion was quashed because a key decision was taken exclusively by the chair of the committee, rather than by the whole committee.

School transport (see chapter 6)

14.60   *George v Devon CC*
[1988] 3 All ER 1002, HL

This House of Lords decision formalised the link between the duty on LEAs to arrange transport where the nearest available school for a child under eight years is more than two miles away and for a child over eight years is more than three miles away, and the fact that a parent would otherwise have an effective defence to a prosecution arising because of his/her failure to send a child to school (now EA 1996 ss444 and 509).

14.61 *Essex CC v Rogers*

[1986] 3 All ER 321, HL

This case concerned the requirements for reasonable safety for a child who was not provided with transport. In determining whether a child was close enough to his/her school so that the LEA was not obliged to provide transport, the route measured must be a safe route.

14.62 *R v East Sussex CC ex p D*

[1991] COD 374

The court confirmed that the definition of what constituted an alternative available school, which may be sufficiently close to home so as to remove any duty on providing transport to the LEA, would not exclude, all other things being equal, a school which a parent does not want. (See also *R v Kent CC ex p C*, para 14.67.)

14.63 *R v Rochdale MBC ex p Schemet*

[1994] ELR 89, QBD

This case considered those circumstances when an LEA may include religious preference in considering whether a nearer alternative school was available, and therefore whether the LEA was obliged to provide transport. In short, parental religious preference was a relevant consideration but not the only one. (See also *R v Essex CC ex p C* [1994] 1 FLR 773.)

14.64 *Re S (minors)*

[1995] ELR 98, CA

This case concerned those circumstances where a court may consider arguments of fact in judicial review. Here, the applicant argued that the school provided by the LEA was not an effective alternative school (because of the use of Welsh as the principal language) and that, because the school chosen by the parent was some distance away, the LEA ought to arrange transport. The application failed. See para 6.60.

14.65 *R v Gwent CC ex p Harris*

[1995] ELR 27, QBD

This case concerned the question of provision of seat belts. The court held that, since there was no question that the vehicle provided by the LEA was not below the ordinary reasonable standard applied throughout the UK, the decision of the LEA not to arrange transport with seat belts was not, of itself, unlawful. However, the Department of Transport has since introduced regulations[5] so that since February 1997, all minibuses and coaches carrying children have to have seatbelts fitted. See para 6.67.

14.66 *R v Hereford and Worcester CC ex p P*
[1992] FLR 207, QBD

This case concerned a child with Down's syndrome who was provided with transport from home to school. The minibus provided took a circuitous route so that the total journey time, from door to door, was about one hour each way. Because of the child's particular needs, it was held that not only was the journey too long but that the child was entitled to 'non-stressful' transport, and that the duties on LEAs to provide transport should be considered as such. See para 6.65.

14.67 *R v Kent CC ex p C*
[1998] ELR 108, QBD

The court held that an LEA's decision to refuse transport for a child to a grammar school, because there was a nearer non-selective school available, was not perverse.

Financial and other support for pupils (see chapter 6)

14.68 *Watt v Kesteven CC*
[1995] 1 All ER 473, CA

This case held that the power of an LEA to pay fees at a non-maintained school (now contained in EA 1996 s18) would not require the LEA to pay such fees at a school selected by a parent, if the LEA could make alternative sufficient arrangements.

14.69 *R v Lambeth LBC ex p G*
[1994] ELR 207, QBD

In this case, the court confirmed that an LEA policy to award maintenance allowances only to students attending a course at an institution within the area of the LEA, unless no suitable course was available, was ultra vires.

---

5   Road Vehicles (Construction and Use) (Amendment) (No 2) Regulations 1996 SI No 163.

14.70   *R v Hampshire Education Authority ex p J*
[1985] LGR 547

This case confirmed that LEAs must not fetter their discretion in determining whether to pay school fees under the extant EA 1944 (now EA 1996 s518). (See also *R v Inner London Education Authority ex p F* (1988) *Times* 16 June, QBD.)

Grants and awards for students (see chapter 12)

14.71   *Shah v Barnet LBC*
[1983] 2 WLR 16, HL

This case considered the meaning of ordinary residence, for the purposes of the regulations governing grants and awards. In short, a person is ordinarily resident if s/he has habitually and normally resided in the place from choice, and for a settled purpose, for the prescribed three-year period.

14.72   *MacMahon v Department of Education and Science*
[1982] 3 WLR 1129, ChD

This case established that the three-year residence requirement imposed on non-UK EC nationals working in the UK in order to obtain domestic status for the purposes of awards and fees was in conflict with the principle of free movement of workers enshrined in article 7 of the Treaty of Rome, and subsequent EC legislation.

14.73   *R v Bexley LBC ex p Jones*
[1995] ELR 42, QBD

An LEA's rigid policy to refuse discretionary awards was an unlawful fettering of its discretion. (See also *R v Warwickshire CC ex p Collymore* [1995] ELR 217, QBD; *R v Warwickshire CC ex p Williams* [1995] ELR 326, QBD; and *R v Southwark LBC ex p Udu* [1996] ELR 390, CA.)

14.74   *R v Portsmouth City Council ex p F*
[1998] ELR 619, QBD; [1999] ELR 116, CA

See para 14.46.

Steps in judicial review proceedings

14.75 This section is intended as a guide but practitioners should always refer to Order 53 of Schedule 1 to the Civil Procedure Rules for the detail.

14.76 When taking instructions where a judicial review may be appropriate, the applicant's solicitor should consider:

1) whether there is a specific decision or decisions which may be amenable;

2) whether the decision was taken so long ago as to fall foul of the requirements to lodge an application for permission 'as soon as possible' and, in any event, within three months (unless there are exceptional circumstances);

3) whether there is an effective alternative remedy.

14.77 Assuming that the above points are satisfactorily met, decide who is the relevant applicant. In many cases, a child may be a relevant applicant and may therefore apply for legal aid, particularly where the material decision affects him/her. Accordingly, families who may otherwise be unable to commence proceedings (perhaps because the parents are not eligible for legal aid but are otherwise of modest means) may do so. Be wary, however, of the first instance decision in *R v Hackney LBC ex p T*[6] where Auld J criticised the child applicant being granted legal aid over a decision regarding the failure of the parent to succeed in an admission appeal. However, the court took a different view in *R v Sheffield County Council ex p H and Others*[7] and in any event it is likely that, given the development in the case-law on standing for judicial review, a child who is directly affected by a decision has sufficient standing to be an applicant.[8]

14.78 Apply for legal aid as soon as possible. Given the very tight deadlines for lodging applications for permission, it will usually be appropriate to lodge an emergency application by completing page 12 of the Form APP1 (and sometimes, in very urgent cases, by faxing the application to the Legal Aid Board).

14.79 Assuming that legal aid is granted, instruct specialist counsel to

---

6 [1991] COD 454.

7 [1999] ELR 242, QBD.

8 See, in particular, *R v Inspectorate of Pollution and Another ex p Greenpeace Ltd (No 2)* [1994] 4 All ER 329, DC; *R v Secretary of State for Foreign Affairs ex p World Development Movement Ltd* [1995] 1 All ER 611, DC and *R v Somerset CC and ARC Southern Limited ex p Dixon* [1997] COD 323. See also para 16.59 note 36.

advise and, if so advised, draft the relevant Form 86A and statement in support (although, especially with respect to statements and exhibits, this may be done by the solicitor).

14.80   Lodge the application for permission to move for judicial review. This should consist of some or all of the following:

1) notice of issue of legal aid;
2) consent of parent to act as litigation friend;
3) certificate of solicitor as to litigation friend of minor;
4) Form 86A;
5) statement and exhibits in support;
6) copies of relevant statutory references.

As well as the originals, a paginated, indexed bundle should also be lodged, containing a list of essential reading, in accordance with the relevant practice directions.[9]

14.81   An application for permission may be conducted without a hearing (on the papers) or with a hearing. The former is the usual procedure but an oral hearing may be sought if the matter is especially urgent. Where interlocutory relief is required, the respondents must be put on notice to give them an opportunity of appearing. Accordingly, unless an oral hearing is sought, there is no need to notify the respondents, at this stage, that an application for permission to move for judicial review has been lodged and no need to serve on them copies of the documents (although there may be strategic reasons for doing so).

14.82   If permission is not granted, it may be renewed at an oral hearing. If leave is refused at an oral hearing, it may be renewed before the Court of Appeal. In these events, separate detailed provisions apply with respect to the lodging of bundles, etc.

14.83   Assuming that permission is granted, a claim form should be served on the respondent, together with copies of the Form 86A and supporting statement and exhibits. The solicitor will then need to make a statement of service and lodge this, together with the claim form and the relevant fee with the Crown Office at the Royal Courts of Justice, within 14 days (or sooner if time is abridged, see para 14.84).

14.84   Generally, the respondent then has 56 days to lodge any evidence in reply but, at the permission stage, this may be abridged, if the matter is urgent.

---

9   Practice Note (Crown Office List : Penalties for Late Papers) [1994] 4 All ER 671 and Practice Note (Judicial Review : Documents to be Lodged) [1997] 1 All ER 128.

14.85   Often the fact of obtaining permission to move for judicial review will result in a settlement. However, if not, eventually, the Crown Office will list the matter for a substantive hearing.

14.86   Interlocutory applications may, in some cases, be required.

14.87   The matter is ready for a substantive hearing on the expiry of the time allowed for the filing of evidence by the respondent. At that stage, the matter will enter part B of the Crown Office warned list and a letter will be sent to the applicant's solicitors informing them that the case has entered part B of the list. The applicant's solicitors should forward a copy of that letter to counsel's clerk and to all other parties. Often, counsel's clerk will approach the Crown Office with suggested dates for the hearing. If the matter is not ready for hearing, it may be necessary to apply to the Crown Office master to have the case stood out into part C of the Crown Office list.

14.88   At least five clear working days before the date fixed for hearing, the applicant's solicitor must lodge with the court a paginated, indexed bundle for the use of the court (two bundles in the case of a matter listed for a Divisional Court). Meanwhile, counsel will, separately, lodge skeleton arguments.

Orders available by way of judicial review

14.89   There are four orders available:
  – declaration;
  – certiorari, an order quashing the decision concerned;
  – prohibition, an order preventing the decision and actions arising;
  – mandamus, an order requiring the respondent to do something.

In some circumstances, it may be possible to obtain damages, but the law in respect of this is complex and counsel's opinion will almost certainly be required.

Statutory appeals against decisions of the SENT

14.90   Since the introduction of the Special Educational Needs Tribunal (SENT) in September 1994, disputes regarding whether a statutory assessment should be made, whether a statement of special educational needs should be made, the contents of Parts 2, 3 or 4 of a statement and whether a statement should cease to be maintained, may now be appealed by a parent to the SENT (see chapter 9). The

Special Educational Needs Tribunal Regulations 1995[10] set out the procedure for appealing and, broadly, appeals will take three to five months between lodgement and hearing.

14.91　　In most cases, the tribunal is the final arbiter in disputes between parents and LEAs but where either party to an appeal to the tribunal (ie, a parent or an LEA) considers that there is a material point of law in issue, the tribunal decision may be appealed to the High Court in accordance with the provisions of Order 55 of Schedule 1 to the Civil Procedure Rules and Tribunals and Inquiries Act 1992 s11 (as amended). *R v Special Educational Needs Tribunal ex p South Glamorgan CC*[11] and *R v Special Educational Needs Tribunal ex p F*[12] confirmed that appeals from the Special Educational Needs Tribunal must be by way of Order 55 and not Order 53 (judicial review) or indeed by way of case stated, pursuant to Order 56 of Schedule 1 to the Civil Procedure Rules.

Procedure

14.92　The procedure for appealing is that a notice of appeal must be lodged with the Crown Office within four weeks of the decision having been served. Accordingly, the steps set out in para 14.78 in respect of an application for legal aid are even more urgent. However, note that, in these cases, it is only a parent (and not a child) who may appeal, in accordance with the Court of Appeal decision in *S v Special Educational Needs Tribunal and City of Westminster*.[13]

14.93　　Once a notice of appeal is lodged, apart from any interlocutory matters, the next stage is the substantive hearing.

14.94　　Currently, there is no provision in the Special Educational Needs Tribunal Regulations for interim relief, pending a full hearing. Practitioners may have thought that judicial review would be available in order, for example, to obtain an order requiring an LEA to maintain the status quo, pending a full court hearing. However, in *Re M (a minor)*,[14] the Court of Appeal refused to grant leave for judicial review to obtain an order requiring specified provision, pending the tribunal appeal. It is likely that this issue will be tested again.

10　1995 SI No 3113. See appendix G.

11　[1996] ELR 326, CA.

12　[1996] ELR 213, QBD.

13　[1996] ELR 228, CA.

14　[1996] ELR 135, CA. See also *R v Oxfordshire CC ex p Roast* [1996] ELR 381, QBD.

Statutory appeal cases

14.95   *Council of the City of Sunderland v P and C*
[1996] ELR 283, QBD

This case determined that the SENT has no power to order an amendment to a child's statement to name a different school, if that school is not authorised by the Secretary of State for Education and Employment to take children of that age. (However, doubts have been raised about this decision in *Ellison v Hampshire County Council* (1999) 30 July (unreported).)

14.96   *Fairpo v Humberside CC*
[1997] ELR 12, QBD

This case confirmed that a foster parent may bring an appeal to the SENT.

14.97   *L v Kensington and Chelsea RLBC*
[1997] ELR 155, QBD

This case concerned, among other things, the refusal of the SENT to adjourn a hearing which had been brought forward so as to result in the parent's witness being unable to attend. The court held that, in this case, the refusal to adjourn was an error of law.

14.98   *R v Kingston upon Thames Council and Hunter*
[1997] ELR 223, QBD

In this case, because the school named in the statement could not meet the provision set out in Part III of the statement, the court quashed the decision of the SENT. (See also *L v Kent CC and Special Educational Needs Tribunal* [1998] ELR 140, QBD.)

14.99   *S and C v Special Educational Needs Tribunal*
[1997] ELR 242, QBD

This case confirmed, amongst other things, that, in an appeal on a point of law against a decision of the SENT, the tribunal chair should be added as a second respondent.

14.100   *B v Isle of Wight Council*
[1997] ELR 279, QBD

The court determined that occupational therapy and physiotherapy need not (although may) be special educational provision so as to be particularised in Part III of a child's statement. (See also *C v Special*

Educational Needs Tribunal [1997] ELR 390, QBD, and *Bromley LBC v Special Educational Needs Tribunal and Others* [1999] ELR 260, CA.)

14.101 *C v Lancashire CC*
[1997] ELR 377, QBD

The appellants were seeking to overturn a decision of the SENT to refuse to amend their son's statement to name a mainstream school, as opposed to a special school. Although the appeal failed, the court determined that, in deciding whether a school was suitable or not, having regard to the efficient use of resources (now set out in EA 1996 s316(2)(c)), the additional cost of the placement in a mainstream school should be weighed against the parent's preference.

14.102 *City of Bradford Metropolitan Council v A*
[1997] ELR 417, QBD

This case determined that nursing care could not be educational provision. In consequence, an LEA is not obliged to specify nursing care in Part III of a statement of special educational needs, nor to arrange it in accordance with EA 1996 s324(5)(a)(i). (See also *Bromley LBC v Special Educational Needs Tribunal and Others* [1999] ELR 260, CA.)

14.103 *Ligouri v City of Salford and Special Educational Needs Tribunal*
[1997] ELR 455, QBD
Phillips v Derbyshire CC
[1997] ELR 461, QBD
Sage v Gloucestershire County Council and Confrey
[1998] ELR 525, QBD
Re F
[1999] ELR 251
S v Jane Williams (Chair of the Special Educational Needs Tribunal) and Oxfordshire County Council
(1999) 26 August (unreported)

These five cases all concerned appeals on a point of law being lodged outside of the 28-day time limit required by RSC Order 55. In all but the second case, the court determined that there were acceptable reasons for the delay and permitted the cases to proceed (although in the first case, the substantive appeal failed) while in the second, the court determined that, because of the unexplained delay (the appeal was four days late), the appellant was barred from proceeding.

14.104 *L v Clarke and Somerset CC*
[1998] ELR 129, QBD

The court underlined the importance of quantifying and particularising amounts of support required, in a statement of special educational needs. The court held that, although the requirement to be specific was not an absolute and universal one, there was a presumption in favour of specificity and so, in most cases, such detail was required. Provision should usually be so specific and clear as to leave no room for doubt about what has been decided was necessary. (See also *Bromley LBC v Special Educational Needs Tribunal and Others* [1999] ELR 260, CA.)

14.105 *Jules v Wandsworth LBC*
[1998] ELR 243, QBD

This case considered the extent of the duty contained in EA 1996 s316 (the requirement to educate a child within a mainstream school, providing certain conditions are met). The appellant sought to argue that if the tribunal had determined that the mainstream school of the parent's choice was not suitable, it should have considered alternative mainstream schools. The court rejected this interpretation.

14.106 *Richardson v Solihull MBC and Special Educational Needs Tribunal; White and Another v Ealing LBC and Special Educational Needs Tribunal; Hereford and Worcester CC v Lane*
[1998] ELR 319, CA

In these cases, the Court of Appeal affirmed the High Court's decision that a statement may provide, in Part IV, not only that a particular school be named but, alternatively, that a description of a type of school be set out. The tribunal's powers of adjournment were also discussed.

14.107 *Wilkin v Goldthorpe and Coventry CC*
[1998] ELR 345, QBD

This case concerned a tribunal decision which had the effect of determining provision for the child for a period of one term only. The court held that the SENT is bound to look at the overall picture, both at the present time and in the near future and that the tribunal should therefore have addressed its mind to the near future as well

14.108 *R v Cheshire CC ex p C*

[1998] ELR 66, QBD

This case held that when exercising powers under EA 1996 s320 in making provision outside of England and Wales, LEAs and tribunals may take account of private funds which might make the costs to the LEA equal to, or less than, that of alternative provision within England and Wales. (The case also overturned the refusal of the tribunal to adjourn, when the appellant's representative was unable to attend, through illness.)

14.109 *B v Harrow LBC and Special Educational Needs Tribunal*

[1998] ELR 351, CA

This case considered the meaning of EA 1996 Sch 27 para 3(3)(b), concerning the efficient use of resources in selection of a school. The court determined that the resources referred to in that paragraph were not only those of the LEA maintaining the statement but, in addition, those of another LEA.

14.110 *Catchpole v Buckinghamshire County Council and Special Educational Needs Tribunal*

[1998] ELR 463, QBD; [1999] ELR 179, CA

This case concerned the relevance of EA 1996 s9 (which gives a general duty to educate pupils in accordance with their parents' wishes) to provision for pupils with special educational needs and considered the interrelation between this section and EA 1996 Part IV (which deals, in detail, with provision for pupils with special educational needs). The case determined that s9 is relevant, especially where parents seek an independent school and therefore when EA 1996 Sch 27 (which deals with choice of a maintained school) does not apply. (See also *S v Bracknell Forest Borough Council and Special Educational Needs Tribunal* [1999] ELR 51, QBD.)

14.111 *G v Barnet LBC and Special Educational Needs Tribunal*

[1998] ELR 480, QBD; [1999] ELR 161, CA

This case held that in considering arrangements for children with special educational needs, religion must be taken into account but may not necessarily constitute special educational provision.

14.112   *Hackney LBC v Silyadin*
[1998] ELR 571, QBD

In the Special Educational Needs Tribunal hearing which formed the subject of this appeal, the parent had sought a place for the child at an independent school and the local education authority had proposed a day maintained school. The tribunal had found that the arrangements proposed by the LEA were not sufficient to meet the child's needs and therefore allowed the appeal, even though it had not determined that the child needed residential provision. The High Court overturned the tribunal decision and stated that the tribunal should have looked at alternative arrangements which may have allowed for the child's needs to be met without necessarily requiring unnecessary residential provision. (See also *Hereford and Worcester County Council v Lane* [1998] ELR 578, QBD and *Bromley LBC v Special Educational Needs Tribunal and Others* [1999] ELR 260, CA.)

14.113   *C v Special Educational Needs Tribunal and Greenwich LBC*
[1999] ELR 5, QBD

This High Court appeal was brought on a number of grounds but, most particularly, the court allowed the appeal because the decision of the tribunal had purported to unlawfully delegate an assessment procedure for determining provision for the child concerned in an extra statutory way. See also para 11.30.

14.114   *S v Cardiff City Council and Another*
[1999] Ed CR 645

This case helpfully reviews the case-law on the duty to give reasons and to explain decisions.

14.115   *Bromley LBC v Special Educational Needs Tribunal and Others*
[1999] ELR 260, QBD and CA

This important case considered three areas. First, it confirmed the requirement for specificity, not only in statements of special educational needs but in Special Educational Needs Tribunal decisions. Second, it affirmed the principle in *Hereford and Worcester v Lane* (see para 14.112) and third, it reviewed the case-law and revisited the question of what precisely is and what is not special educational provision. Unfortunately, the judgment did not determine the issue comprehensively and the question remains open. Incidentally, this appeal was accepted one day late (see para 14.102).

Implications of the Human Rights Act

14.116   The Human Rights Act 1998, which is scheduled to come into effect in autumn 2000, incorporates the European Convention on Human Rights into UK law. Article 2 of the first protocol to the Convention provides that:

> No persons shall be denied the right to education. In the existence of any function which it assumes in relation to education and teaching, the state shall respect the right of parents to ensure such education and teaching in conformity with their own religious and philosophical convictions.

14.117   The UK has a reservation to the effect that the principle affirmed in the second sentence is accepted 'only insofar as it is compatible with efficient instruction and training, and the avoidance of unreasonable public expenditure'. Thus, in cases taken previously by UK citizens (for example seeking to enhance the rights of disabled children to attend mainstream schools) applicants have had limited success. The government has decided that the reservation will remain. Accordingly, it is unclear how much the incorporation of the European Convention will impact on the rights of parents and children in education law but, certainly, practitioners must be alive to the potential implications. See paras 16.7–16.8.[15]

---

15   See also Keir Starmer *European human rights law* (LAG, 1999) chapter 21.

CHAPTER 15

Failure to provide appropriate education

This chapter discusses the developing law in cases where pupils claim that they have not received education appropriate to their needs.

Negligence in schools

15.1   Many issues concerning negligence in schools are not legally distinct from ordinary personal injury principles. Practitioners should have little difficulty in identifying cases concerning faulty equipment, tripping, lack of adequate supervision, etc, for which see standard personal injury textbooks. The law in respect of negligence of teachers, governing bodies and LEAs regarding children who have been bullied is discussed in chapter 6 paras 6.31–6.38. Another area in which the law is developing is failure to make necessary special educational provision. Here, the law is analogous to that of medical negligence, or there may be an action for breach of contract.

Actions in negligence

15.2   Until June 1995, it had generally been considered that individuals may not sue for the negligent provision of education. However, the House of Lords then considered five cases (two concerning alleged negligent provision of social services and three concerning alleged negligent provision of education) which changed the position and opened the door to the possibility of negligence actions in education.[1]

15.3   In the three education cases,[2] the first two plaintiffs had specific learning difficulties (dyslexia and/or dyspraxia). In one way or another, they alleged that the learning difficulties arising from those impairments were not properly met by appropriate provision by the respective LEAs or that necessary education was not arranged otherwise. The House of Lords held that the breach of a public law duty (for example, those contained within EA 1996 Part IV dealing with provision for children with special educational needs) by themselves did not give rise to a claim for damages. However, a private law cause of action may arise if a plaintiff can establish that a statutory duty was imposed for a limited class of the public and that parliament intended to confer on members of that class a private right of action for breach of the duty. At the same time, a cause of

---

1   *X and Others (minors) v Bedfordshire CC; M (a minor) and Another v Newham LBC and Others; E (a minor) v Dorset CC; Christmas v Hampshire CC; Keating v Mayor and Burgesses of Bromley LBC* [1995] ELR 404, HL.

2   *E (a minor) v Dorset CC; Christmas v Hampshire CC; Keating v Mayor and Burgesses of Bromley LBC* [1995] ELR 404, HL.

action may arise if a plaintiff can establish that there was a duty of care at common law which was subsequently breached. The cases were therefore allowed to proceed.

15.4 In deciding whether or not an individual has been negligent, the relevant test was set out in *Bolam v Friern Hospital Management Committee*:[3] Individuals may be found to have acted negligently if they do not provide a service which meets the ordinary skill of a competent headteacher, etc, with the proviso that if they can show that they acted in accordance with the views of a reputable body of opinion within their profession, then they will have discharged their duty of care and will not have been negligent, even though others may disagree with them. Accordingly, it is not sufficient to show that someone or even many people disagree with what the headteacher, etc. did, if that did not fall below the accepted standard of care at the time. It is also important to remember that what happened ten or 20 years ago may have been acceptable then, even if it is not now.

15.5 The High Court has now heard and decided the first two cases involving claims for compensation for harm caused by alleged negligence during school education. Both cases involve dyslexic children. One claim succeeded and but was overturned by the Court of Appeal and the other failed at first instance.

15.6 *Phelps v Hillingdon LBC*
[1998] ELR 38, QBD; [1998] ELR 587, CA

At first instance, the plaintiff succeeded and was awarded damages in the region of £45,000. She argued that a psychologist should have diagnosed her dyslexia in October 1985, when she was aged nearly 12; that subsequently, it should have been diagnosed as she began to experience increasing difficulty; that as a result, she failed to receive necessary provision; and that her standard of literacy was much lower than that which she would have achieved, had she received the necessary provision. On the other hand, the defendant argued that the psychologist had no duty of care to the plaintiff and that the role of the psychologist was only to advise the LEA and the school.

The judge determined that the psychologist did owe a duty of care to the plaintiff. He also found (following the House of Lords decision, see para 15.3) that the LEA was vicariously liable for any breach of duty by the psychologist. In addition, he held that, in fact, the psychologist breached her duty of care in two ways: in failing to diagnose the plaintiff's dyslexia and in failing to think again when

3   [1957] 2 All ER 118, QBD.

the plaintiff was making very little progress, despite support. The judge did, however, determine that school staff were not negligent (in this particular case). Finally, he found that had the plaintiff been diagnosed with dyslexia, she would have received specific provision following the Hornsby method and would have therefore made greater progress in literacy. The defendant appealed.

The Court of Appeal gave judgment on 4 November 1998. The judgment reversed the decision of the High Court and held that, in fact, an individual educational psychologist does not owe a duty of care to a child. The court considered that such a psychologist is part of a multidisciplinary team whose function is to provide information to the LEA, rather than who owes a direct duty of care to the child concerned. Accordingly, as the law currently stands, actions against local education authorities alleging negligence by their educational psychologist (which, in fact, is the basis for many claims for negligence concerning children with special educational needs) may not now be brought, unless it can be shown that there was an assumption of a duty of care by identifiable individuals on behalf of the LEA.

15.7   *Christmas v Hampshire CC*

[1998] ELR 1, QBD

This, of course, was one of the cases that went to the House of Lords in June 1995. Here, the plaintiff also experienced difficulties over the years while at school, which manifested themselves in a number of ways. However, the judge found that, in essence, there was no material breach of duty of care, having regard to the Bolam test (see para 15.4), even though the plaintiff had dyslexia which, arguably, could have been ameliorated by way of special education provision. Again, the reason for this is very much to do with the facts of that particular case. There was no involvement by an educational psychologist and the judge evidently felt that the threshold duty of care was lower for teaching staff.

15.8   *Barrett v Enfield LBC*

[1999] 3 All ER 193, HL

This case concerned an action alleging negligence concerning the provision and nature of social services and care by the defendant to the plaintiff. The judgment reviewed the House of Lords decision in *X v Bedfordshire* (see para 15.2) and also in another case, *Stovin v Wise* [1996] AC 923 (which also considered the extent to which actions may be brought in negligence for breach of statutory duties). It had been hoped that *Barrett* would clarify the law, particularly in the light of the Court of Appeal decision in *Phelps* but, certainly from the point of view of education negligence actions, the position would appear to be broadly unaffected, although practitioners should certainly have regard to this case in considering any negligence actions. In any event, in *Barrett*, the House of Lords held that an action for breach of duty of care by social service officers should not be ruled out, in the same way as it was in the *X v Bedfordshire* case.

15.9   *Osman v UK*

[1999] 1 FLR 193, ECHR

Meanwhile, the European Court of Human Rights gave judgment in this application on 28 October 1998. This case concerned a complaint by the family of a father and child, respectively killed and injured, by a teacher, who had sought to bring an action against the police for failing to take adequate steps to prevent the crimes, but which action was struck out on the ground that public policy required police immunity from suit in relation to the investigation and suppression of crime. The application alleged breach of the family's human rights under the European Convention for the Protection of Human Rights and fundamental freedoms in that, in breach of article 2, the authorities had failed to protect the right of life of the family's father against a threat posed by the teacher, in breach of article 6, the family had been denied their right to access to a court to sue the authorities for damage caused by the police negligence and in breach of article 8, the police had failed to secure the child's personal safety by failing to protect him from harassment. In that regard, particularly with respect to the article 6 claim, the case may have an impact on education negligence actions. In any event, the European Court found against the family with regards to the article 2 claim and the article 8 claim but held that the view that no action could lie against the police for their negligence in the investigation and suppression of crime was a disproportionate restriction on the rights of access to a court and therefore in breach of article 6. The extent to which this may be transplanted to actions currently prohibited by *Phelps* and indeed *X v Bedfordshire* is not yet known.

15.10   *Anderton v Clwyd CC*
[1999] ELR 1, CA

Meanwhile, this case determined that, unless psychiatric injury is alleged, actions for education negligence are not personal injury actions.

15.11   *Holton v Barnet LBC and Another*
[1999] ELR 340, CA

In the light of the House of Lords decision in *X v Bedfordshire CC* and the Court of Appeal decision in *Barrett v Enfield LBC* (see paras 15.2 and 15.8), this case was struck out.

Principles

15.12   Generally, it is very difficult to extract from these cases principles which may be of assistance, particularly as, at the time of writing, *Phelps* and *Anderton* are proceeding to the House of Lords and both *Barrett v Enfield* and *Osman v UK* have not yet filtered into decided cases in education negligence. However, the authors suggest the following:

1) It remains the case that it would appear that there is no right in law for an action for breach of statutory duty of a LEA under EA 1996 Part IV.

2) There would appear also to be no right in common law for an action in negligence concerning an educational psychologist.

3) However, LEAs (and, sometimes, governing bodies of schools) may be held to be vicariously liable for the negligent actions of other individuals – such as head teachers, advisory teachers, etc – arising from their common law duty of care towards children and young people.

4) In addition, psychologists involved other than through LEAs may owe a duty of care, notwithstanding *Phelps*.

5) In any event, negligence actions in education cases may be sustained only if it can be established that:
   – there was a direct relationship between the employee against whom negligence is alleged and the individual concerned;
   – the employee was negligent in the provision of education and/or services, having regard to the *Bolam* test set out above;
   – as a result of that negligence, the individual suffered material and identifiable detriment;

– the consequences to the individual were reasonably foreseeable by the employee.

6) Unless psychiatric injury is alleged, such actions will not be personal injury actions.

7) In proceeding with any cases, it is necessary to identify individuals who either provided incorrect advice or support or failed to provide necessary advice or support. The onus of proof in any action rests with the plaintiff. Thus, the more accurate, comprehensive and detailed records there are – not only school records but also those which relate to matters raised by parents in discussion with schools and LEA staff, etc. – the more likely it is that any action may be sustained. Conversely, the absence of records may make it difficult to establish negligence.

8) There are particular problems in demonstrating the link between alleged negligence and failure to ameliorate specific impairments.

9) Equally, it may be very difficult to establish the level of any quantum for economic loss alleged.

Most critically, because of the complexity of the law, specialist advice will be required, not only from experts but also from counsel.

Actions in breach of contract

15.13   Where there is a dispute over provision of education, damages may separately be obtained if an action in contract can be established. In most instances, such actions may not apply, certainly in the case of provision of education in maintained schools but also in provision of education in most colleges, because students do not usually pay for education. The privity of contract rule may thereby prevent them from having any cause of action. However, particularly in the case where students contribute to the costs of provision (from September 1998), contract law may be of increasing relevance.

15.14   In addition, where private education is involved, a cause of action may arise if a breach can be established. It is unusual for contracts to be sufficiently specific so as to give rise to a breach of an express term and, in that event, the claimant will have to persuade the court of an implied term of a contract.

CHAPTER 16

Practical considerations in running an education case

It is hoped that readers will find the discussion of the tactical considerations and practical background in this chapter useful. For more detail on any particular subject, reference should to be made to the relevant other chapter or part of the book.

For complete chapter contents, see overleaf

Introduction

16.1   Until comparatively recently it might have been thought that there was little scope for or purpose in involving lawyers in what has been seen for generations as an area of activity best left to parents and education professionals, with the state building on the philanthropic tenets of those who established the education system over 100 years ago. The few who used the law to challenge a decision they felt adverse to them or their child were regarded as somewhat misconceived; even when legally justified it was sometimes doubted whether the true interests of the child always took precedence over the parent's sense of grievance. However, as the state has seen fit to legislate increasingly in the last 20 years, functions which hitherto might have continued to run on the basis of common sense or received wisdom have been subjected to formal procedures which have been increasingly refined by new statutes and regulations and have thereby become a fertile ground for the breeding of legal dispute. It is fair to say that this has often become necessary because of the tendency of successive governments to use changes in education law to demonstrate a political message. The emphasis of this chapter is defending the rights of individuals rather than using a legal case to change the system.

16.2   The following are among the issues which will need to be considered in the conduct of any education law case:

1) Who is the client?
2) Who are the other parties?
3) What does the client wish to achieve by seeking legal help?
4) What is the legal framework to use?
5) What is the appropriate remedy, if any?
6) Obtaining and evaluating the evidence and putting the case together.
7) How is the work to be funded?

Who is the client?

Parental rights in education law

16.3   Paradoxically the law of education barely recognises the rights of the child. Parental responsibility governs exercise of statutory rights. So rights belong to parents in relation to:

1) admissions
2) exclusions
3) special educational needs
4) curriculum
5) discipline (consent)
6) consultation about changing character of a school.

16.4   In the Code of Practice for special educational needs (SEN) there is a clear indication that the child's views must be set out. Schools' SEN policy should include using pupil reports and systematic feedback to the child concerned and involve pupils in implementing individual education plans.[1] The adults closest to the child are expected to establish to the best of their ability the wishes and feelings of the child, for example, by interpreting behaviour. But however they are ascertained, the child's views ought to be set out separately from those of the parents and professionals.[2] The Code also contemplates that children under 16 may be competent to give authority for the disclosure of medical information independently of their parents.[3]

16.5   However, there is generally no statutory machinery whereby a child may claim the right to consultation over his/her future.

Children's rights under international convention

16.6   Under the United Nations Convention on the Rights of the Child:

> The best interests of the child shall be a primary consideration in all actions concerning children.[4]

> The child who is capable of forming his or her own views has the right to express those views freely in all matters affecting the child, the views of the child being given due weight in accordance with the age and maturity of the child. For this purpose the child shall have the opportunity to be heard in any judicial and administrative proceedings affecting the child, consistent with procedural rules.[5]

> On the other hand, the rights and duties of parents to give appropriate direction and guidance in the exercise of the above rights are respected.[6]

---

1   *Code of Practice on the Identification and Assessment of Special Educational Needs,* DFE, 1994, paras 2.34-2.37.
2   Ibid para 3.120.
3   Ibid para 2.52.
4   Article 3.
5   Article 12.
6   Article 5.

The Convention came into force in the UK on 15 January 1992. No reservations were entered upon ratification regarding education issues. One of the reasons why it has had so little impact on the framework of education legislation and the practical arrangements may be that there is a lack of co-ordination between government departments and between authorities and departments at local level.

Human Rights Act 1998

16.7   The Act comes into force on 2 October 2000 and it is likely to have a profound impact over the following years on many of the procedures for dealing with disputes about education. UK legislation will have to be compatible with the ECHR. The most significant areas of change will be as a result of articles 6 and 8. The courts are likely to begin to place greater weight on the position of the child, even when not specifically covered by statutory provision.

16.8   Article 6 provides for the right to take a civil dispute before a court or other body. Some examples in the education law field would be: exclusion decisions (denial of full evidence); admissions arrangements; decisions of LEA special needs panels re support, funding or placements; SENT and exclusion appeals (including the present lack of legal aid); and jurisdiction of the local government ombudsman. Article 8 (the right to respect for private and family life) will have a bearing on special needs: children with disabilities; respite care (eg, when not at boarding school); choice of school; and attendance (eg, holidays conflicting with school terms). See paras 14.116–14.117.

The first contact

16.9   Usually the first contact will come from the parent or carer and the issues and client's requirements will be reasonably clear after the first interview. But, according to the nature of the problem and the child's age and capacity to understand and participate in the decision-making about the various options, circumstances could arise where it becomes desirable for the solicitor to meet or even interview the child. It is difficult to set out any firm principles. It must be borne in mind that in the event of proceedings the parent is carrying greater responsibilities as litigation friend than would apply in an accident claim for damages – even in a case of the utmost severity where the prognosis leads to clear consequences in terms of the identification of remedial provision and its expense.

16.10   In an education case, the legal merits have to be viewed against the background of the impact of any decision upon the continuing education and development of the child. Whatever the legal justification for a course of action, the child may still need to deal with the same teachers and other professionals at the end of the day, and the relationship between the child and his/her peers must not be overlooked. Unfortunately there are a significant number of cases where parental aspirations – albeit consistent with legal merit – may be inconsistent with what may be in the child's best interests in any test which a relevant professional (including a lawyer) could apply.

16.11   In other areas – public law children cases, for example – there is machinery for an independent person to be appointed to safeguard the interests of the child and doubt may well have been cast on a person's abilities or judgment. It is rare for such a clear confrontation to emerge in an education case. It is also often difficult to discern from reports and documents unstated reasons and motivations – what may be termed the hidden agenda – which may materially affect decisions and attitudes on the part of all those who have dealings with children and parents, at school or at home.

16.12   The solicitor will usually be able to obtain the cooperation of the parent if it is decided that the child ought to be seen separately. Most parents are ready to acknowledge the reluctance of their children to speak openly about matters which may be distressing or disappointing to the parent. Parents will often be able to acknowledge (particularly as the child grows older) that the child's interests can be separately identified and do take precedence over the parental wishes. In a spirit of frank discussion it should be possible in most cases for the solicitor and the client to agree on a strategy for the resolution of the problem. Hence the importance of identifying at the outset what is sought to be achieved by the legal intervention; and the great value of setting out in writing the agreed case strategy so that the client takes joint responsibility for what has been decided.

Dealing with conflicts

Conflict between the parent's wishes and the child's interests

16.13   When acting for a parent, it is suggested that nothing need be done according to a strict interpretation of the lawyer's duty to the client in exercising the rights which have been conferred on the parent by the legislation and the courts. But it must be acknowledged that the legislation does not fully recognise the child's rights and it is submitted that it may be appropriate for the lawyer to go beyond a consideration of the strict legal rights of the parent in isolation.

16.14   When acting for the child, for example in a dispute about whether a particular school is suitable, expert evidence may suggest that a contributory factor in the child's emotional disturbance is the attitude of the parent who is refusing to send the child to school for the time being. If the parent is resistant to a discussion of this analysis and will not follow the advice being tendered by the expert the solicitor should decline to act further, having explained the basis on which instructions were accepted on behalf of the child. In Children Act 1989 prescribed proceedings, a guardian ad litem (GAL) must be appointed.

16.15   Where judicial review or civil court proceedings are contemplated or under way, consideration might, in exceptional circumstances, have to be given to the appointment of the Official Solicitor as litigation friend in place of the parent. Before this stage is reached, exhaustive efforts will have been made by the lawyer to reach a consensus between the parent and the child about the conduct of the matter. The lawyer has to decide what the issues are and, in respect of each separate issue, whether the child is Gillick-competent.[7] It may be possible to proceed on certain issues only, where it is clear that there is a consensus, and defer the others to a later date. There is guidance on how to find out if there is a conflict.[8]

Conflict in dealings with other people

16.16   It is worth remembering that, by the time the solicitor is consulted, there may have been years of increasingly acrimonious and unsatisfactory exchanges between parents and education officers and headteachers. This provides an opportunity for the solicitor to present him/herself as an independent professional whose brief on behalf of the parents will not be allowed to obscure the lawyer's professional and ethical duties. Some LEA staff are bound to be wary of the involvement of a lawyer and on occasions the reciprocal

---

7   *Gillick v West Norfolk and Wisbech Health Authority* and DHSS [1986] AC 122; [1985] 3 All ER 402, HL. See discussion of this case at para 4.24.

8   See Liddle *Acting for Children* (Law Society, 1992); *The Child as Client: A Handbook for Solicitors who represent Children* (Family Law, 1992) and *Guide to Good Practice when Acting for Children* (Solicitors' Family Law Association, 1994). There is an excellent discussion of this topic and the related problem of recognising the independent rights of children in Judith E Timms *Children's Representation: A Practitioner's Guide* (Sweet and Maxwell, 1995).

instruction of a lawyer by the LEA is not conducive to negotiated outcomes.

16.17   On the other hand the LEA may welcome the opportunity to raise issues which could not be raised solely or directly with the parents because of the history of distrust and animosity. In meetings particularly the lawyer can help to moderate the negative behaviour of the parents whose anger and emotions may hinder them in taking on board what is said. Yet, without undermining the parents' case, the lawyer can generally articulate it in a more effective way, adding weight by the occasional distancing from the inherently emotional appeals by the parents followed by the considered and objective view expressed by the lawyer as an independent-minded third party. LEAs' concern about loss of face is reduced when they are dealing with a negotiator who is obviously consistent and fair-minded.

16.18   It is often necessary to conduct negotiations in a way which will allow the other party to make a dignified exit from his/her entrenched position and the value of a lawyer or a third party effecting a compromise cannot be overestimated.

Who are the other parties?

16.19   Care should be taken to be clear about the identity of the other parties at various times, eg, LEA, governing body, headteacher, vicarious liability of LEAs, parents' statutory rights, appeal committee, Special Educational Needs Tribunal or its president, Secretary of State for Education and Employment.

What does the client wish to achieve?

16.20   There may be one goal or several outcomes, which may be of benefit to the client and others. For example:

1) An admission that the other party was wrong. A written apology from an appropriate person may sometimes be all that is required, though usually it will need to be coupled with undertakings for corrective action.

2) The client may want retribution or to see someone punished for whatever has gone wrong.

3) The client may have a desire to protect others who may learn by his/her experience and benefit from it.

4) The client may still want to get appropriate education together with additional facilities and support which may be necessary to make up for any past deficiency.
5) The client may well want compensation, but this is not usually a dominant motive.

What is the legal framework to use?

16.21 This question can become quite complicated as there may be a mixture, dealing with past events and future provision. The problem can be illustrated with an example:

> A boy, C, who has just turned 14 is permanently excluded from school for hitting a teacher. In the course of this incident the boy sustained a cut to the head which, he says, was inflicted gratuitously by the teacher. There has been mounting history of problematic behaviour. C has a statement of SEN issued two years ago. It describes his emotional and behavioural difficulties (EBD) but, against medical advice at the time, the LEA named his current mainstream school in the statement. No arrangements have been made to review C's statement.

16.22 The lawyer will need to consider, among other things:

1) Advice and possible representation of parents at the exclusion meeting of the school governing body and, later, before the exclusion appeal panel. Should reinstatement be sought or should a more suitable school be found?
2) Whether any report should be made to the police to investigate the allegation of criminal assault on C.
3) In due course, whether criminal injuries compensation is appropriate.
4) Is there a question of judicial review of the LEA on behalf of C for failing to arrange his special education in accordance with his statement under EA 1996 s324(5)(a)(i)?
5) Similarly, on behalf of C and his parents, is there a question of judicial review for the LEA's failure to hold an annual review of C's statement, which by now must include a transition plan meeting.[9]
6) Should the parents (at the same time) be requesting a full statutory reassessment of C's SEN with a view to appealing to the

9 Education (Special Educational Needs) Regulations 1994 SI No 1047 reg 16.

SENT later if the LEA declines or issues an amended statement which is not acceptable to the parents?

7) If the parents have another school in mind, how to persuade the LEA to name the new school as a matter of urgency (eg, by threat of judicial review for not providing suitable education under the statement and under EA 1996 s19) instead of dealing with request under EA 1996 Sch 27 by way of a prospective appeal to the SENT.

8) What does C himself want from his education?

What is the appropriate remedy, if any?

16.23 As has been emphasised elsewhere, there is sometimes a world of difference between the legal solutions which may be proposed and the practical outcome desired by the client. This will mean that, in some cases, the client's instructions will not permit the most effective remedy to be pursued. Subject to this, the client can only be advised on the merits of the evidence presented in the individual case.

16.24 An example of this might be a complaint that the client's son had been kept in a classroom over the lunch break and effectively prevented from having lunch after alleged horseplay in which none of the other participants were similarly treated. The school's policy on discipline is the starting point. Perhaps it was not strictly complied with and the lawfulness of the teacher's action in detaining the pupil can be questioned. Discussion with the client may result in a decision that a letter should be sent to the headteacher reminding him/her of the responsibility of the governing body and headteacher to ensure that disciplinary measures are adequately published and supported by the parents.[10] The parent in this case might not want to prejudice future relations between the child and his teachers by making strict compliance with legal penalties a significant legal issue on this occasion.

16.25 Similarly the client may want to complain about the behaviour of an individual pupil who has abused her son, whereas what is required is an examination of the school's disciplinary code.

16.26 An order of mandamus directing the LEA to arrange an annual review of a SEN statement would be of limited value if the LEA has

---

10 See EA 1996 s154, as amended by EA 1997 s2, now replaced by SSFA 1998 s61 with effect from 1 September 1999.

just issued an amended statement, from which any appeal would be to the SENT.

16.27   Where there are instructions to sue for education negligence it is likely to be essential first to utilise existing statutory rights and remedies to secure effective (remedial) education for a client who can still benefit from it.

Putting the case together

16.28   Instructions may only deal with comparatively recent events, such as an incident which has caused the client to seek legal advice. Sometimes it is possible to focus on such event, analysing the legal issue which arises and disposing of the matter in a few letters. More often it will be necessary to go back further and look at the history over a number of years. In so doing, it is essential to have access to as many contemporary documents and records as the client can possibly produce.

16.29   A chronology should be prepared, which in SEN cases may include significant life events as well as notes of observations about developmental milestones. This will enable the lawyer to be clearer about the dates when disputed events have occurred and the legal framework against which the actions of the protagonists and others may be judged.

16.30   It is recommended that at all times the lawyer should be able to identify in the history the persons and bodies who were involved in, or had responsibility for, the child's education. This will include information on:

1) type of school (as legal procedures may differ);
2) system of funding and management of resources and delegation of budgets;[11]
3) responsible LEA;
4) health authority changes;
5) all follow-up on SEN statements;
6) LEA policy considerations.

16.31   Notes should then be made about the relevant legal principles, which will generally be expressed in some piece of primary or delegated legislation. There are large numbers of circulars but they do not have legislative authority and failure to follow their guidance does not, of

11 See, eg, DFE Circular 2/94 *Local Management of Schools.*

itself, create a legal cause of action, though they are naturally relevant to good practice. Regard must be had to them, see para 12.31.

16.32   Where the dispute requires that the other party take some action, it may be worth trying an informal approach initially. School staff and LEA officers may be wary of dealing with correspondence from solicitors and it is often more productive to telephone first. Regard must be had to the need to advise the unrepresented party to obtain advice, but generally it may be supposed that school and LEA staff will be aware of avenues of advice available to them. If there is a possibility of an early resolution to a dispute, personal contact may be beneficial. But sooner or later it is necessary to set out the facts of what concerns the client, together with a statement of the legal principles governing the outcome which is sought. While there must be emphasis on common sense and pragmatic solutions it must be remembered that, if it is necessary to have recourse to the law to resolve the problem, any correspondence may be considered by a High Court judge and must therefore state the legal principles correctly.

16.33   LEAs vary in how they deal with intervention by lawyers on behalf of a parent. Some will immediately pass the correspondence to the legal department for reply; in others an education officer may continue to handle the matter – even after a letter before action from a solicitor. It is sometimes difficult to preserve a constructive ongoing relationship between parents and school while correspondence is going on with, for example, the LEA legal department, but it is important that this is attempted where educational services are still required. Much depends on the balance of power between the other party and its legal advisers. Sometimes the awareness of a possible legal intervention does not encourage co-operation with lawyers. Where proceedings for negligence are contemplated, an insurer or lawyer will be involved at an early stage.

16.34   Generally, LEAs are highly bureaucratic institutions whose structure and decision-making machinery has evolved over a long period of time and has been slow to adapt to the changes brought about by the legislation of the last few years. Policies tend to be applied with insufficient regard for exceptions. This may be in the interests of certainty and good administration, yet it rarely seems to eliminate delay. Decisions may be expressed as made by panels – for example, the Special Needs Panel. These have no statutory basis but probably reflect the desire of the LEA to consult particular expert opinion, sometimes on a multidisciplinary basis. But they may turn out to be insufficiently involved in discussions and consultation to be seen to have acted fairly.

16.35 The person to contact at the school is clearly the headteacher, who is the manager in charge of the school but is always accountable to the governing body, which retains all the statutory duties. The headteacher will usually be a teacher governor.[12]

16.36 In special needs cases, the special educational needs co-ordinator should be approached. In small schools this may be the headteacher or the deputy head.[13] In a larger mainstream secondary school, this may be a full-time post. In all schools, there will be a governor designated to ensure that special needs requirements are met.[14]

16.37 Questions of management of the school should be at least copied to the chair of the governing body, if not directly addressed to him/her. The school secretary probably acts as secretary to the governing body. There are clerks at the LEA allocated to each governing body and they deal with formal correspondence and circulating information from the LEA and the DfEE, as well as clerking formal governors' meetings. Both in schools and LEAs there is a dramatic decrease in activity during the school holidays. LEAs may need to consult school staff who are absent on holiday and this is an important factor to bear in mind when calling for a response.

How is the work to be funded?

Legal advice and assistance scheme (Claim 10)[15]

16.38 Education law will soon be a franchised category of work, whereupon different rules will apply. Until then, the procedure is as for other non-franchised work, although the Legal Aid Board (LAB) has issued some guidance in its manual on the exercise of devolved powers. A personal application for advice and assistance must be

---

12 EA 1996 ss79, 84 and 225 – unless s/he chooses not to be a governor. Headteacher members of the governing body are treated as ex officio (SSFA 1998 Sch 9 para 8).

13 Code of Practice paras 2.14–2.15.

14 EA 1996 s317(2) and Code of Practice paras 2.7–2.9.

15 Still often called the green form scheme following its replacement by the 'photocopier friendly' Claim 10 form on 19 October 1998.

made.[16] Where the client cannot for good reason get to the office there are two alternatives for getting instructions:

1) The client can give authority to another person to make the application on his/her behalf.[17] This is best done by a relative or close friend with access to the client's financial information and it is prudent for the authority to be put into writing, although not a statutory requirement.[18]

2) If the client is disabled and not far distant, prior authority to exceed the two-hour limit may be obtained, by telephone if the matter is urgent. It will not cover the time taken on the outward journey.[19]

16.39   Where the client is a child under compulsory school leaving age, the parent, guardian or carer signs the Claim 10 on behalf of the child and the means assessment is that of the parent/carer liable to maintain him/her.[20] Generally it is not possible to accept an application direct from a child under 16.[21] But NFG 2-09 makes it clear that where the child is 'Gillick-competent' and there is a conflict of interest with the parent or guardian, or the child is in care and needs separate representation, prior authority to advise a child directly will be given.[22] This has the advantage that the child's own

16 Legal Advice and Assistance Regulations 1989 SI No 340 reg 9(3). The LAB's distinction whereby franchise holders are able to receive applications by letter or telephone has been questioned on the grounds of discrimination in the provision of legal services under the Legal Aid Act 1988. There are no reported cases on this point.

17 Legal Advice and Assistance Regulations 1989 reg 10(1). As a result of a successful costs appeal published in March 1996 (LAB reference LAA10), the LAB agreed that another member of the solicitor's firm may be appointed by the prospective client for the purposes of reg 10(1). See now *Legal Aid Handbook 1998/99* (Sweet & Maxwell, 1998) Notes for Guidance (NFG) 2-12 and 2-62. This has improved access to the legal advice and assistance scheme but the solicitor's task under reg 13 of assessing financial eligibility is not eased by the absence of a distinct form of application in such cases (see reg 10(4)). Under exclusive contracting arrangements, it will no longer be permissible for a member of the solicitor's firm to be authorised under reg 10.

18 See NFG 2-12 and 2-62.

19 As the Claim 10 has not yet been signed and cover cannot be backdated. Arguably this is another piece of discrimination (against disabled people) by the LAB, although this does not breach the provisions of the Disability Discrimination Act 1995.

20 See Legal Advice and Assistance Regulations 1989 SI No 340 Sch 2 para 5.

21 Ibid reg 14 and NFG 2-09.

22 NFG 2-09 states that 'authority to advise a child direct will be given if: (a) there is good reason why the parent or guardian is not applying (eg, conflict of

means are assessed and not aggregated with those of the adult liable to maintain them. In case of doubt it is prudent to obtain prior authority, under reg 14(1). Note also that reg 14(3)(d) allows the solicitor to obtain prior authority from the area office where it is reasonable in the circumstances for someone who is neither a parent nor a carer to obtain advice and assistance on behalf of a child.[23]

16.40   The assessment of resources is a matter for the solicitor, having regard to guidance (eg, the Notes for Guidance) given by the LAB. Schedule 2 para 5 of the Legal Advice and Assistance Regulations 1989 entitles the solicitor to have regard to 'all the circumstances' and to decide whether it is just and equitable to treat the child's resources as separate from the adult.[24] If it is proposed to separate the resources in this way, it would be prudent to inform the LAB of the assessment decision so as to prevent the point being taken against the solicitor later. The true construction of para 5, it is to be submitted, may not limit the 'just and equitable' decision to cases where (a) and (b) of NFG 2-09 are both satisfied. A person over 16 years of age (compulsory school age) can sign a Claim 10 form in his/her own right. It is suggested that the legal advice and assistance scheme can be used without an extension to advise someone who has an interest in the legal problem, eg, the parent of 17-year-old trying to secure further education.

16.41   Unless clear grounds for legal aid already exist, it will be necessary to do more preparatory work under the legal advice and assistance scheme, often including obtaining expert reports. These can be very expensive and the LAB is, understandably, reluctant to authorise this expenditure. The area office is not likely to be particularly familiar with education statutes and practical problems. It is helpful to set out the law at some length in an initial letter to the other side, which can then be copied to the LAB when making an extension application.

16.42   For expert reports, hourly and daily rates must always be quoted, together with a breakdown of the anticipated time. It may not be

interest, or the child is in care and needs separate representation) ; and (b) the child is old enough to give instructions and understand the nature of the advice and assistance'. See also *LAB Guidance on General Issues: Advice and Assistance* Issue 6: April 1998, paras 2.3.4–2.3.5.

23   See NFG 2-10. The LAB points out that it is essential for the person applying to indicate his/her full name and the capacity in which the form is signed. The means assessment is again according to Sch 2 para 5. It is arguable that the means of foster parents, for example, should not be included where application is made under reg 14(3)(d).

24   This is now covered in NFG 2-09.

necessary to shop around for quotations if there is a good reason for using a particular expert. But it may save time to provide alternative quotations as well as information about the particular advantages of a desired expert. The LAB is unlikely to approve expenditure exceeding about £400 in the first instance. If this is enough to get started, a useful tactic is to submit a further Claim 10 as this extension is becoming exhausted. This may be met with the suggestion that legal aid should be applied for instead. But it is often difficult to find grounds for possible proceedings at a particular stage and the expert report may be a vital part of the pre-certificate investigative work. There is authority for using an extension for a costly expert report.[25]

Multiple applications

16.43   The LAB issued revised guidance and costs guidelines to area offices on 1 May 1996, now NFG 2-16 to 2-22 in the *Legal Aid Handbook 1998/9*. Unfortunately there is no specific guidance on education cases here. Regulation 17 of the Legal Advice and Assistance Regulations 1989 requires separate forms to be used for separate matters. The LAB expects a single form to be used to identify all the issues and provide general, preliminary advice, but 'if other separate legal issues are identified or subsequently arise requiring separate progression, then a further form or forms should be used'.[26]

16.44   By analogy with housing and welfare benefits cases, it seems reasonable to proceed on the footing that a separate Claim 10 may be used for separate advice and assistance once a specific legal regime or jurisdiction is pursued and the work undertaken and the issues involved are separate. An example might be assistance with a forthcoming SENT appeal on a separate Claim 10 while seeking legal aid to challenge a failure to secure the statemented provision in the statement under appeal.

16.45   The practice of area offices is likely to differ and it is not known to what extent decisions are made on the basis of aggregate costs or costs per form. The safest course would appear to be to seek extensions on a single form as far as possible. This should reduce the chance of the LAB deciding that work had been duplicated when assessing the costs. Unfortunately this is also likely to delay the date when the first costs claim can be made.

25   *R v Legal Aid Board ex p Higgins* (1993) *Times* 19 November, QBD.
26   NFG 2-16.

Extensions of legal advice and assistance authority

16.46 Even when education work is franchised, the nature of the expenditure would persuade most practitioners that authority ought to be obtained as a precaution. The experts most likely to be used are educational psychologists (EPs). Most are members of the British Association of Chartered Psychologists and their fees reflect this. £70–£90 per hour is quite common, though some will provide an assessment report based on a single consultation for an inclusive fee of £200–£250. However, often this is insufficient.

16.47 It can be invaluable in certain circumstances for the independent EP to visit and assess the child at home in the family setting, for example, to assist in dealing with or rebutting implied suggestions that problems have an origin in some factors in relationships at home. Where the EP can visit and observe the child in the school setting it is possible to obtain much better evidence on questions such as: the training and experience of the teaching staff, teaching methods, the amount and quality of classroom support, the existence or failure of the special educational provision in a statement. Where parents are seeking an assessment under EA 1996 s323, the opinion of an independent EP is likely to be vital once the LEA has refused one. This is appropriate Claim 10 work in preparation for an SENT appeal or hearing.

16.48 Another advantage of using an independent professional is that it will usually be impractical, and probably unethical, for the family's solicitor to be interviewing teaching staff, whereas they will be more forthcoming with the EP, who may even be in a position to gain their sympathy for changes in attitudes to needs or support. EPs employed by the LEA are invariably under constraints from LEA policies or funding. Some observers feel that this has an impact on their professional recommendations for a particular child. An independent expert can sometimes elicit tacit support for an alternative view.

16.49 Preparation of a comprehensive assessment report incorporating observation visits etc can take up to 15 hours of the expert's time. Even if this is charged on a daily basis, the cost is likely to be in the region of £500–£1,000. A clear and detailed justification for the use of the expert will have to be provided to the LAB if funding is to approved. Sometimes the expert's work can be split up. Sometimes it is possible to undertake it later under a legal aid certificate – but even here the same need for justification arises, and it would be wise to obtain an APP6 authority before proceeding.

16.50   Unfortunately the LAB does not always display a realistic attitude to the expense of education law work. Without any comparable evidence apparently available (despite its computerised facilities), individual officers may decide that a limit of, say, £300 will be placed on expenditure on an EP – often irrespective of the amount of work required. And the amount of work required from the solicitor in these cases is seriously undervalued by the LAB. Practitioners have to recognise that the majority of their cases may involve as much a long drawn out battle with the LAB over funding as a dispute with the other party about education. Unhappily, there is no right of appeal against a decision to refuse or limit a Claim 10 extension.

16.51   It should not be overlooked that a Claim 10 extension can be granted to obtain counsel's opinion. Because of the complexities of the education statutes, regulations and circulars this may be the best way of persuading the LAB of the merits of a legal aid application. But there are many situations where specialist counsel's advice could usefully be sought by the general practitioner where it may be premature or inappropriate to apply for legal aid. For example, for a parent making the difficult decision whether to request a full reassessment of special educational needs (SEN) or to rely on the less thorough process of the annual review in a shorter timescale. See also chapter 7 on exclusions – the merits of an appeal against exclusion and the consequences of not pursuing it. The LAB contemplates this in SEN cases in its devolved powers guidance reissued in January 1998.[27]

16.52   Examples of situations when help can be given under the legal advice and assistance scheme include:

1)   complaint to local councillor, MP or parent teacher association;
2)   admissions;
3)   complaint to governing body and/or LEA (can include attendance at meetings to progress the matter);
4)   independent assessment of SEN;
5)   representations to monitoring officer;
6)   complaint to local ombudsman;
7)   complaint to secretary of state;
8)   obtaining educational (and health) records;
9)   access to social services files;[28]

---

27 Legal Aid Board *Guidance: Exercise of Devolved Powers*, section 16 paras 1.1.2–1.1.4.

28 Where emotional and behavioural difficulties problems are involved or alleged, it is often helpful to check what information the social services department

10) curriculum problems;

11) bullying cases;

12) exclusions;

13) health and safety issues;

14) disputes about academic assessment;

15) disciplinary appeals and procedures;

16) participation in statutory consultation procedures.

16.53   It should be noted that, where the legal issue is one in which other people have the same or a similar interest, it is often difficult to obtain an extension. There is no obvious parallel to Civil Legal Aid (General) Regulations 1989 reg 32, where the area director can require that other interested parties contribute to the costs. The question for the area director appears to be limited to justifying the advice and whether the costs estimate is reasonable.[29] The LAB would need to be satisfied that the other people did not together have the necessary financial resources.[30] The area director will undoubtedly have this in mind when limiting the scope and funding of the extension 'as he sees fit'.[31] The extension application form will need to address this issue.[32]

Representation under the legal advice and assistance scheme

16.54   Preparatory work, including formulation of written grounds and representations, can be carried out for SENT hearings, exclusion appeals, admission appeals etc. It is not possible to use the scheme for representation at the hearing or for paying witnesses to attend. An application can, however, be made for representation by a McKenzie friend,[33] although it will be difficult to demonstrate the benefit of this without transgressing the no representation rule.[34]

16.55   Legal Aid Act 1988 s2(4) defines 'representation' as follows:

'Representation' means representation for the purposes of proceedings and it includes –

were working on. In practice, if not in law, LEAs depend on decisions and funding from social services departments.

29 Legal Advice and Assistance Regulations 1989 reg 21(2).

30 NFG 2-23(g).

31 Reg 21(3).

32 See *Guidance*, January 1998 (see note 27), para 1.3.2.

33 NFG para 2-27.

34 Note that the London Legal Aid Office states that a claim for attending as a McKenzie friend will not be entertained where an advocate provides services (even on a pro bono basis). See NFG 2-27 and the factors outlined therein.

(a) all such assistance as is usually given by a legal representative in the steps preliminary or incidental to any proceedings;

(b) all such assistance as is usually given in civil proceedings in arriving at or giving effect to a compromise to avoid or bring to an end any proceedings; ...

This obviously includes advice and assistance, anticipating that regulations may specify what is included. Representation and advice and assistance are not defined in the regulations. However, the helpful guidance given in NFG 2-26 confirms that everything short of preparing instructions to an advocate, and advocacy, will be allowed. Accordingly, the authors are of the view that 'representation' for these purposes may be defined as advocacy at a court hearing or a hearing covered by the Tribunals and Inquiries Act 1992 Sch 1 para 15. Thus, full representation at a meeting (even if part of an appeal process) can be undertaken provided that a legal representative's attendance at the meeting can be justified.[35] See the factors outlined in NFG 2-20 paras (a), (b) and (c).

Civil legal aid

Applications

16.56   The attractions of a legal aid certificate are obvious to most lawyers: significant funding and a virtual guarantee that the client will not have to pay the costs of the other side. In addition, the statutory charge may apply to any money recovered. The effect of the client's financial contribution must not be overlooked. The continuing monthly contributions do at least encourage the lawyer to progress the case without delay.

16.57   Where the applicant is under 18, the certificate will be issued with an adult, usually a parent, acting as litigation friend. A check should be made to ensure that there is no actual conflict between these two. This is unlikely to present a problem where the child is under (say) 12, but the solicitor will have to make an individual judgment.

16.58   Financial eligibility may be determined using the figures issued each April by the LAB. Where the child is under 16, form Means 4 is used. Usually the child has no income in his/her own right. If the parent/carer receives disability living allowance it is useful to

---

35 This is within the definition of 'assistance' in Legal Aid Act 1988 s2(3). It specifically includes assistance in taking steps with respect to proceedings.

mention this on the Means 4 instead of completing a form APP1. It is arguable that this income has been received by the parent for the child, rather than by the child.

16.59   If judicial review is contemplated, proceedings may be brought by anyone who has sufficient interest.[36] Thus, if judicial review of a direction of the president of the SENT is sought, proceedings could be brought by the child, even though it was the parent's appeal. This avenue is not likely to be open where there has been a SENT hearing. In *R v Special Educational Needs Tribunal ex p South Glamorgan CC*,[37] the Court of Appeal ruled that a challenge to a decision of the SENT should be by an appeal under RSC Order 55, so that the appellant is the parent. This was confirmed a few days later when the Court of Appeal held that the High Court had no jurisdiction to entertain an appeal brought by the child.[38] The court did not accept that a child could be a party in reliance on Tribunals and Inquiries Act 1992 s11(1) because the 1993 Act and subsequent regulations were inconsistent with that view. Though doubtless this was the draftsman's intention, there can in some cases be a serious injustice to the teenage 'Gillick-competent' child who cannot be heard by the court on such a fundamentally important matter. In the absence of amending legislation it would be surprising if this situation were not taken up in the European Court. The fact that someone aged up to 19 has no right to be heard in a proceeding which is of such fundamental importance provides compelling ground for the application of article 6 once the Human Rights Act 1998 is in force.

16.60   Where it is proposed to bring a representative action in which others have the same interest in the outcome, the LAB will look at the ability of the other persons to fund the action.[39] Under the Funding Code it seems likely that there will be much greater scope for public interest judicial review cases, though the role of private practice in such challenges under the Community Legal Service is uncertain.

---

36   *R v Secretary of State for Foreign and Commonwealth Affairs ex p World Development Movement Ltd* [1995] 1 WLR 386. Rose LJ suggested a number of factors determining standing: the importance of vindicating the rule of law, the importance of the issue raised, the likely absence of any other responsible challenger, the nature of the breach of duty against which relief is sought, and the prominent role of the applicants.

37   [1996] ELR 326, CA.

38   *S v Special Educational Needs Tribunal and Another* [1996] ELR 102, QBD.

39   Civil Legal Aid (General) Regulations 1989 reg 32.

Urgent cases

16.61   It is usually impracticable to try and get emergency legal aid over the telephone because of the complexity of education cases. The degree of urgency is rarely comparable with, say, a domestic violence case. Also, there is little point in trying to get legal aid until the problem has been fully explained to the other side in a comprehensive letter before action and a reasonable time has been allowed for response. There is usually a mass of documentation presented to the solicitor who is preparing the legal aid application. It is really only necessary to send the following:

1) Succinct statement of client giving brief family and personal details, brief milestones, and a more detailed section on the effect of a current legal problem on the client and family. The nature of the proceedings, the reason for joining the parties and relief sought can be outlined at the end.

2) Copies of any decision letters and letter before action.

3) The latest statement or draft in a special needs case. The appendices are sometimes voluminous and any which are not central to the application should be omitted.

4) Independent EP's report (if available). Where there is a dispute about SEN or provision it is as well to include the LEA EP's report. There is insufficient space on form APP1 to explain enough about the proceedings and this is best dealt with in the covering letter, if it is not in the applicant's statement.

Usual scope of legal aid

Judicial review

16.62   In a judicial review case the certificate might cover, 'applying for a judicial review of a decision of the ABC authority and if permission is granted to include service of the claim form'. Unless it is a question of a policy decision, there are usually many decisions in all education cases. Often these will have been taken outside the three-month period under Order 53 (see chapter 13). But such decisions frequently result in an ongoing breach of duty for which there is no time limit. Care should be taken to ensure that the legal aid certificate is issued or amended with the words 'breach of duty' after 'decision'. The certificate will sometimes have a financial limit of £5,000, but more often the limit is £2,500.

Judicial review of admissions/exclusion appeal

16.63   The appeal committee should be joined as a respondent. It has been held that, since the appeal committee is a creature of the LEA, there is no need to add it as a respondent, but this may not be the view of every LEA.

16.64   Time is of the essence. Added to the normal stringent rule about timeousness, there is the problem that the quashing of a decision in such a case is bound to have implications for significant numbers of innocent parties who may now be prejudiced by a fresh consideration of the matter. This applies especially in admissions cases.[41] It has recently been held that delay in obtaining legal aid is not a ground for extending time under RSC Order 53.[41]

Claim for damages

16.65   If the claim concerns a child of school age, it is likely to be against the education authority concerned, which is vicariously liable for torts committed by headteachers and EPs, in particular.[42]

Work under certificate

16.66   It may be that the education authority, for example, will soon correct the breach of duty or undertake to do so within a reasonable time. This will often still leave outstanding other functions which need to be completed before the duty has belatedly been performed. In those circumstances, once it is clear that an application to the court is not going to be required, it is not possible to retain the certificate while monitoring the situation. Education cases often run for several years, with successive certificates being issued, punctuated by periods when no legal aid is required. Where a technical decision is taken to leave a legal aid certificate on foot, it is desirable to write to the LAB to explain why. This is a useful contemporaneous record of the decision taken at that time by the solicitor which can be referred to by the costs draftsman and the costs judge.

---

40   See *R v Leicestershire CC Education Appeals Committee ex p Tarmomohamed* [1997] ELR 48, QBD, and para 5.88.

41   *R v University of Portsmouth ex p Lakareber* [1999] ELR 135, CA.

42   This area of the law is likely to be clarified by the forthcoming House of Lords decision in *Phelps v Hillingdon BC*. See chapter 15.

Representations about legal aid

16.67   There is no obligation to notify the other side about the grant of legal aid until proceedings are started. However, frequently it is tactically wise to do so. Usually the grant of legal aid acts as a strong incentive for the authority or other party to take corrective action. Sometimes the LEA lawyers will write to the LAB making representations about why there should be no legal aid. This correspondence will always be sent to the solicitor for the legally assisted person and comments will be invited. This provides another good opportunity to show what the case is about and to justify continued funding.

Some further points

16.68   In the case of a possible judicial review, legal aid is often granted for counsel's opinion. Perhaps this needs to be obtained as a matter of urgency because of some time limit. If the case is urgent it is unlikely that all the necessary material will have been assembled at an early stage. It is desirable for counsel to give an informed opinion, where appropriate, having had recourse to all the educational records, expert reports and response from the other side to correspondence. This can take several months. With such cases it is helpful to inform the LAB of any initial view of counsel and the steps now necessary, and if appropriate, obtain an amendment of legal aid to permit a further conference or opinion of counsel at a future date. This will help to ensure that the work done is covered by the certificate.

16.69   Another important practical consideration is having a meeting with the other side, but it should not be assumed that a meeting will be covered under the legal aid certificate without a specific extension for the purpose. Sometimes this can be obtained easily by telephone if time is short. The great advantage of meetings is that they can help to clarify the issues in dispute, put pressure on the other side to give concessions, permit peripheral matters to be explored and, finally, to make progress which would otherwise have to await many months of preparation before proceeding. On the other hand, particularly where multidisciplinary meetings are involved, there can be greater delays and the original legal points can become overtaken. If the LAB suggests that attending meetings may not be within the scope of the certificate it is worth mentioning Legal Aid Act 1988 s2(4) and the meaning of representation under the certificate.

16.70   It follows from the foregoing that the first consideration initially and at all times thereafter is to identify a legal cause of action which will justify the grant of legal aid. It is unnecessary for the precise proceedings to be identified. It is sufficient that there should be a legal problem worthy of investigation. The novelty and complexity of some education legal issues will often justify the involvement of counsel at an early stage. The practicalities of working under a certificate as opposed to the vagaries of the green form are substantially easier and the remuneration is obviously higher.

16.71   A case may be started with a view to judicial review, but turn out ultimately to involve a private law claim for damages for breach of contract or negligence. For example:

> A student at an FE college complains about an academic assessment 15 months earlier which led to a failure. He then pursued the college's appeals procedure, which was defective, with no success. Investigation showed poor teaching methods and reliance by the college on a discredited external assessor.

Before a decision can be made about what (if any) remedy there may be, it will be necessary to consider the delay and the reasons for not seeking advice earlier, the effect on the student, the effort subsequently made to continue with his course, his performance on any further course and any financial loss. The certificate can then be amended, replaced with a fresh certificate or discharged.

Costs

16.72   As with any other tort, a case of education negligence which succeeds will result in an order for costs against the defendant.

16.73   In the case of judicial review, costs should usually follow an application which is not dismissed by the court, unless there is no outstanding breach of duty at the date of the hearing, but judges are sometimes reluctant to award costs even when satisfied that a remedy should be granted because there is a continuing breach of duty. This seems to be because of the perception that LEAs are short of money and their hard-pressed finances should not be used to pay costs to benefit another government department, namely the legal aid fund.[43] It may depend on the extent that the court's intervention was needed by the time the case comes on for hearing.

16.74   The best tactic is therefore to press on with the proceedings as long as there is a reasonable prospect of the court granting some

---

43 *R v Gloucestershire CC ex p P* (1994) ELR 334, QBD.

form of remedy[44] and, once the other party backs down, to insist on a consent order including an order that the applicant's costs are paid. The consent order can agree that the application for permission is withdrawn or even dismissed, while still providing for the payment of the applicant's costs by the respondent. Reasons for the matter being dealt with by way of a consent order must always be stated on a separate schedule signed by the parties.[45] It should be noted that generally the LAB is reluctant to support litigation simply to recover the costs, so it is as well to provide for them beforehand. In practice it is not always possible to negotiate the most favourable terms for a consent order for the applicant's benefit without compromising the claim for inter partes costs.

16.75   Where the local ombudsman has been involved, it is sometimes possible to obtain the recommendation that the applicant's legal costs are paid by the authority. These recommendations are not legally binding but are usually followed. The local authority will only pay costs and expenses for which the client is personally directly liable. This does not include legal aid costs.

16.76   Costs awarded or agreed will usually be on the basis that the client is indemnified against any expenditure reasonably paid out on the case, including legal fees. Where there is a legal aid certificate, the regulations permit payment by a third party.[46] Pre-legal aid costs where the green form/Claim 10 has been used are usually reimbursed up to the amount of the claim.

16.77   Where no arrangements have been made for private funding, there may be problems in recovering party and party costs. In the absence of a taxation, the point would have to be taken by the paying party.[47] It is therefore desirable to agree instructions with the client making it clear that the client is liable to pay costs which are not covered by the advice and assistance scheme (where financially eligible). See precedents in appendix L.

44   A declaration is likely to be of little value to an individual applicant who brought proceedings for a prerogative orders of certiorari, prohibition or mandamus (see chapter 13).

45   Practice Statement (Supreme Court's Judgments) [1998] 2 All ER 638.

46   Legal Advice and Assistance Regulations 1989 reg 107B, applicable to all certificates granted on or after 25 February 1994: Civil Legal Aid (General) (Amendment) Regulations 1994 SI No 229..

47   *British Waterways Board v Norman* [1994] COD 262. In *Thai Trading Co v Taylor* [1998] 3 All ER 65, CA, the Court of Appeal held that *Norman* was wrongly decided and that it was lawful for a solicitor to make an agreement with his client providing for the payment of fees in the event of success and no fee or a nominal fee otherwise. The solicitors' practice rule which prohibits

Other funding sources

Household insurance

16.78 Household insurance policies sometimes contain an optional extension covering legal expenses insurance. There may be restrictions on the choice of solicitor but these may be overcome in this specialised field. Unfortunately, there are likely to be exclusions affecting most of the education law field – judicial review and disputes with local authorities being excluded altogether.

Pressure groups

16.79 Some pressure groups may be prepared to assist with costs, or expenses, for example in obtaining expert reports.

Conditional fees

16.80 Where there is a personal injury claim, legal aid is going to be withdrawn in the coming months as a result of the Access to Justice Act 1999 and a conditional fee arrangement may be entered into using an insurance company to protect the client against his/her own costs and an award of costs to the other side. Those arrangements are outside the present scope of this book.[48]

16.81 At the time of going to press, it appears doubtful that education negligence cases will be classified as personal injury claims from the funding point of view – notwithstanding the view expressed by the judges trying the first two cases coming to trial, to the effect that failure to ameliorate a congenital defect amounts to a personal injury. It is likely that they will be treated as other negligence cases, particularly as a distinction has already been made as regards legal aid funding in the case of medical negligence.

Contingency fees

16.82 As a result of the Court of Appeal decision in *Thai Trading*[49] there may be an extension in the use of contingency fees. In the context of education there is very little scope for their application.

this was amended on 7 January 1999 to permit this. See Law Society *Guide to Professional Conduct of Solicitors 1999* paras 14.03–14.04.

48 See Napier and Bawdon *Conditional Fees – A Survival Guide* (Law Society 1996). See also the bi-monthly journal *Litigation Funding*, edited by Fiona Bawdon and available from the Law Society.

49 See note 47.

After the event insurance

16.83   Another type of insurance is developing, known as 'after the event' insurance where for an agreed premium a block of cover is purchased to cover some or all of the costs as above (para 16.80). This is payable only where the proceedings are wholly unsuccessful. Success in proceedings before a court or tribunal which can award costs will result in an order for costs, to be agreed or assessed in the usual way. But in other cases, even where the LAB is not impressed by the cost/benefit analysis which may be necessary in a judicial review, or where there is no legal aid, such as the SENT, insurance may be taken out to cover the client's likely costs in the event of failure of the proceedings. This could be an attractive proposition for SENT work, where it would be very rare for the tribunal to award costs against an unsuccessful appellant. Unfortunately, underwriting advice seems to have already persuaded insurers not to fund SENT appeals. Insurance products available on the market are likely to continue to develop and change over the next few years. Practitioners will have to remain alert to these.

APPENDICES

Local Government Act 1974 ss26 and 31

PART III: LOCAL GOVERNMENT ADMINISTRATION
Matters subject to investigation

26 (1) Subject to the provisions of this Part of this Act where a written complaint is made by or on behalf of a member of the public who claims to have sustained injustice in consequence of maladministration in connection with action taken by or on behalf of an authority to which this Part of this Act applies, being action taken in the exercise of administrative functions of that authority, a Local Commissioner may investigate that complaint.

(2) A complaint shall not be entertained under this Part of this Act unless it is made in writing to the Local Commissioner specifying the action alleged to constitute maladministration or –

(a) it is made in writing to a member of the authority, or of any other authority concerned, specifying the action alleged to constitute maladministration, and

(b) it is referred to the Local Commissioner, with the consent of the person aggrieved, or of a person acting on his behalf, by that member, or by any other person who is a member of any authority concerned, with a request to investigate the complaint.

(3) If the Local Commissioner is satisfied that any member of any authority concerned has been requested to refer the complaint to a Local Commissioner, and has not done so, the Local Commissioner may, if he thinks fit, dispense with the requirements in subsection (2) (b) above.

(4) A complaint shall not be entertained unless it was made to the Local Commissioner or a member of any authority concerned within twelve months from the day on which the person aggrieved first had notice of the matters alleged in the complaint, but a Local Commissioner may conduct an investigation pursuant to a complaint not made within that period if he considers that it is reasonable to do so.

(5) Before proceeding to investigate a complaint, a Local Commissioner shall satisfy himself that the complaint has been brought, by or on behalf of the person aggrieved, to the notice of the authority to which the complaint relates and that that authority has been afforded a reasonable opportunity to investigate, and reply to, the complaint.

(6) A Local Commissioner shall not conduct an investigation under this Part of this Act in respect of any of the following matters, that is to say, –

(a) any action in respect of which the person aggrieved has or had a right of appeal, reference or review to or before a tribunal constituted by or under any enactment;

(b) any action in respect of which the person aggrieved has or had a right of appeal to a Minister of the Crown or the National Assembly for Wales; or

(c) any action in respect of which the person aggrieved has or had a remedy by way of proceedings in any court of law:

Provided that a Local Commissioner may conduct an investigation notwithstanding the existence of such a right or remedy if satisfied that in the particular circumstances it is not reasonable to expect the person aggrieved to resort or have resorted to it.

(7) A Local Commissioner shall not conduct an investigation in respect of any action which in his opinion affects all or most of the inhabitants of the following area –

(aa) where the complaint relates to a National Park authority, the area of the Park for which it is such an authority;

(a) where the complaint relates to the Commission for the New Towns, the area of the new town or towns to which the complaint relates;

(ba) where the complaint relates to the Urban Regeneration Agency, any designated area within the meaning of Part III of the Leasehold Reform, Housing and Urban Development Act 1993;

(8) Without prejudice to the preceding provisions of this section, a Local Commissioner shall not conduct an investigation under this Part of this Act in respect of any such action or matter as is described in Schedule 5 to this Act.

(9) Her Majesty may by Order in Council amend the said Schedule 5 so as to add to or exclude from the provisions of that Schedule (as it has effect for the time being) such actions or matters as may be described in the Order; and any Order made by virtue of this subsection shall be subject to annulment in pursuance of a resolution of either House of Parliament.

(10) In determining whether to initiate, continue or discontinue an investigation, a Local Commissioner shall, subject to the preceding provisions of this section, act at discretion; and any question whether a complaint is duly made under this Part of this Act shall be determined by the Local Commissioner.

(11) In this section –

(a) references to a person aggrieved include references to his personal representatives; and

(b) references to a member of an authority concerned include, in the case of a complaint relating to a joint authority established by Part IV of the Local Government Act 1985, references to a member of a constituent council of that authority.

(12) A complaint shall not be entertained under this Part of this Act if and so far as it is in respect of anything done before 1st April 1974, or in respect of any default or alleged default first arising before that date.

(13) A complaint as regards an authority mentioned in section 25(1)(ba), (bb) or (bd) above shall not be entertained under this Part of this Act if and so far

as it is in respect of anything done before the coming into force of Schedule 3 to the Local Government Act 1988, or in respect of any default or alleged default first arising before its coming into force; and subsection (12) above shall have effect subject to this.

Reports on investigations: further provisions

31 (1) This section applies where a Local Commissioner reports that injustice has been caused to a person aggrieved in consequence of maladministration.

(2) The report shall be laid before the authority concerned and it shall be the duty of that authority to consider the report and, within the period of three months beginning with the date on which they received the report, or such longer period as the Local Commissioner may agree in writing, to notify the Local Commissioner of the action which the authority have taken or propose to take.

(2A) If the Local Commissioner –

(a) does not receive the notification required by subsection (2) above within the period allowed by or under that subsection, or

(b) is not satisfied with the action which the authority concerned have taken or propose to take, or

(c) does not within a period of three months beginning with the end of the period so allowed, or such longer period as the Local Commissioner may agree in writing, receive confirmation from the authority concerned that they have taken action, as proposed, to the satisfaction of the Local Commissioner,

he shall make a further report setting out those facts and making recommendations.

(2B) Those recommendations are such recommendations as the Local Commissioner thinks fit to make with respect to action which, in his opinion, the authority concerned should take to remedy the injustice to the person aggrieved and to prevent similar injustice being caused in the future.

(2C) Section 30 above, with any necessary modifications, and sub-section (2) above shall apply to a report under subsection (2A) above as the apply to a report under that section.

(2D) If the Local Commissioner –

(a) does not receive the notification required by subsection (2) above as applied by subsection (2C) above within the period allowed by or under that subsection or is satisfied before the period allowed by that subsection has expired that the authority concerned have decided to take no action, or

(b) is not satisfied with the action which the authority concerned have taken or propose to take, or

(c) does not within a period of three months beginning with the end of the period allowed by or under subsection (2) above as applied by subsection (2C) above, or such longer period as the Local Commissioner may agree in writing, receive confirmation from the authority concerned that they have taken action, as proposed, to the satisfaction of the Local Commissioner, he may by notice to the authority, require them to arrange for a statement to be published in accordance with subsections (2E) and (2F) below.

(2E) The statement referred to in subsection (2D) above is a statement, in such form as the authority concerned and the Local Commissioner may agree, consisting of –

(a) details of any action recommended by the Local Commissioner in his further report which the authority have not taken;

(b) such supporting material as the Local Commissioner may require; and

(c) if the authority so require, a statement of the reasons for their having taken no action on, or not the action recommended in, the report.

(2F) The requirements for the publication of the statement are that –

(a) publication shall be in any two editions within a fortnight of a newspaper circulating in the area of the authority agreed with the Local Commissioner or, in default of agreement, nominated by him; and

(b) publication in the first such edition shall be arranged for the earliest practicable date.

(2G) If the authority concerned –

(a) fail to arrange for the publication of the statement in accordance with subsections (2E) and (2F) above, or

(b) are unable, within the period of one month beginning with the date on which they received the notice under subsection (2D) above, or such longer period as the Local Commissioner may agree in writing, to agree with the Local Commissioner the form of the statement to be published,

the Local Commissioner shall arrange for such a statement as is mentioned in subsection (2E) above to be published in any two editions within a fortnight of a newspaper circulating within the authority's area.

(2H) The authority concerned shall reimburse the Commission on demand any reasonable expenses incurred by the Local Commissioner in performing his duty under subsection (2G) above.

Amendments

Sections 26 and 31 have been amended by Local Government Acts 1985 and 1988, Local Government and Housing Act 1989, Leasehold Reform, Housing and Urban Development Act 1993, Environment Act 1995 and Government of Wales Act 1998.

Education Act 1996 ss312–349, 409 and 496–497B and Schs 26 and 27

PART IV: SPECIAL EDUCATIONAL NEEDS
CHAPTER I: CHILDREN WITH SPECIAL EDUCATIONAL NEEDS
INTRODUCTORY
Meaning of 'special educational needs' and 'special educational provision' etc.

312(1) A child has 'special educational needs' for the purposes of this Act if he has a learning difficulty which calls for special educational provision to be made for him.

(2) Subject to subsection (3) (and except for the purposes of section 15(5)) a child has a 'learning difficulty' for the purposes of this Act if –

(a) he has a significantly greater difficulty in learning than the majority of children of his age,

(b) he has a disability which either prevents or hinders him from making use of educational facilities of a kind generally provided for children of his age in schools within the area of the local education authority, or

(c) he is under the age of five and is, or would be if special educational provision were not made for him, likely to fall within paragraph (a) or (b) when of or over that age.

(3) A child is not to be taken as having a learning difficulty solely because the language (or form of the language) in which he is, or will be, taught is different from a language (or form of a language) which has at any time been spoken in his home.

(4) In this Act 'special educational provision' means –

(a) in relation to a child who has attained the age of two, educational provision which is additional to, or otherwise different from, the educational provision made generally for children of his age in schools maintained by the local education authority (other than special schools), and

(b) in relation to a child under that age, educational provision of any kind.

(5) In this Part –

'child' includes any person who has not attained the age of 19 and is a registered pupil at a school;

'maintained school' means any community, foundation or voluntary school or any community or foundation special school not established in a hospital.

CODE OF PRACTICE
Code of Practice

313(1) The Secretary of State shall issue, and may from time to time revise, a code of practice giving practical guidance in respect of the discharge by local education authorities and the governing bodies of maintained schools of their functions under this Part.

(2) It shall be the duty of –
  (a) local education authorities, and such governing bodies, exercising functions under this Part, and
  (b) any other person exercising any function for the purpose of the discharge by local education authorities, and such governing bodies, of functions under this Part, to have regard to the provisions of the code.

(3) On any appeal under this Part to the Tribunal, the Tribunal shall have regard to any provision of the code which appears to the Tribunal to be relevant to any question arising on the appeal.

(4) The Secretary of State shall publish the code as for the time being in force.

(5) In this Part 'the Tribunal' means the Special Educational Needs Tribunal.

Making and approval of code

314(1) Where the Secretary of State proposes to issue or revise a code of practice, he shall prepare a draft of the code (or revised code).

(2) The Secretary of State shall consult such persons about the draft as he thinks fit and shall consider any representations made by them.

(3) If he determines to proceed with the draft (either in its original form or with such modifications as he thinks fit) he shall lay it before both Houses of Parliament.

(4) If the draft is approved by resolution of each House, the Secretary of State shall issue the code in the form of the draft, and the code shall come into effect on such day as the Secretary of State may by order appoint.

SPECIAL EDUCATIONAL PROVISION: GENERAL
Review of arrangements

315(1) A local education authority shall keep under review the arrangements made by them for special educational provision.

(2) In doing so the authority shall, to the extent that it appears necessary or desirable for the purpose of co-ordinating provision for children with special educational needs, consult the governing bodies of community, foundation and voluntary and community and foundation special schools in their area.

Children with special educational needs normally to be educated in mainstream schools

316(1) Any person exercising any functions under this Part in respect of a child with special educational needs who should be educated in a school shall secure that, if the conditions mentioned in subsection (2) are satisfied, the child is educated in a school which is not a special school unless that is incompatible with the wishes of his parent.

(2) The conditions are that educating the child in a school which is not a special

school is compatible with –

(a) his receiving the special educational provision which his learning difficulty calls for,

(b) the provision of efficient education for the children with whom he will be educated, and

(c) the efficient use of resources.

Duties of governing body or LEA in relation to pupils with special educational needs

317(1) The governing body, in the case of a community, foundation or voluntary school and the local education authority, in the case of a maintained nursery school, shall –

(a) use their best endeavours, in exercising their functions in relation to the school, to secure that, if any registered pupil has special educational needs, the special educational provision which his learning difficulty calls for is made,

(b) secure that, where the responsible person has been informed by the local education authority that a registered pupil has special educational needs, those needs are made known to all who are likely to teach him, and

(c) secure that the teachers in the school are aware of the importance of identifying, and providing for, those registered pupils who have special educational needs.

(2) In subsection (1)(b) 'the responsible person' means –

(a) in the case of a community, foundation or voluntary school, the head teacher or the appropriate governor (that is, the chairman of the governing body or, where the governing body have designated another governor for the purposes of this paragraph, that other governor), and

(b) in the case of a nursery school, the head teacher.

(3) To the extent that it appears necessary or desirable for the purpose of co-ordinating provision for children with special educational needs –

(a) the governing bodies of community, foundation and voluntary schools shall, in exercising functions relating to the provision for such children, consult the local education authority and the governing bodies of other such schools, and

(b) in relation to maintained nursery schools, the local education authority shall, in exercising those functions, consult the governing bodies of community, foundation and voluntary schools.

(4) Where a child who has special educational needs is being educated in a community, foundation or voluntary school or a maintained nursery school, those concerned with making special educational provision for the child shall secure, so far as is reasonably practicable and is compatible with –

(a) the child receiving the special educational provision which his learning difficulty calls for,

(b) the provision of efficient education for the children with whom he will be educated, and

(c) the efficient use of resources, that the child engages in the activities of the school together with children who do not have special educational needs.

(5) The annual report for each community, foundation or voluntary or community or foundation special school shall include a report containing such information as may be prescribed about the implementation of the governing body's policy for pupils with special educational needs.

(6) The annual report for each community, foundation or voluntary school shall also include a report containing information as to –
   (a) the arrangements for the admission of disabled pupils;
   (b) the steps taken to prevent disabled pupils from being treated less favourably than other pupils; and
   (c) the facilities provided to assist access to the school by disabled pupils; and for this purpose 'disabled pupils' means pupils who are disabled persons for the purposes of the Disability Discrimination Act 1995.

(7) In this section 'annual report' means the report prepared under section 42 of the School Standards and Framework Act 1998.

Provision of goods and services in connection with special educational needs

318(1) A local education authority may, for the purpose only of assisting –
   (a) the governing bodies of community, foundation or voluntary schools (in their or any other area) in the performance of the governing bodies' duties under section 317(1)(a), or
   (b) the governing bodies of community or foundation special schools (in their or any other area) in the performance of the governing bodies' duties, supply goods or services to those bodies.

(2) The terms on which goods or services are supplied by local education authorities under this section to the governing bodies of community, foundation or voluntary schools or community or foundation special schools in any other area may, in such circumstances as may be prescribed, include such terms as to payment as may be prescribed.

(3) A local education authority may supply goods and services to any authority or other person (other than a governing body within subsection (1) for the purpose only of assisting them in making for any child to whom subsection (3A) applies any special educational provision which any learning difficulty of the child calls for.

(3A)This subsection applies to any child –
   (a) who is receiving relevant nursery education within the meaning of section 123 of the School Standards and Framework Act 1998, or;
   (b) in respect of whose education grants are (or are to be) made under section 1 of the Nursery Education and Grant-Maintained Schools Act 1996.

(4) This section is without prejudice to the generality of any other power of local education authorities to supply goods or services.

Special educational provision otherwise than in schools

319(1) Where a local education authority are satisfied that it would be inappropriate for –

(a) the special educational provision which a learning difficulty of a child in their area calls for, or

(b) any part of any such provision,

to be made in a school, they may arrange for the provision (or, as the case may be, for that part of it) to be made otherwise than in a school.

(2) Before making an arrangement under this section, a local education authority shall consult the child's parent.

Provision outside England and Wales for certain children

320(1) A local education authority may make such arrangements as they think fit to enable a child for whom they maintain a statement under section 324 to attend an institution outside England and Wales which specialises in providing for children with special needs.

(2) In subsection (1) 'children with special needs' means children who have particular needs which would be special educational needs if those children were in England and Wales.

(3) Where a local education authority make arrangements under this section in respect of a child, those arrangements may in particular include contributing to or paying –

(a) fees charged by the institution,

(b) expenses reasonably incurred in maintaining him while he is at the institution or travelling to or from it,

(c) his travelling expenses, and

(d) expenses reasonably incurred by any person accompanying him while he is travelling or staying at the institution.

(4) This section is without prejudice to any other powers of a local education authority.

IDENTIFICATION AND ASSESSMENT OF CHILDREN WITH SPECIAL EDUCATIONAL NEEDS
General duty of local education authority towards children for whom they are responsible

321(1) A local education authority shall exercise their powers with a view to securing that, of the children for whom they are responsible, they identify those to whom subsection (2) below applies.

(2) This subsection applies to a child if –

(a) he has special educational needs, and

(b) it is necessary for the authority to determine the special educational provision which any learning difficulty he may have calls for.

(3) For the purposes of this Part a local education authority are responsible for a child if he is in their area and –

(a) he is a registered pupil at a maintained school,

(b) education is provided for him at a school which is not a maintained school but is so provided at the expense of the authority,

(c) he does not come within paragraph (a) or (b) above but is a registered pupil at a school and has been brought to the authority's attention as having (or probably having) special educational needs, or

(d) he is not a registered pupil at a school but is not under the age of two or

over compulsory school age and has been brought to their attention as
having (or probably having) special educational needs.

Duty of Health Authority or local authority to help local education authority.

322(1) Where it appears to a local education authority that any Health Authority or
local authority could, by taking any specified action, help in the exercise of
any of their functions under this Part, they may request the help of the
authority, specifying the action in question.

(2) An authority whose help is so requested shall comply with the request
unless –
  (a) they consider that the help requested is not necessary for the purpose of
  the exercise by the local education authority of those functions, or
  (b) subsection (3) applies.

(3) This subsection applies –
  (a) in the case of a Health Authority, if that authority consider that, having
  regard to the resources available to them for the purpose of the exercise
  of their functions under the National Health Service Act 1977, it is not
  reasonable for them to comply with the request, or
  (b) in the case of a local authority, if that authority consider that the request
  is not compatible with their own statutory or other duties and
  obligations or unduly prejudices the discharge of any of their functions.

(4) Regulations may provide that, where an authority are under a duty by virtue
of subsection (2) to comply with a request to help a local education authority
in the making of an assessment under section 323 or a statement under
section 324 of this Act, they must, subject to prescribed exceptions, comply
with the request within the prescribed period.

(5) In this section 'local authority' means a county council, a county borough
council, a district council (other than one for an area for which there is a
county council), a London borough council or the Common Council of the
City of London.

Assessment of educational needs

323(1) Where a local education authority are of the opinion that a child for whom
they are responsible falls, or probably falls, within subsection (2), they shall
serve a notice on the child's parent informing him –
  (a) that they propose to make an assessment of the child's educational
  needs,
  (b) of the procedure to be followed in making the assessment,
  (c) of the name of the officer of the authority from whom further
  information may be obtained, and
  (d) of the parent's right to make representations, and submit written
  evidence, to the authority within such period (which must not be less
  than 29 days beginning with the date on which the notice is served) as
  may be specified in the notice.

(2) A child falls within this subsection if –
  (a) he has special educational needs, and
  (b) it is necessary for the authority to determine the special educational

provision which any learning difficulty he may have calls for.

(3) Where –

    (a) a local education authority have served a notice under subsection (1) and the period specified in the notice in accordance with subsection (1)(d) has expired, and

    (b) the authority remain of the opinion, after taking into account any representations made and any evidence submitted to them in response to the notice, that the child falls, or probably falls, within subsection (2),

they shall make an assessment of his educational needs.

(4) Where a local education authority decide to make an assessment under this section, they shall give notice in writing to the child's parent of that decision and of their reasons for making it.

(5) Schedule 26 has effect in relation to the making of assessments under this section.

(6) Where, at any time after serving a notice under subsection (1), a local education authority decide not to assess the educational needs of the child concerned they shall give notice in writing to the child's parent of their decision.

Statement of special educational needs

324(1) If, in the light of an assessment under section 323 of any child's educational needs and of any representations made by the child's parent in pursuance of Schedule 27, it is necessary for the local education authority to determine the special educational provision which any learning difficulty he may have calls for, the authority shall make and maintain a statement of his special educational needs.

(2) The statement shall be in such form and contain such information as may be prescribed.

(3) In particular, the statement shall –

    (a) give details of the authority's assessment of the child's special educational needs, and

    (b) specify the special educational provision to be made for the purpose of meeting those needs, including the particulars required by subsection (4).

(4) The statement shall –

    (a) specify the type of school or other institution which the local education authority consider would be appropriate for the child,

    (b) if they are not required under Schedule 27 to specify the name of any school in the statement, specify the name of any school or institution (whether in the United Kingdom or elsewhere) which they consider would be appropriate for the child and should be specified in the statement, and

    (c) specify any provision for the child for which they make arrangements under section 319 and which they consider should be specified in the statement.

(5) Where a local education authority maintain a statement under this section, then –

    (a) unless the child's parent has made suitable arrangements, the authority

(i) shall arrange that the special educational provision specified in the statement is made for the child, and

(ii) may arrange that any non-educational provision specified in the statement is made for him in such manner as they consider appropriate, and

(b) if the name of a maintained school is specified in the statement, the governing body of the school shall admit the child to the school.

(5A) Subsection (5)(b) has effect regardless of any duty imposed on the governing body of a school by section 1(6) of the School Standards and Framework Act 1998.

(6) Subsection (5)(b) does not affect any power to exclude from a school a pupil who is already a registered pupil there.

(7) Schedule 27 has effect in relation to the making and maintenance of statements under this section.

Appeal against decision not to make statement

325(1) If, after making an assessment under section 323 of the educational needs of any child for whom no statement is maintained under section 324, the local education authority do not propose to make such a statement, they shall give notice in writing of their decision, and of the effect of subsection (2) below, to the child's parent.

(2) In such a case, the child's parent may appeal to the Tribunal against the decision.

(3) On an appeal under this section, the Tribunal may –

(a) dismiss the appeal,

(b) order the local education authority to make and maintain such a statement, or

(c) remit the case to the authority for them to reconsider whether, having regard to any observations made by the Tribunal, it is necessary for the authority to determine the special educational provision which any learning difficulty the child may have calls for.

Appeal against contents of statement

326(1) The parent of a child for whom a local education authority maintain a statement under section 324 may –

(a) when the statement is first made,

(b) where the description in the statement of the authority's assessment of the child's special educational needs, or the special educational provision specified in the statement, is amended, or

(c) where, after conducting an assessment of the educational needs of the child under section 323, the local education authority determine not to amend the statement, appeal to the Tribunal against the description in the statement of the authority's assessment of the child's special educational needs, the special educational provision specified in the statement or, if no school is named in the statement, that fact.

(2) Subsection (1)(b) does not apply where the amendment is made in pursuance of –

(a) paragraph 8 (change of named school) or 11(3)(b) (amendment ordered

by Tribunal) of Schedule 27, or
(b) directions under section 442 (revocation of school attendance order);
and subsection (1)(c) does not apply to a determination made following the service of notice under paragraph 10 (amendment by LEA) of Schedule 27 of a proposal to amend the statement.

(3) On an appeal under this section, the Tribunal may –
   (a) dismiss the appeal,
   (b) order the authority to amend the statement, so far as it describes the authority's assessment of the child's special educational needs or specifies the special educational provision, and make such other consequential amendments to the statement as the Tribunal think fit, or
   (c) order the authority to cease to maintain the statement.

(4) On an appeal under this section the Tribunal shall not order the local education authority to specify the name of any school in the statement (either in substitution for an existing name or in a case where no school is named) unless –
   (a) the parent has expressed a preference for the school in pursuance of arrangements under paragraph 3 (choice of school) of Schedule 27, or
   (b) in the proceedings the parent, the local education authority, or both have proposed the school.

(5) Before determining any appeal under this section the Tribunal may, with the agreement of the parties, correct any deficiency in the statement.

Access for local education authority to certain schools

327(1) This section applies where –
   (a) a local education authority maintain a statement for a child under section 324, and
   (b) in pursuance of the statement education is provided for the child at a school maintained by another local education authority.

(2) Any person authorised by the local education authority shall be entitled to have access at any reasonable time to the premises of any such school for the purpose of monitoring the special educational provision made in pursuance of the statement for the child at the school.

Reviews of educational needs

328(1) Regulations may prescribe the frequency with which assessments under section 323 are to be repeated in respect of children for whom statements are maintained under section 324.

(2) Where –
   (a) the parent of a child for whom a statement is maintained under section 324 asks the local education authority to arrange for an assessment to be made in respect of the child under section 323,
   (b) no such assessment has been made within the period of six months ending with the date on which the request is made, and
   (c) it is necessary for the authority to make a further assessment under section 323,
   the authority shall comply with the request.

(3) If in any case where subsection (2)(a) and (b) applies the authority determine not to comply with the request –
   (a) they shall give notice of that fact and of the effect of paragraph (b) below to the child's parent, and
   (b) the parent may appeal to the Tribunal against the determination.
(4) On an appeal under subsection (3) the Tribunal may –
   (a) dismiss the appeal, or
   (b) order the authority to arrange for an assessment to be made in respect of the child under section 323.
(5) A statement under section 324 shall be reviewed by the local education authority –
   (a) on the making of an assessment in respect of the child concerned under section 323, and
   (b) in any event, within the period of 12 months beginning with the making of the statement or, as the case may be, with the previous review.
(6) Regulations may make provision –
   (a) as to the manner in which reviews of such statements are to be conducted,
   (b) as to the participation in such reviews of such persons as may be prescribed, and
   (c) in connection with such other matters relating to such reviews as the Secretary of State considers appropriate.

Assessment of educational needs at request of child's parent

329(1) Where –
   (a) the parent of a child for whom a local education authority are responsible but for whom no statement is maintained under section 324 asks the authority to arrange for an assessment to be made in respect of the child under section 323,
   (b) no such assessment has been made within the period of six months ending with the date on which the request is made, and
   (c) it is necessary for the authority to make an assessment under that section,
   the authority shall comply with the request.
(2) If in any case where subsection (1)(a) and (b) applies the authority determine not to comply with the request –
   (a) they shall give notice of that fact and of the effect of paragraph (b) below to the child's parent, and
   (b) the parent may appeal to the Tribunal against the determination.
(3) On an appeal under subsection (2) the Tribunal may –
   (a) dismiss the appeal, or
   (b) order the authority to arrange for an assessment to be made in respect of the child under section 323.

Assessment of educational needs of children under two

331(1) Where a local education authority are of the opinion that a child in their area who is under the age of two falls, or probably falls, within subsection (2) –

    (a) they may, with the consent of his parent, make an assessment of the child's educational needs, and

    (b) they shall make such an assessment if requested to do so by his parent.

(2) A child falls within this subsection if –

    (a) he has special educational needs, and

    (b) it is necessary for the authority to determine the special educational provision which any learning difficulty he may have calls for.

(3) An assessment under this section shall be made in such manner as the authority consider appropriate.

(4) After making an assessment under this section, the authority –

    (a) may make a statement of the child's special educational needs, and

    (b) may maintain that statement,

in such manner as they consider appropriate.

Duty of Health Authority or National Health Service trust to notify parent etc

332(1) This section applies where a Health Authority or a National Health Service trust, in the course of exercising any of their functions in relation to a child who is under the age of five, form the opinion that he has (or probably has) special educational needs.

(2) The Authority or trust –

    (a) shall inform the child's parent of their opinion and of their duty under paragraph (b), and

    (b) after giving the parent an opportunity to discuss that opinion with an officer of the Authority or trust, shall bring it to the attention of the appropriate local education authority.

(3) If the Authority or trust are of the opinion that a particular voluntary organisation is likely to be able to give the parent advice or assistance in connection with any special educational needs that the child may have, they shall inform the parent accordingly.

SPECIAL EDUCATIONAL NEEDS TRIBUNAL
Constitution of Tribunal

333(1) There shall continue to be a tribunal known as the Special Educational Needs Tribunal which shall exercise the jurisdiction conferred on it by this Part.

(2) There shall be appointed –

    (a) a President of the Tribunal (referred to in this Part as 'the President'),

    (b) a panel of persons (referred to in this Part as 'the chairmen's panel') who may serve as chairman of the Tribunal, and

    (c) a panel of persons (referred to in this Part as 'the lay panel') who may serve as the other two members of the Tribunal apart from the chairman.

(3) The President and the members of the chairmen's panel shall each be appointed by the Lord Chancellor.

(4) The members of the lay panel shall each be appointed by the Secretary of State.

(5) Regulations may –

(a) provide for the jurisdiction of the Tribunal to be exercised by such number of tribunals as may be determined from time to time by the President, and

(b) make such other provision in connection with the establishment and continuation of the Tribunal as the Secretary of State considers necessary or desirable.

(6) The Secretary of State may, with the consent of the Treasury, provide such staff and accommodation as the Tribunal may require.

The President and members of the panels

334(1) No person may be appointed President or member of the chairmen's panel unless he has a seven year general qualification (within the meaning of section 71 of the Courts and Legal Services Act 1990).

(2) No person may be appointed member of the lay panel unless he satisfies such requirements as may be prescribed.

(3) If, in the opinion of the Lord Chancellor, the President is unfit to continue in office or is incapable of performing his duties, the Lord Chancellor may revoke his appointment.

(4) Each member of the chairmen's panel or lay panel shall hold and vacate office under the terms of the instrument under which he is appointed.

(5) The President or a member of the chairmen's panel or lay panel –

(a) may resign office by notice in writing to the Lord Chancellor or (as the case may be) the Secretary of State, and

(b) is eligible for re-appointment if he ceases to hold office.

Remuneration and expenses

335(1) The Secretary of State may pay to the President, and to any other person in respect of his service as a member of the Tribunal, such remuneration and allowances as the Secretary of State may, with the consent of the Treasury, determine.

(2) The Secretary of State may defray the expenses of the Tribunal to such amount as he may, with the consent of the Treasury, determine.

Tribunal procedure

336 (1) Regulations may make provision about the proceedings of the Tribunal on an appeal under this Part and the initiation of such an appeal.

(2) The regulations may, in particular, include provision –

(a) as to the period within which, and the manner in which, appeals are to be instituted,

(b) where the jurisdiction of the Tribunal is being exercised by more than one tribunal –

(i) for determining by which tribunal any appeal is to be heard, and

(ii) for the transfer of proceedings from one tribunal to another,

(c) for enabling any functions which relate to matters preliminary or incidental to an appeal to be performed by the President, or by the chairman,

(d) for the holding of hearings in private in prescribed circumstances,

(e) for hearings to be conducted in the absence of any member other than

the chairman,
(f) as to the persons who may appear on behalf of the parties,
(g) for granting any person such discovery or inspection of documents or right to further particulars as might be granted by a county court,
(h) requiring persons to attend to give evidence and produce documents,
(i) for authorising the administration of oaths to witnesses,
(j) for the determination of appeals without a hearing in prescribed circumstances,
(k) as to the withdrawal of appeals,
(l) for the award of costs or expenses,
(m)for taxing or otherwise settling any such costs or expenses (and, in particular, for enabling such costs to be taxed in the county court),
(n) for the registration and proof of decisions and orders, and
(o) for enabling the Tribunal to review its decisions, or revoke or vary its orders, in such circumstances as may be determined in accordance with the regulations.
(3) The Secretary of State may pay such allowances for the purpose of or in connection with the attendance of persons at the Tribunal as he may, with the consent of the Treasury, determine.
(4) Part I of the Arbitration Act 1996 shall not apply to any proceedings before the Tribunal but regulations may make provision corresponding to any provision of that Act.
(5) Any person who without reasonable excuse fails to comply with –
(a) any requirement in respect of the discovery or inspection of documents imposed by the regulations by virtue of subsection (2)(g), or
(b) any requirement imposed by the regulations by virtue of subsection (2)(h),
is guilty of an offence.
(6) A person guilty of an offence under subsection (5) is liable on summary conviction to a fine not exceeding level 3 on the standard scale.

CHAPTER II: SCHOOLS PROVIDING FOR SPECIAL EDUCATIONAL NEEDS
SPECIAL SCHOOLS
Special schools
337(1) A school is a special school if it is specially organised to make special educational provision for pupils with special educational needs.
(2) There are the following categories of special school–
(a) special schools maintained by local education authorities, comprising –
(i) community special schools, and
(ii) foundation special schools; and
(b) special schools which are not so maintained but are for the time being approved by the Secretary of State under section 342.

APPROVAL OF NON-MAINTAINED SPECIAL SCHOOLS
Approval of non-maintained special schools
342(1) The Secretary of State may approve under this section any school which–

(a) is specially organised to make special educational provision for pupils with special educational needs, and

(b) is not a community or foundation special school,

and may give his approval before or after the school is established.

(2) Regulations may make provision as to the requirements which are to be complied with as a condition of approval under subsection (1) above.

(3) Any school which was a special school immediately before 1st April 1994 shall be treated, subject to subsection (4) below, as approved under this section.

(4) Regulations may make provision as to–

(a) the requirements which are to be complied with by a school while approved under this section, and

(b) the withdrawal of approval from a school (including approval treated as given under subsection (3)) at the request of the proprietor or on the ground that there has been a failure to comply with any prescribed requirement.

(5) Without prejudice to the generality of subsections (2) and (4), the requirements which may be imposed by the regulations include requirements–

(a) which call for arrangements to be approved by the Secretary of State, or

(b) as to the organisation of any special school as a primary school or as a secondary school.

(6) Regulations shall make provision for securing that, so far as practicable, every pupil attending a special school approved under this section–

(a) receives religious education and attends religious worship, or

(b) is withdrawn from receiving such education or from attendance at such worship in accordance with the wishes of his parent.

INDEPENDENT SCHOOLS PROVIDING SPECIAL EDUCATION
Approval of independent schools

347(1) The Secretary of State may approve an independent school as suitable for the admission of children for whom statements are maintained under section 324.

(2) Regulations may make provision as to –

(a) the requirements which are to be complied with by a school as a condition of its approval under this section,

(b) the requirements which are to be complied with by a school while an approval under this section is in force in respect of it, and

(c) the withdrawal of approval from a school at the request of the proprietor or on the ground that there has been a failure to comply with any prescribed requirement.

(3) An approval under this section may be given subject to such conditions (in addition to those prescribed) as the Secretary of State sees fit to impose.

(4) In any case where there is a failure to comply with such a condition imposed under subsection (3), the Secretary of State may withdraw his approval.

(5) No person shall so exercise his functions under this Part that a child with

special educational needs is educated in an independent school unless –

(a) the school is for the time being approved by the Secretary of State as suitable for the admission of children for whom statements are maintained under section 324, or

(b) the Secretary of State consents to the child being educated there.

Provision of special education at non-maintained schools

348(1) This section applies where –

(a) special educational provision in respect of a child with special educational needs is made at a school which is not a maintained school, and

(b) either the name of the school is specified in a statement in respect of the child under section 324 or the local education authority are satisfied –

(i) that his interests require the necessary special educational provision to be made for him at a school which is not a maintained school, and

(ii) that it is appropriate for the child to be provided with education at the particular school.

(2) Where this section applies, the local education authority shall pay the whole of the fees payable in respect of the education provided for the child at the school, and if –

(a) board and lodging are provided for him at the school, and

(b) the authority are satisfied that the necessary special educational provision cannot be provided for him at the school unless the board and lodging are also provided,

the authority shall pay the whole of the fees payable in respect of the board and lodging.

(3) In this section 'maintained school' means a school maintained by a local education authority.

VARIATION OF DEEDS
Variation of trust deeds etc. by order

349(1) The Secretary of State may by order make such modifications of any trust deed or other instrument relating to a school as, after consultation with the governing body or other proprietor of the school, appear to him to be necessary to enable the governing body or proprietor to meet any requirement imposed by regulations under section 342 or 347.

(2) Any modification made by an order under this section may be made to have permanent effect or to have effect for such period as may be specified in the order.

Amendments

Sections 312, 313, 315, 317, 318, 321, 324, 327, 330, 337 were amended by School Standards and Framework Act 1998 Sch 30 paras 71–80. Sections 338–341 were omitted by ibid para 81. Section 342 was amended by ibid para 82. Sections 343–346 were omitted by ibid para 83. Section 348 was amended by ibid para 84.

PART V: THE CURRICULUM
CHAPTER IV: MISCELLANEOUS AND SUPPLEMENTARY PROVISIONS
COMPLAINTS AND ENFORCEMENT
Complaints and enforcement: maintained schools

409(1) A local education authority shall, with the approval of the Secretary of State and after consultation with governing bodies of foundation and voluntary aided schools, make arrangements for the consideration and disposal of any complaint to which subsection (2) applies.

(2) This subsection applies to any complaint which is to the effect that the authority, or the governing body of any community, foundation or voluntary school maintained by the authority or any community or foundation special school so maintained which is not established in a hospital –

(a) have acted or are proposing to act unreasonably in relation to the exercise of a power conferred on them by or under a relevant enactment, or

(b) have acted or are proposing to act unreasonably in relation to the performance of, or have failed to discharge, a duty imposed on them by or under a relevant enactment.

(3) In subsection (2) 'relevant enactment' means –

(a) any provision which by virtue of section 408(4) is a relevant provision of this Part for the purposes of section 408(1), and

(b) any other enactment (whether contained in this Part or otherwise) so far as relating to the curriculum for, or religious worship in, maintained schools.

(4) The Secretary of State shall not entertain under section 496 (power to prevent unreasonable exercise of functions) or 497 (powers where a local education authority or governing body fail to discharge their duties) any complaint to which subsection (2) applies, unless a complaint concerning the same matter has been made and disposed of in accordance with arrangements made under subsection (1).

Amendments

Section 409 was amended by School Standards and Framework Act 1998 Sch 30 para 107.

PART IX: ANCILLARY FUNCTIONS
CHAPTER 1: ANCILLARY FUNCTIONS OF SECRETARY OF STATE
GENERAL FUNCTIONS
Power to prevent unreasonable exercise of functions

496(1) If the Secretary of State is satisfied (either on a complaint by any person or otherwise) that a body to which this section applies have acted or are proposing to act unreasonably with respect to the exercise of any power conferred or the performance of any duty imposed by or under this Act, he may give such directions as to the exercise of the power or the performance of the duty as appear to him to be expedient (and may do so despite any enactment which makes the exercise of the power or the performance of the duty contingent upon the opinion of the body).

(2) The bodies to which this section applies are –
   (a) any local authority, and
   (b) the governing body of any community, foundation or voluntary school or any community or foundation special school.

General default powers

497(1) If the Secretary of State is satisfied (either on a complaint by any person interested or otherwise) that a body to which this section applies have failed to discharge any duty imposed on them by or for the purposes of this Act, he may make an order –
   (a) declaring the body to be in default in respect of that duty, and
   (b) giving such directions for the purpose of enforcing the performance of the duty as appear to him to be expedient.

(2) The bodies to which this section applies are –
   (a) any local education authority, and
   (b) the governing body of any community, foundation or voluntary school or any community or foundation special school.

(3) Any directions given under subsection (1)(b) shall be enforceable, on an application made on behalf of the Secretary of State, by an order of mandamus.

Power to secure proper performance of LEA's functions

497A(1) This section applies to a local education authority's functions (of whatever nature) which relate to the provision of education –
   (a) for persons of compulsory school age (whether at school or otherwise), or
   (b) for persons of any age above or below that age who are registered as pupils at schools maintained by the authority.

(2) If the Secretary of State is satisfied (either on a complaint by any person interested or otherwise) that a local education authority are failing in any respect to perform any function to which this section applies to an adequate standard (or at all), he may exercise his powers under subsection (3) or (4).

(3) The Secretary of State may under this subsection direct an officer of the authority to secure that that function is performed in such way as to achieve such objectives as are specified in the direction.

(4) The Secretary of State may under this subsection give an officer of the authority such directions as the Secretary of State thinks expedient for the purpose of securing that the function–
   (a is performed, on behalf of the authority and at their expense, by such person as is specified in the direction, and
   (b) is so performed in such a way as to achieve such objectives as are so specified;

and such directions may require that any contract or other arrangement made by the authority with that person contains such terms and conditions as may be so specified.

(5) Where the Secretary of State considers it expedient that the person specified in directions under subsection (4) should perform other functions to which this section applies in addition to the function to which subsection (2) applies, the directions under subsection (4) may relate to the performance of those other functions as well; and in considering whether it is expedient that that person should perform any such additional functions, the Secretary of State may have regard to financial considerations.

(6) Any direction under this section may either–

(a) have effect for an indefinite period until revoked by the Secretary of State, or

(b) have effect until any objectives specified in the direction have been achieved (as determined in accordance with the direction).

(7) Any direction given under subsection (3) or (4) shall be enforceable, on an application made on behalf of the Secretary of State, by an order of mandamus.

Power to secure proper performance: further provisions

497B(1) Where the Secretary of State gives directions under section 497A(4) to an officer of a local education authority, the person specified in those directions shall, in the performance of the function or functions specified in the directions, be entitled to exercise the powers conferred by this section.

(2) The specified person shall have at all reasonable times–

(a) a right of entry to the premises of the authority, and

(b) a right to inspect, and take copies of, any records or other documents kept by the authority, and any other documents containing information relating to the authority, which he considers relevant to the performance of the specified function or functions.

(3) In exercising the right to inspect records or other documents under subsection (2), the specified person–

(a) shall be entitled at any reasonable time to have access to, and inspect and check the operation of, any computer and any associated apparatus or material which is or has been in use in connection with the records or other documents in question, and

(b) may require–

(i) the person by whom or on whose behalf the computer is or has been so used, or

(ii) any person having charge of, or otherwise concerned with the operation of, the computer, apparatus or material, to afford him such assistance as he may reasonably require (including, in particular, the making of information available for inspection or copying in a legible form).

(4) Without prejudice to subsection (2), the authority shall give the specified person all assistance in connection with the performance of the specified function or functions which they are reasonably able to give.

(5) Subsection (2) shall apply in relation to any school maintained by the authority as it applies in relation to the authority; and without prejudice to that subsection (as it so applies) –

(a) the governing body of any such school shall give the specified person all assistance in connection with the exercise of his functions which they are reasonably able to give; and

(b) the governing body of any such school and the authority shall secure that all such assistance is also given by persons who work at the school.

(6) Any reference in this section to the specified person includes a reference to any person assisting him in the performance of the specified function or functions.

(7) In this section 'document' and 'records' each include information recorded in any form.

Amendments

Sections 496 and 497 were amended by School Standards and Framework Act 1998 Sch 30 paras 129 and 130. Sections 297A and B were added by School Standards and Framework Act 1998 Part I Chapter II s8.

SCHEDULE 26: MAKING OF ASSESSMENTS UNDER SECTION 323

Introductory

1   In this Schedule 'assessment' means an assessment of a child's educational needs under section 323.

Medical and other advice

2 (1) Regulations shall make provision as to the advice which a local education authority are to seek in making assessments.

(2) Without prejudice to the generality of sub-paragraph (1), the regulations shall require the authority, except in such circumstances as may be prescribed, to seek medical, psychological and educational advice and such other advice as may be prescribed.

Manner, and timing, of assessments, etc.

3 (1) Regulations may make provision –

(a) as to the manner in which assessments are to be conducted,

(b) requiring the local education authority, where, after conducting an assessment under section 323 of the educational needs of a child for whom a statement is maintained under section 324, they determine not to amend the statement, to serve on the parent of the child a notice giving the prescribed information, and

(c) in connection with such other matters relating to the making of assessments as the Secretary of State considers appropriate.

(2) Sub-paragraph (1)(b) does not apply to a determination made following the service of notice under paragraph 10 of Schedule 27 (amendment of statement by LEA) of a proposal to amend the statement.

(3) Regulations may provide that, where a local education authority are under a duty to make an assessment, the duty must, subject to prescribed exceptions, be performed within the prescribed period.

(4) Such provision shall not relieve the authority of the duty to make an assessment which has not been performed within that period.

Attendance at examinations

4 (1) Where a local education authority propose to make an assessment, they may serve a notice on the parent of the child concerned requiring the child's attendance for examination in accordance with the provisions of the notice.

(2) The parent of a child examined under this paragraph may be present at the examination if he so desires.

(3) A notice under this paragraph shall –
(a) state the purpose of the examination,
(b) state the time and place at which the examination will be held,
(c) name an officer of the authority from whom further information may be obtained,
(d) inform the parent that he may submit such information to the authority as he may wish, and
(e) inform the parent of his right to be present at the examination.

Offence

5 (1) Any parent who fails without reasonable excuse to comply with any requirements of a notice served on him under paragraph 4 commits an offence if the notice relates to a child who is not over compulsory school age at the time stated in it as the time for holding the examination.

(2) A person guilty of an offence under this paragraph is liable on summary conviction to a fine not exceeding level 2 on the standard scale.

SCHEDULE 27: MAKING AND MAINTENANCE OF STATEMENTS UNDER SECTION 324

Introductory

1   In this Schedule 'statement' means statement of a child's special educational needs under section 324.

Copy of proposed statement

2   Before making a statement, a local education authority shall serve on the parent of the child concerned –
(a) a copy of the proposed statement, and
(b) a written notice explaining the arrangements under paragraph 3, the effect of paragraph 4 and the right to appeal under section 326 and containing such other information as may be prescribed,
but the copy of the proposed statement shall not specify any matter in pursuance of section 324(4) or any prescribed matter.

Choice of school

3 (1) Every local education authority shall make arrangements for enabling a parent on whom a copy of a proposed statement has been served under paragraph 2 to express a preference as to the maintained school at which he wishes education to be provided for his child and to give reasons for his preference.

(2) Any such preference must be expressed or made within the period of 15 days beginning –
(a) with the date on which the written notice mentioned in paragraph 2(b)

was served on the parent, or

(b) if a meeting has (or meetings have) been arranged under paragraph 4(1)(b) or (2), with the date fixed for that meeting (or the last of those meetings).

(3) Where a local education authority make a statement in a case where the parent of the child concerned has expressed a preference in pursuance of such arrangements as to the school at which he wishes education to be provided for his child, they shall specify the name of that school in the statement unless –

(a) the school is unsuitable to the child's age, ability or aptitude or to his special educational needs, or

(b) the attendance of the child at the school would be incompatible with the provision of efficient education for the children with whom he would be educated or the efficient use of resources,

(4) A local education authority shall, before specifying the name of any maintained school in a statement, consult the governing body of the school and, if the school is maintained by another local education authority, that authority.

Representations

4 (1) A parent on whom a copy of a proposed statement has been served under paragraph 2 may –

(a) make representations (or further representations) to the local education authority about the content of the statement, and

(b) require the authority to arrange a meeting between him and an officer of the authority at which the statement can be discussed.

(2) Where a parent, having attended a meeting arranged by a local education authority under sub-paragraph (1)(b), disagrees with any part of the assessment in question, he may require the authority to arrange such meeting or meetings as they consider will enable him to discuss the relevant advice with the appropriate person or persons.

(3) In this paragraph –

'relevant advice' means such of the advice given to the authority in connection with the assessment as they consider to be relevant to that part of the assessment with which the parent disagrees, and

'appropriate person' means the person who gave the relevant advice or any other person who, in the opinion of the authority, is the appropriate person to discuss it with the parent.

(4) Any representations under sub-paragraph (1)(a) must be made within the period of 15 days beginning –

(a) with the date on which the written notice mentioned in paragraph 2(b) was served on the parent, or

(b) if a meeting has (or meetings have) been arranged under sub-paragraph (1)(b) or (2), with the date fixed for that meeting (or the last of those meetings).

(5) A requirement under sub-paragraph (1)(b) must be made within the period of 15 days beginning with the date on which the written notice mentioned in paragraph 2(b) was served on the parent.

(6) A requirement under sub-paragraph (2) must be made within the period of 15 days beginning with the date fixed for the meeting arranged under sub-paragraph (1)(b).

Making the statement

5 (1) Where representations are made to a local education authority under paragraph 4(1)(a), the authority shall not make the statement until they have considered the representations and the period or the last of the periods allowed by paragraph 4 for making requirements or further representations has expired.

(2) The statement may be in the form originally proposed (except as to the matters required to be excluded from the copy of the proposed statement) or in a form modified in the light of the representations.

(3) Regulations may provide that, where a local education authority are under a duty (subject to compliance with the preceding requirements of this Schedule) to make a statement, the duty, or any step required to be taken for performance of the duty, must, subject to prescribed exceptions, be performed within the prescribed period.

(4) Such provision shall not relieve the authority of the duty to make a statement, or take any step, which has not been performed or taken within that period.

Service of statement

6   Where a local education authority make a statement they shall serve a copy of the statement on the parent of the child concerned and shall give notice in writing to him –

(a) of his right under section 326(1) to appeal against –
  (i) the description in the statement of the authority's assessment of the child's special educational needs,
  (ii) the special educational provision specified in the statement, or
  (iii) if no school is named in the statement, that fact, and

(b) of the name of the person to whom he may apply for information and advice about the child's special educational needs.

Keeping, disclosure and transfer of statements

7 (1) Regulations may make provision as to the keeping and disclosure of statements.

(2) Regulations may make provision, where a local education authority become responsible for a child for whom a statement is maintained by another authority, for the transfer of the statement to them and for Part IV to have effect as if the duty to maintain the transferred statement were their duty.

Change of named school

8 (1) Sub-paragraph (2) applies where –

(a) the parent of a child for whom a statement is maintained which specifies the name of a school or institution asks the local education authority to substitute for that name the name of a maintained school specified by the parent, and

(b) the request is not made less than 12 months after –

      (i) an earlier request under this paragraph,

      (ii) the service of a copy of the statement under paragraph 6,

      (iii) if the statement has been amended, the date when notice of the amendment is given under paragraph 10(3)(b), or

      (iv) if the parent has appealed to the Tribunal, under section 326 or this paragraph, the date when the appeal is concluded,

    whichever is the later.

(2) The local education authority shall comply with the request unless –

    (a) the school is unsuitable to the child's age, ability or aptitude or to his special educational needs, or

    (b) the attendance of the child at the school would be incompatible with the provision of efficient education for the children with whom he would be educated or the efficient use of resources.

(3) Where the local education authority determine not to comply with the request –

    (a) they shall give notice of that fact and of the effect of paragraph (b) below to the parent of the child. and

    (b) the parent of the child may appeal to the Tribunal against the determination.

(4) On the appeal the Tribunal may –

    (a) dismiss the appeal, or

    (b) order the local education authority to substitute for the name of the school or other institution specified in the statement the name of the school specified by the parent.

(5) Regulations may provide that, where a local education authority are under a duty to comply with a request under this paragraph, the duty must, subject to prescribed exceptions, be performed within the prescribed period.

(6) Such provision shall not relieve the authority of the duty to comply with such a request which has not been complied with within that period.

Procedure for amending or ceasing to maintain a statement

9 (1) A local education authority may not amend, or cease to maintain, a statement except in accordance with paragraph 10 or 11.

  (2) Sub-paragraph (1) does not apply where the local education authority –

    (a) cease to maintain a statement for a child who has ceased to be a child for whom they are responsible,

    (b) amend a statement in pursuance of paragraph 8,

    (c) are ordered to cease to maintain a statement under section 326(3)(c), or

    (d) amend a statement in pursuance of directions under section 442 (revocation of school attendance order).

10 (1) Before amending a statement, a local education authority shall serve on the parent of the child concerned a notice informing him –

    (a) of their proposal, and

    (b) of his right to make representations under sub-paragraph (2).

  (2) A parent on whom a notice has been served under sub-paragraph (1) may, within the period of 15 days beginning with the date on which the notice is served, make representations to the local education authority about their

proposal.

(3) The local education authority –
  (a) shall consider any representations made to them under sub-paragraph (2), and
  (b) on taking a decision on the proposal to which the representations relate, shall give notice in writing to the parent of their decision.

(4) Where a local education authority make an amendment under this paragraph to the description in a statement of the authority's assessment of a child's special educational needs or to the special educational provision specified in a statement, they shall give notice in writing to the parent of his right under section 326(1) to appeal against –
  (a) the description in the statement of the authority's assessment of the child's special educational needs,
  (b) the special educational provision specified in the statement, or
  (c) if no school is named in the statement, that fact.

(5) A local education authority may only amend a statement under this paragraph within the prescribed period beginning with the service of the notice under sub-paragraph (1).

11 (1) A local education authority may cease to maintain a statement only if it is no longer necessary to maintain it.

(2) Where the local education authority determine to cease to maintain a statement –
  (a) they shall give notice of that fact and of the effect of paragraph (b) below to the parent of the child, and
  (b) the parent of the child may appeal to the Tribunal against the determination.

(3) On an appeal under this paragraph the Tribunal may
  (a) dismiss the appeal, or
  (b) order the local education authority to continue to maintain the statement in its existing form or with such amendments of –
    (i) the description in the statement of the authority's assessment of the child's special educational needs, or
    (ii) the special educational provision specified in the statement, and such other consequential amendments, as the Tribunal may determine.

(4) Except where the parent of the child appeals to the Tribunal under this paragraph, a local education authority may only cease to maintain a statement under this paragraph within the prescribed period beginning with the service of the notice under sub-paragraph (2).

Amendments

Schedule 27 was amended by School Standards and Framework Act 1998 Sch 30 para 186.

School Standards and Framework Act 1998 ss38–39 and Sch 24

PART II: NEW FRAMEWORK FOR MAINTAINED SCHOOLS
CHAPTER III: GOVERNMENT OF MAINTAINED SCHOOLS
FUNCTIONS OF GOVERNING BODY
General responsibility of governing body for conduct of school

38 (1) Subject to any other statutory provision, the conduct of a maintained school shall be under the direction of the school's governing body.

(2) The governing body shall conduct the school with a view to promoting high standards of educational achievement at the school.

(3) Regulations may –
   (a) set out terms of reference for governing bodies of maintained schools;
   (b) define the respective roles and responsibilities of governing bodies and head teachers of such schools, whether generally or with respect to particular matters, including the curriculum for such schools;
   (c) confer functions of governing bodies and head teachers of such schools.

(4) The governing body of a maintained school shall, in discharging their functions, comply with –
   (a) the instrument of government; and
   (b) (subject to any other statutory provision) any trust deed relating to the school.

Additional functions of governing body

39 (1) The governing body of a maintained school shall in accordance with regulations–
   (a) establish procedures for dealing with all complaints relating to the school other than those falling to be dealt with in accordance with any procedures required to be established in relation to the school by virtue of any other statutory provision; and
   (b) publicise the procedures so established.

(2) The governing body of a maintained school may require pupils in attendance at the school to attend at any place outside the school premises for the purpose of receiving any instruction or training included in the secular curriculum for the school.

(3) The governing body and head teacher of –
   (a) a community or voluntary controlled school, or

(b) a community special school,

shall comply with any direction given to them by the local education authority concerning the health or safety of persons in the school's premises or taking part in any school activities elsewhere.

SCHEDULE 24: ADMISSION APPEALS
PART 1: CONSTITUTION OF APPEAL PANELS
Appeal arrangements made by local education authorities

1 (1) An appeal pursuant to arrangements made by a local education authority under section 94(1) shall be to an appeal panel constituted in accordance with this paragraph.

(2) An appeal panel shall consist of three or five members appointed by the authority from –
   (a) persons who are eligible to be lay members; and
   (b) persons who have experience in education, are acquainted with educational conditions in the area of the authority or are parents of registered pupils at a school.

(3) Of the members of an appeal panel –
   (a) at least one must be a person who is eligible to be a lay member and is appointed as such; and
   (b) at least one must be a person failing within sub-paragraph (2)(b).

(4) For the purposes of this paragraph a person is eligible to be a lay member if he is a person without personal experience in the management of any school or the provision of education in any school (disregarding any such experience as a governor or in any other voluntary capacity).

(5) Sufficient persons may be appointed by the authority under this paragraph to enable two or more appeal panels to sit at the same time.

(6) No person shall be a member of an appeal panel if he is disqualified by virtue of sub-paragraph (7).

(7) The following persons are disqualified for membership of an appeal panel –
   (a) any member of the authority or of the governing body of the school in question;
   (b) any person employed by the authority or the governing body, other than a person employed as a teacher,
   (c) any person who has, or at any time has had, any connection with the authority or the school, or with any person within paragraph (b), of a kind which might reasonably be taken to raise doubts about his ability to act impartially in relation to the authority or the school.

(8) A person employed as a teacher by the authority shall not be taken, by reason only of that employment, to have such a connection with the authority as is mentioned in sub-paragraph (7)(c).

(9) A person shall not be a member of an appeal panel for the consideration of an appeal against a decision if he was among those who made the decision or took part in discussions as to whether the decision should be made.

(10) A person who is a teacher at a school shall not be a member of an appeal panel for the consideration of an appeal involving a question whether a

child is to be admitted to that school.

(11) Where, at any time after an appeal panel consisting of five members have begun to consider an appeal, any of the members –

(a) dies, or

(b) becomes unable through illness to continue as a member, the panel may continue with their consideration and determination of the appeal so long as the number of the remaining members is not less than three and the requirements of sub-paragraph (3) are satisfied.

Appeal arrangements made by governing bodies

2 (1) An appeal pursuant to arrangements made by the governing body of a foundation or voluntary aided school under section 94(2) shall be to an appeal panel constituted in accordance with this paragraph.

(2) An appeal panel shall consist of three or five members appointed by the governing body from –

(a) persons who are eligible to be lay members; and

(b) persons who have experience in education, are acquainted with educational conditions in the area of the school or are parents of registered pupils at a school.

(3) Of the members of an appeal panel –

(a) at least one must be a person who is eligible to be a lay member and is appointed as such; and

(b) at least one must be a person falling within sub-paragraph (2)(b).

(4) For the purposes of this paragraph a person is eligible to be a lay member if he is a person without personal experience in the management of any school or the provision of education in any school (disregarding any such experience as a governor or in any other voluntary capacity).

(5) Sufficient persons may be appointed by the governing body under this paragraph to enable two or more appeal panels to sit at the same time.

(6) No person shall be a member of an appeal panel if he is disqualified by virtue of sub-paragraph (7).

(7) The following persons are disqualified for membership of an appeal panel –

(a) any member of the local education authority by whom the school is maintained or of the governing body;

(b) any person employed by the authority or the governing body, other than a person employed as a teacher;

(c) any person who has, or at any time has had, any connection with the authority or the school, or with any person within paragraph (b), of a kind which might reasonably be taken to raise doubts about his ability to act impartially in relation to the authority or the school.

(8) A person employed as a teacher by the authority shall not be taken, by reason only of that employment, to have such a connection with the authority as is mentioned in sub-paragraph (7)(c).

(9) A person who is a teacher at a school shall not be a member of an appeal panel for the consideration of an appeal involving a question whether a child is to be admitted to that school.

(10) Where, at any time after an appeal panel consisting of five members have begun to consider an appeal, any of the members –

(a) dies, or

(b) becomes unable through illness to continue as a member, the panel may continue with their consideration and determination of the appeal so long as the number of the remaining members is not less than three and the requirements of sub-paragraph (3) are satisfied.

3 (1) Where (by virtue of section 94(3)) joint arrangements are made under section 94(2) by the governing bodies of two or more schools, paragraph 2 shall apply as if –

(a) (except in sub-paragraph (7)) any reference to the governing body were a reference to the governing bodies of both or all the schools; and

(b) in sub-paragraph (7), any reference to the governing body of the school in question or to that school were a reference to any of those governing bodies or to any of those schools (as the case may be).

(2) An appeal pursuant to such joint arrangements shall be to an appeal panel constituted in accordance with paragraph 2 as it so applies.

Joint arrangements by local education authorities and governing bodies

4 (1) Where (by virtue of section 94(4)) joint arrangements are made by a local education authority and the governing body or bodies of one or more schools, paragraph 1 shall apply in relation to those arrangements as it applies in relation to arrangements made by a local education authority under section 94(1), but as if in sub-paragraph (7) any reference to the governing body of the school in question or to that school were a reference to the governing body of any school to which the arrangements relate or to any such school (as the case may be).

(2) An appeal pursuant to such joint arrangements shall be to an appeal panel constituted in accordance with paragraph 1 as it so applies.

Allowances for members

5 (1) For the purpose of the payment of financial loss allowance under section 173(4) of the Local Government Act 1972, that provision shall apply, with any necessary modifications, to any member of an appeal panel constituted in accordance with paragraph 1 or 2 (or in accordance with either of those paragraphs as it applies by virtue of paragraph 3 or 4) as it applies to any member of a parish or community council; and such an appeal panel shall be included in the bodies to which section 174 of that Act (travelling and subsistence allowances) applies.

(2) In section 174(1) of that Act, in its application to a panel in accordance with sub-paragraph (1), the reference to payments at rates determined by the body in question shall be read as a reference to payments at rates determined –

(a) by the authority, if the panel is constituted in accordance with paragraph 1 (or in accordance with that paragraph as it applies by virtue of paragraph 4); and

(b) otherwise by the governing body or bodies of the school or schools in question.

Duty to advertise for lay members

6   Secretary of State may by regulations require any local education authority or governing body who are required by section 94(1) or (2) to make arrangements under that provision –

   (a) to advertise, in such manner and at such times as may be prescribed, for persons eligible to be lay members of any appeal panel required to be constituted for the purposes of such arrangements to apply to the authority or body for appointment as such members, and

   (b) in appointing persons as such members, to consider any persons eligible to be so appointed who have applied to the authority or body in response to an advertisement placed in pursuance of sub-paragraph (a) above.

Indemnity

7   (1) Any local education authority or governing body required to make arrangements under section 94(1) or (2) shall indemnify the members of any appeal panel required to be constituted for the purposes of those arrangements against any reasonable legal costs and expenses reasonably incurred by those members in connection with any decision or action taken by them in good faith in pursuance of their functions as members of that panel.

   (2) Where any such panel is constituted in accordance with –

   (a) paragraph 1 as it applies by virtue of paragraph 4, or

   (b) paragraph 2 as it applies by virtue of paragraph 3, any liability arising under sub-paragraph (1) above shall be a joint and several liability of the bodies by whom the joint arrangements are made unless otherwise previously agreed in writing between those bodies.

PART II: PROCEDURE

8   In this Part of this Schedule 'appeal' means an appeal pursuant to any arrangements made under section 94.

9   An appeal shall be by notice in writing setting out the grounds on which it is made.

10   An appeal panel shall give the appellant an opportunity of appearing and making oral representations, and may allow him to be accompanied by a friend or to be represented.

11   The matters to be taken into account by an appeal panel in considering an appeal shall include –

   (a) any preference expressed by the appellant in respect of the child as mentioned in section 86, and

   (b) the arrangements for the admission of pupils published by the local education authority or the governing body under section 92.

12   Where the decision under appeal was made on the ground that prejudice of the kind referred to in section 86(3)(a) would arise as mentioned in subsection (4) of that section, an appeal panel shall determine that a place is to be offered to the child only if they are satisfied –

   (a) that the decision was not one which a reasonable admission authority would make in the circumstances of the case; or

(b) that the child would have been offered a place if the admission arrangements (as published under section 92) had been properly implemented.

13 (1) Appeals shall be heard in private except when the body or bodies by whom the arrangements under section 94 are made direct otherwise; but –

(a) if the panel so direct, one member of the local education authority may attend, as an observer, any hearing of an appeal by an appeal panel constituted in accordance with paragraph 1;

(b) if the panel so direct, one member of the governing body of the school in question may attend, as an observer, any hearing of an appeal by an appeal panel constituted in accordance with paragraph 1 or 2 (or in accordance with paragraph 2 as it applies by virtue of paragraph 3); and

(c) one member of the Council on Tribunals may attend, as an observer, any meeting of any appeal panel at which an appeal is considered.

(2) For the purposes of sub-paragraph (1), an appeal to an appeal panel constituted in accordance with paragraph 1 as it applies by virtue of paragraph 4 shall be treated –

(a) as an appeal to an appeal panel constituted in accordance with paragraph 1 if it relates to a community or voluntary controlled school; and

(b) as an appeal to an appeal panel constituted in accordance with paragraph 2 if it relates to a foundation or voluntary aided school.

14 In the event of a disagreement between the members of an appeal panel, the appeal under consideration shall be decided by a simple majority of the votes cast and, in the case of an equality of votes, the chairman of the panel shall have a second or casting vote.

15 (1) The decision of an appeal panel and the grounds on which it is made shall be communicated by the panel in writing to –

(a) the appellant and the local education authority;

(b) in the case of an appeal to an appeal panel constituted in accordance with paragraph 2 (or in accordance with that paragraph as it applies by virtue of paragraph 3), to the governing body by whom or on whose behalf the decision appealed against was made.

(2) For the purposes of sub-paragraph (1), an appeal to an appeal panel constituted in accordance with paragraph 1 as it applies by virtue of paragraph 4 shall be treated as an appeal to an appeal panel constituted in accordance with paragraph 2, if it relates to a foundation or voluntary aided school.

16 Subject to paragraphs 9 to 15, all matters relating to the procedure on appeals, including the time within which they are to be brought, shall be determined by the body or bodies by whom the arrangements under section 94 are made.

Power of Secretary of State to make amendments

17 The Secretary of State may by order make such amendments of this Schedule as he considers expedient.

Education (School Records) Regulations 1989 SI No 1261

Citation
1   These Regulations may be cited as the Education (School Records) Regulations 1989.

Commencement
2 (1) Except for the regulations referred to in paragraph (2), these Regulations shall come into force on Ist September 1989.

   (2) Regulations 6(1)(b) and (c), (2), (3) and (4), 7 (insofar as it relates to disclosure and amendment of records), and 8 (insofar as aforesaid) shall c me into force on Ist September 1990.

Revocation
3   Regulation 13 of the Education (Schools and Further Education) Regulations 1981 (transfer of educational records) is hereby revoked.

Definitions
4 (1) In these Regulations –
    'child abuse' includes physical injury (other than accidental injury) to, and
       physical and emotional neglect, ill-treatment or sexual abuse of a child;
    'entitled person', in relation to a registered pupil at a school, means –
      (a) a parent of the pupil, where that pupil is under the age of 16 years, or
      (b) the pupil or his parent, where that pupil is aged 16 or 17 years, or
      (c) the pupil himself, where he is aged 18 years or more;
    'institution of further or higher education' means any institution falling
       within subsection (10) of section 218 of the Education Reform Act 1988;
    'curricular record' means a formal record of a pupil's academic
       achievements, his other skills and abilities and his progress in school;
    'responsible person' means –
      (a) the head teacher of an independent school, or
      (b) the governing body of any other school, or
      (c) the person responsible for the conduct of any institution of or
         higher education or other place of education or training to which a
         pupil transfers or may transfer;
    'school day' means a day on which the school meets; and 'teacher' includes
       head teacher.

   (2) In these Regulations, unless the context otherwise requires, any reference

to a numbered regulation is a reference to the regulation bearing that number in these Regulations and any reference in a regulation to a numbered paragraph is to the paragraph of that regulation bearing that number.

Schools to which Regulations apply

5   In these Regulations, unless the context otherwise requires, a reference to a school is to a school maintained by,a local education authority, a special school (whether or not so maintained) or a grant-maintained school.

Duties of Governing Body

6 (1) It shall be the duty of the governing body of every school to make arrangements whereunder –

(a) in respect of every registered pupil at that school there is kept a curricular record and that record is updated at least once a year;

(b) upon receipt of a request made in writing by an entitled person, the relevant pupil's curricular record is disclosed free of charge to the person making the request and, on payment of such fee (not exceeding the cost of supply), if any, as the governing body may prescribe, a copy of it is supplied to him;

(c) upon receipt of a notice given in writing by an entitled person that he regards any part of the relevant pupil's curricular record as inaccurate then –

  (i) if the holder of the record is satisfied that the record is inaccurate, the record is amended by the removal or correction of that part which is regarded as inaccurate, or

  (ii) if the holder of the record is not satisfied that the record is inaccurate, the notice is appended to the record and subsequently treated as forming part of it; and

(d) in every case where the pupil ceases to be a registered pupil at that school and becomes a registered pupil at another school (including an independent school) or a student at an institution of further or higher education or any other place of education or training, that pupil's curricular record and the records referred to in paragraph (5) are transferred to the responsible person, if that person so requests in writing.

(2) Arrangements made in pursuance of paragraph (1)(b) shall secure that the request is complied with within 15 school days of its receipt or, if the request is received on a day which is not a school day, within 15 school days of the first school day following the day on which the request was received.

(3) In any case where the pupil is under consideration for admission to another school (including an independent school) or to an institution of further or higher education, the arrangements for disclosure and supply of a copy of that pupil's curricular record made in pursuance of paragraph (1)(b) shall have effect as if the responsible person were an entitled person in relation to the pupil save that he shall not be required to pay any fee in respect of the supply [and the curricular record shall not include the results of any assessment of the pupil's achievements (whether under Chapter 1 of Part I of the Education Reform Act 1988 or otherwise)].

[(4) Paragraph (1)(c) does not apply to that part of a curricular record consisting of the results of any assessment of a pupil's achievements (whether under Chapter 1 of Part 1 of the Education Reform Act 1988 or otherwise), and in that sub-paragraph 'inaccurate' means inaccurate or misleading as to any matter of fact.]

(5) The records referred to in paragraph (1)(d) are such educational records, or parts thereof, relating to a pupil and kept before 1st September 1989 as appear to the governing body to be appropriate for transfer.

[(6) Nothing in paragraph (3) shall be taken to prevent the disclosure and supply of copies of the results of a pupil's assessment to the head teacher of a school to which a pupil transfers following his consideration for admission thereto.] Amendment The words within square brackets at the end of para (3) were added, para (4) was substituted and para (6) was inserted, in relation to England, by the Education (Individual Pupils' Achievements) (Information) Regulations 1992, SI 1992/3168, with effect from 4 January 1993; and, in relation to Wales, by the Education (Individual Pupils' Achievements) (Information) (Wales) Regulations 1993, SI 1993/835, with effect from 20 April 1993.

7 (1) It shall be the duty of the governing body of every school to make arrangements where under –

(a) any other educational records relating to a registered pupil (including a teacher's record) which are kept at the school in addition to the pupil's curricular record shall be as liable to disclosure or transfer to, and (to a copy thereof being supplied to, and to amendment upon notice being given by, the parent or pupil or responsible person as if they formed part of the pupil's curricular record; and

(b) a record of the arrangements made in pursuance of regulation 6 other than regulation 6(1)(a)) and this regulation is kept and available for inspection free of charge at all reasonable times on a school day by an entitled person and on payment of such fee (not exceeding the cost of supply), if any, as the governing body may prescribe a copy of the arrangements is supplied to him.

(2) In paragraph (1) 'teacher's record' means any record kept at the school by a teacher other than a record kept and intended to be kept solely for that teacher's own use.

8 The arrangements required to be made by regulations 6 and 7 shall make provision enabling the parent, pupil or responsible person (as the case may be) to appeal to the governing body of the school against any decision refusing disclosure or transfer or the supply of a copy of the whole or any part of the pupil's curricular record or a record mentioned in regulation 7(1)(a) or any decision refusing amendment of any such record in those cases where the arrangements provide for those decisions to be taken by a teacher of the school.

Savings

9 Nothing in these Regulations shall authorise or require arrangements to be made for the disclosure of any information –

[(a) originating from or supplied by or on behalf of any person other than –

(i) an employee of the local education authority which maintains the school;

(ii) in the case of a grant-maintained or voluntary aided school, a teacher or other employee at the school (including an educational psychologist engaged by the governing body under a contract for services);

(iii) an education welfare officer (within the meaning of the Education (No 2) Act 1986), or

(iv) the person requesting disclosure;]

(b) to the extent that it would reveal, or enable to be deduced, the identity of a person (other than the pupil to whom that information relates or a person mentioned in sub-paragraph (a)) as the source of the information or as a person to whom that information relates; or

(c) to the extent that disclosure would in the opinion of the holder of the information be likely to cause serious harm to the physical or mental health or emotional condition of the pupil to whom the information relates or of any other person; or

(d) to the extent that in the opinion of the holder of the information it is relevant to the question whether the pupil to which it relates is or has been the subject of or may be at risk of child abuse.

Amendment

Para (a) was substituted, in relation to England, by the Education (Individual Pupils' Achievements, School Records and School Curriculum) (Amendment) Regulations 1992, SI 1992 No 1089, with effect from 1 June 1992; and, in relation to Wales, by the Education (Individual Pupils' Achievements) (Information) (Wales) Regulations 1992, SI 1992 No 1205, with effect from 11 June 1992.

10 Nothing in these Regulations shall require arrangements to be made for the disclosure or supply of a copy of any reference given by a teacher in respect of a registered pupil at the school in response to a request from potential employers of the pupil, from the Polytechnics Central Admissions System, the Universities Central Council on Admissions, or any other national body concerned with student admissions, from another school (including an independent school), from an institution of further or higher education or from any other place of education and training.

11 Nothing in regulation 6(1)(b) to (d) or 7 shall apply to educational records which are data for the purposes of the Data Protection Act 1984.

12 (1) Nothing in these Regulations shall empower or authorise the governing body of any school to make arrangements for the disclosure, supply of copies of or transfer of –

(a) statements of special educational needs maintained under the Education Act 1981;

(b) ... ;

(c) any report prepared for the purposes of proceedings to which the Magistrates' Courts (Children and Young Persons) Rules 1988 apply;

(d) information as to the racial group to which a pupil belongs, the language spoken in his home, and his religious persuasion, otherwise than to an entitled person.

(2) In paragraph (1)(d) 'racial group' means a group of persons defined by reference to colour, race, nationality or ethnic or national origins.

Amendment

Para (1)(b) was revoked, in relation to England, by the Education (Individual Pupils' Achievements) (Information) Regulations 1992, SI 1992 No 3168, with effect from 4 January 1993; and, in relation to Wales, by the Education (Individual Pupils' Achievements) (Information) (Wales) Regulations 1993, SI 1993 No 835, with effect from 20 April 1993.

13 Nothing in these Regulations shall require arrangements to be made for the disclosure or supply of a copy of a pupil's curricular record or a record of the kind mentioned in regulation 7(1)(a) to the extent that those records comprise records made before 1 September 1989.

Translation of documents

14 (1) This regulation applies to any document containing a record of disclosure and transfer arrangements kept in pursuance of regulation 7(1)(b)

(2) If it appears requisite to the governing body of any school in Wales that any such document should be translated into Welsh, it shall be so translated and subject to paragraph (4) these Regulations shall apply to the translated document as they apply to the original document.

(3) If it appears requisite to the governing body of any school that any such document should be translated into a language other than English or Welsh, it shall be so translated and subject to paragraph (4) these Regulations shall apply to the translated document as they apply to the original document.

(4) Where a charge is made for a copy of the original document, no greater charge shall be made for a copy of the document so translated.

Education (Special Educational Needs) Regulations 1994 SI No 1047

PART I: GENERAL
Title and commencement

1   These Regulations may be cited as the Education (Special Educational Needs) Regulations 1994 and shall come into force on 1st September 1994.

Interpretation

2   (1) In these Regulations –
'the Act' means the Education Act 1993;
'authority' means a local education authority;
'district health authority' has the same meaning as in the National Health Service Act 1977;
'head teacher' includes any person to whom the duties or functions of a head teacher under these Regulations have been delegated by the head teacher in accordance with regulation 3;
'social services authority' means a local authority for the purposes of the Local Authority Social Services Act 1970 acting in the discharge of such functions as are referred to in section 2(1) of that Act;
'target' means the knowledge, skills and understanding which a child is expected to have by the end of a particular period;
'transition plan' means a document prepared pursuant to regulation 16(9) or 17(9) which sets out the arrangements which an authority consider appropriate for a young person during the period when he is aged 14 to 19 years, including arrangements for special educational provision and for any other necessary provision, for suitable employment and accommodation and for leisure activities, and which will facilitate a satisfactory transition from childhood to adulthood;
'working day' means a day other than a Saturday, Sunday, Christmas Day, Good Friday or Bank Holiday within the meaning of the Banking and Financial Dealings Act 1971;
'the 1981 Act' means the Education Act 1981;
'the 1983 Regulations' means the Education (Special Educational Needs) Regulations 1983.

(2) In these Regulations any reference to the district health authority or the social services authority is, in relation to a particular child, a reference to the district health authority or social services authority in whose area that child lives.

(3) Where a thing is required to be done under these Regulations –

(a) within a period after an action is taken, the day on which that action was taken shall not be counted in the calculation of that period; and

(b) within a period and the last day of that period is not a working day, the period shall be extended to include the following working day.

(4) References in these Regulations to a section are references to a section of the Act.

(5) References in these Regulations to a regulation are references to a regulation in these Regulations and references to a Schedule are references to the Schedule to these Regulations.

Delegation of functions

3 Where a head teacher has any functions or duties under these Regulations he may delegate those functions or duties –

(a) generally to a member of the staff of the school who is a qualified teacher within the meaning of section 218 of the Education Reform Act 1988, or

(b) in a particular case to a member of the staff of the school who teaches the child in question.

Service of documents

4 (1) Where any provision in Part III of the Act or in these Regulations authorises or requires any document to be served or sent to a person or any written notice to be given to a person the document may be served or sent or the notice may be given by properly addressing, pre-paying and posting a letter containing the document or notice.

(2) For the purposes of this regulation, the proper address of a person is –

(a) in the case of the child's parent, his last known address;

(b) in the case of a head teacher or other member of the staff of a school, the school's address;

(c) in the case of any other person, the last known address of the place where he carries on his business, profession or other employment.

(3) Where first class post is used, the document or notice hall be treated as served, sent or given on the second working day after the date of posting, unless the contrary is shown.

(4) Where second class post is used, the document or notice shall be treated as served, sent or given on the fourth working day after the date of posting, unless the contrary is shown.

(5) The date of posting shall be presumed, unless the contrary is shown, to be the date shown in the post-mark on the envelope in which the document is contained.

PART II: ASSESSMENTS
Notices relating to assessment

5 (1) Where under section 167(1) or 174(2) an authority give notice to a child's parent that they propose to make an assessment, or under section 167(4) give notice to a child's parent of their decision to make an assessment, they shall send copies of the relevant notice to –

    (a) the social services authority,

    (b) the district health authority, and

    (c) if the child is registered at a school, the head teacher of that school.

(2) Where a copy of a notice is sent under paragraph (1) an endorsement on the copy or a notice accompanying that copy shall inform the recipient what help the authority are likely to request.

(3) Where under section 172(2) or 173(1) a child's parent asks the authority to arrange for an assessment to be made the authority shall give notice in writing to the persons referred to in paragraph (1)(a) to (c) of the fact that the request has been made and inform them what help they are likely to request.

Advice to be sought

6 (1) For the purpose of making an assessment under section 167 an authority shall seek –

    (a) advice from the child's parent;

    (b) educational advice as provided for in regulation 7;

    (c) medical advice from the district health authority as provided for in regulation 8;

    (d) psychological advice as provided for in regulation 9;

    (e) advice from the social services authority; and

    (f) any other advice which the authority consider appropriate for the purpose of arriving at a satisfactory assessment.

(2) The advice referred to in paragraph (1) shall be written advice relating to –

    (a) the educational, medical, psychological or other features of the case (according to the nature of the advice sought) which appear to be relevant to the child's educational needs (including his likely future needs);

    (b) how those features could affect the child's educational needs, and

    (c) the provision which is appropriate for the child in light of those features of the child's case, whether by way of special educational provision or non-educational provision, but not relating to any matter which is required to be specified in a statement by virtue of section 168(4)(b).

(3) A person from whom the advice referred to in paragraph (1) is sought may in connection therewith consult such persons as it appears to him expedient to consult; and he shall consult such persons, if any, as are specified in the particular case by the authority as persons who have relevant knowledge of, or information relating to, the child.

(4) When seeking the advice referred to in paragraph (1)(b) to (f) an authority shall provide the person from whom it is sought with copies of –

    (a) any representations made by the parent, and

    (b) any evidence submitted by, or at the request of, the parent under section 167(1)(d).

(5) The authority need not seek the advice referred to in paragraph (1)(b), (c), (d), (e) or (f) if –

    (a) the authority have obtained advice under paragraph (1)(b), (c), (d), (e) or (f) respectively within the preceding 12 months, and

    (b) the authority, the person from whom the advice was obtained and the child's parent are satisfied that the existing advice is sufficient for the purpose of arriving at a satisfactory assessment.

Educational advice

7 (1) The educational advice referred to in regulation 6(1)(b) shall, subject to paragraphs (2) to (5), be sought –

(a) from the head teacher of each school which the child is currently attending or which he has attended at any time within the preceding 18 months;

(b) if advice cannot be obtained from a head teacher of a school which the child is currently attending (because the child is not attending a school or otherwise) from a person who the authority are satisfied has experience of teaching children with special educational needs or knowledge of the differing provision which may be called for in different cases to meet those needs;

(c) if the child is not currently attending a school and if advice obtained under sub-paragraph (b) is not advice from such a person, from a person responsible for educational provision for him; and

(d) if any of the child's parents is a serving member of Her Majesty's armed forces, from the Service Children's Education Authority.

(2) The advice sought as provided in paragraph (1)(a) to (c) shall not be sought from any person who is not a qualified teacher within the meaning of section 218 of the Education Reform Act 1988.

(3) The advice sought from a head teacher as provided in paragraph (1)(a) shall, if the head teacher has not himself taught the child within the preceding 18 months, be advice given after consultation with a teacher who has so taught the child.

(4) The advice sought from a head teacher as provided in paragraph (1)(a) shall include advice relating to the steps which have been taken by the school to identify and assess the special educational needs of the child and to make provision for the purpose of meeting those needs.

(5) Where it appears to the authority, in consequence of medical advice or otherwise, that the child in question is –

(a) hearing impaired, or

(b) visually impaired, or

(c) both hearing impaired and visually impaired,

and any person from whom advice is sought as provided in paragraph (1) is not qualified to teach pupils who are so impaired then the advice sought shall be advice given after consultation with a person who is so qualified.

(6) For the purposes of paragraph (5) a person shall be considered to be qualified to teach pupils who are hearing impaired or visually impaired or who are both hearing impaired and visually impaired if he is qualified to be employed at a school as a teacher of a class for pupils who are so impaired otherwise than to give instruction in a craft, trade, or domestic subject.

(7) Paragraphs (3) and (5) are without prejudice to regulation 6(3).

Medical advice

8   The advice referred to in paragraph 6(1)(c) shall be sought from the district

health authority, who shall obtain the advice from a fully registered medical practitioner.

Psychological advice

9 (1) The psychological advice referred to in regulation 6(1)(d) shall be sought from a person –
   (a) regularly employed by the authority as an educational psychologist, or
   (b) engaged by the authority as an educational psychologist in the case in question.

(2) The advice sought from a person as provided in paragraph (1) shall, if that person has reason to believe that another psychologist has relevant 'knowledge of, or information relating to, the child, be advice given after consultation with that other psychologist.

(3) Paragraph (2) is without prejudice to regulation 6(3).

Matters to be taken into account in making an assessment

10 When making an assessment an authority shall take into consideration –
   (a) any representations made by the child's parent under section 167(1)(d);
   (b) any evidence submitted by, or at the request of, the child's parent under section 167(1)(d); and
   (c) the advice obtained under regulation 6.

Time limits

11 (1) Where under section 167(1) the authority serve a notice on the child's parent informing him that they propose to make an assessment of the child's educational needs under section 167 they shall within 6 weeks of the date of service of the notice give notice to the child's parent –
   (a) under section 167(4) of their decision to make an assessment, and of their reasons for making that decision, or
   (b) under section 167(6) of their decision not to assess the educational needs of the child.

(2) Where under section 174(2) the authority serve a notice on the child's parent informing him that they propose to make an assessment of the child's educational needs under section 167 they shall within 6 weeks of the date of service of notice give notice to the child's parent and to the governing body of the grant-maintained school which asked the authority to make an assessment –
   (a) under section 174(5) of their decision to make an assessment and their reasons for making that decision, or
   (b) under section 174(6) of their decision not to assess the educational needs of the child.

(3) Where under sections 172(2) or 173(1) a parent asks the authority to arrange for an assessment to be made under section 167 they shall within 6 weeks of the date of receipt of the request give notice to the child's parent –
   (a) under section 167(4) of their decision to make an assessment, or
   (b) under section 172(3)(a) or 173(2)(a) respectively of their decision not to comply with the request and of the parent's right to appeal to the Tribunal against the determination.

(4) An authority need not comply with the time limits referred to in paragraphs (1) to (3) if it is impractical to do so because –

    (a) the authority have requested advice from the head teacher of a school during a period beginning one week before any date on which that school was closed for a continuous period of not less than 4 weeks from that date and ending one week before the date on which it re-opens;

    (b) exceptional personal circumstances affect the child or his parent during the 6 week period referred to in paragraphs (1) to (3); or

    (c) the child or his parent are absent from the area of the authority for a continuous period of not less than 4 weeks during the 6 week period referred to in (1) to (3).

(5) Subject to paragraph (6), where under section 167(4) an authority have given notice to the child's parent of their decision to make an assessment they shall complete that assessment within 10 weeks of the date on which such notice was given.

(6) An authority need not comply with the time limit referred to in paragraph (5) if it is impractical to do so because –

    (a) in exceptional cases after receiving advice sought under regulation 6 it is necessary for the authority to seek further advice;

    (b) the child's parent has indicated to the authority that he wishes to provide advice to the authority after the expiry of 6 weeks from the date on which a request for such advice under regulation 6(a) was received, and the authority have agreed to consider such advice before completing the assessment;

    (c) the authority have requested advice from the head teacher of a school under regulation 6(1)(b) during a period beginning one week before any date on which that school was closed for a continuous period of not less than 4 weeks from that date and ending one week before the date on which it re-opens;

    (d) the authority have requested advice from a district health authority or a social services authority under regulation 6(c) or (e) respectively and the district health authority or the social services authority have not complied with that request within 6 weeks from the date on which it was made;

    (e) exceptional personal circumstances affect the child or his parent during the 10 week period referred to in paragraph (5);

    (f) the child or his parent are absent from the area of the authority for a continuous period of not less than 4 weeks during the 10 week period referred to in paragraph (5); or

    (g) the child fails to keep an appointment for an examination or a test during the 10 week period referred to in paragraph (5).

(7) Subject to paragraph (8), where an authority have requested advice from a district health authority or a social services authority under regulation 6(1)(c) or (e) respectively they shall comply with that request within 6 weeks of the date on which they receive it.

(8) A district health authority or a social services authority need not comply with the time limit referred to in paragraph (7) if it is impractical to do so because –

(a) exceptional personal circumstances affect the child or his parent during the 6 week period referred to in paragraph (7);

(b) the child or his parent are absent from the area of the authority for a continuous period of not less than 4 weeks during the 6 week period referred to in paragraph (7);

(c) the child fails to keep an appointment for an examination or a test made by the district health authority or the social services authority respectively during the 6 week period referred to in paragraph (7); or

(d) they have not before the date on which a copy of a notice has been served on them in accordance with regulation 5(1) or a notice bas been served on them in accordance with regulation 5(3) produced or maintained any information or records relevant to the assessment of the child under section 167.

PART III: STATEMENTS
Notice accompanying a proposed statement

12   The notice which shall accompany a copy of a proposed statement served on the parent pursuant to paragraph 2 of Schedule 10 to the Act shall be in a form substantially corresponding to that set out in Part A of the Schedule and shall contain the information therein specified.

Statement of special educational needs

13   A statement of a child's special educational needs made under section 168(1) shall be in a form substantially corresponding to that set out in Part B of the Schedule, shall contain the information therein specified, and shall be dated and authenticated by the signature of a duly authorised officer of the authority concerned.

Time limits

14 (1) Where under section 167 an authority have made an assessment of the educational needs of a child for whom no statement is maintained they shall within two weeks of the date on which the assessment was completed either –

(a) serve a copy of a proposed statement and a written notice on the child's parent under paragraph 2 of Schedule 10 to the Act, or

(b) give notice in writing to the child's parent under section 169(1) that they have decided not to make a statement and that he may appeal against that decision to the Tribunal.

(2) Where under section 167 an authority have made an assessment of the educational needs of a child for whom a statement is maintained they shall within two weeks of the date on which the assessment was completed –

(a) under paragraph 10(1) of Schedule 10 to the Act serve on the child's parent a notice that they propose to amend the statement and of his right to make representations;

(b) under paragraph 11(2) of Schedule 10 to the Act give notice to the child's parent that they have determined to cease to maintain the statement and of his right of appeal to the Tribunal; or

(c) serve on the child's parent a notice which informs him that they have determined not to amend the statement and their reasons for that determination, which is accompanied by copies of the professional advice obtained during the assessment, and which informs the child's parent that under section 170(1)(c) he may appeal to the Tribunal against the description in the statement of the authority's assessment of the child's special educational needs, the special educational provision specified in the statement or, if no school is named in the statement, that fact.

(3) Subject to paragraph (4), where an authority have served a copy of a proposed statement on the child's parent under paragraph 2 of Schedule 10 to the Act they shall within 8 weeks of the date on which the proposed statement was served serve a copy of the completed statement and a written notice on the child's parent under paragraph 6 of that Schedule, or give notice to the child's parent that they have decided not to make a statement.

(4) The authority need not comply with the time limit referred to in paragraph (3) if it is impractical to do so because –

(a) exceptional personal circumstances affect the child or his parent during the 8 week period referred to in paragraph (3);

(b) the child or his parent are absent from the area of the authority for continuous period of not less than 4 weeks during the 8 week period referred to in paragraph (3);

(c) the child's parent indicates that he wishes to make representations to the authority about the content of the statement under paragraph 4(1)(a) of Schedule 10 to the Act after the expiry of the 15 day period for making such representations provided for in paragraph 4(4) of that Schedule;

(d) a meeting between the child's parent and an officer of the authority has been held pursuant to paragraph 4(1)(b) of Schedule 10 to the Act and the child's parent has required that another such meeting be arranged or under paragraph 4(2) of that Schedule has required a meeting with the appropriate person to be arranged; or

(e) the authority have sent a written request to the Secretary of State seeking his consent under section 189(5)(b) to the child being educated at an independent school which is not approved by him and such consent has not been received by the authority within two weeks of the date on which the request was sent.

(5) Where under paragraph 8(1) of Schedule 10 to the Act the child's parent asks the authority to substitute for the name of a school or institution specified in a statement the name of another school specified by him and where the condition referred to in paragraph 8(1)(b) of that Schedule has been satisfied the authority shall within weeks of the date on which the request was received either –

(a) comply with the request; or

(b) give notice to the child's parent under paragraph 8(3) of that Schedule that they have determined not to comply with the request and that may appeal against that determination to the Tribunal.

(6) Where under paragraph 10(1) of Schedule 10 to the Act an authority serve a notice on the child's parent informing him of their proposal to amend a statement they shall not amend the statement after the expiry of 8 weeks

from the date on which the notice was served.

(7) Where under paragraph 11(2) of Schedule 10 to the Act an authority give notice to the child's parent that they have determined to cease to maintain a statement they shall not cease to maintain the statement –

(a) before the expiry of the prescribed period during which the parent may appeal to the Tribunal against the determination, or

(b) after the expiry of 4 weeks from the end of that period.

Review of statement where child not aged 14 attends school

15 (1) This regulation applies where –

(a) an authority review a statement under section 172(5) other an on the making of an assessment,

(b) the child concerned attends a school, and

(c) regulation 16 does not apply.

(2) The authority shall by notice in writing require the head teacher of the child's school to submit a report to them under this regulation by a specified date not less than two months from the date the notice is given and shall send a copy of the notice to the child's parent.

(3) The head teacher shall for the purpose of preparing the report referred to in paragraph (2) seek advice as to the matters referred to in paragraph (4) from –

(a) the child's parent;

(b) any person whose advice the authority consider appropriate for the purpose of arriving at a satisfactory report and whom they specify in the notice referred to in paragraph (2), and

(c) any person whose advice the head teacher considers appropriate for the purpose of arriving at a satisfactory report.

(4) The advice referred to in paragraph (3) shall be written advice as to –

(a) the child's progress towards meeting the objectives specified in the statement;

(b) the child's progress towards attaining any targets established in furtherance of the objectives specified in the statement;

(c) where the school is not established in a hospital and is a maintained, grant-maintained or grant-maintained special school, the application of the provisions of the National Curriculum to the child;

(d) where the school is not established in a hospital and is a maintained, grant-maintained or grant-maintained special school, the application of any provisions substituted for the provisions of the National Curriculum in order to maintain a balanced and broadly based curriculum;

(e) where appropriate, and in any case where a transition plan exists, any matters which are the appropriate subject of such a plan;

(f) whether the statement continues to be appropriate;

(g) any amendments to the statement which would be appropriate; and

(h) whether the authority should cease to maintain the statement.

(5) The notice referred to in paragraph (2) shall require the head teacher to invite the following persons to attend a meeting to be held on a date before the report referred to in that paragraph is submitted –

(a) the representative of the authority specified in the notice,

(b) the child's parent,

(c) a member or members of the staff of the school who teach the child or who are otherwise responsible for the provision of education for the child whose attendance the head teacher considers appropriate,

(d) any other person whose attendance the head teacher considers appropriate, and

(e) any person whose attendance the authority consider appropriate and who is specified in the notice.

(6) The head teacher shall not later than two weeks before the date on which a meeting referred to in paragraph (5) is to be held send to all the persons invited to that meeting copies of the advice he has received pursuant to his request under paragraph (3) and by written notice accompanying the copies shall request the recipients to submit to him before or at the meeting written comments on that advice and any other advice which they think appropriate.

(7) The meeting referred to in paragraph (5) shall consider –

(a) the matters referred to in paragraph (4); and

(b) any significant changes in the child's circumstances since the date on which the statement was made or last reviewed.

(8) The meeting shall recommend –

(a) any steps which it concludes ought to be taken, including whether the authority should amend or cease to maintain the statement,

(b) any targets to be established in furtherance of the objectives specified in the statement which it concludes the child ought to meet during the period until the next review, and

(c) where a transition plan exists, the matters which it concludes ought to be included in that plan.

(9) If the meeting cannot agree the recommendations to be made under paragraph (8) the persons who attended the meeting shall make differing recommendations as appears necessary to each of them.

(10) The report to be submitted under paragraph (2) shall be completed after the meeting is held and shall include the head teacher's assessment of the matters referred to in paragraph (7) and his recommendations as to the matter referred to in paragraph (8), and shall refer to any difference between his assessment and recommendations and those of the meeting.

(11) When the head teacher submits his report to the authority under paragraph (2) he shall at the same time send copies to –

(a) the child's parent,

(b) the persons from whom the head teacher sought advice under paragraph (3),

(c) the persons who were invited to attend the meeting in accordance with paragraph (5),

(d) any other person to whom the authority consider it appropriate that a copy be sent and to whom they direct him to send a copy, and

(e) any other person to whom the head teacher considers it appropriate that a copy be sent.

(12) The authority shall review the statement under section 172(5) in light of the

report and any other information or advice which they consider relevant, shall make written recommendations as to the matters referred to in paragraph (8)(a) and (b) and, where a transition plan exists, shall amend the plan as they consider appropriate.

(13) The authority shall within one week of completing the review under section 172(5) send copies of the recommendations and any transition plan referred to in paragraph (12) to –
   (a) the child's parent;
   (b) the head teacher;
   (c) the persons from whom the head teacher sought advice under paragraph (3);
   (d) the persons who were invited to attend the meeting in accordance with paragraph (5), and
   (e) any other person to whom the authority consider it appropriate that a copy be sent.

Review of statement where child aged 14 attends school

16 (1) This regulation applies where –
   (a) an authority review a statement under section 172(5) other than on the making of an assessment,
   (b) the child concerned attends a school, and
   (c) the review is the first review commenced after the child has attained the age of 14 years.

   (2) The authority shall for the purpose of preparing a report under this regulation by notice in writing require the head teacher of the child's school to seek the advice referred to in regulation 15(4), including in all cases advice as to the matters referred to in regulation 15(4)(e), from –
   (a) the child's parent,
   (b) any person whose advice the authority consider appropriate for the purpose of arriving at a satisfactory report and whom they specify in the notice referred to above, and
   (c) any person whose advice the head teacher considers appropriate for the purpose of arriving at a satisfactory report.

   (3) The authority shall invite the following persons to attend a meeting to be held on a date before the review referred to in paragraph (1) is required to be completed –
   (a) the child's parent;
   (b) a member or members of the staff of the school who teach the child or who are otherwise responsible for the provision of education for the child whose attendance the head teacher considers appropriate and whom he has asked the authority to invite;
   (c) a representative of the social services authority;
   (d) a person providing careers services under sections 8 to 10 of the Employment and Training Act 1973;
   (e) any person whose attendance the head teacher considers appropriate and whom he has asked the authority to invite; and
   (f) any person whose attendance the authority consider appropriate.

   (4) The head teacher shall not later than two weeks before the date on which

the meeting referred to in paragraph (3) is to be held serve on all the persons invited to attend that meeting copies of the advice he has received pursuant to his request under paragraph (2) and shall by written notice request the recipients to submit to him before or at the meeting written comments on that advice and any other advice which they think appropriate.

(5) A representative of the authority shall attend the meeting.

(6) The meeting shall consider the matters referred to in regulation 15(7), in all cases including the matters referred to in regulation 15(4)(e), and shall make recommendations in accordance with regulation 15(8) and (9), in all cases including recommendations as to the matters referred to in regulation 15(8)(c).

(7) The report to be prepared by the authority under paragraph (2) shall be completed after the meeting, shall contain the authority's assessment of the matters required to be considered by the meeting and their recommendations as to the matters required to be recommended by it and shall refer to any difference between their assessment and recommendations and those of the meeting.

(8) The authority shall within one week of the date on which the meeting was held send copies of the report completed under paragraph (7) to –

(a) the child's parent;

(b) the head teacher;

(c) the persons from whom the head teacher sought advice under paragraph (2);

(d) the persons who were invited to attend the meeting under paragraph (3); and

(e) any person to whom they consider it appropriate to send a copy.

(9) The authority shall review the statement under section 172(5) in light of the report and any other information or advice which it considers relevant, shall make written recommendations as to the matters referred to in regulation 15(8)(a) and (b), and shall prepare a transition plan.

(10) The authority shall within one week of completing the review under section 172(5) send copies of the recommendations and the transition plan referred to in paragraph (9) to the persons referred to in paragraph (8).

Review of statement where child does not attend school

17 (1) This regulation applies where an authority review statement under section 172(5) other than on the making of an assessment and the child concerned does not attend a school.

(2) The authority shall prepare a report addressing the matters referred to in regulation 15(4), including the matters referred to in regulation 15(4)(e) in any case where the review referred to in paragraph (1) is commenced after the child has attained the age of 14 years or older, and for that purpose shall seek advice on those matters from the child's parent and any other person whose advice they consider appropriate it the case in question for the purpose of arriving at a satisfactory report.

(3) The authority shall invite the following persons to attend a meeting to be held on a date before the review referred to in paragraph (1) is required to

be completed –
(a) the child's parent;
(b) where the review referred to in paragraph (1) is the first review commenced after
the child has attained the age of 14 years, a representative of the social services authority;
(c) where sub-paragraph (b) applies, a person providing careers services under sections 8 to 10 of the Employment and Training Act 1973; and
(d) any person or persons whose attendance the authority consider appropriate.

(4) The authority shall not later than two weeks before the date on which the meeting referred to in paragraph (3) is to be held send to all the persons invited to that meeting a copy of the report which they propose to make under paragraph (2) and by written notice accompanying the copies shall request the recipients to submit to the authority written comments on the report and any other advice which they think appropriate.

(5) A representative of the authority shall attend the meeting.

(6) The meeting shall consider the matters referred to in regulation 15(7), including in any case where the review is commenced after the child has attained the age of 14 years the matters referred to in regulation 15(4)(e), and shall make recommendations in accordance with regulation 15(8) and (9), including in any case where the child has attained the age) of 14 years or older as aforesaid recommendations as to the matters referred to in regulation 15(8)(c).

(7) The report prepared by the authority under paragraph (2) shall be completed after the meeting referred to in paragraph (3) is held, shall contain the authority's assessment of the matters required to be considered by the meeting and their recommendations as to the matters required to be recommended by it, and shall refer to any difference between their assessment and recommendations and those of the meeting.

(8) The authority shall within one week of the date on which the meeting referred to in paragraph (3) was held send copies of the report completed under paragraph (7) to –
(a) the child's parent;
(b) the persons from whom they sought advice under paragraph (2);
(c) the persons who were invited to attend the meeting under paragraph (3) and
(d) any person to whom they consider it appropriate to send a copy.

(9) The authority shall review the statement under section 172(5) in light of the report and any other information or advice which it considers relevant, shall make written recommendations as to the matters referred to in regulation 15(8)(a) and (b), in any case when the review is the first review commenced after the child has attained the age of 14 years prepare a transition plan, and in any case where a transition plan exists amend the plan as they consider appropriate.

(10) The authority shall within one week of completing the review under section 172(5) send copies of the recommendations and any transition plan referred to in paragraph (9) to the persons referred to in paragraph (8).

Transfer of statements

18 (1) This regulation applies where a child in respect of whom a statement is maintained moves from the area of the authority which maintains the statement ('the old authority') into that of another ('the new authority').

(2) The old authority shall transfer the statement to the new authority, and from the date of the transfer –

(a) the statement shall be treated for the purposes of the new authority's duties and functions under Part III of the Act and these Regulations as if it had been made by the new authority on the date on which it was made by the old authority, and

(b) where the new authority make an assessment under section 167 and the old authority have supplied the new authority with advice obtained in pursuance of a previous assessment regulation 6(5) shall apply as if the new authority had obtained the advice on the date on which the old authority obtained it.

(3) The new authority shall within 6 weeks of the date of the transfer serve a notice on the child's parent informing him –

(a) that the statement has been transferred,

(b) whether they proposed to make an assessment under section 167, and

(c) when they propose to review the statement in accordance with paragraph (4).

(4) The new authority shall review the statement under section 172(5) before the expiry of whichever of the following two periods expires later – ,

(a) the period of twelve months beginning with the making of the statement, or as the case may be, with the previous review, or

(b) the period of three months beginning with the date of the transfer.

(5) Whereby virtue of the transfer the new authority come under a duty to arrange the child's attendance at a school specified in the statement but in light of child's move that attendance is no longer practicable the new authority may arrange for the child's attendance at another school appropriate for the child until such time as it is possible to amend the statement in accordance with paragraph 10 of Schedule 10 to the Act.

Restriction on disclosure of statements

19 (1) Subject to the provisions of the Act and of these Regulations, a statement in respect of a child shall not be disclosed without the parent's consent except –

(a) to persons to whom, in the opinion of the authority concerned, the statement should be disclosed in the interests of the child;

(b) for the purposes of any appeal under the Act;

(c) for the purposes of educational research which, in opinion of the authority, may advance the education of children with special educational needs, if, but only if, the person engaged in that research undertakes not to publish anything contained in, or derived from, a statement other than in a form which does not identify any individual concerned including, in particular, the child concerned and his parent;

(d) on the order of any court or for the purposes of any criminal proceedings;

(e) for the purposes of any investigation under Part III of the Local Government Act 1974 (investigation of maladministration);

(f) to the Secretary of State when he requests such disclosure for the purposes of deciding whether to give directions or make an order under section 68 or 99 of the Education Act 1944;

(g) for the purposes of an assessment of the needs of the child with respect to the provision of any statutory services for him being carried out by officers of a social services authority by virtue of arrangements made under section 5(5) of the Disabled Persons (Services, Consultation and Representation) Act 1986;

(h) for the purposes of a local authority in the performance of their duties under sections 22(3)(a), 85(4)(a), 86(3)(a) and 87(3) of the Children Act 1989; or

(i) to one of Her Majesty's Inspectors of Schools, or, to a registered inspector or a member of an inspection team, who requests the right to inspect or take copies of a statement in accordance with section 3(3) of or paragraph 7 of Schedule 2 to the Education (Schools) Act 1992 respectively.

(2) The arrangements for keeping such statements shall be such as to ensure, so far as is reasonably practicable, that unauthorised persons do not have access to them.

(3) In this regulation any reference to a statement includes a reference to any representations, evidence, advice or information which is set out in the appendices to a statement.

PART IV: REVOCATION AND TRANSITIONAL PROVISIONS
Revocation of the 1983 Regulations

20 Subject to regulation 21, the 1983 Regulations, the Education (Special Educational Needs) (Amendment) Regulations 1988 and the Education (Special Educational Needs) (Amendment) Regulations 1990 are hereby revoked.

Transitional provisions

21 (1) Subject to the following provisions of this regulation references in these Regulations to anything done under the Act or these Regulations shall be read in relation to the times, circumstances or purposes in relation to which a corresponding provision of the 1981 Act or the 1983 Regulations had effect and so far as the nature of the reference permits as including a reference to that corresponding provision.

(2) Regulations 3 to 8 of the 1983 Regulations shall continue to apply in relation to any assessment where before 1st September 1994 in pursuance section 5(5) of the 1981 Act the authority notify the parent that they have decided to make an assessment, and Part II of these Regulations shall not apply in relation to any such assessment.

(3) Where regulations 3 to 8 of the 1983 Regulations continue to apply in relation to any assessment but the authority have not before 1st January 1995 –

(a) notified the parent of their decision that they are not required to determine the special educational provision of the child in accordance with section 5(7) of the 1981 Act, or

(b) served on the parent a copy of a proposed statement in accordance with section 7(3) of the 1981 Act

Part II of these Regulations shall apply in relation to the assessment from 1st January 1995 as if on that date the authority had given notice to the parent under section 167(4) of their decision to make an assessment.

(4) Where in accordance with paragraph (3) above Part II of these Regulations applies in relation to an assessment the authority shall obtain advice in accordance with Part II, but advice obtained in accordance with the 1983 Regulations shall be considered to have been obtained under Part II if such advice is appropriate for the purpose of arriving at a satisfactory assessment under that Part.

(5) Where before 1st September 1994 in accordance with section 5(3) of the 1981 Act the authority have served notice on the child's parent that they propose to make an assessment but they have not before that date notified the parent under section 5(5) of the 1981 Act that they have decided to make the assessment or notified them that they have decided not to make the assessment, the authority shall decide whether or not to make the assessment in accordance with section 167 and not later than 13th October 1994 give notice to the child's parent –

(a) under section 167(4) of their decision to make an assessment, and of their reasons for making that decision, or

(b) under section 167(6) of their decision not to assess the educational needs of the child, and Part II of these Regulations shall apply to any such assessment.

(6) Where before 1st September 1994 in accordance with section 9 of the 1981 Act a parent has asked the authority to arrange for an assessment to be made of the child's educational needs but the authority have not before that date notified the parent under section 5(5) of the 1981 Act that they have decided to make the assessment or notified them that they have decided not to make the assessment, the authority shall decide whether or not to make the assessment in accordance with section 167 and not later than 13th October 1994 give notice to the child's parent –

(a) under section 167(4) of their decision to make an assessment, or

(b) under section 172(3)(a) or 173(2)(a) of their decision not to comply with the request and of the parent's right to appeal to the Tribunal again the the determination, and Part II of these Regulations shall apply to any such assessment.

(7) Regulation 10 of the 1983 Regulations shall continue to apply to the making of any statement where before 1st January 1995 the authority have served on the parent a copy of a proposed statement in accordance with section 7(3) of the 1981 Act, and regulations 12, 13 and 14(1) to (4) of these Regulations shall not apply to making of any such statement.

(8) Regulation 14(6) and (7) shall not apply in relation to a proposal, to amend or cease to maintain a statement where an authority serve a notice under paragraph of Schedule 1 to the 1981 Act before 1st September 1994.

(9) Regulations 15 to 17 shall not apply to any review of a statement which is

required to be completed before 1st December 1994.

(10) Regulations 15 to 17 shall apply to a review of a statement which is not required to be completed before 1st December 1994, but where the statement was made under the 1981 Act they shall apply with any necessary modifications, including the following:

(a) where the review is the first review to which regulations 15 to 17 apply
—

   (i) the authority shall seek advice as to the objective which the special educational provision for the child should meet rather than as to the child's progress towards meeting the objectives specified in statement;

   (ii) the authority shall seek advice as to the target, which should be established in furtherance of those objectives rather than as to the child's progress towards attaining any such targets;

   (iii) where the child has attained the age of 14 years before the date on which the review is commenced the authority shall in any event seek advice as to any matters which are the appropriate subject of a transition plan;

   (iv) the meeting held in accordance with regulation 15(7), 16(6) or 17(6) shall consider the matters referred to in those regulations as modified by sub-paragraphs (i) to (iii) above as appropriate, and shall make recommendations under regulation 15(8), 16(7) or 17(7) but including recommendations as to the objectives referred to in sub-paragraph (i), the targets referred to in sub-paragraph (ii) and where appropriate the transition plan referred to in paragraph (iii); and

   (v) the authority shall review the statement in accordance with regulation 15(12) 16(9) or 17(9), shall make recommendations as to the matters referred to in those regulations read in light of the modifications in this sub-paragraph, shall prepare a transition plan where sub-paragraph (iii) above applies, and shall in any event specify the objectives referred to in sub-paragraph (i) above;

and

(b) where the review is not the first review to which regulations 15 to 17 apply any reference to objectives shall include a reference to objectives specified in accordance with sub-paragraph (a)(v) above in addition to objectives specified in a statement.

(11) Subject to paragraphs (12) and (13), regulation 12 of the 1983 Regulations shall continue to apply in relation to a transfer on a date before 1st September 1994, and regulation 18 of these Regulations shall not apply in relation to such a transfer.

(12) Notwithstanding paragraph (11), where a statement has been transferred on a date before 1st September 1994 and the new authority has not before that date either –

(a) in pursuance of section 5(3) of the 1981 Act served notice on the child's parent that they propose to make an assessment, or

(b) in pursuance of regulation 12(4) of the 1983 Regulations notified the child's parent that they do not propose to make an assessment, they shall comply with regulation 18(3) of these Regulation before 13th October 1994.

(13) Notwithstanding paragraph (11), where a statement has been referred on a date before 1st September 1994 the new authority shall review the statement under section 172(5) before the expiry of whichever of the following two periods expires later –

(a) the period of twelve months beginning with the making of the statement, or as the case may be, with the previous review, or

(b) the period ending on 30th November 1994.

(14) Regulation 11 of the 1983 Regulations shall not apply 'to statements made before or after 1st September 1994 and regulation 19 of these Regulations shall apply, except that a statement may be disclosed for the purposes of, any appeal under section 8 of the 1981 Act as well as for the purposes of any appeal under the Act.

SCHEDULE Regulations 12 and 13

PART A: NOTICE TO PARENT

To: [name and address of parent]

1   Accompanying this notice is a copy of a statement of the special educational needs of [name of child] which [name of authority]('the authority') propose to make under the Education Act 1993.

2   You may express a preference for the maintained, grant-maintained or grant-maintained special school you wish your child to attend and may give reasons for your preference.

3   If you wish to express such a preference you must do so not later than 15 days from the date on which you receive this notice and the copy of the statement or 15 days from the date on which you last attend a meeting in accordance with paragraph 10 or 11 below, which ever is later. If the 15th day falls on a weekend or a bank holiday you must do so not later than the following working day.

4   If you express a preference in accordance with paragraphs 2 and 3 above the authority are required to specify the name of the school you prefer in the statement, and accordingly to arrange special educational provision at that school, unless –

(a) the school is unsuitable to your child's age, ability or aptitude or to his/her special educational needs, or

(b) the attendance of your child at the school would be incompatible with the provision of efficient education for the children with whom he/she would be educated or the efficient use of resources.

5   The authority will normally arrange special educational provision in a maintained, grant-maintained or grant-maintained special school. However, if you believe that the authority should arrange special educational provision for your child at a non-maintained special school or an independent school you may make representations to that effect.

6   The following maintained, grant-maintained and grant-maintained special schools provide [primary/secondary] education in the area of the authority:

[Here list all maintained, grant-maintained, and grant-maintained special

schools in the authority's area which provide primary education, or list all such schools which provide secondary education, depending on whether the child requires primary or secondary education. Alternatively, list the required information in a list attached to this notice].

7   A list of the non-maintained special schools which make special educational provision for pupils with special educational needs in England and Wales and are approved by the Secretary of State for Education or the Secretary of State for Wales is attached to this notice.

8   A list of the independent schools in England and Wales which are approved by the Secretary of State for Education or the Secretary of State for Wales as suitable for the admission of children for whom statements of special educational needs are maintained is attached to this notice.

9   You are entitled to make representations to the authority about the content of the statement. If you wish to make such representations you must do so not later than 15 days from the date on which you receive this notice, or 15 days from the date on which you last attended a meeting in accordance with the next paragraph, whichever is the later date.

10 You are entitled, not later than 15 days from the date on which you receive this notice, to require the authority to arrange a meeting between you and an officer of the authority at which any part of the statement, or all of it, may be discussed. In particular, any advice on which the statement is based may be discussed.

11 If having attended a meeting in accordance with paragraph 10 above you still disagree with any part of the assessment in question, you may within 15 days of the date of the meeting require the authority to arrange a meeting or meetings to discuss the advice which they consider relevant to the part of the assessment you disagree with. They will arrange for the person who gave the advice, or some other person whom they think appropriate, to attend the meeting.

12 If at the conclusion of the procedure referred to above the authority serve on you a statement with which you disagree you may appeal to the Special Educational Needs Tribunal against the description of your child's special educational needs, against the special educational provision specified including the school named, or, if no school is named, against that fact.

13 All correspondence with the authority should be addressed to the officer responsible for this case:
    [Here set out name, address and telephone number of case officer, and any reference number which should be quoted]

PART B: STATEMENT OF SPECIAL EDUCATIONAL NEEDS

PART 1: INTRODUCTION

1   In accordance with section 168 of the Education Act 1993 ('the Act') and the Education (Special Educational Needs) Regulations 1994 ('the Regulations'), the following statement is made by *[here set out name of authority]* ('the authority') in respect of the child whose name and other particulars are mentioned below.
    Child

Surname
Other names
Home address
Sex
Religion
Date of birth
Home language
Child's parent or person responsible
Surname
Other names.
Home address
Relationship to child
Telephone No

2   When assessing the child's special educational needs the authority took into consideration, in accordance with regulation 8 of the Regulations, the representations, evidence and advice set out in the Appendices to this statement.

PART 2: SPECIAL EDUCATIONAL NEEDS

[Here set out the child's special educational needs, in terms of the child's learning difficulties which call for special educational provision, as assessed by the authority.]

PART 3: SPECIAL EDUCATIONAL PROVISION

Objectives

[Here specify the objectives which the special educational provision for the child should aim to meet.]

Educational provision to meet needs and objectives

[Here specify the special educational provision which the authority consider appropriate to meet the needs specified in Part 2 and to meet the objectives specified in this Part, and in particular specify –
(a) any appropriate facilities and equipment, staffing arrangements and curriculum,
(b) any appropriate modifications to the application of the National Curriculum,
(c) any appropriate exclusions from the application of the National Curriculum, in detail, and the provision which it is proposed to substitute for any such exclusions in order to maintain a balanced and broadly based curriculum and
(d) where residential accommodation is appropriate, that fact.]

Monitoring

[Here specify the arrangements to be made for –
(a) regularly monitoring progress in meeting the objectives specified in this Part,
(b) establishing targets in furtherance of those objectives,
(c) regularly monitoring the targets referred to in (b),
(d) regularly monitoring the appropriateness of any modifications to the

application of the National Curriculum, and
(e) regularly monitoring the appropriateness of any provision substituted for exclusions from the application of the National Curriculum.
[Here also specify any special arrangements for reviewing this statement.]

PART 4: PLACEMENT

[Here specify –
(a) the type of school which the authority consider appropriate for the child and the name of the school for which the parent has expressed a preference or, where the authority are required to specify the name of a school, the name of the school which they consider, would be appropriate for the child and should be specified, or
(b) the provision for his education otherwise than at a school which the authority consider appropriate.]

PART 5: NON-EDUCATIONAL NEEDS

[Here specify the non-educational needs of the child for which the authority consider provision is appropriate if the child is to properly benefit from the special educational provision specified in Part 3.]

PART 6: NON-EDUCATIONAL PROVISION

[Here specify any non-educational provision which the authority propose to available or which they are satisfied will be made available by a district health authority, a social services authority or some other body, including the arrangements for its provision. Also specify the objectives of the provision, and the arrangements for monitoring progress in meeting those objectives.]

Appendix A: Parental Representations

[Here set out any written representations made by the parent of the child under section 167(1) (d) of or paragraph 4(1) of Schedule 10 to the Act and a summary which the parent has accepted as accurate of any oral representations so made or record that no such representations were made.]

Appendix B: Parental Evidence

[Here set out any written evidence either submitted by the parent of the child under section 167(1)(d) of the Act or record that no such evidence was submitted.]

Appendix C: Advice from the Child's Parent

[Here set out the advice obtained under regulation 6(1) (a).]

Appendix D: Educational Advice

[Here set out the advice obtained under regulation 6(1) (b).]

Appendix E: Medical Advice

[Here set out the advice obtained under regulation 6(1) (c).]

Appendix F: Psychological Advice

[Here set out the advice obtained under regulation 6(1) (d).]

Appendix G: Advice from the Social Services Authority
[Here set out the advice obtained under regulation 6(1) (e).]

Appendix H: Other Advice Obtained by the Authority
[Here set out the advice obtained under regulation 6(1)]

Education (Pupil Registration) Regulations 1995 SI No 2089

Citation and commencement

1 These Regulations may be cited as the Education (Pupil Registration) Regulations 1995 and shall come into force on 1st September 1995.

Interpretation

2 In these Regulations –
'maintained school' means a school maintained by a local education authority, a grant-maintained school and a grant-maintained special school;
'proprietor' in the case of a maintained school means the governing body of the school and otherwise has the meaning assigned to it by section 114 of the Education Act 1944.

Revocation

3 The Pupils' Registration Regulations 1956 shall be revoked.

Amendment of the Education (Schools and Further Education) Regulations 1981

4 Regulations 11 and 12 of the Education (Schools and Further Education) Regulations 1981 shall be omitted.

Registers to be kept

5 The proprietor of every school shall cause to be kept –
(a) an admission register; and
(b) except in the case of a school of which all the pupils are boarders, an attendance register.

Contents of Admission Register

6 (1) The admission register for every school shall contain an index in alphabetical order of all the pupils at the school and shall also contain the following particulars in respect of every such pupil –
(a) name in full;
(b) sex;
(c) the name and address of every person known to the proprietor of the school to be a parent of the pupil and, against the entry on the register of the particulars of any parent with whom the pupil normally resides, an indication of that fact and a note of at least one telephone number at which the parent can be contacted in an emergency;

(d) day, month and year of birth;

(e) day, month and year of admission or re-admission to the school; and

(f) name and address of the school last attended, if any.

(2) In the case of every school which includes boarding pupils a statement as to whether each pupil of compulsory school age is a boarder or a day pupil shall be added to the particulars specified in paragraph (1), and that statement shall be amended accordingly where a registered pupil at the school becomes or ceases to be a boarder at the school.

Contents of Attendance Register

7 (1) There shall be recorded in the attendance register at the commencement of each morning and afternoon session the following particulars –

(a) the presence or absence of every pupil whose name is entered in and not deleted from the admission register; and

(b) in the case of any such pupil of compulsory school age who is absent, a statement whether or not his absence is authorised in accordance paragraph (3):

but this paragraph does not apply in respect of a pupil who is a boarder.

(2) For the purposes of this regulation only a pupil is of compulsory school age unless –

(a) he has not attained the age of five years before the commencement of the term of which the session forms part; or

(b) he has attained the age of sixteen years before 1st September in the school year of which the session forms part.

(3) In the case of a pupil who is not a boarder, his absence shall be treated as authorised for the purposes of this regulation if –

(a) he has been granted leave of absence in accordance with regulation 8;

(b) he is unable to attend –

(i) by reason of sickness or any unavoidable cause;

(ii) on a day exclusively set apart for religious observation by the religious body to which his parent belongs; or

(iii) because the school is not within walking distance of the pupil's home, and no suitable arrangements have been made by the local education authority either for his transport to and from the school, or for boarding accommodation for him at or near the school or for enabling him to become a registered pupil at a school nearer to his home; or

(c) in the case of a pupil who is registered as a pupil at more than one school in accordance with regulation 10, because he is attending another school at which he is a registered pupil.

(4) Where the reason for a pupil's absence cannot be established at the commencement of a session, that absence shall be recorded as unauthorised and any subsequent correction to the register recording that absence as authorised shall be made in accordance with regulation 14 and as soon as practicable after the reason for the absence is established by the person with responsibility for completing the register.

(5) The name of a pupil may only be deleted from the attendance register when that pupil's name has been deleted from the admission register for that

school in accordance with regulation 9.

(6) For the purposes of this regulation 'walking distance' has the meaning given to that expression in section 199(5) of the Education Act 1993.

Leave of absence

8   (1)   Leave of absence may only be granted by a person authorised in that behalf by the proprietor of the school.

(2)   Leave of absence shall not be granted to enable a pupil to undertake employment (whether paid or unpaid) during school hours except –

(a) employment in pursuance of arrangements made or approved under the Education (Work Experience) Act 1973;

(b) employment for the purpose of taking part in a performance within the meaning of section 37 of the Children and Young Persons Act 1963 under the authority of a licence granted by the local authority under that; or

(c) employment abroad for a purpose mentioned in section 25 of the Children and Young Persons Act 1933 where a licence has been granted under that section by a police magistrate as defined in paragraph (9) of that section.

(3)   Subject to paragraph (4), on application made by a parent with whom the pupil normally resides, a pupil may be granted leave of absence from school to enable him to go away on holiday.

(4)   Save in exceptional circumstances, a pupil shall not in pursuance of paragraph (3) be granted more than ten school days leave of absence in any school year.

Deletions from Admission Register

9   (1)   The following are prescribed as the grounds on which the name of a pupil of compulsory school age shall be deleted from the admission register –

(a) where the pupil is registered at the school in accordance with the requirements of a school attendance order, that another school is substituted by the local education authority for that named in the order or the order is revoked by the local education authority on the ground that arrangements have been made for the child to receive efficient full-time education suitable to his age, ability and aptitude otherwise than at school;

(b) except as provided in regulation 10, in a case not falling within sub-paragraph (a) of this paragraph, that he has been registered as a pupil of another school;

(c) in a case not falling within sub-paragraph (a) of this paragraph, that he has ceased to attend the school and the proprietor has received written notification from the parent that the pupil is receiving education otherwise than at school;

(d) except in the case of a boarder, that he has ceased to attend the school and no longer ordinarily resides at a place which is a reasonable distance from the school at which he is registered;

(e) in the case of a pupil granted leave of absence exceeding ten school days for the purpose of a holiday in accordance with regulation 8(3), that the pupil has failed to attend the school within the ten school days immediately following the expiry of the period for which such leave was granted, and tho proprietor is not satisfied that the pupil is unable to attend the school by reason of sickness or any unavoidable cause;

(f) that he is certified by the school medical officer as unlikely to be in a fit state of health to attend school before ceasing to be of compulsory school age;

(g) that he has been continuously absent from school for a period of not less than four weeks and both the proprietor of the school and the local education authority have failed, after reasonable enquiry, to locate the pupil;

(h) that the pupil has died;

(i) that he will cease to be of compulsory school age before the school next meets and intends to cease to attend the school;

(j) in the case of a pupil at a school other than a maintained school, that he has ceased to be a pupil of the school;

(k) where the pupil is registered at a maintained school, that he has been permanently excluded from the school; or

(l) where the pupil has been admitted to the school to receive nursery education, he has not on completing such education transferred to a reception class at the school.

(2) In a case not covered by paragraph (1)(a), (h) or (k), or regulation 10, the name of a child who has under arrangements made by a local education authority become a registered pupil at a special school shall not be removed from the admission register of that school without the consent of that authority or, if that authority refuse to give consent, without a direction of the Secretary of State.

(3) The following are prescribed as the grounds on which the name of a pupil not of compulsory school age is to be deleted from the admission register –

(a) that he has ceased to attend the school, or, in the case of a boarder, that he has ceased to be a pupil of the school;

(b) that he has been continuously absent from the school for a period of not less that four weeks and the proprietor of the school has failed, after reasonable enquiry, to locate the pupil;

(c) that the pupil has died;

(d) where the pupil has been admitted to the school to receive nursery education, he has not on completing such education transferred to a reception class at the school; or

(e) where the pupil is registered at a maintained school, that he has been permanently excluded from the school.

(4) For the purposes of this regulation –

(a) a pupil shall be treated as ordinarily residing at a place where the pupil is habitually and normally resident apart from temporary or occasional absences;

(b) 'reception class' means a class in which education is provided which is suitable to the requirements of pupils aged five and any pupils under or over that age whom it is expedient to educate together with pupils of that age;

(c) children are to be regarded as having been admitted to a school to receive nursery education if they were placed on admission in a nursery class; and

(d) the permanent exclusion of a pupil does not take effect until –
(i) any review under the articles of government for the school of the decision to exclude him has been completed, and
(ii) any time for appealing under section 26 of the Education (No. 2) Act 1986 or those articles has expired without such an appeal being made, such an appeal has been finally concluded or the parents have given notice in writing that they do not intend to appeal.

Dual registration

10 (1) Where a pupil is registered as a pupil at a pupil referral unit and at a school other than a pupil referral unit, the name of that pupil shall not be removed from the admission register of either the unit or the school pursuant to regulation 9(1)(b) without the consent of both the local education authority by which the unit is maintained and the proprietor of the school.

(2) Subject to paragraph (3) where a pupil –
(a) is registered as a pupil at a special school (including a special school established in a hospital) and at another school (other than a pupil referral unit), and
(b) there is not maintained for that pupil a statement of special educational needs specifying the name of the special school only,

the name of that pupil shall not be removed from the admission register of either school pursuant to regulation 9(1)(b) without the consent of the proprietor of both schools.

(3) Where a pupil is registered as a pupil at a special school established in a hospital and at another special school the name of that pupil shall not be removed from the admission register of either school pursuant to regulation 9(1)(b) without the consent of the proprietor of both schools.

(4) The requirements to obtain consent in paragraphs (1) to (3) do not apply in cases covered by regulation 9(1)(h) and (k).

Inspection of registers

11 (1) The admission register and the attendance register of every school shall be available for inspection during school hours by –
(a) any of Her Majesty's Inspectors of Schools appointed under section 1(2) or 5(2) of the Education (Schools) Act 1992(a);
(b) any inspector registered under section 10 of that Act; and
(c) in the case of a school maintained by a local education authority, any officer of the local education authority authorised for the purpose.

Extracts from registers

12 The persons authorised by regulation 11 to inspect the admission register and attendance register of any school shall be permitted to make extracts from those registers for the purposes of the Education Acts 1944 to 1994.

Returns

13 (1) Subject to paragraph (2), the proprietor of every school shall make, in the case of a school maintained by a local education authority to that authority, and in every other case to the local education authority for the area in which the school is situated, at such intervals as may be agreed between the proprietor and the local education authority, or as may be determined by the Secretary of State in default of agreement, a return giving the full name and address of every registered pupil of compulsory school age who –

(a) fails to attend the school regularly; or

(b) has been absent from the school for a continuous period of not less than ten school days, and specifying the cause of absence if known to the proprietor.

(2) Paragraph (1) shall not apply with respect to any absence from the school –

(a) due to sickness of the pupil in respect of which a medical certificate has been furnished to the head teacher,

(b) due to leave of absence granted by a person authorised in that behalf by the proprietor of the school in accordance with regulation 8, and

(c) of a pupil who is registered at more than one school in accordance with regulation 10, due to the pupil attending another school at which he is a registered pupil.

(3) When the name of a pupil has been deleted from the admission register in accordance with regulation 9(1)(c) the proprietor shall make a return to the local education authority giving the full name and address of that pupil within the ten school days immediately following the date on which the pupil's name was so deleted.

Method of making entries

14   Every entry in an admission register or attendance register shall be written in ink and any correction shall be made in such a manner that the original entry and the correction are both clearly distinguishable.

Preservation of registers

15   Every entry in an admission register or attendance register shall be preserved for a period of three years after the date on which the entry was made.

Use of computers

16 (1) Nothing in these Regulations shall be taken to prevent the keeping of an admission register or an attendance register by means of a computer, but where such a register is so kept the following paragraphs of this regulation shall apply for the purpose of modifying the requirements of these Regulations.

(2) The requirements of regulation 5 shall not be treated as, satisfied unless a print is made of the attendance register not less than once a month and of the admission register not less than once a year.

(3) The requirements of regulation 14 shall not be treated as satisfied unless, where any correction to an original entry in the registers is made, prints of the register in question made after the correction distinguish clearly between the original entry and the correction.

(4) The requirements of regulation 15 shall not be treated as satisfied, in the

case of an attendance register, unless each print of the attendance register relating to a particular school year is retained in a single volume for that year and that volume is retained for a period of three years after the end of that school year.

(5) A print of a register produced by means of a computer shall for the purposes of regulation 14 be taken to be made in ink.

(6) The provisions of this regulation are without prejudice to the requirements of the Data Protection Act 1984.

Special Educational Needs Tribunal Regulations 1995 SI No 3113

PART 1: GENERAL

Citation and commencement

1 These Regulations may be cited as the Special Educational Needs Tribunal Regulations 1995 and shall come into force on 1st January 1996.

Interpretation

2 In these Regulations, unless the context otherwise requires –

'the 1993 Act' means the Education Act 1993;

'the authority' means the local education authority which made the disputed decision;

'child' means the child in respect of whom the appeal is brought;

'disputed decision' means the decision or determination in respect of which the appeal is brought;

'the clerk to the tribunal' means the person appointed by the Secretary of the Tribunal to act in that capacity at one or more hearings;

'hearing' means a sitting of the tribunal duly constituted for the purpose of receiving evidence, hearing addresses and witnesses or doing anything lawfully requisite to enable the tribunal to reach a decision on any question;

'parent' means a parent who has made an appeal to the Special Educational Needs Tribunal under the 1993 Act;

'records' means the records of the Special Educational Needs Tribunal;

'the Secretary of the Tribunal' means the person for the time being acting as the Secretary of the office of the Special Educational Needs Tribunal;

'the tribunal' means the Special Educational Needs Tribunal but where the President has determined pursuant to regulation 4(1) that the jurisdiction of the Special Educational Needs Tribunal is to be exercised by more than one tribunal, it means, in relation to any proceedings, the tribunal to which the proceedings have been referred by the President;

'working day', except in regulation 24, means any day other than –

(a) a Saturday, a Sunday, Christmas Day, Good Friday or a day which is a bank holiday within the meaning of the Banking and Financial Dealings Act 1971; or

(b) a day in August.

Members of lay panel

3 No person may be appointed as a member of the lay panel unless the

Secretary of State is satisfied that he has knowledge and experience in respect of –

(a) children with special educational needs; or

(b) local government.

Establishment of tribunals

4 (1) Such number of tribunals shall be established to exercise the jurisdiction of the Special Educational Needs Tribunal as the President may from time to time determine.

(2) The tribunals shall sit at such times and in such places as may from time to time be determined by the President.

Membership of tribunal

5 (1) Subject to the provisions of regulation 28(5), the tribunal shall consist of a chairman and two other members.

(2) For each hearing –

(a) the chairman shall be the President or a person selected from the chairman's panel by the President; and

(b) the two other members of the tribunal other than the chairman shall be selected from the lay panel by the President.

Proof of documents and certification of decisions

6 (1) A document purporting to be a document issued by the Secretary of the Tribunal on behalf of the Special Educational Needs Tribunal shall, unless the contrary is proved, be deemed to be a document so issued.

(2) A document purporting to be certified by the Secretary of the Tribunal to be a true copy of a document containing a decision of the tribunal shall, unless the contrary is proved, be sufficient evidence of matters contained therein.

PART 2: MAKING AN APPEAL TO THE TRIBUNAL AND REPLY BY THE AUTHORITY

(A) THE PARENT

Notice of appeal

7 (1) An appeal to the Special Educational Needs Tribunal shall be made by notice which –

(a) shall state –

(i) the name and address of the parent making the appeal and if more than one address is given, the address to which the tribunal should send replies or notices concerning the appeal;

(ii) the name of the child;

(iii) that the notice is a notice of appeal;

(iv) the name of the authority which made the disputed decision and the date on which the parent was notified of it;

(v) the grounds of the appeal;

(vi) if the parent seeks an order that a school (other than one already named in the statement of special educational needs relating to the child) be named in the child's statement, the name and address of that school;

(b) shall be accompanied by –
  (i) a copy of the notice of the disputed decision;
  (ii) where the appeal is made under section 170 of, or paragraph 8 of Schedule 10 to, the 1993 Act, a copy of the statement of special educational needs relating to the child; and
(c) may state the name, address and profession of any representative of the parent to whom the tribunal should (subject to any notice under regulation 42(2)(a)) send replies or notices concerning the appeal instead of the parent.

(2) The parent shall sign the notice of appeal.

(3) The parent must deliver the notice of appeal to the Secretary of the Tribunal so that it is received no later than the first working day after the expiry of 2 months from the date on which the authority gave him notice, under Part III of the 1993 Act, that he had a right of appeal.

Response, and supplementary provisions

8 (1) If the authority delivers a reply under regulation 12 the parent may deliver a written response to it.

(2) A response under paragraph (1) above must be delivered to the Secretary of the Tribunal not later than 15 working days from the date on which the parent receives a copy of the authority's written reply from the Secretary of the Tribunal.

(3) Subject to paragraph (5) below a response under paragraph (1) shall include all written evidence which the parent wishes to submit to the tribunal (unless such evidence was delivered with the notice of appeal);

(4) The parent may in exceptional cases (in addition to delivering a response under paragraph (1) above) –
(a) with the permission of the President, at any time before the hearing; or
(b) with the permission of the tribunal at the hearing itself –
amend the notice of appeal or any response, deliver a supplementary statement of grounds of appeal or amend a supplementary statement of grounds of appeal.

(5) The parent may in exceptional cases –
(a) with the permission of the President at any time within 15 working days from the date on which a response under paragraph (2) above could have been delivered, or
(b) with the permission of the tribunal at the hearing itself –
deliver written evidence (if he has not previously done so) or further written evidence.

(6) The parent shall deliver a copy of every amendment and supplementary statement made under paragraph (4)(a) above and any written evidence delivered under paragraph (5)(a) above to the Secretary of the Tribunal.

Withdrawal of appeal

9 The parent may –
(a) at any time before the hearing of the appeal withdraw his appeal by sending to the Secretary of the Tribunal a notice signed by him stating that he withdraws his appeal;

(b) at the hearing of the appeal, withdraw his appeal.

Further action by parent

10 (1) The parent shall supply the Secretary of the Tribunal with the information requested in the enquiry made under regulation 17.

(2) If the parent does not intend to attend or be represented at the hearing, he may, not less than 5 working days before the hearing, send to the Secretary of the Tribunal additional written representations in support of his appeal.

Representatives of the parent: further provisions

11 (1) Where a parent has not stated the name of a representative in the notice of appeal pursuant to regulation 7(1)(c) he may at any time before the hearing notify the Secretary of the Tribunal in writing of the name, address and profession of a representative to whom the tribunal should (subject to any notice under regulation 42(2)(a)) send any subsequent documents or notices concerning the appeal instead of to the parent;

(2) Where a parent has stated the name of a representative, whether in the notice of appeal pursuant to regulation 7(1)(c) or pursuant to paragraph (1) above, he may at any time notify the Secretary of the Tribunal in writing –

(a) of the name, address and profession of a new representative of the parent to whom the tribunal should send documents or notices concerning the appeal instead of to the representative previously notified; or

(b) that no person is acting as a representative of the parent and accordingly any subsequent documents or notices concerning the appeal should be sent to the parent himself.

(3) If the person named by the parent as a representative under regulation 7(1)(c) or paragraphs (1) or (2)(a) above notifies the Secretary of the Tribunal in writing that he is not prepared, or is no longer prepared, to act in that capacity –

(a) the Secretary of the Tribunal shall notify the parent, and

(b) any subsequent documents or notices concerning the appeal shall be sent to the parent himself.

(4) At a hearing, the parent may conduct his case himself (with assistance from one person if he wishes) or may appear and be represented by one person whether or not legally qualified:

Provided that, if the President gives permission before the hearing or the tribunal gives permission at the hearing, the parent may obtain assistance or be represented by more than one person.

(B) THE REPLY BY THE AUTHORITY
Action by the authority on receipt of a notice of appeal

12 (1) An authority which receives a copy of a notice of appeal shall deliver to the Secretary of the Tribunal a written reply acknowledging service upon it of the notice of appeal and stating –

(a) whether or not the authority intends to oppose the appeal and, if it does intend to oppose the appeal, the grounds on which it relies; and

(b) the name and profession of the representative of the authority and the address for service of the authority for the purposes of the appeal.

(2) The authority's reply shall include –
   (a) a statement summarising the facts relating to the disputed decision;
   (b) if they are not part of the decision, the reasons for the disputed decision; and
   (c) subject to regulation 13(3) all written evidence which the authority wishes to submit to the tribunal.

(3) Every such reply shall be signed by an officer of the authority who is authorised to sign such documents and shall be delivered to the Secretary of the Tribunal not later than 20 working days after the date on which the copy of the notice of appeal was received by the authority from the Secretary of the Tribunal.

Amendment of reply by the authority

13 (1) The authority, if it has delivered a reply pursuant to regulation 12, may, in exceptional cases –
   (a) with the permission of the President at any time before the hearing; or
   (b) with the permission of the tribunal at the hearing itself
   amend its reply, deliver a supplementary reply or amend a supplementary reply.

(2) The President or, as the case may be, the tribunal may give permission under paragraph (1) above on such terms as he or it thinks fit including the payment of costs or expenses.

(3) The authority may, in exceptional cases –
   (a) with the permission of the President at any time within 15 working days from the date on which the parent could have delivered a response under regulation 8(1); or
   (b) with the permission of the tribunal at the hearing itself
   deliver written evidence (if it has not previously done so) or further written evidence.

(4) The authority shall send a copy of every amendment and supplementary statement made before the hearing to the Secretary of the Tribunal.

Failure to reply and absence of opposition

14 If no reply is received by the Secretary of the Tribunal within the time appointed by regulation 12(3) or if the authority states in writing that it does not resist the appeal, or withdraws its opposition to the appeal the tribunal shall –
   (a) determine the appeal on the basis of the notice of appeal without a hearing; or
   (b) without notifying the authority hold a hearing at which the authority is not represented.

Representation at bearing and further action by the authority

15 (1) At a hearing or part of a hearing the authority may be represented by one person whether or not legally qualified:
   Provided that if the President gives permission before the hearing or the tribunal gives permission at the hearing the authority may be represented

by more than one person.

(2) The authority shall supply the Secretary of the Tribunal with the information requested in the enquiry made under Regulation 17.

(3) If the authority does not intend to attend or be represented at the hearing it may, not less than 5 working days before the hearing, send to the Secretary of the Tribunal additional written representations in support of its reply.

PART 3: PREPARATION FOR A HEARING
Acknowledgement of appeal and service of documents by the Secretary of the Tribunal

16 (1) Upon receiving a notice of appeal the Secretary of the Tribunal shall –
  (a) enter particulars of it in the records;
  (b) send to the parent –
    (i) an acknowledgement of its receipt and a note of case number entered in the records;
    (ii) a note of the address to which notices and communications to the Special Educational Needs Tribunal or to the Secretary of the Tribunal should be sent; and
    (iii) notification that advice about the appeal procedure may be obtained from the office of the Special Educational Needs Tribunal;
  (c) subject to paragraph (6) below, send to the authority –
    (i) a copy of the notice of appeal and any accompanying papers;
    (ii) a note of the address to which notices and communications to the Special Educational Needs Tribunal or to the Secretary of the Tribunal should be sent, and
    (iii) a notice stating the time for replying and the consequences of failure to do so.

(2) Where the Secretary of the Tribunal is of the opinion that, on the basis of the notice of appeal, the parent is asking the Special Educational Needs Tribunal to do something which it cannot, he may give notice to that effect to the parent stating the reasons for his opinion and informing him that the notice of appeal will not be entered in the records unless the parent notifies the Secretary of the Tribunal that he wishes to proceed with it.

(3) Where the Secretary of the Tribunal is of the opinion that there is an obvious error in the notice of appeal –
  (a) he may correct that error and if he does so shall notify the parent accordingly and such notification shall state the effect of sub-paragraph (b) below; and
  (b) unless within 5 working days the parent notifies the Secretary of the Tribunal that he objects to the correction, the notice of appeal as so corrected shall be treated as the notice of appeal for the purposes of these Regulations.

(4) An appeal, as respects which a notice has been given under paragraph (2) above, shall only be treated as having been received for the purposes of paragraph (1) when the parent notifies the Secretary of the Tribunal that he wishes to proceed with it.

(5) Subject to paragraph (6) below, the Secretary of the Tribunal shall forthwith

send a copy of a reply by the authority under regulation 12 and of a response under regulation 8 together with any amendments or supplementary statements, written representations, written evidence or other documents received from a party, to the other party to the proceedings.

(6) If a notice of appeal, reply by the authority under regulation 12 or response by the parent under regulation 8 is delivered to the Secretary of the Tribunal after the time prescribed by these Regulations, the Secretary of the Tribunal shall defer the sending of the copies referred to in paragraph (1)(c) or (5) above pending a decision by the President as to an extension of the time limit pursuant to regulation 41.

Enquiries by the Secretary of the Tribunal

17 The Secretary of the Tribunal shall, at any time after he has received the notice of appeal –

(a) enquire of each party –

(i) whether or not the party intends to attend the hearing;

(ii) whether the party wishes to be represented at the hearing in accordance with regulation 11(4) or 15(1) and if so the name of the: representative;

(iii) whether the party wishes the hearing to be in public;

(iv) whether the party intends to call witnesses and if so the names of the proposed witnesses; and

(v) whether the party or a witness will require the assistance of an interpreter; and

(b) enquire of the parent whether he wishes any persons (other than a person who will represent him or any witness which he proposes to call) to attend the hearing if the hearing is to be in private and if so the names of such persons.

Directions in preparation for a hearing

18 (1) The President may at any time before the hearing give such directions (including the issue of a witness summons) as are provided in this Part of these Regulations to enable the parties to prepare for the hearing or to assist the tribunal to determine the issues.

(2) Directions given pursuant to regulations 20 and 21 may be given on the application of a party or of the President's own motion.

(3) A witness summons issued pursuant to regulation 22 may only be issued on the application of a party.

(4) An application by a party for directions shall be made in writing to the Secretary of the Tribunal and, unless it is accompanied by the written consent of the other party, shall be served by the Secretary of the Tribunal on that other party. If the other party objects to the directions sought, the President shall consider the objection and, if he considers it necessary for the determination of the application, shall give the parties an opportunity of appearing before him.

(5) Directions containing a requirement under this Part of these Regulations shall, as appropriate –

(a) include a statement of the possible consequences for the appeal, as provided by regulation 23, of a party's failure to comply with the requirement within the time allowed by the President; and

(b) contain a reference to the fact that, under section 180(5) of the 1993 Act, any person who without reasonable excuse fails to comply with requirements regarding discovery or inspection of documents, or regarding attendance to give evidence and produce documents, shall be liable on summary conviction to a fine not exceeding level 3 on the standard scale and shall, unless the person to whom the direction is addressed had an opportunity of objecting to the direction, contain a statement to the effect that that person may apply to the President under regulation 19 to vary or set aside the direction.

Varying or setting aside of directions

19   Where a person to whom a direction (including any summons) given under this Part of these Regulations is addressed had no opportunity to object to the giving of such direction, he may apply to the President, by notice to the Secretary to the Tribunal, to vary it or set it aside, but the President shall not so do without first notifying the person who applied for the direction and considering any representations made by him.

Particulars and supplementary statements

20   The President may give directions requiring any party to provide such particulars or supplementary statements as may be reasonably required for the determination of the appeal.

Disclosure of documents and other material

21 (1) The President may give directions requiring a party to deliver to the tribunal any document or other material which the tribunal may require and which it is in the power of that party to deliver. The President shall make such provision as he thinks necessary to supply copies of any document obtained under this paragraph to the other party to the proceedings, and it shall be a condition of such supply that that party shall use such a document only for the purposes of the appeal.

(2) The President may grant to a party such discovery or inspection of documents (including the taking of copies) as might be granted by a county court.

Summoning of witnesses

22   The President may by summons require any person in England and Wales to attend as a witness at a hearing of an appeal at such time and places may be specified in the summons and at the hearing to answer any questions or produce any documents or other material in his custody or under his control which relate to any matter in question in the appeal:

Provided that –

(a) no person shall be compelled to give any evidence or produce any document or other material that he could not be compelled to give or produce at a trial of an action in a Court of law;

(b) in exercising the powers conferred by this regulation, the President shall take into account the need to protect any matter that relates to intimate personal or financial circumstances or consists of information communicated or obtained in confidence;

(c) no person shall be required to attend in obedience to such a summons unless he has been given at least 5 working days' notice of the hearing or, if less than 5 working days, he has informed the President that he accepts such notice as he has been given; and

(d) no person shall be required in obedience to such a summons to attend and give evidence or to produce any document unless the necessary expenses of his attendance are paid or tendered to him.

Failure to comply with directions

23 (1) If a party has not complied with a direction to it under this Part of these Regulations within the time specified in the direction the tribunal may –

(a) where the party in default is the parent, dismiss the appeal without a hearing;

(b) where the party in default is the authority, determine the appeal without a hearing; or

(c) hold a hearing (without notifying the party in default) at which the party in default is not represented or, where the parties have been notified of the hearing under regulation 24, direct that neither the party in default nor any person whom he intends should represent him be entitled to attend the hearing;

(2) In this regulation 'the party in default' means the party which has failed to comply with the direction.

Notice of place and time of bearing and adjournments

24 (1) Subject to the provisions of regulation 25, the Secretary of the Tribunal shall, after consultation with the parties, fix the time and place of the hearing and send to each party a notice that the hearing is to be at such time and place.

(2) The notice referred to in paragraph (1) above shall be sent –

(a) not less than 5 working days before the date fixed for the hearing where the hearing is held under regulation 14, 31 or 36;

(b) not less than 10 working days before the date fixed for the hearing in any other case

or within such shorter period before the date fixed for the hearing as the parties may agree.

(3) The Secretary of the Tribunal shall include in or with the notice of hearing –

(a) information and guidance, in a form approved by the President, as to attendance at the hearing of the parties and witnesses, the bringing of documents, and the right of representation or assistance as provided by regulation 11(4) or 15(1); and

(b) a statement explaining the possible consequence non-attendance and of the right of –

(i) a parent; and

(ii) the authority, if it has presented a reply,

who does not attend and is not represented, to make representations in writing.

(4) The tribunal may alter the time and place of any hearing and the Secretary of the Tribunal shall give the parties not less than 5 working days (or such shorter time as the parties agree) notice of the altered hearing date:

Provided that any altered hearing date shall not (unless the parties agree) be before the date notified under paragraph (1).

(5) The tribunal may from time to time adjourn the hearing and, if the time and place of the adjourned hearing are announced before the adjournment, no further notice shall be required.

(6) Nothing in paragraphs (1) or (4) above shall oblige the Secretary of the Tribunal to consult, or send a notice to any party who by virtue of any provision of these Regulations is not entitled to be represented at the hearing.

(7) In this regulation 'working day' means any day other than a Saturday, a Sunday, Christmas Day, Good Friday or a day which is a bank holiday within the meaning of the Banking and Financial Dealings Act 1971.

PART 4: DETERMINATION OF APPEALS
Power to determine an appeal without a bearing

25 (1) The tribunal may –

(a) if the parties so agree in writing; or

(b) in the circumstances described in regulations 14 and 23,

determine an appeal or any particular issue without a hearing.

(2) The provisions of regulation 27(2) shall apply in respect of the determination of an appeal, or any particular issue, under this regulation.

Hearings to be in private: exceptions

26 (1) A hearing by the tribunal shall be in private unless –

(a) both the parent and the authority request that the hearing be in public; or

(b) the President, at any time before the hearing, or the tribunal at the hearing, orders that the hearing should be in public.

(2) The following persons (as well as the parties and their representatives and witnesses) shall be entitled to attend the hearing of an appeal, even though it is in private –

(a) subject to the provisions of paragraph (8), below, any person named by the parent in response to the enquiry under regulation 17(b) unless the President has determined that any such person should not be entitled to attend the hearing and notified the parent accordingly;

(b) a parent of the child who is not a party to the appeal;

(c) the clerk to the tribunal and the Secretary of the Tribunal;

(d) the President and any member of the chairmen's or lay panel (when not sitting as members of the tribunal);

(e) a member of the Council on Tribunals;

(f) any person undergoing training as a member of the chairmen's or lay panel or as a clerk to the tribunal;

(g) any person acting on behalf of the President in the training or

supervision of clerks to tribunals;
(h) an interpreter.

(3) The tribunal, with the consent of the parties or their representatives actually present, may permit any other person to attend the hearing of an appeal which is held in private.

(4) Without prejudice to any other powers it may have, the tribunal may exclude from the hearing, or part of it, any person whose conduct has disrupted or is likely, in the opinion of the tribunal, to disrupt the hearing.

(5) For the purposes of arriving at its decision a tribunal shall, and for the purposes of discussing any question of procedure may, notwithstanding anything contained in these Regulations, order all persons to withdraw from the sitting of the tribunal other than the members of the tribunal or any of the persons mentioned in paragraph (2)(c) to (f) above.

(6) Except as provided in paragraph (7) below none of the persons mentioned in paragraphs (2) or (3) above shall, save in the case of the clerk to the tribunal or an interpreter as their respective duties require, take any part in the hearing or (where entitled or permitted to remain) in the deliberations of the tribunal.

(7) The tribunal may permit a parent of the child who is not a party to the appeal to address the tribunal on the subject matter of the appeal.

(8) Where the parent has named more than two persons in response to the enquiry under regulation 17(b) only two persons shall be entitled to attend the hearing unless the President has given permission before the hearing or the tribunal gives permission at the hearing for a greater number to attend.

Failure of parties to attend bearing

27 (1) If a party fails to attend or be represented at a hearing of which he has been duly notified, the tribunal may –
   (a) unless it is satisfied that there is sufficient reason for such absence, hear and determine the appeal in the party's absence; or
   (b) adjourn the hearing.

(2) Before disposing of an appeal in the absence of a party, the tribunal shall consider any representations in writing submitted by that party in response to the notice of hearing and, for the purpose of this regulation the notice of appeal, any reply by the authority under regulations 12 or 13 and any response by the parent under regulation 8 shall be treated as representations in writing.

Procedure at bearing

28 (1) At the beginning of the hearing the chairman shall explain the order of proceeding which the tribunal proposes to adopt.

(2) The tribunal shall conduct the hearing in such manner as it considers most suitable to the clarification of the issues and generally to the just handling of the proceedings; it shall, so far as appears to it appropriate, seek to avoid formality in its proceedings.

(3) The tribunal shall determine the order in which the parties are heard and the issues determined.

(4) The tribunal may, if it is satisfied that it is just and reasonable to do so, permit a party to rely on grounds not stated in his notice of appeal or, as the, case may be, his reply or response and to adduce any evidence not presented to the authority before or at the time it took the disputed decision.

(5) If at or after the commencement of any hearing a member of the tribunal other than the chairman is absent, the hearing may, with the consent of the parties, be conducted by the other two members and in that event the tribunal shall be deemed to be properly constituted and the decision of the tribunal shall be taken by those two members.

Evidence at hearing

29 (1) In the course of the hearing the parties shall be entitled o give evidence, to call witnesses, to question any witnesses and to address the tribunal both on the evidence and generally on the subject matter of the appeal:

Provided that neither party shall be entitled to call more that two witnesses to give evidence orally (in addition to any witnesses whose attendance is required pursuant to paragraph (2) below) unless the President has given permission before the hearing or the tribunal gives permission at the hearing.

(2) Evidence before the tribunal may be given orally or by written statement, but the tribunal may at any stage of the proceedings require the personal attendance of any maker of any written statement:

Provided that neither party shall be entitled to give evidence by written statement if such evidence was not submitted with the notice of appeal or submitted in accordance with regulation 8 or (as appropriate) regulations 12 or 13.

(3) The tribunal may receive evidence of any fact which pears to the tribunal to be relevant.

(4) The tribunal may require any witness to give evidence on oath or affirmation, and for that purpose there may be administered an oath or affirmation in due form, or may require any evidence given by written statement to be given by affidavit.

Decision of the tribunal

30 (1) A decision of the tribunal may be taken by a majority and where the tribunal is constituted by two members only under regulation 28(5) the chairman shall have a second or casting vote.

(2) The decision of the tribunal may be given orally at the end of the hearing or reserved and, in any event, whether there has been a hearing or not shall be recorded forthwith in a document which, save in the case of a decision by consent, shall also contain, or have annexed to it, a statement of the reasons (in summary form) for the tribunal's decision, and each such document shall be signed and dated by the chairman.

(3) Neither a decision given orally nor the document referred to in paragraph (2) above shall contain any reference to the decision being by majority (if that be the case) or to any opinion of a minority.

(4) Every decision of the tribunal shall be entered in the records.

(5) As soon as may be the Secretary of the Tribunal shall send a copy of the

document referred to in paragraph (2) above to each party, accompanied by guidance, in a form approved by the President, about the circumstances in which there is a right to appeal against a tribunal decision and the procedure to be followed.

(6) Where, under regulations 7(1)(c), or 11(1) or (2)(a) a parent has stated the name of a representative the Secretary of the Tribunal shall (notwithstanding regulation 42) send a copy of the documents referred to in paragraph (5) above to the parent as well as to the representative.

(7) Every decision shall be treated as having been made on the date on which a copy of the document recording it is sent to the parent (whether or not the decision has been previously announced at the end of the hearing).

Review of the tribunal's decision

31 (1) Any party may apply to the Secretary of the Tribunal for the decision of the tribunal to be reviewed on the grounds that –

(a) its decision was wrongly made as a result of an error on the part of the tribunal staff;

(b) a party, who was entitled to be heard at a hearing but failed to appear or to be represented, had good and sufficient reason for failing to appear;

(c) there was an obvious error in the decision of the tribunal which decided the case; or

(d) the interests of justice require.

(2) An application for the purposes of paragraph (1) above shall be made not later than 10 working days after the date on which the decision was sent to the parties and shall be in writing stating the grounds in full.

(3) An application for the purposes of paragraph (1) above may be refused by the President, or by the chairman of the tribunal which decided the case, if in his opinion it has no reasonable prospect of success, but if such an application is not refused –

(a) the parties shall have an opportunity to be heard on the: application for review; and

(b) the review shall be determined by the tribunal which decided the case or, where it is not practicable for it to be heard by that tribunal, by a tribunal appointed by the President.

(4) The tribunal may of its own motion review its decision on any of the grounds referred to in sub-paragraphs (a) to (d) of paragraph (1) above, and if it proposes to do so –

(a) it shall serve notice on the parties not later than ten working days after the date on which the decision was sent to the parties; and

(b) the parties shall have an opportunity to be heard on the proposal for review.

(5) If, on the application of a party under paragraphs (1) to (3) above or of its own motion under paragraph (4) above the tribunal is satisfied as to any of the grounds referred to in sub-paragraphs (a) to (d) of paragraph (1) above, the tribunal may review and, by certificate under the chairman's hand, set aside or vary the relevant decision.

(6) If, having reviewed the decision, the decision is set aside, the tribunal shall substitute such decision as it thinks fit or order a rehearing before either

the same or a differently constituted tribunal.

(7) If any decision is set aside or varied under this regulation or altered in any way by order of a superior court, the Secretary of the Tribunal shall alter the entry in the records to conform with the chairman's certificate or order of a superior court and shall notify the parties accordingly.

Review of the President's decision

32 (1) If, on the application of a party to the Secretary of the Tribunal or of his own motion the President is satisfied that –

(a) a decision by him was wrongly made as a result of an error on the part of the tribunal staff,

(b) there was an obvious error in his decision; or

(c) the interests of justice require,

the President may review and set aside or vary the relevant decision of his.

(2) An application for the purposes of paragraph (1) above shall be made not later than 10 working days after the date on which the party making the application was notified of the decision and shall be in writing stating the grounds in full. Where the President proposes to review his decision of his own motion he shall serve notice of that proposal on the parties within the same period.

(3) The parties shall have an opportunity to be heard on any application or proposal for review under this regulation and the review shall be determined the President.

(4) If any decision is set aside or varied under this regulation the Secretary of the Tribunal shall alter the entry in the records and shall notify the parties accordingly.

Orders for costs and expenses

33 (1) The tribunal shall not normally make an order in respect of costs and expenses, but may, subject to paragraph (2) below, make such an order –

(a) against a party (including any party who has withdrawn his appeal or reply) if it is of the opinion that that party has acted frivolously or vexatiously or that his conduct in making, pursuing or resisting an appeal was wholly unreasonable;

(b) against a party which has failed to attend or be represented at a hearing of which he has been duly notified;

(c) against the authority where it has not delivered a written reply under regulation 12; or

(d) against the authority, where it considers that the disputed decision was wholly unreasonable.

(2) Any order in respect of costs and expenses may be made –

(a) as respects any costs or expenses incurred, or any allowances paid; or

(b) as respects the whole, or any part, of any allowance (other than allowances paid to members of tribunals) paid by the Secretary of State under section 180(3) of the 1993 Act to any person for the purposes of, or in connection with, his attendance at the tribunal.

(3) No order shall be made under paragraph (1) above against a party without first giving that party an opportunity of making representations against the

making of the order.

(4) An order under paragraph (1) above may require the party against whom it is made to pay the other party either a specified sum in respect of the costs and expenses incurred by that other party in connection with the proceedings or the whole or part of such costs as taxed (if not otherwise agreed).

(5) Any costs required by an order under this regulation to be taxed may be taxed in the county court according to such of the scales prescribed by the county court rules for proceedings in the county court as shall be directed in the order.

PART 5: ADDITIONAL POWERS OF AND PROVISIONS RELATING TO THE TRIBUNAL

Transfer of proceedings

34 Where it appears to the President that an appeal pending before a tribunal could be determined more conveniently in another tribunal he may at any time, upon the application of a party or of his own motion, direct that the said proceedings be transferred so as to be determined in that other tribunal:

Provided that no such direction shall be given unless notice has been sent to all parties concerned giving them an opportunity to show cause why such a direction should not be given.

Miscellaneous powers of the tribunal

35 (1) Subject to the provisions of the 1993 Act and these regulations, a tribunal may regulate its own procedure.

(2) A tribunal may, if it thinks fit, if both parties agree in writing upon the terms of a decision to be made by the tribunal, decide accordingly.

Power to strike out

36 (1) The Secretary of the Tribunal shall, at any stage of the proceedings if the authority applies or the President so directs serve a notice on the parent stating that it appears that the appeal should be struck out on one or both of the grounds specified in paragraph (2) below or for want of prosecution.

(2) The grounds referred to in paragraph (1) above are that –
   (a) the appeal is not, or is no longer, within the jurisdiction of the Special Educational Needs Tribunal;
   (b) the notice of the appeal is, or the appeal is or has become, scandalous, frivolous or vexatious.

(3) The notice under paragraph (1) above shall state that the parent may make representations in accordance with paragraph (8) below.

(4) The tribunal, after considering any representations duly made, may order that the appeal should be struck out on one or both of the grounds specified in paragraph (2) above or for want of prosecution.

(5) The tribunal may make such an order without holding hearing unless either party requests the opportunity to make oral representations, and if the tribunal holds a hearing it may be held at the beginning of the hearing

of the substantive appeal.

(6) The President may, if he thinks fit, at any stage of the proceedings order that a reply, response or statement should be struck out or amended on the grounds that it is scandalous, frivolous or vexatious.

(7) Before making an order under paragraph (6) above, the President shall give to the party against whom he proposes to make the order a notice inviting representations and shall consider any representations duly made.

(8) For the purposes of this regulation –
   (a) a notice inviting representations must inform the recipient that he may, within a period (not being less than 5 working days) specified in the notice, either make written representations or request an opportunity to make oral representations;
   (b) representations are duly made if –
     (i) in the case of written representations, they are made within the period so specified; and
     (ii) in the case of oral representations, the party proposing to make them has requested an opportunity to do so within the period so specified.

Power to exercise powers of President and Chairman

37 (1) An act required or authorised by these Regulations to be done by the President may be done by a member of the chairman's panel authorised by the President.

(2) Where, pursuant to paragraph (1) above, a member of the chairman's panel carries out the function under regulation 5(2) of selecting the chairman of a burial, he may select himself.

(3) Where, pursuant to paragraph (1) above a member of the chairman's panel makes a decision, regulation 32 shall apply in relation to that decision taking the reference in that regulation to the President as a reference to the member of the chairman's panel by whom the decision was taken.

(4) Subject to regulation 39(6) in the event of the death or incapacity of the chairman following the decision of the tribunal in any matter, the functions of the chairman for the completion of the proceedings, including any review of the decision may be exercised by the President or any member of the chairman's panel.

The Secretary of the Tribunal

38   A function of the Secretary of the Tribunal may be performed by another member of the staff of the Tribunal authorised for the purpose of carrying out that function by the President.

Irregularities

39 (1) An irregularity resulting from failure to comply with any provisions of these Regulations or of any direction of the tribunal before the tribunal has reached its decision shall not of itself render the proceedings void.

(2) Where any such irregularity comes to the attention of the tribunal, the tribunal may, and shall, if it considers that any person may have been prejudiced by the irregularity, give such directions as it thinks just before

reaching its decision to cure or waive the irregularity.

(3) Clerical mistakes in any document recording a decision of the tribunal or a direction or decision of the President produced by or on behalf of the tribunal of errors arising in such documents from accidental slips or omissions may at any time be corrected by the chairman or the President (as the case may be) by certificate under his hand.

(4) The Secretary of the Tribunal shall as soon as may be send a copy of any corrected document containing reasons for the tribunal's decision, to each party.

(5) Where under regulations 7(1)(c) or 11(1) or (2)(a) a parent has stated the name of a representative the Secretary of the Tribunal shall (notwithstanding regulation 42) send a copy of the document referred to in paragraph (4) above to the parent as well as to the representative.

(6) Where by these Regulations a document is required to be signed by the chairman but by reason of death or incapacity the chairman is unable to sign such a document, it shall be signed by the other members of the tribunal, who shall certify that the chairman is unable to sign.

Method of sending, delivering or serving notices and documents

40 (1) A notice given under these Regulations shall be in writing and where under these Regulations provision is made for a party to notify the Secretary of the Tribunal of any matter he shall do so in writing.

(2) All notices and documents required by these Regulations to be sent or delivered to the Secretary of the Tribunal or the tribunal may be sent by post or by facsimile or delivered to or at the office of the Special Educational Needs Tribunal or such other office as may be notified by the Secretary of the Tribunal to the parties.

(3) All notices and documents required or authorised by these Regulations to be sent or given to any person mentioned in sub-paragraph (a) or (b) below may (subject to paragraph (5) below) either be sent by first class post or by facsimile or delivered to or at –

(a) in the case of a notice or document directed to a party –
  (i) his address for service specified in the notice of appeal or in a written reply or in a notice under paragraph (4) below, or
  (ii) if no address for service has been so specified his last known address; and

(b) in the case of a notice or document directed to any person other than a party, his address or place of business or if such a person is a corporation, the corporation's registered or principal office and if sent or given to the authorised representative of a party shall be deemed to have been sent or given, to that party.

(4) A party may at any time by notice to the Secretary of the Tribunal change his address for service under these Regulations.

(5) The recorded delivery service shall be used instead of the first class post for service of a summons issued under regulation 22 requiring the attendance of a witness.

(6) A notice or document sent by the Secretary of the Tribunal by post in accordance with these Regulations, and not returned, shall be taken to have

been delivered to the addressee on the second working day after it was posted.

(7) A notice or document sent by facsimile shall be taken to have been delivered when it is received in legible form.

(8) Where for any sufficient reason service of any document or notice cannot be effected in the manner prescribed under this regulation, the President may dispense with service or make an order for substituted service in such manner as he may deem fit and such service shall have the same effect as service in the manner prescribed under this regulation.

Extensions of time

41 (1) Where, pursuant to any provision of these Regulations anything is required to be done by a party within a period of time the President may, on the application of the party in question or of his own motion, in exceptional circumstances extend any period of time.

(2) Where a period of time has been extended pursuant to paragraph (1) above any reference in these Regulations to that period of time shall be construed as a reference to the period of time as so extended.

Parent's representative

42 (1) Subject to paragraph (2) below where, pursuant to regulations 7(1)(c) or 11(1) or (2)(a) a parent has stated the name of a representative, any reference in Parts 3, 4 or 5 of these Regulations (however expressed) to sending document to, or giving notice to, the parent shall be construed as a reference to sending documents to or giving notice to the representative and any such reference to sending documents to or giving notice to a party or the parties shall in the context of the parent be likewise construed as a reference to sending documents to, or giving notice to the representative.

(2) Paragraph (1) above does not apply if –

(a) the parent has notified the Secretary of the Tribunal that he does not wish it to apply;

(b) the parent has notified the Secretary of the Tribunal under regulation 11 (2)(b) that no person is acting as a representative; or

(c) the representative named has notified the Secretary the Tribunal under regulation 11(3) that he is not prepared or no longer prepared to act in that capacity.

Revocation and Transitional Provisions

43 (1) The Special Educational Needs Tribunal Regulations 1994(a) (in this regulation referred to as 'the 1994 Regulations') are hereby revoked.

(2) Notwithstanding paragraph (1) above –

(a) any notice of appeal received before Ist March 1996 may comply either with regulation 7 of the 1994 Regulations or with regulation 7 of these Regulations; and

(b) the 1994 Regulations shall continue to apply in relation to any appeal where the notice of appeal was entered in the records under regulation 17(2) of the 1994 Regulations before 1st January 1996.

Education (Areas to which Pupils and Students Belong) Regulations 1996 SI No 615

Citation and Commencement

1   These Regulations may be cited as the Education (Areas to which Pupils and Students Belong) Regulations 1996 and shall come into force on 1st April 1996.

Interpretation

2   (1)   In these Regulations –

'child looked after by a local authority' has the meaning assigned to it by section 22(1) of the Children Act 1989;

'education authority' means a local education authority;

'further education student' means a person in respect of whom provision for further education is made;

'hospital' includes a nursing home or other establishment (not being a school) for the care of persons who are sick or disabled (including persons whose sickness or disability makes special educational provision requisite) and, in relation to such an establishment, 'patient' includes any sick or disabled person cared for therein;

'parent' includes a person who is not a parent of a person but who has parental responsibility for him;

'parental responsibility' has the meaning assigned to it by section 3 of the Children Act 1989; and

'school pupil' means a person in respect of whom provision for primary or secondary education is made and includes a person for whom such provision is made otherwise than at a school.

(2)   References in these Regulations to the place where a person is ordinarily resident are references to the address where that person is habitually and normally resident apart from temporary or occasional absences, except that no school pupil shall be treated as being ordinarily resident in the area of an education authority by reason only of his residing as a boarder at a school which is situated in the area of that authority.

(3)   References in these Regulations to the person responsible for a school pupil are to –

(a) the parent with parental responsibility for him,

provided that if the parents of a school pupil with parental responsibility for him live in different education authority areas –

(i) the person responsible for the pupil shall be the parent with parental 413 responsibility for him with whom the pupil is habitually and normally resident,

(ii) if the pupil is habitually and normally resident with more than one parent with parental responsibility for him, the person responsible for the pupil shall be the parent who is ordinarily resident nearest to the school attended by the pupil or to the place at which the pupil receives education otherwise than at school,

(iii) if the pupil is not habitually and normally resident with a parent with parental responsibility for him, the person responsible for the pupil shall be the parent who is ordinarily resident nearest to the school attended by the pupil or to the place at which the pupil receives education otherwise than at school; or

(b) where there is no parent with parental responsibility for him, to the person (not being a local authority) who has care of him when be is not attending school or living in boarding accommodation or in hospital.

General principle

3   Subject to regulations 4 to 10 below, a person shall be treated as belonging to the area of the education authority in which he is ordinarily resident or, where he has no ordinary residence, the area of the authority in which he is for the time being resident.

School pupils with statements of special educational needs living in boarding accommodation

4   (1) This regulation shall not apply where regulation 7 below applies.

(2) This regulation shall apply in the case of a school pupil –

(a) for whom a statement of special educational needs is maintained under Part III of the Education Act 1993; and

(b) who attends a boarding school or who is provided with boarding accommodation in pursuance of section 50(1) of the Education Act 1944; and

(c) who does not spend his holidays with the person responsible for him.

(3) Where the person responsible for such a pupil is ordinarily resident in the area of an education authority the pupil shall be treated as belonging to that area.

(4) Where the person responsible for such a pupil is not ordinarily resident in the area of an education authority, or there is no person responsible for the pupil, the pupil shall be treated as belonging to the area of the education authority which maintains the statement.

School pupils with statements of special educational needs and pupils at special schools

5   (1) This regulation shall not apply where regulation 4 above, 6 or 7 below applies.

(2) This regulation shall apply in the case of a school pupil –

(a) for whom a statement of special educational needs is maintained under Part 111 of the Education Act 1993; or

(b) who is registered as a pupil at a special school.

(3) Where the person responsible for such a pupil is ordinarily resident in the area of an education authority the pupil shall be treated as belonging to that area.

(4) Where the person responsible for such a pupil is resident in England or Wales but is not ordinarily resident in the area of an education authority, the pupil shall be treated as belonging to the area of the authority in which the person responsible for such a pupil is for the time being resident.

(5) Where –
  (a) the person responsible for such a pupil is not resident in England or Wales, and
  (b) there is a person who has care of the pupil who is ordinarily resident in England or Wales,
  the pupil shall be treated as belonging to the area of the education authority in England or Wales where such person is ordinarily resident.

(6) Where the person responsible for the pupil is not resident in England and Wales and there is no person who has care of the pupil in England or Wales, the pupil shall be treated as belonging to the area of the education authority making provision for his education.

School pupils resident in hospital

6 (1) This regulation shall not apply where regulation 7 below applies.

(2) This regulation shall apply in the case of a school pupil who –
  (a) is a patient in hospital; and
  (b) receives education in a special school established in hospital, or education referred to in section 298(1) of the Education Act 1993 otherwise than at school.

(3) Where the person responsible for such a pupil is ordinarily resident in the area of an education authority the pupil shall be treated as belonging to that are area.

(4) Where the person responsible for such a pupil is not ordinarily resident in the area of an education authority, the pupil shall be treated as belonging to the area of the authority in which the person responsible for such a pupil is for the time being resident.

(5) Where the person responsible for such a pupil is neither ordinarily nor for the time being resident in the area of an education authority, or there is no person responsible for the pupil, the pupil shall be treated as belonging to the area of the education authority in which the hospital is situated.

Children looked after by a local authority

7 (1) This regulation shall apply to the exclusion of any other regulation which would otherwise apply to such a person.

(2) This regulation shall apply in the case of a child who is looked after by a local authority –
  (a) for whom a statement of special educational needs is maintained under Part III of the Education Act 1993, or
  (b) who is registered as a pupil at a special school, or
  (c) who is a patient in hospital, and receives education either in a special school established in a hospital or education referred to in section

298(1) of the Education Act 1993 otherwise than at school, or

(d) who is a further education student.

(3) Such a person shall be treated as belonging to the education authority area which coincides with or includes the area of the local authority which looks after him.

Further education students becoming ordinarily resident for educational purposes

8 (1) This regulation shall apply in the case of a further education student attending a course of further education (his 'current course') who moved to become ordinarily resident in the area of an education authority for the purpose of attending either his current course or such a previous course as is mentioned in paragraph (3) below.

(2) (a) where immediately before so moving such a student was ordinarily resident in the area of another education authority he shall be treated as belonging to the area of that other authority for so long as he attends his current course; and

(b) where immediately before so moving such a student was not ordinarily resident in the area of another education authority, he shall be treated as belonging to the area of the education authority in which he attends his current course.

(3) The reference in paragraph (1) above and in regulation 9(1) below to a previous course is a reference to a course of further education or higher education which, disregarding an intervening vacation, the student was attending immediately before commencing his current course.

Further education students who change ordinary residence while attending courses

9 (1) This regulation shall apply in the case of a student whose ordinary residence changes while he is attending a course of further education (his 'current course') or such a previous course as is mentioned in regulation 8(3) above.

(2) Where the student was treated as belonging to the area of an education authority immediately before his change of ordinary residence he shall continue to be treated as belonging to that area for so long as he attends his current course.

Further education students in receipt of awards

10 (1) This regulation shall apply to the exclusion of an preceding regulation which would otherwise apply to such a student.

(2) This regulation shall apply in the case of a further education student attending a course of further education in respect of which he is granted an award by an education authority otherwise than pursuant to section 1 of the Education Act 1962(a).

(3) The student shall be treated as belonging to the area of the authority by whom the award was granted so long as he attends the course in question.

Revocation of regulations and transitional provisions

11 (1) The Education (Areas to which Pupils and Students Belong) Regulations 1989 (in this regulation referred to as 'the 1989 Regulations') and the Education (Areas to which Pupils and Students Belong) (Amendment) Regulations 1990 are hereby revoked.

(2) Notwithstanding paragraph (1) above the 1989 Regulations shall continue to apply in relation to any claim for payment made –

(a) before 1st April 1995, under section 51(1) of the Education (No 2) Act 1986 as originally enacted; or

(b) on or after 1st April 1995, under regulation 5 of the Education (Inter-authority Recoupment) Regulations 1994.

Education (School Information) (England) Regulations 1998 SI No 2526

PART I: GENERAL

Citation, commencement and application

1 (1) These Regulations may be cited as the Education (School Information) (England) Regulations 1998 and shall come into force on 5th November 1998.

(2) These Regulations apply in relation to maintained schools in England.

Revocation

2 The Education (School Information) (England) Regulations 1996[2] are hereby revoked.

Interpretation

3 (1) In these Regulations, unless the context otherwise requires –

'the 1996 Act' means the Education Act 1996;

'admission school year' means a school year at the beginning of which pupils are to be admitted to any school;

'assess' means assess pursuant to orders made under section 356(2)(c) of the 1996 Act[3] and 'assessment' shall be construed accordingly;

'associated documents' means the documents published by Her Majesty's Stationery Office, setting out any levels of attainment and attainment targets in relation to the core subjects, which documents have effect by virtue of the respective section 356(2)(a) and (b) orders for those subjects for the time being in force[4];

'authority' means a local education authority and, in relation to an authority, 'the offices' means the education offices;

'core subjects' means English, mathematics and science;

'GCE 'A' level examinations' and 'GCE 'AS' examinations' means General Certificate of Education advanced level and advanced supplementary examinations respectively;

'GCSE' means General Certificate of Secondary Education;

'GNVQ' means a General National Vocational Qualification;

'local average figures' means the average figures for all schools maintained by the relevant authority (other than any special school established in a hospital), all grant-maintained schools, grant-maintained special schools (other than any established in a hospital), and all city technology colleges and city colleges for the technology of the arts, in the area of that relevant authority;

419

'maintained school' means:
(a) any county or voluntary school;
(b) any special school maintained by an authority which is not established in a hospital;
(c) any grant-maintained school or grant-maintained special school which is not established in a hospital, but excludes any nursery school;
'national average figures' means the average figures for all schools in England;
'national summary figures' means the summary figures in respect of National Curriculum assessments of pupils for all schools in England;
'NC tasks' means National Curriculum standard tasks administered to pupils in the final year of the first key stage pursuant to article 5 of the Education (National Curriculum) (Assessment Arrangements for the Core Subjects) (Key Stage 1) (England) Order 1995[5];
'NC tests' means National Curriculum tests administered to pupils in, as the case may be, the final year of the second key stage or the final year of the third key stage pursuant to, respectively, article 5 of the Education (National Curriculum) (Assessment Arrangements for the Core Subjects) (Key Stage 2) (England) Order 1995[6] and article 10 of the Education (National Curriculum) (Key Stage 3 Assessment Arrangements) (England) Order 1996[7];
'non-maintained special school' means a special school which is neither maintained by an authority nor a grant-maintained special school (and which is not established in a hospital);
'previous school year' means the school year immediately preceding the reporting school year;
'publication school year' means the school year immediately preceding the admission school year;
'public examinations' means public examinations which are for the time being prescribed by regulations made under sections 402, 451, 453 and 454 of the 1996 Act[8];
'primary education' does not include such education provided at a middle school;
'relevant authority', in relation to a county or voluntary school or a special school maintained by an authority which is not established in a hospital, means the authority by which the school is maintained and, in relation to a grant-maintained school or a grant-maintained special school which is not established in a hospital, means the authority in whose area the school is situated;
'reporting school year' means the school year immediately preceding the publication school year;
'school prospectus' means the document described in regulation 11;
'special educational needs' and 'special educational provision' have the same meanings as in section 312 of the 1996 Act;
'special school' has the meaning assigned to it by section 337(1) of the 1996 Act;
'the statutory arrangements' means assessment arrangements specified by

orders made under section 356(2)(c) of the 1996 Act;

'teacher assessment' means assessment of a pupil by a teacher as specified in the statutory arrangements;

'unit' in relation to a vocational qualification, means a module or part of a course leading to that qualification which, when successfully completed, can be counted together with other modules or parts towards obtaining that qualification; and references to levels and attainment targets are references to, respectively, the levels of attainment of the National Curriculum level scale and attainment targets set out in the associated documents.

(2) In these Regulations, unless the context otherwise requires, a reference to a numbered regulation or Schedule is a reference to a regulation in, or a Schedule to, these Regulations so numbered and any reference to a paragraph is to a paragraph of the regulation or Schedule in which the reference is made and, any reference to a sub-paragraph is a reference to a sub-paragraph of the paragraph in which the reference is made.

(3) In these Regulations, any reference to a date up to which parents may express a preference for a school is a reference to the date by which, in accordance with arrangements made by the relevant local education authority under section 411(1) of the 1996 Act, a parent wishing education to be provided for his child in the exercise of the authority's functions should express such a preference.

(4) In these Regulations, unless the context otherwise requires, a reference to publication by the governing body of a school includes a reference to publication on behalf of the governing body by the relevant authority by virtue of section 414(8) of the 1996 Act.

(5) In these Regulations, references to the first key stage, the second key stage, the third key stage and the fourth key stage are references to the periods set out in paragraphs (a) to (d) of section 355(1) of the 1996 Act.

(6) In these Regulations, unless the context otherwise requires, references to pupils of a particular age are to pupils who attained that age during the period of twelve months ending on the 31st August immediately preceding the commencement of the reporting school year and who were registered pupils at the school on the third Thursday in January in the reporting school year.

(7) In these Regulations –
(a) except where otherwise provided, where a percentage which is required to be calculated by virtue of these Regulations is not a whole number it shall be rounded to the nearest whole number, the fraction of one half being rounded upwards to the next whole number;
(b) where an average point score which is required to be calculated by virtue of these Regulations is not a whole number, it shall be calculated to one decimal place.

(8) In these Regulations, references to examinations for which pupils at the school were entered include examinations for which they were entered otherwise than in pursuance of section 402 of the 1996 Act.

(9) For the purposes of these Regulations, any examination for the GCSE for

which a pupil aged 15 was entered during the previous school year or any earlier school year shall be treated as such an examination for which the pupil was entered during the reporting school year.

Qualification of duties

4   The duties imposed on governing bodies and authorities by virtue of these Regulations in respect of provision, publication or making available of information apply only to the extent that that information is available to the governing body or the authority in time for it to be reasonably practicable to provide, publish or make available the information before the latest occasion on which the information is required to be provided, published or made available as the case may be.

PART II: PROVISION OF INFORMATION BY HEAD TEACHER

Provision of information by head teacher to governing body

5   For the purpose of enabling the governing body to comply with their obligations under these Regulations, the head teacher of every maintained school shall make available to the governing body information about the matters mentioned in Schedule 2.

PART III: INFORMATION TO BE PUBLISHED OR PROVIDED BY AUTHORITIES

General information to be published by authorities

6 (1) An authority shall publish with respect to its policy and arrangements in respect of primary and secondary education (including such education provided in a middle school) in its area information in respect of each of the matters specified in Schedule 1.

   (2) Where changes in respect of any of those matters have been decided on by the authority but not yet implemented, the authority shall also publish information about those changes.

   (3) This information shall be published as provided in regulation 7.

Time and manner of publication by authorities of general information and particulars of school admission arrangements and related matters

7 (1) This regulation shall apply in relation to the publication by an authority of
   –

   (a) information in respect of the matters specified in Schedule 1;

   (b) particulars of the arrangements mentioned in section 414(1), (3), (4) and (5) of the 1996 Act; and

   (c) particulars of the arrangements relating to voluntary aided or special agreement schools mentioned in section 414(2), (3) and (4) of the 1996 Act where those particulars are being published by the authority on behalf of the governing body of the school pursuant to subsection (8) of that section.

   (2) Such information and particulars shall be published during the publication school year and, except in so far as they relate exclusively to primary

education or special educational provision, they shall be published no later than six weeks before the date up to which parents may express a preference for a school in respect of the admission school year.

(3) Subject to paragraphs (4) to (9), such information and particulars shall be published –

  (a) by copies being made available for distribution without charge to parents on request, and for reference by parents and other persons –

    (i) at the offices of the relevant authority, and

    (ii) at every school maintained by that authority, other than a nursery school or a special school;

  (b) by copies being distributed without charge to parents of pupils at schools maintained by the relevant authority, other than nursery schools or special schools, who, in the publication school year, are in the final year at such schools and who might transfer to other schools so maintained; and

  (c) by copies being made available for reference by parents and other persons at the public libraries in the area of the relevant authority.

(4) So far as the information in respect of the matters specified in paragraphs 3, 4 and 5 of Schedule 1 is concerned (schools maintained by the authority), the information in respect of schools in a particular part of the relevant local education authority's area need not –

  (a) be made available at offices, schools and libraries outside that part; or

  (b) be distributed to the parents of pupils who are at schools outside that part, if information about how it may be obtained is available at those offices, schools and libraries or, as the case may be, is distributed to those parents.

(5) It shall be a sufficient compliance with paragraph (3)(a)(ii) if so much of the information and particulars as relates to schools classified as –

  (a) primary schools;

  (b) middle schools; or

  (c) secondary schools, (irrespective of the terminology used) is available only in schools of the classification in question.

(6) It shall be a sufficient compliance with paragraph (3)(b) if there is published so much of the information and particulars as is relevant having regard to the schools to which pupils in the final year at that school might transfer.

(7) So far as the particulars specified in Part II of Schedule 1 are concerned (special educational provision), paragraphs (3), (4), (5) and (6) shall not apply but the particulars shall be published –

  (a) by copies being available for distribution without charge to parents on request, and for reference by parents and other persons, at the offices of the relevant authority; and

  (b) by copies being available for reference by parents and other persons –

    (i) at every school maintained by the relevant authority, and

    (ii) at the public libraries in the area of that authority.

(8) Without prejudice to the foregoing provisions of this regulation, such particulars of the arrangements made by the relevant authority under section 423(1) of the 1996 Act (appeals against admission decisions) and mentioned in section 414(1)(c) of that Act shall also be published by being

set out in any document containing a notification to parents of a decision referred to in section 423(1) of that Act refusing their child admission to a school for which the parents have expressed a preference in accordance with arrangements made under section 411(1) of that Act.

(9) Information about the matters mentioned in paragraphs 7(2) and 18 of Schedule 1 (transport arrangements and policies) shall also be published by copies being distributed without charge to institutions within the further education sector or at which a further education funding council has secured provision which (in either case) the authority consider students resident within its area may wish to attend.

(10) The particulars referred to in paragraph (1)(c) shall be supplied to the authority by the governing body and shall be published without material alteration.

PART IV: INFORMATION TO BE PUBLISHED BY GOVERNING BODIES

General information to be published by governing bodies

8 (1) Subject to regulation 9, the governing body of a maintained school shall publish as respects that school the information specified in Schedule 2.

(2) Subject to regulation 9, this information shall be published as provided in regulation 11.

Determination of examination results particulars and equivalency between GCSE examinations and vocational qualifications

9 (1) The provisions of this regulation have effect for the purpose of determining the information specified in Schedule 2.

(2) Subject to paragraph (14), if a pupil has been entered for two or more examinations in the same subject in the same school year, or in different school years which are treated as the same school year by virtue of regulation 3(9), only the examination in which he achieved the higher or highest grade shall be taken into account.

(3) In the case of an examination leading to the award of GCSE in two subjects, a pupil shall be included only once in the number of pupils entered for the examination and taken into account only once in calculating the relevant percentages, but each grade awarded to him shall be treated as having been awarded in a separate subject.

(4) In the case of any GCSE examination for which pupils aged 15 were entered, the information shall commence with the subjects listed in the first column of Schedule 4 in the order in which they are so listed.

(5) For the purposes of this regulation, any GCSE examination in a subject listed in the first column of Schedule 4 is not to be treated as such unless the examination is in a syllabus referred to in the second column opposite that subject.

(6) For the purposes of paragraph 12(1)(e) of Schedule 2, where a pupil is awarded a grade in an examination relating to a GCSE short course, he shall be treated as having achieved that grade in half a GCSE subject.

(7) For the purposes of paragraph 12(1)(e) and (2) of Schedule 2, questions as

to –
(a) which vocational qualification award corresponds to which GCSE examination grade, and
(b) the equivalency between GCSE examination results and vocational qualifications, shall be determined in accordance with paragraphs (8) to (13) below.

(8) Where a pupil is awarded a Part One GNVQ (Intermediate level), he shall be treated as having achieved grade A* to C in two GCSE subjects.

(9) Where a pupil is awarded a Part One GNVQ (Foundation level), he shall be treated as having achieved grade D to G in two GCSE subjects.

(10) Where a pupil is awarded an Intermediate GNVQ, he shall be treated as having achieved grade A* to C in four GCSE subjects.

(11) Where a pupil is awarded a Foundation GNVQ, he shall be treated as having achieved grade D to G in four GCSE subjects.

(12) Where a pupil is awarded a GNVQ Language Unit (Intermediate level), he shall be treated as having achieved grade A* to C in half a GCSE subject.

(13) Where a pupil is awarded a GNVQ Language Unit (Foundation level), he shall be treated as having achieved grade D to G in half a GCSE subject.

(14) In the case of a pupil who has been entered for both GCE 'A' level and GCE 'AS' examinations in the same subject –
(a) except in the circumstances described in sub-paragraph (b), only the GCE 'A' level examination result shall be taken into account;
(b) where the pupil achieves grade N or fails to achieve a grade in the GCE 'A' level examination but achieves a grade between A and E inclusive in the GCE 'AS' examination, only the GCE 'AS' examination result shall be taken into account.

(15) Subject to paragraph (14), in calculating the number of GCE 'A' levels a pupil is entered for, one GCE 'AS' shall be treated as the equivalent of half a GCE 'A' level.

(16) Subject to paragraph (14), for the purpose of determining point scores in GCE 'A' level and GCE 'AS' examinations, the following grades of achievement equate to the following points, namely:
GCE 'A' level: grade A=10 points; grade B=8 points; grade C=6 points; grade D=4 points; and grade E=2 points;
GCE 'AS': grade A=5 points; grade B=4 points; grade C=3 points; grade D=2 points; and grade E=1 point.

Derivations

Owing to the plethora of primary and delegated legislation which has appeared, particularly since 1992, many regulations and circulars (which are still in effect), as well as law reports, contain references to statutory provisions which have since been re-enacted or repealed. In a work of this nature it would be impossible to provide an accurate and comprehensive guide to the changes. Much more detail may be found in *The Law of Education* (Butterworth, loose-leaf). This appendix traces the more significant sections of the Education Reform Act 1988 and the Education Acts 1993 and 1996 to their current statutory provisions.

Education Reform Act 1988

ss1–5 now EA 1996 ss350–357: National Curriculum

ss6–13 now EA 1996 ss375–384: religious education and worship

s14 now EA 1996 ss358–361: curriculum assessment councils (now Curriculum and Assessment Authority)

s22 now EA 1996 s458: information

s23 now EA 1996 s409: complaints

Chapter II

ss26–32 then EA 1996 ss416–422, Sch 32, now SSFA 1998 Part III ss84–109 and Schs 23–25: admissions and standard number

ss33–43 then EA 1996 ss101–122, now SSFA ss49–50: delegated budgets

s44–46 then EA 1996 ss136–142 and Sch 3, repealed by SSFA 1998 Sch 30 paras 69 and 70: staffing consequences

Chapter IV

ss53–104 now EA 1996 ss183–311: grant-maintained schools

ss106–111, 118 now EA 1996 ss449–462: charges in maintained schools

Education Act 1993

s3 now EA 1996 s20: Funding Agency for Schools (FAS) – to be dissolved by order under SSFA 1998 s132

s12 then EA 1996 s27: LEA sharing responsibility for school place provision with the FAS, repealed from 1 April 1999 by SSFA Sch 30 paras 57 and 66, Sch 31

Education Act 1993 *continued*

s13 then EA 1996 ss431–432, now SSFA 1998 ss96–97: direction to admit child

ss55–155 then EA 1996 ss183–311: grant-maintained schools (various sections 30–311 prospectively repealed by SSFA 1998)

Part III (ss156–191 and Schs 9 and 10) replaced by EA 1996 Part IV (ss312 –349 and Schs 26 and 27) from 1 November 1996: special educational needs (SEN)

s156 now EA 1996 s312: meaning of SEN and SEP

s159 now EA 1996 s315: LEA to review arrangements

s160 now EA 1996 s316: SEN children in mainstream schools

s161 now EA 1996 s317: duties of governing body

s163 now EA 1996 s319: provision otherwise than in a school

s164 now EA 1996 s320: provision outside England and Wales

s165 now EA 1996 s321: LEA duty towards SEN children

s166 now EA 1996 s322: health authority duty to help LEA

s167 now EA 1996 s323: assessment of educational needs

s168 now EA 1996 s324: statement of SEN

ss169, 170 and Sch 10 now EA 1996 ss325, 326 and Sch 27: appeals to SENT

s172 now EA 1996 s328: annual reviews and reassessment

s173 now EA 1996 s329: parental request for assessment

s175 now EA 1996 s331: children under two,

s177 now EA 1996 s333: the tribunal

ss182–188 now EA 1996 ss337–342: special schools

s189 now EA 1996 s347: approval of independent schools

s190 now EA 1996 s348: provision at non-maintained school

ss192–199 now EA 1996 ss437–444: school attendance and offences

s202 now EA 1996 s447: education supervision orders

s232 now EA 1996 s500 (prospectively repealed by SSFA 1998): rationalisation of excessive school places

s266–268 then EA 1996 s308 and Sch 33, now SSFA 1998 s94 and Sch 24: appeal committees

s298 now EA 1996 s19: exceptional provision of education in PRU or elsewhere

Education Act 1996

Discipline

s154: responsibility of governing body and headteacher

s155 now SSFA 1998 s62: LEA's reserve power to prevent a breakdown

s156 now SSFA 1998 s64: power of headteacher to exclude pupils

s157 now SSFA 1998 s65: duty to inform parents of exclusions

s158 and Sch 15: reinstatement of excluded pupils

Education Act 1996 *continued*

s159 and Sch 16 now SSFA 1998 s67 and Sch 18: appeals against exclusion, and s68: guidance from secretary of state

Admissions

s411 now SSFA 1998 s86: parental preferences

s411A now SSFA 1998 s87: children permanently excluded from two or more schools

s412 now SSFA 1998 s89: procedure for determining admission arrangements, and s90: reference to adjudicator or secretary of state

s413 now SSFA 1998 s91: special arrangements to preserve religious character

s414 now SSFA 1998 s92: information about admissions

s415 now SSFA 1998 s88: admission authority

s416 now SSFA 1998 s93: fixing admission numbers

ss417–422 now SSFA 1998 Sch 23: standard number

s423 and Sch 33 now SSFA 1998 s94 and Sch 24: appeal arrangements

s423A now SSFA 1998 s94 and Sch 25: school appeal re excluded children

s431 now SSFA 1998 s96: LEA direction to admit

Checklists

General
Full name and title of instructing client
Previous name
Date of birth
National insurance no
Address
Telephone no home/work

Full name of child client
Previous name
Date of birth
National insurance no
Address and telephone no (where different)
Previous family address

Family
Parent 1 age, occupation
Parent 2 name, age, occupation (present status and involvement where absent)
Siblings: names, sex, present age, brief educational details

Conflict
Issue(s) raised by instructions
Is the child client Gillick competent?

Development
(Check against existing reports – eg, from educational psychologist)
Reports of concern – client's comments

Special educational needs
Birth history
Relevant family history (eg, mental health problems)
Dates of all statements under 1981, 1993 or 1996 Act
List appendices by category, maker, status, date of advice
Client's comments on adequacy of Part 3 provision
Details of relevant meetings and reviews in the past two years
Timetable of any current assessment procedure
Relevant decisions by LEA
Dates which will trigger SENT appeal

Education negligence
Dates of all schools attended, from nursery school up
All school records
Summary of reports:
    over the last three years
    upon secondary transfer
    upon leaving school
Public examinations taken and results
Best subjects
Favourite subjects
Specimens of work
Problems encountered/comments on problems highlighted:
    from parent
    from child
    from LEA educational psychologist and senior teachers (identify)
    with dates (compare with reports)
All statements of SEN and appendices
Professional involvement – medical, psychological, legal
Ombudsman, councillor
Correspondence and reports relied on to show problem

Medical history
Details of GP and any relevant hospital treatment/investigations
Decide whether this is a PI case and the limitation period

Further/higher education history
Details of subjects studied
Grades obtained
Support given

Employment history
List chronologically posts held
Description of duties
Salary
Reason for leaving
Explain any gaps in employment

Further education and career plans

Public law/complaints cases
Time limits
Date and details of decision complained of
Documents considered
Letter of notification
Representations made to date by client
Previous representation at hearing/meetings
Parties to decision and their interests
Rules or published procedure
What client seeks to achieve
Involvement by MP, councillor, doctor, previous solicitors

Correspondence with other parties
Seeking information
Information about, eg, school information, curricular records, policy, progress of administrative actions
Education committee papers
Resolutions
Policy document for each year
Info re numbers of comparable cases and outcomes
Asking for statement of reason(s) where not yet given
Letter before action
This should set out the legal framework following a brief summary of the facts relied on and their source. The letter should make it clear what is being sought and state the sanctions if this outcome is not achieved.

Admissions disputes
Which authority?
Admissions criteria
Correspondence re admission and refusal
Prospectus of school
Precise reasons for refusal

If oversubscribed the standard number and admissions number
How many admitted?
What is the physical layout of the school like?
Would it easily accommodate more?
Particular factors re the child (for stage II of the process)
Were the criteria properly applied, eg, mistake as to distance?
Religious case:
Same, except admissions number
What are the religious qualifications and who decides whether the child meets them or not?
Academic ability case:
Did they make a mistake in the assessment?
Aptitude:
Has the 15% limit been reached in music, art, drama or sport or in general ability – maintaining the character?

Appeal to SENT

Statement of SEN
Letter/notice from LEA
Date of receipt
Appendices
Previous statement(s)
Previous appeals
What does the parent want?
School registration
Age of child
Expert report?
Evidence of hardship
Consider:
   Obtaining discovery
   Witness summons
   When to lodge appeal in view of time limits and evidence

Exclusions appeals

Did you do it?
What exactly happened?
School discipline policy
Promulgation of policy
Previous incidents and children
Previous treatment of others

Was guidance in Circular 10/99 appropriately applied?

Consider:

    Will the child be at the appeal?

    Are there excuses for the behaviour?

    Pastoral care policy

    Does the child wish to return to the school? If not, why not?

    Has a place been offered at an alternative school?

    Strength and nature of evidence gathered by the headteacher following the exclusion decision

    Identifying pupil witnesses

For the panel appeal:

No disqualified members or apparent bias

Notes of governing body/LEA meetings re exclusion

Obtaining curricular records

Precedent letters

L1   Private client funding and costs letter

(Different types of work for which costs estimates might be given):

- Admissions: representation at appeal
- Exclusion: governors' meeting and appeal
- Obtaining and examining school records
- Arranging independent psychological assessment and report
- Making representations and monitoring statutory assessment of special educational needs
- Reassessment
- Attending annual SEN review meeting
- Representations on review of statement
- Attending special needs panel/complex case meeting
- Advice on failure of SEN provision and letter before action
- Application for legal aid (parent)
- Application for legal aid (child)
- Attendance at Legal Aid Board appeal
- Application for permission for judicial review
- SENT appeals
- Appeal to High Court (RSC Order 55)

L2   Authority

[Address]

Name . . . .   **d.o.b.** . . . .
parent/carer of

Name of pupil/student . . . .   **d.o.b.** . . . .
Address (where different)

. . . .

. . . .

Names of other children . . . .   **d.o.b.** . . . .
(if applicable)

I hereby authorise my solicitors Edsol and Partners of [address] to obtain information about me and/or the above-named child including but not limited to all correspondence, records, reports, memoranda and files from [delete where inapplicable]:

- Any school attended.
- Any education authority which has had responsibility for providing education, including files and reports of the educational psychology

service and any statements of special educational needs or documents arising from a statutory assessment or request for one.

- Local authority social services department.
- Any medical practitioner who has attended me/him/her.
- Any college of further education.
- Further Education Funding Council (FEFC).

Signed . . . . **Date** . . . .

L3   Form of authority for child's social services file

To . . . .

Re: Access to Personal Files (Social Services) Regulations 1989

I am . . . . of . . . .

I am the mother/father of . . . . d.o.b. . . . .

I declare that . . . . lacks the capacity to make an application set out below/consents to the application set out below.

I request that you give access to me and my solicitor [solicitor's name] at [solicitor's address]

all personal information and files held by . . . . Authority relating to:

a)   me [name]

b)   my son/daughter

within 40 days of receipt of this request.

I authorise [solicitor's name] to inspect and/or take copies of documents.

Signed . . . . **Date** . . . .

L4   Request for child's education files (paras 4.47 and 8.53)

To the Secretary of the Governing Body

. . . . **School**

Re: AB . . . . **d.o.b.** . . . .

Education (School Records) Regulations 1989

We act for [X, the parent of AB/AB now aged (over 16)] who has a right of access to AB's curricular and other records under regulations 6 and 7 of the Regulations.

On behalf of our client we hereby request copies of the above records, for which we are willing to pay any reasonable fee prescribed by the governing body (not exceeding the cost of supply). We enclose a copy of an authority from our client.

If any such records are no longer kept by your governing body, please let us have full details of when and to whom they were transferred.[1]

As you are aware, our request must be complied with within 15 school days.[2] We calculate that this period expires on [date].

We would be grateful if you would telephone us if you anticipate any difficulty. If we think that we do not need to have the entire records in question we will telephone you to arrange to inspect the records first.

---

1   There is a duty to pass the appropriate parts of the record to the next place of education: Education (Schools and Further Education) Regulations 1981 SI No 1086 reg 13.

2   A 'school day' means any day on which that school has a school session. Education Act 1996 s579.

L5   Letter requesting SEN information from LEA (para 9.31)

To the Education Officer (Special Needs)

. . . .   LEA

Re: AB . . . .   d.o.b. . . . .

We have been consulted by X, A's [mother/father], and we are looking into the level of provision for A's special educational needs. In order that we can have access to all the relevant material we would like copies of all of the following, except where we have indicated that we already have them:

Statements, advices, correspondence regarding assessments, reports, reviews, minutes of [SEN Panel] meetings.

We enclose a copy of our client's signed authority for us to receive this information. If you propose to make a charge for supplying these copies kindly let us know.

L6   Request for information about LEA policy/decision

The letter could include requests for the following:

– Education Committee papers.
– Resolutions.
– Policy document for each year.
– Information regarding numbers of comparable cases and outcomes.
– Statement of reason(s) where not yet given.

L7   Information re school (para 5.31)

To the Headteacher

. . . .   School

Education (School Information) Regulations 1998/99

We write to request a copy of the school's prospectus. (parent)

If you are unable to send a copy free of charge, please advise us of the fee or arrangements for inspection. (non-parent)

L8   Request for annual report of governing body (paras 5.31 and 9.24)

To the Headteacher or to the Secretary to the Governing Body

.... School

We would be grateful if you would let us have copies of the last [three] annual reports to parents or the arrangements for inspection.[3]

3   Under EA 1996 s161. The report is free to parents (EA 1993 Sch 6 para 8) and deals with the school activities over the previous year. By EA 1996 s317(5), all reports since 1 August 1995 must cover the implementation of the governing body's special educational needs policy. For special educational needs see also Education (Special Educational Needs) (Information) Regulations 1994 SI No 1048 and DfEE Circular 6/94.

L9   Letter to LEA re deficiency in statemented provision (paras 9.33 and 16.22)

We have been considering with our client the Statement of special educational needs issued on [date].

We have copies of all the appendices referred to therein. [It is not clear what documents constitute the parental advice and we would be grateful if you could provide us with a list of those documents so that we may identify them.]

As you are aware, your LEA has a statutory duty under Education Act 1996 s324(5) to arrange that the statemented SEN provision is made in the school attended by AB. [This applies even where the provision is delivered by another authority.] According to our instructions, however, the provision is not being made in the following specific areas covered by part 3 of the statement. The list is not meant to be exhaustive, because we have yet to receive [expert advice about the provision which is required to meet AB's needs and] independent confirmation of the arrangements which have been implemented.

1   Under paragraph (1) of the statement: We understand that none of AB's teachers have been trained in the tuition of pupils with specific learning difficulty.

2   AB does not have 2 hours per week access to a computer as required by paragraph 4 of the statement. Only 15 minutes is provided weekly.

(List items by reference to statement)

Before we decide how to advise our clients we would like to hear from you with your observations on these apparent breaches of statutory duty on the part of your authority. Please give full details of the steps which your LEA proposes to take to rectify the situation. If you do not accept that any of the provision falls below the required level please give details of the way in which the provision meets the requirements of the statement in your view. We look forward to hearing from you in the next 14 days.

[See L16 for subsequent action.]

L10   Letter to LEA re help from district health authority

The statement of special educational needs provides for (inter alia):

1 (in part 3) an individual programme designed by a speech and language therapist delivered by teachers and other staff under the supervision of the SALT who shall monitor the progress and revise the programme termly;

2 (in part 5) additional support for emotional needs by means of weekly counselling sessions by a child psychologist at the Children and Families' Centre.

We are instructed that it is more than 4 months since a SALT saw AB and that following the resignation of the regular postholder's maternity locum there has been no SALT in post for the last 2 months. In order to comply with its duty under s324(5) to arrange that the statemented provision is made, your authority must either make a successful request to the district health authority for help under s322(1) Education Act 1996 or employ a SALT to undertake the work. It is not sufficient to rely on the DHA in the circumstances.[4] If we do not receive evidence within the next 14 days that the LEA has made the necessary arrangements we regret that we shall have to advise our clients to commence proceedings for a judicial review.

It is understood that no appointment for counselling has been made since the date of the statement and thus your LEA would appear to be failing in its its duty with regard to the non-educational provision under s324(5)(a)(ii) Education Act 1996.

In order that we can consider the position kindly let us have within the next 14 days:

1 Copies of any correspondence with the DHA and the social services department with a view to arranging this provision;

2 If none, details of any decision not to arrange the provision, with a full statement of reasons.

---

4   The duty cannot be delegated. See *R v Harrow LBC ex p M* (1996) *Times* 15 October, and para 9.49.

L11   Letter to LEA re local social services authority help

Part 6 of AB's statement of special educational needs provides for him/her to have access to play facilities after school. This is to assist him/her to develop his social skills. The Family Link project, run by the Bowford Social Services department, have informed our client that they cannot accommodate AB because of the degree of supervision s/he requires. Our client would like you to use your statutory powers to request further assistance from the social services department.

Under s322(1) Education Act 1996 you have the power to request specified action from the social services department to help in the exercise of any of your functions. This includes arranging appropriate non-educational provision in the statement. We enclose the relevant reports (which you have already seen) dealing with the desirability of this out of school provision for AB and we would be grateful if you would now pass them to the social services department with your request.

Please confirm within 14 days that you agree to make this request under s322 and let us have copies of your request and the response of the social services department. If you decide not to make the request kindly let us have a full explanation and reasons for your decision.

Your authority is vicariously liable for the acts and omissions of its servants and agents in breach of their duty of care and our client holds you responsible for what has occurred.

[In our view this is a prospective action for personal injury so that our client is entitled to pre-action discovery of all relevant documents under Civil Procedure Rule 31 (formerly RSC Order 24 Rule 7A, s33(2) Supreme Court Act 1981).] We therefore request copies of all educational and curricular records relating to our client, together with all correspondence, statements, advices, reports, minutes and notes affecting him/her.

In respect of education records which have come into existence since 1 September 1989 and are in your custody, kindly note that this request is made under regulations 6 and 7 of the Education (School Records) Regulations 1989.

We look forward to hearing from you within the next 21 days.

L12   Letter to SENT re appeal (para 9.75)

Re: AB

We are advising Mrs CD, mother of the above named. We enclose the parent's notice of appeal against [the provision in the statement issued on [date]]. Please advise us as soon as possible that this appeal has been registered.

Please ensure that we are provided promptly with copies of any relevant correspondence and documents you receive from the LEA.[5]

---

5   If the appeal form so specifies, the SENT will write to the solicitor. Funding must therefore be arranged to enable the solicitor to deal with all routine correspondence as well as to present the appeal.

L13   Parental request for statutory assessment (paras 9.36–9.39)

To the Head of Special Educational Needs

. . . .   LEA

Re: AB

As AB's parent, I am writing to you formally to request that you arrange for an assessment of AB's special educational needs under section 323 Education Act 1996.

[Set out reasons.]

In order to save time if you agree with my request,[6] I am waiving my right to the 29-day notice period in section 330 for making representations and submitting evidence, so that you can proceed to give me formal notice straight away.

---

6   Education (Special Educational Needs) Regulations 1994 give the LEA six weeks to notify its decision (reg 11(3)). See paras 9.59 and 9.65.

L14   Parental request for reassessment of statemented child (para 9.95)

Re: AB

I am not satisfied that AB's statement reflects his/her current needs and the appropriate provision for them and I would like you to treat this letter as formal notice under section 328 Education Act 1996 for a full assessment to be made under section 323.

[Set out reasons.]

L15   Letter to LEA about SEN time limits (para 9.58)

Re: AB

We are acting for AB through his/her mother Mrs CB and we are writing about the statutory assessment which you commenced by notice on [date].

At the time of writing it appears to us that the LEA is not complying with the statutory timetable under regulation 11 of the Education (Special Educational Needs) Regulations 1994.

[Set out relevant steps and time limits, take account of the relevant factors permitting any exceptions to the time limits and set out calculation of a revised timetable.]

AB's mother is anxious that the assessment/statementing process should be completed within the prescribed time limits so that she may exercise her right of appeal to the SENT if she is dissatisfied with the outcome. Accordingly we wish to notify you that we are instructed that if the above timetable is not complied with we are to take the necessary steps to apply for a judicial review of your authority in this matter.

L16 Letter before action to LEA for failure to arrange SEN provision etc (paras 9.33 and 16.22)

We refer to our previous correspondence in which we expressed our concern that your authority was not carrying out its statutory obligation under section 324(5)(a)(i) Education Act 1996 to arrange that the special educational provision in AB's statement is made.

[On the information available to us it appears that your authority has not made a decision or has inappropriately exercised its discretion concerning the non-educational needs specified in the statement.]

[Set out, in particular, items about which there is no factual dispute.]

The result of this is that our client is still not receiving the SEN provision to which he/she is entitled. Therefore we are instructed to inform you that preparations are being commenced with a view to an application for permission for a judicial review of your authority in this matter, without further notice to you.

L17 Letter to maintained school refusing to admit statemented pupil (para 9.26)

To the Clerk to the Governing Body

c/o .... School

Re: AB

We act for AB who has a statement of special educational needs issued by [name] LEA on [date]. In part 4 of the statement your school is named. By virtue of section 324(5)(b) Education Act 1996 there is a statutory duty to admit AB to your school. This is irrespective of any restriction on class sizes. You should be aware that the LEA which maintains the statement also has a statutory obligation to ensure that any school SEN support which AB requires is arranged.

[Refer to parental contact and any attempts to enrol pupil.]

This letter will serve to notify you that if we do not receive confirmation by [date and time 48 hours hence] that AB is a registered pupil at the school, we have instructions to prepare for a judicial review of the governing body, without further notice to you. This will include an application for an injunction. In the circumstances we respectfully suggest that the governing body obtains legal advice.

L18 Letter to LEA re failure to review statement (paras 9.97–9.100)

Re: AB

We are instructed by AB and his mother, Mrs CB, concerning the arrangements which are required to be made by your authority, as the LEA maintaining AB's statement of special educational needs, for the annual review of his/her statement. We draw your attention to regulation (15/16)

of the Education (Special Educational Needs) Regulations 1994.
The last annual review appears to have taken place in [month, year].[7]
[Mention any previous failure by the LEA to take the initiative, failure to obtain relevant advices, failure of headteacher to convene meeting, failure of invitees to attend, failure by LEA to heed advice.]
We are instructed that no meeting has yet been arranged. The 12-month anniversary of [the making of the statement/the last annual review] will fall on [date].[8] We refer you to section 328(5) Education Act 1996. The regulations require that you [give notice to the headteacher to prepare a report by a specified date (child under 14)/seek advice and convene the meeting (child aged 14 at school or child out of school)] and the review cannot now take place within the statutory time limit.
We write to notify you that if we do not receive, by [date]:
(delete as appropriate)

– details of the meeting to be held, copies of all advices and reports not yet provided to the parent and a list of persons invited and attending
– a copy of the report of the meeting held on [date]
– notification of the LEA's decision upon the annual review

we are instructed to prepare for judicial review proceedings without any further reference to you.

---

7   As stated in para 9.98(6), there is no time limit for the review following the meeting.

8   It is not always easy to say when the review (reg 15(12) or 16 (10)) actually took place. There is a very common misconception that the review meeting is the review by the LEA, whereas in the case of a meeting convened by the headteacher under reg 15(5) it is simply a forum for making recommendations to the LEA. Furthermore, there is no time limit for the headteacher's report to be submitted to the LEA under reg 15(10). Where the child is over 14, the LEA convenes the meeting and prepares and circulates its report within seven days.

Useful names and addresses

Advisory Centre for Education
Unit 1B
Aberdeen Studios
22 Highbury Grove
London N5 2DQ
tel: 0171 354 8321

Children's Legal Centre
University of Essex
Wivenhoe Park
Colchester
Essex
CO4 3SQ
tel: 01206 873820

Contact-a-Family
(charity for children with special needs and disabilities)
170 Tottenham Court Road
London W1P 0HA
tel: 0171 383 3555

Department for Education and Employment (DfEE)
Sanctuary Buildings
Great Smith Street
Westminster
London SW1P 3BT
tel: 0171 925 5000

DfEE Publications Centre
PO Box 5050
Sherwood Park
Annesley
Nottinghamshire
NG15 8BY
tel: 0845 602 2260

Disability Law Service
2nd Floor
High Holborn House
52–54 High Holborn
London WC1V 6RL
tel: 0171 831 8031

**Downs' Syndrome
Association**
155 Mitcham Road
London SW17 9PG •
tel: 0181 682 4001

Dyslexia Institute
133 Gresham Road
Staines
Middlesex
TW18 2AJ
tel: 01784 463935

**Independent Panel for
Special Educational Advice**
4 Ancient House Mews
Woodbridge
Suffolk
tel: 01394 382814

**Local Government
Ombudsman (England)**
21 Queen Anne's Gate
London SW1H 9BU
tel: 0171 222 5622

**Local Ombudsman for
Wales**
Derwen House
Court Road
Bridgend
Mid Glamorgan
CF31 1BN
tel: 01656 611325

**MENCAP (Royal Society for
Mentally Handicapped
Children and Adults)**
117–123 Golden Lane
London EC1Y 0RT
tel: 0171 454 0454

**MIND (National Association
for Mental Health)**
Granta House
15–19 Broadway
Stratford
London E15 4BQ
tel: 0181 519 2122

**SCOPE (former Spastics
Society)**
6 Market Road
London N7 9PW
tel: 0171 619 7100

**Special Educational Needs
Tribunal**
50 Victoria Street
London SW1H 0HW
tel: 0171 925 6925

**Special Educational Needs
Tribunal**
Mowden Hall
Staindrop Road
Darlington
County Durham
DL3 9BG
tel: 01325 391046

Index

LAG Legal Action Group

Working with lawyers and advisers to promote equal access to justice

Legal Action magazine

The only monthly magazine published specifically for legal aid practitioners and the advice sector. *Legal Action* features 'Recent developments in education law' in its March and September issues.

Annual subscription: £75
Concessionary rates available for students and trainees – call the LAG office for details

Books

LAG's catalogue includes a range of titles covering:

- community care
- crime
- debt
- education
- family
- housing
- human rights
- immigration
- personal injury
- practice & procedure
- welfare benefits
- LAG policy

Community Care Law Reports

The only law reports devoted entirely to community care issues. Compiled by an expert team and published quarterly, each issue contains:

- editorial review
- community care law update
- law reports
- cumulative index
- full tables

Training

Accredited with the Law Society, the Bar Council and the Institute of Legal Executives, LAG has been providing pioneering courses in continuing professional development for many years.

Conferences

LAG runs major conferences to examine issues at the cutting-edge of legal services policy and to inform practitioners of their implications.

For further information about any of Legal Action Group's activities please contact:

Legal Action Group
242 Pentonville Road
London
N1 9UN
DX 130400 London (Pentonville Road)
Telephone: 0171 833 2931
Fax: 0171 837 6094
e-mail: lag@lag.org.uk